Buddhist Nuns and Gendered Practice

Buddhist Nuns and Gendered Practice

In Search of the Female Renunciant

NIRMALA S. SALGADO

OXFORD
UNIVERSITY PRESS

OXFORD
UNIVERSITY PRESS

Oxford University Press is a department of the University of Oxford.
It furthers the University's objective of excellence in research,
scholarship, and education by publishing worldwide.

Oxford   New York

Auckland   Cape Town   Dar es Salaam   Hong Kong   Karachi
Kuala Lumpur   Madrid   Melbourne   Mexico City   Nairobi
New Delhi   Shanghai   Taipei   Toronto

With offices in

Argentina   Austria   Brazil   Chile   Czech Republic   France   Greece
Guatemala   Hungary   Italy   Japan   Poland   Portugal   Singapore
South Korea   Switzerland   Thailand   Turkey   Ukraine   Vietnam

Oxford is a registered trademark of Oxford University Press
in the UK and certain other countries.

Published in the United States of America by
Oxford University Press
198 Madison Avenue, New York, NY 10016

© Oxford University Press 2013

Library of Congress Cataloging-in-Publication Data
Salgado, Nirmala S.
Buddhist nuns and gendered practice: in search of the female renunciant/
Nirmala S. Salgado.
pages cm
Includes bibliographical references and index.
ISBN 978–0–19–976001–5 (pbk. : alk. paper)—ISBN 978–0–19–976002–2
(hardcover : alk. paper)—ISBN (invalid) 978–0–19–998623–1 (ebook)
1. Buddhist nuns.   2. Buddhist monasticism and religious orders for women.
3. Women in Buddhism.   I. Title.
BQ6150.S25 2013
294.3'657082—dc23
2012036573

1 3 5 7 9 8 6 4 2
Printed in the United States of America
on acid-free paper

For my mother Indira Siromani Salgado

and in memory of
my father
Chandrasena Aladin Kenneth Salgado
and my uncle
Ananda Salgado Kulasuriya

Contents

Acknowledgments   ix

Introduction: Buddhist Nuns and Gendered Practice   1

PART I: *Narration*

1. Decolonizing Female Renunciation   21
2. Institutional Discourse and Everyday Practice   49
3. Buddhism, Power, and Practice   77

PART II: *Identity*

4. Invisible Nuns   103
5. Subjects of Renunciation   123
6. Becoming *Bhikkhunis,* Becoming Theravada   149

PART III: *Empowerment*

7. Renunciation and "Empowerment"   185
8. Global Empowerment and the Renunciant Everyday   211

Notes   235
Works Cited   277
Index   297

Acknowledgments

To adequately recognize and thank all those who have helped me with my research for this project would be impossible. My conversations with Buddhist nuns began in December 1983 as part of a research project I undertook at the International Center for Ethnic Studies (ICES) in Colombo, Sri Lanka, with the encouragement of Radhika Coomaraswamy, who remained supportive of my work for several years even after I had left ICES and Sri Lanka for graduate study in the United States. While at ICES I benefited from the support of Neelan Tiruchelvam and Reggie/Regi Siriwardene as well as from many conversations with Jagath Senaratne, Yasmin Tambiah, Jani De Silva, Nireka Weeratunge, D.B.S Jeyaraj, and Sunil Bastian during a time of unforgettable civil unrest and tension in the country. I am grateful for their friendship during those troubled times.

I appreciate the help of Anuradha Malalasekara and Amali Boralugoda in locating important sources in Sri Lanka and providing translations. I am indebted to Daya Wickramasinghe for the many hours she spent helping me translate Sinhalese-language public debates and articles on nuns and for her prompt, patient responses to my linguistic queries about Sinhalese. I thank Sandagomi Coperahewa and Tilak Weerasekera for their extensive archival research of newspaper articles covering the 1980–1997 period and for their help in summarizing and translating important documents. They translated many of the Sinhalese-language sources for Chapters 4, 5, and 6. The translations I completed for those chapters as well as others benefited from Daya's guidance. I am also grateful to Gisela Krey for assistance in translating the Eight Conditions from the Pali for Chapter 3 and to K. D. Paranavitana for help in rechecking archival sources during the final stages of this work. Amy Jegerski Bovi, Amber Mollenbeck, and Faith Leaich helped me organize crucial documents that spanned several years.

I am appreciative of Lham Purevjav for her hospitality when I visited Mongolia and for her translations from Mongolian. I am also thankful to Abhaya Weerakoon, Padma Dinapala, Amarasiri Weeraratne, Kusuma Devendra, Raja Dharmapala, Jehan Perera, and the late Ratna Dias, who spent precious time with me in conversation, providing me with important resources and updates throughout the 1980s and 1990s. I am also grateful for the assistance, time, and resources, made available to me by Eardley Ratwatte, who passed away in 2001, just as higher ordination of nuns was becoming a regular event in Sri Lanka, and to Kumar Piyasena, whose sudden death shortly before that time stalled his work on behalf of Sri Lankan nuns. My gratitude to the mostly unnamed female renunciants in Sri Lanka knows no bounds. I briefly left the idea of researching Buddhist nuns while doing graduate work at Northwestern University. During a visit I made to Sri Lanka in the summer of 1988, the civil unrest there made me wary of traveling far from my base; I quickly abandoned the thought of visiting distant hermitages to do research. But when I returned there in the early 1990s, the enthusiasm and warmth with which the nuns welcomed me reignited my interest in researching questions about them. If not for those nuns, this work would not have continued. When my family members and I traveled to visit them in remote locations, they gave us food and shelter and often went out of their way to help me meet informants and locate sources.

Many people encouraged me to work on a book-length project on nuns before I gave it serious thought. I am grateful to Ananda Kulasuriya, Ratna Handurukande, Daya Wickramasinghe, Minoli Salgado, Dilesh Jayanntha, and Indira Salgado for such encouragement. Ratna was a constant source of support through the years; she and Dilesh consistently collected and sent me relevant newspaper articles. Dilesh also assisted in checking important archival sources and guided my thinking in important ways. I thank Steve Berkwitz and Joseph Walser for their comments during the early stages of writing, and I am deeply indebted to George Bond, Robert Launay, and Martha Reineke for taking time out of their hectic schedules to give me essential scholarly advice on drafts of individual chapters.

I am grateful for the encouragement of colleagues, past and present, at Augustana College, including Van J. Symons for his friendship and support over the years and also Pramod Mishra, Mwenda Ntarangwi, Sushmita Chatterjee, Anette Ejsing, Ritva Williams, Peter Kivisto, Molly Todd, Adam Kaul, Dan Lee, Eric Stewart, Cyrus Zargar, Peter Xiao, and Roman Bonzon for their assistance and their constructive conversations with me. I am especially thankful to Peter Kivisto, Pramod, and Sushmita for reading drafts of individual chapters and offering thoughtful critiques. This work has benefited from Jeff Abernathy's commitment to faculty research. I appreciate his encouragement as well as the support given to me by Pareena Lawrence. I am grateful for funds from numerous sources, including Faculty Research Grants, Presidential Research Fellowships, and a Sabbatical Leave Grant from Augustana as well as grants from the David. E. Nudd Fund, the William E. Freistat Center, and the American Academy of Religion. My thanks to the librarians at Augustana's Thomas Tredway Library, especially Stefanie Bluemle for her patience in working with me and Sherrie Herbst for her promptness in obtaining materials through interlibrary loan. I am also thankful for Wendy Ramsdale and other ITS staff at Augustana for their eagerness to help me with computer issues.

I am greatly indebted to Ananda Abeysekara for the intellectual contribution he has made to the field of religion in general and to Buddhism in particular. His scholarship has encouraged me to think about Buddhism in new ways. The impact of Ananda's thinking on my work is unmistakable, and I thank him for his incisive, constructive comments on drafts of chapters of this manuscript. Paul Westman patiently read, commented on, critiqued, and edited every draft of this manuscript. I thank him for his insightful comments and for our many conversations on my research. I am grateful to Robert Green for his careful editing in the final stages of this work. I am indebted to Theo Calderara, Charlotte Steinhardt, and the anonymous reviewers from Oxford for their helpful suggestions as my manuscript made the transition to a book publication. The responsibility for errors of omission and commission in this book lies with me alone.

I thank Al Westman and Marilyn Borden Westman for their kindness and support over the years. I received much inspiration from my late uncle Ananda Kulasuriya, who, from the inception of my research, assisted me in many ways, including helping with translations and reading and commenting on my earlier work on female renunciation, and from my aunt Rukmini Kulasuriya, who consistently supported my research. They long encouraged my writing a book on nuns and assisted me in arranging travels to isolated areas of Sri Lanka in search of female renunciants. I am grateful to my late grandmother Dorothy Dias for her interactions with nuns and her pointed comments on my encounters with them. I owe an immense debt to my parents, Kenneth and Indira Salgado, who nurtured my work from the beginning. I am especially thankful to my mother, who over the years insisted on accompanying me on sometimes long and arduous travels. Her presence during many of my communications with nuns gave my rapport with them a dimension that would otherwise have been lacking. As one ages, it becomes increasingly difficult to endure the demands of traveling through rugged terrain and sitting on hard wooden chairs for hours at a time. Thank you, Amma.

Last but not least, I thank my son, Arjun, for his patience and for his reminders that there is more to a lived life than the writing of a book.

Buddhist Nuns and Gendered Practice

Introduction

BUDDHIST NUNS AND GENDERED PRACTICE

The world today speaks Latin.
—JACQUES DERRIDA, *Acts of Religion* 64.[1]

This book is the outcome of about twenty-five years of conversations with female renunciants mainly living in Sri Lanka.[2] Studies of gender and women in Buddhism have become increasingly popular since the 1980s. Some studies have tended to refract Buddhist women's identity through "images" or rules of relevance in textual traditions (Barnes; Gross, *Buddhism after Patriarchy*; Murcott; Paul and Wilson; Sponberg; Trainor). Others have included field research that seeks to understand (the relation between texts and) the contemporary world of Buddhist nuns (Arai; Bartholomeusz; S. Brown; M. Falk; Gutschow; Havnevik; Kawanami, "Changing World", "Religious Standing"; Van Esterik). In the first decade of the twenty-first century, when some touted the higher ordination (*upasampadā*) of Buddhist women as a feminist "movement," studies on the subject of nuns proliferated (Cheng, *Buddhist Nuns*; Cook; Mohr and Tsedroen; M. Falk; Tsomo, *Innovative Buddhist Women*; Tsomo, *Buddhist Women and Social Justice*). Although my book includes interviews and "field research," it is not intended as an "ethnography," in which one might *seek* to represent and interpret nuns' identity in terms of who they are and by way of what they do. Rather, it attempts to raise some questions about representing nuns in stories about them that appear both in scholarly discourse and in the writings of Buddhist practitioners. While my focus in this work is on accounts of nuns within what is generally known as Theravada Buddhism, I also address the broader implications of such questions in narratives about Tibetan Buddhist nuns, because the recent debates about the higher ordination of Tibetan nuns in particular have had a significant impact on the representation of Buddhist nuns in general.

Buddhist women renounce and live apart from family members because of what one may, however inadequately, call "religious" and "personal" reasons. The texts of the Buddhist canon and recent ethnographic studies, as is well known, recount some of the reasons women renounce. In considering the conditions of the lives and practices of contemporary nuns, I argue that renunciant narratives can be misinterpreted and misunderstood when placed, as they often have been, within a theoretical framework of liberal feminism. Studies using such frameworks, though they claim to represent the lives of nuns, tend to neglect nuns' everyday concerns, which center on such duties as maintaining and running a hermitage, cooking, cleaning, meditating, accepting alms from supporters, counseling, performing religious services, and teaching. I refer to the conditions of nuns' engagement in such daily work (vāḍa) as the "renunciant everyday."[3] Talal Asad argues that everyday lives tend to elude representation in narratives on culture: "Everyday life is not so easily invented, abandoned, reinhabited, as this notion of culture...suggests.... Life is essentially itself. Only the part of it that can be narrativized may be said to be 'made up' like a story by an artist" (Genealogies 289–290).[4] Albeit with some trepidation in creating yet another "made up" story, I attempt to articulate complications that derive from superimposing liberal feminist frameworks on the renunciant everyday of Buddhist nuns. Textual and historical evidence suggests that fully ordained nuns (bhikkhunīs or bhikṣuṇīs) lived in the time of the Buddha and that their ordination lineage was introduced to Sri Lanka in the third century B.C.E. Bhikkhunis are recorded as having practiced in Sri Lanka until sometime in the tenth century,[5] after which a lack of evidence hints at the demise of the bhikkhuni sāsana (also śāsana or sasna; "order" or "dispensation").[6] The late nineteenth century began to witness records of the establishment of renunciant hermitages for women living in community and the growing visibility of renunciant women in the country. Although those women practiced renunciation, they did not receive the bhikkhuni upasampada. In the late nineteenth century and throughout the twentieth century, some Buddhist leaders have occasionally questioned why Buddhist women who renounce cannot receive the upasampada, but it was often assumed that without the necessary quorum of ten bhikkhunis for the upasampada, implementing the upasampada would simply be impossible. However, since the 1980s, scholarship on Buddhist nuns has begun to debate that question more intensely. How such studies raise that question and what they say about

Buddhist nuns in terms of the conceptual paradigms that they adopt constitute main concerns of this book.

Questions about the colonial[7] and postcolonial politics of representation vis-à-vis "native" identities have emerged within and across disciplines over the course of the past several decades, especially since the publication in 1978 of Edward Said's *Orientalism*.[8] Since that publication, an examination of the representation of the gendered subject and its relationship to notions of agency, resistance, and ideology has also received considerable attention (Bannerji; Sunder Rajan, *Real and Imagined*; Spivak, "Can the Subaltern Speak?").[9] Scholars in the social sciences and humanities, though avowedly representing their subjects, are often better at being "ventriloquists" than at being the cultural mediators they claim to be. To some extent, any narrative construed about subjects studied is just that—a construction that speaks more to the disciplines that it addresses than to the human subjects that a body of "material" analyzes. My study cannot escape such disciplinary limitations as I write within such limits. It too provides a construction that needs to make sense within academic parameters. In addition, though, this book intends to promote a better understanding of how narratives on contemporary female renunciants have been constructed and to suggest other possibilities for thinking about their lives. In doing so, it calls into question how the subject of "the female renunciant," or "the nun," is *conceptualized*, in many senses of that word, arguing that assumptions about cross-cultural comparisons are embedded in nomenclature that is intrinsic to a certain way of theorizing religion. Central to my work is the problem of cultural translation vis-à-vis religion and culture that has come to attract some attention lately (Abeysekara, "Un-translatability"; Asad, *Genealogies*; Bermann and Wood; Dubuisson; Fitzgerald, *Ideology*; Mandair; Mas). In *Religion and the Specter of the West*, Arvind-Pal Mandair argues that the concept of globalatinization, a neologism introduced by Jacques Derrida, proves useful in questioning how scholars think about religion. According to Derrida, globalatinization assumes a translatability of language, concepts, culture, religion, secularity, and so on that in fact resist translation. More specifically, as Mandair says, globalatinization "enables...the core mechanism of Christianity and its language, to retain its hegemony....It can be seen as the global re-Christianization of the planet through the discourse of secular conceptuality" (104). In other words, the conceptual vocabulary of Christianity, modernity, secularism, and the Latin idiom to which they are indebted have become integral to the translation and interpretation of religion, both in colonial and postcolonial ("native") discourses as well as in the academy. The problem for Mandair centers on the repetition of such a translation that continues to inform how one thinks about and studies religion. That repetition, which pervades the academy and still instructs how practitioners throughout the world define themselves and others, is what Mandair calls the "repetition of the colonial event" (1–6). The concern is that "even when it is not the West, but the non-West, that is being evoked, the West is being automatically constituted" via a self-referential evocation of the West's other (Mandair 5). I seek to understand how the concepts, paradigms, and language used to articulate and translate religion—particularly in terms of renunciation and gender—have influenced our understanding of Buddhism. My intention is to make a modest contribution to interrupting the "repetition of the colonial event" where Orientalist and now globalatinized narratives about religion in academic disciplines tend to be repeated and translated into seemingly "local" discourses. Such translation and repetition must involve, as Mandair and others have argued, rethinking the very language we use to talk about secularism, religion, tradition, and culture. With that in mind, my study foregrounds the practice of nuns who do not speak a globalatinized idiom. In doing so, I am not suggesting that those nuns are somehow more "authentic" or "traditional" in their Buddhist practice than more cosmopolitan English-speaking renunciants with international connections;[10] what I want to suggest is that their primary concerns as well as the disciplinary paradigms that scholars (and English-speaking nuns) use to frame nuns' lives need to be reassessed. In that vein, I appraise the concepts used and taken for granted in talking about Buddhist nuns. I also consider how the dominant scholarly narratives of nuns are connected with the larger politics of identity, conceptualized in terms of liberal discourses and Western feminist categories. Distinctions scholars often use to understand Buddhism—for example, Theravada versus Mahayana—are generally based on understandings of religion that neglect the particularities that give rise to debates about such categories in the first place. Such a historicist understanding of religious lives invariably turns the lived lives of religious practitioners into a "problem" requiring a "resolution" framed according to liberal and liberating secular assumptions about the need to affirm gender equality or equal rights. Once the lives of nuns (and Buddhists in general) are seen from the perspective of secular feminist politics as *problems* to be solved, however differently conceptualized and qualified they may be, those lives inevitably give rise to a "curative project" one must think about (Asad, *Genealogies*; Abeysekara, *Colors*; *Politics*).

The question of *empowerment*—with its associations with such notions as agency, autonomy, and independence—remains central to secular feminist senses of politics. Nevertheless, that question needs to be better understood with reference to what is most central to the lived lives of female renunciants.[11] Those lives remain inseparable from the Buddhist practices that constitute them, including the concern with realizing nibbana/nirvana, the end of the cycle of rebirth and redeath (samsara). In other words, renunciant *practice* in itself is empowering, if we use that word to convey a sense of religious *fulfillment* or realization. That does not mean that nuns are somehow lacking in a power that they will somehow realize upon renouncing. Rather, their practice of renunciation is intrinsically fulfilling; it is not the product of some *external* activity which they must strive to achieve. Put differently, although the question of what female renunciants supposedly can or cannot do may figure into their departure from the household life to take up a life of monastic practice, such a departure needs to be grounded in renunciants' affirmation of that life and in their new relationships with family rather than in a rejection of family per se that may be attributed to a sense of self-assertion. To understand and frame nuns' lives in terms of dichotomies such as lay/monastic, householder/renunciant, or world affirmation/world renunciation or of something unsatisfactorily "in-between" is to continue to produce narratives about nuns that turn them in advance into putative problems centered on their social or religious "status." But those kinds of framing do not attend to thinking about nuns themselves as they engage in *sīla* (moral or disciplinary practices).[12] The scholarly narratives as well as the ongoing debates about the higher ordination for women must be contrasted with nuns' practice of *sila* in their renunciant everyday.

Using works that scholars of Buddhism and gender have hitherto largely overlooked, such as those by Talal Asad, Arvind-Pal Mandair, Saba Mahmood, Chandra T. Mohanty, and Dorothy E. Smith, and giving some attention to the intellectual influences of Michel Foucault and select social-movement and subaltern-studies theorists, this book considers contemporary female renunciation in Buddhism differently from the existing literature. It questions the relevance of liberal and feminist theories in relation to narratives about Buddhist nuns, and it raises a doubt about the idea that the higher ordination of women in Buddhism instantiates an essentially global or transnational "movement." A study of contemporary female renunciation cannot ignore the postcolonial, globalizing present informed by discourses on "women in development" as well as images of the "third world." And yet the nuns I study here, do not, for the most part, equate receiving the higher ordination with secular senses of opportunity. Rather, their receiving the higher ordination depends more on the exigencies of their renunciant everyday than on some desire to acquire a status of equality. I argue that, contrary to what some claim, the establishment of the *bhikkhuni upasampada* in Sri Lanka is not an expression of a *social movement*, making nuns primary agents of "reform" or "revival." The idea of a movement implies notions of intentionality, responsibility, and agency on the part of nuns. But that idea is a construct of scholars and some practitioners, not of the Sinhalese-speaking nuns I interviewed in the 1980s and '90s, some of whom were among the first to be ordained as *bhikkhunis*.[13] Simply put, despite efforts to understand what those nuns themselves say, what they say is often not *heard* by those who write about them.

G. C. Spivak's renowned essay "Can the Subaltern Speak?" considers the question of understanding what the subaltern (non-elite) says.[14] Spivak states that to say "'the subaltern cannot speak' means that even when the subaltern makes an effort to the death to speak, she is not able to be heard, and speaking and hearing complete the speech act" ("Subaltern Talk" 292). Moreover, the "non-speaking" of the subaltern has to do with the *failure* of others to *hear* her (De Kock 44–46; Sunder Rajan, "Death" 121). In the attempts to communicate with the subaltern, what is left are the gaps and the silences, and even those remain unacknowledged or forgotten in studies of Buddhist nuns. As noted by Pierre Macherey, "What is important in a work is what it does not say.... What the work *cannot* say is important, because there the elaboration of the utterance is carried out, in a sort of journey to silence" (qtd. in Spivak, "Can the Subaltern Speak?" [1988] 286; emphasis in original). But, as Spivak said, the distinction between speech and silence is not unproblematic.[15] What remains to be thought is the question of the inaccessibility of subaltern speech and representation, and the limitations of language. Here I am reminded of a conversation I had with a senior Sri Lankan *bhikkhuni* who was engaged in a program to prepare nuns for the *upasampada*. I interviewed her shortly after her own *upasampada*. She had spent most of her life as a *dasa sil mātā/dasa sil māniyō* (Ten [Training] Precept Mother) rather than a *bhikkhuni*. I asked her if she thought that the attempts to institute the *bhikkhuni upasampada* in Sri Lanka could be considered feminist (*strīvādī*, literally "woman-ism"). Her immediate response was, "We are not women (*strī*); we are renunciant[s] (*pāvidi*)." Taken aback by this seeming denial of her "womanhood," I remained acquiescent, in silent acknowledgment of her words. I have often pondered what she meant. The monastic code of conduct (*Vinaya*) stipulates that a female ordinand must affirm her sexuality as a woman by responding to a series of questions; she must have what is considered a normatively female body and a clear-cut sexual identity as a woman in order to enter the community of *bhikkhunis*.[16] Well versed in these *vinaya* codes, this senior *bhikkhuni* appeared to reject her womanhood. But perhaps her response was a refusal to engage my suggestion that Buddhist nuns were somehow comparable to women who were not renunciants. I have come to realize that she, like other nuns I have known, did not see herself as having a gendered identity in the way that one might expect. A nun is first and foremost a *celibate* renunciant. *Sil mātās* (Precept Mothers) in Sri Lanka, with their shaved heads and their robes typically ranging from yellow or orange to dark brown, look almost indistinguishable from monks. One may notice that Sri Lankan nuns wear long sleeves regardless of the heat and that some of them have robes that are cut and sewn differently from those of monks. By saying that she was not a woman, the *bhikkhuni* perhaps implied that her body defied definition in terms of conventional notions about gender. In leading celibate lives and adopting attire similar to that of monks, nuns see themselves as being beyond gender—or at least as being beyond gender as it is generally conceptualized.[17] By stating that she was not a woman, the *bhikkhuni* was making it difficult if not impossible to be understood using a modern secular sense of the word "woman," that is, a word associated with "women's issues" as recognized (and appropriated) by the state,— issues pertaining to education, labor, sexuality, and domestic violence.

Conventionally, scholars have perceived nuns as religious women whose renunciant lives might be seen through feminist lenses. Perhaps, however, the focus should not be on the "status" and "role" of nuns as gendered renunciants but rather on the articulation of their everyday practice, or their renunciant everyday, which includes the rules and rituals they follow in renunciation, their training in meditation, their studies, their ongoing relationships with neighbors, kinfolk, supporters, and other renunciants. My reference to the renunciant everyday is not to some notion or "concept" of everyday practice that can simply be accessible to scholarly narratives. Rather, the reference is to a living practice that is heterogeneous and intrinsic to the living of a renunciant life. I propose that although nuns may not consider themselves gendered, their practice, which differs from that of monks, is in fact gendered. (Nuns, for example, have closer associations with women than monks do.) Perhaps it was the conflation of gendered identity with gendered practice that explains my surprise at the *bhikkhuni* who asserted: "We are not women." That same conflation has likely led scholars to position nuns, despite their renunciation of what we generally understand as gender, in feminist frameworks of interpretation—frameworks that, I argue throughout this book, are often misplaced.

This study is divided into three interrelated parts centering on narrative, identity, and empowerment as each plays out in representations of female renunciation. The first three chapters focus on the construction of scholarly narratives about Buddhist nuns. Here I suggest that such narratives, framed with reference to feminist and liberal paradigms, should not be understood as self-explanatory depictions of social reality, in which the subject of "the nun" is readily available for scholarly narration. The next three chapters center on nuns as subjects of discourse and on articulations of female renunciant identities. Those chapters explain how the "subject" of female renunciation in Theravada was largely constructed by the Sri Lankan state, prominent monastics, and scholars. That subject was often conceptualized as an *indigent* (in various senses) in need of (economic, political, and other forms of) betterment, which, according to some practitioners and scholars, could be achieved by her receiving the *upasampada*. But the prospect of the *upasampada* was entertained differently by nuns whose focus remained on the cultivation of moral or disciplinary practices (*sila*) and renunciation. The final two chapters argue for rethinking concepts of empowerment and secular notions of agency and freedom that have become intrinsic to colonial and Orientalist narratives. Such articulations about nuns involve an assessment of non-Western others in terms of a problem-solution paradigm, as noted earlier. Those two chapters center on the various ways that empowerment may be understood both by nuns who, for the sake of simplicity we may say, speak in a globalatinized idiom and by those who do not, suggesting why it is misleading to read seemingly universal notions into the lives of nuns.

Chapter Overview

Chapter 1 sets the stage for this book with a general as well as a specific focus on narration. It establishes the need to question how academic writings represent the topic of women in Buddhism in general and female renunciation in particular. I do a close reading of narratives by three academics who have written on women and Buddhism—Rita Gross, Tessa Bartholomeusz, and Wei-Yi Cheng—and I argue that they address gender and women's studies in Buddhism by using master narratives that are of questionable relevance to the everyday lives of women living in Buddhist countries.[18] Gross, whose understanding of Buddhist women is informed primarily by texts, is often cited in ethnographic studies of women in Buddhism. I propose that her works are of limited use insofar as they instantiate a liberal feminism as well as what Timothy Fitzgerald calls a "liberal ecumenical theology" (6–7), in which an ostensibly objective study of religion veils a theological enterprise. I argue that Gross's works, though instructive in their approach to the subject, relate better to Buddhist practitioners of a certain profile living in the "developed" world rather than to those living elsewhere. I also read Gross's works in relation to the theoretical frameworks of Arvind-Pal Mandair and Tomoko Masuzawa, who argue for the importance of questioning current disciplinary paradigms used in scholarship on Asian religions. The works of Bartholomeusz and Cheng claim to speak of the "realities" of nuns living in Asia; Bartholomeusz focuses on nuns in Sri Lanka, while Cheng attempts a comparative study of nuns in Sri Lanka and Taiwan. Both studies raise questions that are set in frameworks recognizably different from those in which the nuns see themselves. That creates a problem I call *narrative disjunction,* in which a narrative provides frameworks for understanding the lives of nuns to which the nuns themselves clearly do not subscribe. I suggest that the problem of narrative disjunction has to be recognized in the scholarly attempts to construct, represent, and even assess the lives of renunciant subjects. The works of the scholars considered in this chapter use a language of secular liberalism in their accounts of Buddhist women. The narrative disjunction that emerges in their works results, I argue, in a misreading of how Asian women who do not articulate themselves in such language respond to questions of renunciant practice.

Chapter 2 continues to discuss the implications of narrative disjunction in academic representations of Buddhist nuns. Here I propose that dichotomous structures such as lay/renunciant and this-worldly/otherworldly, which are often used to identify nuns and their practices, echo variations on a liberal feminist distinction between the private and the public. Such dualities lend themselves to asking and answering questions that articulate a colonial discourse on the subject of female renunciation in particular and Buddhism in general. By colonial (Orientalist) discourse I mean a persistent hegemonic, albeit seemingly universal, account about the construction of religion and religious lives (that nevertheless continues to inform our so called post-colonial age). The dichotomies written into narratives about nuns continue to make possible, perhaps inadvertently on the part of their authors, what Mandair has called the repetition of the colonial event. Viewed from a perspective rooted in the politics of a curative project, the lives of nuns have been seen as lacking in political, ethical, or liberationist realizations and thus as needing correction. This chapter questions the usefulness of categories, such as "lay" and "monastic," and suggests that the English rendering of those terms inadequately reflects the practices of contemporary female renunciants. I single out important works on contemporary nuns in Theravada and Tibetan Buddhism and show that thinking of nuns in terms of such dualities positions them in a secular-liberal narrative that does not measure up to their lived lives, which center on the contemplation of *dukkha* (questions of suffering or dis-ease). I include interviews with contemporary Sri Lankan nuns to indicate the complications inherent in the dichotomous frames characteristically used to interpret who nuns *are* and what they *do*. In particular, I argue that the *questions* nuns face (and respond to) in their lives must not be interpreted as *problems* that need to be solved (as part of a curative project). I propose rather, that they be understood as questions that have contributed to deepening nuns' understanding of the meaning of key Buddhist notions such as *dukkha* and samsara—an understanding that cannot be situated in a liberal feminist story about feminism. This chapter, which owes much to critiques of liberal feminism developed by scholars such as Saba Mahmood, Carole Pateman, and Wendy Brown, also identifies in narratives on nuns the kinds of institutional discourses and representations of life that Dorothy E. Smith has censured. Overall, this chapter argues that it is important to acknowledge authorial complicity in the production of narrative disjunction and imperialistic interpretations of nuns' lives. This is necessary if we are to interrupt the repetition of the colonial event in accounts of those lives

Chapter 3 centers on the controversial Eight Revered Conditions, an iteration of regulations allegedly constituting nuns' subordination to monks.[19] As such, they have become central to debates concerning ideas about male domination and gender inequality in Buddhist monasticism. I question how Western scholars, as well some Sri Lanka practitioners, have interpreted the Conditions in so far as they serve to inform our presumptions about feminist notions of identity, equality, and agency among nuns. Assumptions about the controversial Conditions vis-à-vis the question of agency and subordination bespeak an ideological complicity that reinforces a supposedly patriarchal Buddhism. Those assumptions are grounded in a dubious reconstruction of earlier Buddhist realities, in which textual Buddhism tends to be conflated with early Buddhism as an expression of normative praxis. But the focus of this chapter is not on the difference between theory and practice or texts and lived lives; rather, it is on how scholarly reconstructions of a text lend themselves to secular feminist interpretations superimposed on nuns' practice. Such reconstructions are self-referential, in that they speak more to liberal concerns about gender than they do to attitudes and practices embodied by nuns. I argue that narratives on the Eight Conditions that focus too narrowly on whether the conditions are *Buddhavacana* (the word of the Buddha) have abetted the production of an epistemic (a "knowing" or an "unknowing") female renunciant subject. In contemporary Sri Lanka, nuns' reflections on the Eight Conditions differ from the ways many scholars represent them. In effect, the Conditions function less as imperatives or injunctions than as a discourse about identity, in terms of which monastics inhabit a world where questions of gender equality and agency do not figure in the manner assumed by secular-liberal thinking. My contention is that the narratives of contemporary *bhikkhunis* suggest the presence of a very different kind of "subject" of renunciation than the one hitherto supposed in accounts of the Eight Conditions. Far from being "subordinate" or "unequal," those female renunciants tend to either challenge, ignore, or simply bypass apparent structures of male dominance. Questioning the ideological complicity inscribed in scholarly debates on the Eight Conditions and their focus on *Buddhavacana*, this chapter argues that nuns' articulations of the Conditions diverge significantly from those intimated in accounts about them.

Chapter 4 includes specific arguments that are central to how one thinks of female renunciation in Buddhism.[20] Studies about nuns often situate them between members of the sangha (fully ordained community of monastics) and householders. However, an understanding of nuns' position—if one can even talk of such a thing—is better served by an inquiry into the meaning of "renunciation" *(pävidi)* that can only be thought in relation to the daily practices that make it possible. In particular, this chapter looks at public debates about nuns (in both Sinhalese- and English-language news media) in Sri Lanka during the 1980s and '90s. Although some of the debates centered on the appropriateness of conferring the *upasampada* on nuns, others addressed more fundamentally the very character of renunciants' identity as articulated by renunciant attire, the nomenclature used for renunciants, and the precepts they observed. Those debates, though seemingly "authenticating" nuns' identity (in terms of their renunciant or householder status), were more about contesting what nuns could or could not do. On the basis of Pali textual sources, Sri Lankan publications, and interviews with monks, nuns, and householders, I argue not only that the apparent indicators (both in texts and in contemporary times) of female renunciation are far from definitive but also that, in Sri Lanka, recent attempts to assert what they *do* mean are inseparable from the debates about what they supposedly *should* mean. For example, those who opposed the possibility of the *bhikkhuni upasampada*, unlike those who supported it, tended to see nuns as householders rather than as renunciants. In other words, the affirmation of nuns' so-called position cannot be considered a self-evident representation of a socio-cultural reality; rather, it must be seen as an assertion made within certain "conjunctures," or specific convergences of discourses and debates.[21]

I also propose that the use of terms such as *nun, lay nun,* and *female renunciant*, though perhaps inevitable in studies articulated in English, creates (political and ethical) complications for scholars and practitioners alike. Thinking about the lives of nuns as resisting translation helps one understand why pre-conceptualized notions of gender, identity, and religion should be re-considered. More simply put, the English translations of the Sinhalese terms used for nuns, such as *māṇiyō* ("mother"), *meheṇi* (ordained female renunciant), *sil mātā/māṇiyō* (Training Precept Mother), and *bhikkhuni*, prove inadequate. Ultimately, even as debates about nuns' identity attest to the lack of a clear-cut notion of female renunciation among Buddhists in Sri Lanka, nuns' identities and practices cannot simply be translated into articulations about their renunciant or householder "status."

Chapter 5 explains how the subject of the *bhikkhuni* emerges as the instantiation of a particular social ideal in Sri Lanka. In a related vein, it critiques the attempt to represent Buddhist nuns as participants and agents in some kind of movement for the *upasampada*. While outlining the arguments of select social-movement theorists and subaltern-studies scholars, I suggest that the construction of the renunciant subject, by the state as well as researchers, bears witness to a programmatic model moored in a rhetoric of "development" that reinscribes prevailing debates about the suitability of the *bhikkhuni upasampada*. I am indebted to the work of Arturo Escobar, who has developed Foucault's thinking to better explain how one might understand the idea of development in the so-called third world. Specifically, the focus on female renunciation in recent decades—partly prompted by views on how third-world development, reflected in the development rhetoric prevalent in Sri Lanka throughout the 1970s and 1980s and related to the idea of "women and development"—directly influenced perceptions of *sil matas* as deprived subjects worthy of "aid," and ultimately, of the *upasampada*. Within the parameters of that discourse, the state sponsored nation- and district-wide organizations of *sil matas* while evading the topic of their *upasampada*. Although the debates on the identity of female renunciants and their suitability for the *upasampada* continued throughout the '90s, few female renunciants sought the *upasampada*. Moreover, renunciants who were *sil matas* in the 1980s and were later given the *bhikkhuni upasampada* had had little if any interest in receiving it at the outset; they had focused instead on the everyday religious practices of their home hermitages. *Sil matas'* lack of consensus about the *bhikkhuni upasampada* throughout the 1980s and '90s, despite the endeavors of others to initiate such an *upasampada*, inhibited a widespread mobilization of *sil matas* seeking it. Nevertheless, some *sil matas* did accept it. I argue that that acceptance bears witness more to *sil matas'* readiness to accommodate the programmatic models of others than to their initiating a movement of collective action. If one must interpret the attempts to introduce the *bhikkhuni upasampada* in Sri Lanka as some sort of movement, I propose that those attempts would be seen better as something promoted by a few intellectuals, monks, and activists than as part of a large-scale resistance movement pioneered by *sil matas* to overcome male dominance.

Chapter 6 continues to question the construction of female renunciant identity by focusing on what "Theravada" and the "higher ordination" mean for monks and nuns in relation to debates on the *bhikkhuni upasampada* in Sri Lanka. Sri Lankan monks living abroad who have recently organized international higher ordinations for Sri Lankan nuns clearly see the establishment of a Theravada identity for *bhikkhunis* as central to Buddhist missions outside Sri Lanka. Within Sri Lanka, Theravada "authenticity" is upheld by all parties in the debate, whether or not they approve of the *bhikkhuni upasampada*. Those who reject the viability of the *bhikkhuni upasampada* do so on the grounds that the participation of Mahayana monastics—considered necessary to ensure the "re-establishment" of a "lost" or "broken" lineage of *bhikkhunis*—would compromise the "Theravada" character of the *upasampada*. Those who favor the *upasampada* argue about Theravada in different ways. For example, they suggest that because the Mahayana *bhikkhuni* ordination lineage currently known in East Asian countries can be traced to that which was originally known in Sri Lanka (even though it is no longer extant there), the transmission of the ordination lineage from contemporary Mahayana *bhikkhunis* to Theravada nuns is valid. Although there are Sri Lankan monastics who approve of the idea of a *bhikkhuni* ordination for Sri Lankan nuns and are conducting ordinations regularly in Sri Lanka, some of them argue that only certain ordinations can be considered authentically Theravada while those in which Mahayana nuns participate are not. Drawing on Ananda Abeysekara's *The Colors of the Robe,* and on recent discussions with monks and nuns living in Sri Lanka, I argue that competing narratives that lay claim to Theravada identity center less on defining the meaning of Theravada than on staking claims to monastic precedence and seniority. The observance of such seniority and precedence among nuns living in Sri Lanka is central to the internal organization of monastic communities and is connected with the recent *bhikkhuni* ordinations, which have altered the previously existing order of seniority among nuns. I suggest that the debates about Theravada authenticity effectively represent competing claims to monastic precedence among recently ordained *bhikkhunis* and the monks who support them. Although some monastics wish to identify different lineages among recently ordained *bhikkhunis* in Sri Lanka, others assert that such distinctions are of little importance. Overall, this chapter argues that the category of Theravada is not self-explanatory; it can be understood only in the context of the competing debates that attempt to define it.

Chapter 7 asks how questions of empowerment might be understood in the renunciant everyday of nuns who do not speak in a globalatinized idiom. Central to the chapter remain critiques of liberal feminist notions that tend to theorize female renunciation by way of seeing the very idea of renunciation as a form of resistance against and freedom from the supposed patriarchal politics of the household life. The chapter also looks closely at the question of what constitutes freedom for nuns, giving some attention to works by Pierre Bourdieu, Michel de Certeau, and David Scott. In keeping with arguments about gender transformation and colonialism advanced by Ashis Nandy and Carla Risseeuw, I suggest that in the late nineteenth century, legal changes wrought by colonial administrators that affected marriage laws and the definition of land ownership rendered women's family and work life increasingly difficult. In those circumstances, renunciation—even the very idea of it—plausibly became increasingly attractive. As I point out, however, contemporary nuns do not, as many studies assume, sever family ties; rather, they maintain relations with family members, who often provide them with the support they need as renunciants. Moreover, women who decide to renounce have often done so despite having been in the position to secure employment outside the home; their work was not necessarily restricted to child rearing and household chores. In other words, renunciation is not the *only* means of "livelihood" or "vocation" open to them. Seeing renunciation in that light casts doubt on liberal and feminist paradigms, which tend to interpret female renunciation as a means of attaining freedom from patriarchy. The *sil matas* associate the land on which they live with their religious practices. Despite their apparent struggle to find and maintain a physical space in which to establish renunciant practices, they shy away from owning land—at least as defined by a legalized concept of property. For *sil matas*, renunciation is about the cultivation of moral practice (literally grounded in living in a space of their own) that is intrinsically empowering (for want of a better word). Their attitudes to land—privileging *religious* practice over the legal ownership of property—help us understand that nuns' empowerment cannot simply be translated into some political affirmation of feminist freedom.

Chapter 8 continues to focus on the question of female renunciants' supposed empowerment, with reference to the proceedings of transnational forums. Here I analyze reports emerging from Sakyadhita International Conferences and the International Congress on Buddhist Women in Hamburg in 2007. I also conduct interviews with nuns living in Myanmar, Thailand, Nepal, Sri Lanka, and the United States. Participants who engage in transnational conversations (mainly in latinized idioms) about nuns focus on promoting the higher ordination for women. Yet, most nuns living throughout Asia understand the higher ordination quite differently from the way English-educated practitioners (mostly of non-Asian origin) do.[22] Rather than suggesting that this difference of perspectives be interpreted in terms of a feminism in which nuns from Asia need *education* in order to support the higher ordination, I argue that transnational forums of and about Buddhist nuns are based on a liberal feminism that attempts to project the fully ordained *bhikkhuni* as the ideal and universal model of a nun. Nuns of different Buddhist traditions who are well established, materially self-sufficient, and English *educated* enjoy membership in an array of global networks and engage in practices and debates that differ from what is known to most Asian monastics whom one encounters in this book. In this chapter I argue that ideas about the higher ordination are understood differently by Buddhist nuns, some speaking in a globalatinized idiom that others reject. I focus on Tibetan Buddhist nuns' articulations about the higher ordination in relation to secular-liberal values. Tibetan nuns who are not conversant with a liberal feminist paradigm are somewhat similar to other such nuns in prioritizing the renunciant everyday over a concern about the higher ordination. Nevertheless, certain comparisons of Tibetan and Theravada nuns—comparisons that have dominated transnational forums promoting the higher ordination—remain highly problematic. In general, this chapter seeks to raise doubts about widely held assumptions that Buddhist nuns represent a global sisterhood and to rethink the notion of empowerment in relation to nuns who do not even describe themselves in such a way.

Conclusion

This book makes a case for reassessing theories and frameworks that have portrayed contemporary female renunciation in Buddhism. Recent scholarship on Buddhist nuns tends to be guided by norms of canonical texts, supplemented by feminist presuppositions and liberal theories, in understanding the meaning of renunciant freedom and of debates about the higher ordination; it is also guided by a supposed *need* to find comparative categories of analysis across Buddhist traditions. That is, feminist notions of freedom are often perceived as valid not because they are universally valid; they gain their validity precisely in the comparative applications of them elsewhere, away from their birthplace. The model of comparison effectively produces a universalist *necessity* in an unending play of iterations referencing such a model. Studies guided by that universalist necessity are at best limited in scope and at worst condoning an underlying if not explicit legacy of Orientalism. (After all, comparativism remains heir to the Orientalist construction of religion.) This book argues for understandings of female renunciation beyond such comparative perspectives of seemingly universal values of freedom and equality and suggests that translations of renunciation and renunciant practice in terms of the categories used in such analyses be rethought.

This is not to promote cultural relativism or to extol an idealized "native" culture "out there" but rather to emphasize that religious lives, about which one may like to make grand claims in terms of seemingly universal notions, simply resist or remain unavailable for facile comparison and the application of such notions. In claiming the unavailability of such lives for comparison, I am also arguing that the presumed availability of the current analytical categories in the lives of those who live "elsewhere" is merely a presumption, not a reality that matches something that exists out there. I suggest that the very idea of what has been considered a so-called global sisterhood of Buddhism, the apparently self-evident category of "Theravada" when applied to renunciants who supposedly share a *common* heritage, and even the notion of *"bhikkhuni"* be reconsidered. This study provides no easy answers but raises questions that may help scholars rethink contemporary Buddhism and the responsibility of scholarship that seeks to represent it. What I am calling for is not more "ethnography," but more self-critical evaluation of how one reflects on everyday lives, and the practices that make them possible.

PART I

Narration

I

Decolonizing Female Renunciation

Introduction

In this chapter I seek to question scholarly narratives on gender and female renunciation in Buddhism. Those narratives forge feminist Buddhisms that address a Western academic audience while presenting new ways of thinking about texts and providing new empirical data. I discuss the works of three select scholars: Rita Gross, Tessa Bartholomeusz, and Wei-Yi Cheng.[1] Their studies have been influential in attempting to further the field of inquiry on the topic of gender in Buddhism, both in theory and in practice. To varying extents, all three scholars, who ground their studies in liberal notions of feminism and equality, are complicit in reinscribing master narratives that are for the most part privileged over the concerns of the Buddhist women who are the subjects of their research. The works of those three scholars, albeit written at different points in time and in differing contexts of gender, embrace a notion of Buddhist feminist "agency," which suggests how Buddhist practitioners act or might act to achieve a feminist "freedom." However, the conceptualization of such a notion of agency, rather than addressing the central concerns of their (predominantly Asian) subjects, who do not think in such ways, effectively places the subjects in a feminist narrative in which their thoughts and actions are considered to be deficient with reference to what they *should* be. In some cases, that agency can play out only on puppet strings—tied as it is to concepts of a non-Buddhist (and possibly Christian) heritage, or a secular articulation of liberal feminism, or Buddhist practitioners of such persuasion. In general, this chapter also identifies the relation between those narratives and the politics of colonialist discourse with reference to certain specificities.

In an interview with Saba Mahmood, Talal Asad states that it is important to question grand narratives because they may encourage a certain type of teleological thinking that overshadows conditions that are more immediate to the subjects of study:

> Once we get out of the habit of seeing everything in relation to the universal path to the future which the West has supposedly discovered, then it may be possible to describe things in their own terms. This is an eminently anthropological enterprise....The anthropologist must describe ways of life in appropriate terms. To begin with, at least, this means terms intrinsic to the social practices, beliefs, movements and traditions of the people being referred to and not in relation to some supposed future the people are moving towards. (Asad, "Modern Power")

Scholars writing about Buddhist feminism tend to seek a Buddhism that produces a freedom that involves liberation from structures of male-dominated constraints, which may be present in familial relations, monastic institutions, or Buddhist soteriology. Consequently, such scholars assess Buddhist practitioners in terms of their feminist awareness or consciousness. Asad notes in the same interview that in focusing on consciousness, which is invariably seen as either a "forced/oppressed" or "consenting" consciousness, we tend to overlook that (as in a game of chess) "there are certain circumstances and conditions that may or may not be immediately available to the consciousness of the person engaged in those activities but which constrain and structure the possibilities of his/her own actions....What is crucial here is what it is that one is in a sense obliged to do by the structuration of conditions and possibilities, not the consciousness, with which one does them" (Asad, "Modern Power"). In other words, he suggests that rather than focusing on consciousness of a particular kind—or on its absence—we need to consider the conditions and possibilities in which effective action (agency) can take place in the lived lives of individuals. Hence, Asad proceeds to argue that "the sense in which a theory gives scope to agency is quite different from the sense in which actual conditions give scope to agency" (Asad, "Modern Power"). In stating this, Asad cautions us against prioritizing theoretical interpretations that downplay conditions of life itself.

The narrative frameworks that are construed in the works of Gross, Bartholomeusz, and Cheng are not identical, but they share some assumptions about how feminism and Buddhism interrelate in theory and practice and how agency might be expressed. Though Gross's studies

of gender and Buddhism focus on the analysis of texts, they also reference comparative methodologies which appear to ground dialogue across
traditions. Bartholomeusz adopts frameworks based on particular texts
(known among Sri Lankan practitioners) to help explain the meaning
of female renunciation. Cheng, who admits having misgivings about
"Western feminist critiques of Buddhism," relies on the assumptions of
the very critiques she seeks to question. Those three scholars, rather than
thinking carefully about the conditions that make disciplinary practices
and renunciant lives possible, focus on how a feminist consciousness
(and agency) might be expressed in the texts and among the subjects they
discuss. By neglecting to address concerns embedded in the everyday lives
of practitioners, the works of those scholars bear witness to a narrative
disjunction between the lives of their subjects and the scholarly analyses
they forward. Albeit to different extents, their accounts dovetail in producing and reinforcing discourses that seem to recommend how a feminist
Buddhism should work.

Reading Feminist Buddhisms

Rita Gross has written prolifically about women and feminism in both
Buddhism and other religions. Her pioneering works continue to roil theoretical and empirical studies in these areas. Here I assess the usefulness
of Gross's works to scholarship on Buddhist women. Gross's contributions
need to be appreciated for what they are. She, together with Nancy A. Falk,
edited *Unspoken Worlds: Women's Religious Lives*, an interdisciplinary work
about cross-cultural studies of women's religious practices, and she published the first book-length study that reflects on the possibilities of envi-
sioning a more "egalitarian" Buddhism. A later work of hers, *Feminism
and Religion: An Introduction*, provides a survey of literature on the topic,
serving as a basic introduction for a general audience with little knowledge about feminism or religion. Gross's publications emerged within the
evolving discipline of religion in the Western academy when empirical
studies of women in religion, feminist theologies, and feminist critiques
of Buddhism were incipient.[2] Her work is pathbreaking in that she was
among the first scholars who provided introductory materials on feminist
religion and feminist Buddhism accessible to students in Western academia.[3] For that very reason, however, her studies need to be read with cir-
cumspection and with an appreciation for her stated strategies as well as
her audience. Gross writes about Buddhism both as an "insider" convert

and as an academic teaching at a state school in the United States where the teaching of religion claims to uphold "objectivity" and "neutrality." It is her attempt to express herself as a Buddhist feminist theologian (as she calls herself) and a teacher of American university students that results in writings that present inconsistencies or contradictions and at times evoke disturbingly Orientalist or colonial themes. Koppedrayer appropriately places Gross's works in "a longer history of forays into Asian religions that reflect the interior and individualistic preoccupations of North American seekers" (125). Her writings in the discipline are circumscribed, for as Kwok Pui-Lan notes about her thoughts on feminism, they concern "the tradition of liberalism and the modernist discourse on humanism" (Kwok, "Gender" 24). The discussion of Gross's works in the following pages will focus first on appraising the limitations of her studies within the discipline of religion and second on assessing their contributions to the field of gender studies in Buddhism.

Gross's contributions need to be seen in light of studies by scholars such as Tomoko Masuzawa, Arvind-Pal Mandair, and Timothy Fitzgerald, who question the conditions that gave rise to concepts of "world religions" and of "religion" itself. Those scholars think about the histories and implications of comparative inquiry that have become the hallmark of the discipline of religion (and religious studies). Masuzawa in her work *The Invention of World Religions; or, How European Universalism Was Preserved in the Language of Pluralism* argues that the very idea of world religions emerged from an attempt to classify religions and that such classifications were conditioned throughout time by specific models of modernity and secularism. According to Masuzawa, that enabled the West to ensure an ideological and seemingly "universal" sovereignty that resulted in "a new discourse of world religions, couched in the language of pluralism and diversity" (29) that is still present today. Mandair, whose work is based on Jacques Derrida's question "What if *religio* remained untranslatable?" (1) explains how what most scholars somewhat naively assumed as an objective phenomenon—"religion"—is in fact inseparable from political, capitalist, and secular matrices that are rooted in colonial ways of thinking. Timothy Fitzgerald was writing earlier than Mandair, but like both Mandair and Masuzawa, he is intent on questioning the academic construct that gave rise to the concept and discipline known as religion (and religious studies). Fitzgerald states that religion should not be studied "as though it were some objective feature of societies; it should instead be studied as an ideological category, an aspect of modern western ideology, with a specific location in history, including the nineteenth-century period of European colonization.... The confusion generated by the concept of religion cannot be explained only as a category mistake. Religion is really the basis of a modern form of theology" (4). That is what Fitzgerald goes on to call a "liberal ecumenical theology," which is a product of "western liberal capitalist ideology" and which includes "the so-called study of religion (also called the science of religion, religious studies, comparative religion and phenomenology of religion)" (6). Gross's works on gender in Buddhism are part of a discourse that is indebted to the "comparative study" of religion and the conceptualization of "world religions." In the following pages, I want to question Gross's works for their grounding in that discourse.

Gross's interest in the scholarship of diverse religions is informed by an idea attributed to Max Muller: To "know one religion is to know none" (*Feminism* 7–8).[4] Muller, who is known for his attempts to introduce a taxonomy of world religions, has associated such classifications with a loose translation of *divide et impera*, rendered by him as "classify and understand" (Muller 68). Sugirtharajah (citing Muller) has this to say about him:

> Max Muller... not only spoke in favour of territorial and political colonization of India but also called for its cultural and intellectual colonization. He saw "Sanskrit scholarship" in terms of "discovery and conquest" (Muller 1892: vi) and was keen that Britain should not stop with the "material conquest of India"; it should not "leave the laurels of its intellectual conquest entirely to other countries" (Muller 1982: viii). He pronounced that when the last two volumes of the Veda were published, it would signal the "conquest of the world by means of commerce, colonization, education, and conversion" (Muller 1902a: 289). (Sugirtharajah 69–70)[5]

Muller is considered one of the founding scholars of the discipline of comparative religion. Gross, building on the works of such scholars, proposes that religions share an "equivalence" in their common recognition of a "sacred" (*Feminism* 9).[6] She engages that notion of equivalence in her attempt to further "dialogue" with different religions. Yet the attribution of such equivalence defies the recognition that the historical processes that gave rise to the discipline of the comparative study of religion are grounded in Western imperialism. It is perhaps for that reason that, as Kwok has aptly observed, Gross notes the need to "avoid cultural imperialism,

ethnocentrism and colonialism" (Kwok, "Gender" 25) yet does not follow
through; she fails to reflect on just how those processes actually affect
scholarship on religion (Kwok, "Gender" 25–28). Gross's insensitivity to
the missionary and colonial impact of religion in Asian countries is evident in how she makes broad distinctions between the category of "world
religions" and "native" or "indigenous" traditions. Whereas the latter
include Native American and aboriginal religions, in which "colonialist
persecutions" and "missionary activities" have played a part (*Feminism*
63), the "world religions" rubric, under which Buddhism and other traditions in Asia fall, is (in keeping with a somewhat North American–centric
understanding) not seen in that light (*Feminism* 56–64). A certain lack of
understanding is also present in her statements about those apparently
different types of religion that supposedly entertain a liberal egalitarianism: "None of the major world religions…treat women and men equally,
though they fail to a greater or lesser extent.…Whether such evaluations
apply to small-scale tribal and ethnic traditions, such as Native American
or African traditional religions, is a much more complex question" (106).
For Gross, egalitarianism becomes the *norm* by which religions are judged
and "fail to a greater or lesser extent."[7]

In her analysis of religion, Gross tends to dismiss essential questions
related to the idea of comparative religion. Such questions, raised by
Timothy Fitzgerald among others, focus on how the study of religion is
rooted in specific ideological and colonial processes (Fitzgerald 17–19,
31). Gross grounds her work in the assumption that the discipline of religion has an "inherently comparative character" (*Garland* 80) and goes
on to adopt a phenomenological perspective in her study of religion.
For example, in keeping with the phenomenologists, Gross suggests in
her book *Feminism and Religion* that "knowing about and understanding a religion is quite different from believing it. The academic study of
religion depends on that distinction" (7). Moreover, according to her, the
academic study of religion should take into account "the neutral setting
of the academic classroom" (*Feminism* 8). Attempting to move beyond
the framework of the discipline while effectively working within it
results in the inconsistencies of her approach to objectivity in the study
of religion—for example, when she asserts that one should "develop
what objectivity is possible and… treat all religions even-handedly and
with empathy" (*Feminism* 101); and also when she states that "objectivity and neutrality prove to be impossible ideals" (*Feminism* 73), particularly in the scholarship of women's studies in religion (*Feminism* 83)!

As a teacher who is a Western Buddhist feminist, Gross faces a tension between, on the one hand, attempting to construct a feminist religion at a deeply personal level and integrate that as a social vision for students in a North American state university and, on the other hand, maintaining the necessary neutrality of the classroom setting. It is Gross's attempting to resolve that tension that both informs and directs her writing, ultimately giving rise to inconsistencies and colonial discourse. As Chandra T. Mohanty argues, "feminist scholarly practices...are inscribed in relations of power—relations that they counter, resist, or even perhaps implicitly support. There can, of course, be no apolitical scholarship" (19). Mohanty's comments remind us that claims to neutrality and objectivity, claims that are supposedly necessary in a certain academic setting, are not what they seem to be and may even be detrimental to feminist scholarship.

Gross's disregard for how the dynamics of power determine the construction and study of religion becomes particularly prevalent in her discussion of gender. She suggests a somewhat questionable distinction between "feminism as an academic method," which she names "women's studies," and "feminism as a social vision" ("Feminism" 16–28). That distinction became the subject of a well-known debate with Katherine Young, which, for want of space, I will not recapitulate (Kwok, "Gender" 24–26; Gross, "A Rose"; Young). According to Gross, women's studies involves collecting more data for the purposes of accuracy in the representation of women and the construction of new paradigms; it remains neutral and, according to her, "does not inherently make judgments about what women's position in society should be" (*Feminism* 21). She proposes that, unlike feminism as an academic method, feminism as a social vision can be judgmental, or "radically critical of current conventional norms and expectations" (*Feminism* 22). It is within that description of feminism as a social vision that Gross develops her thinking on feminist religion, which in turn informs her academic investigations within the discipline. In her thinking, the need for the collection of information about women is also intrinsically related to feminism as a social vision (*Feminism* 21). Such data collection was deemed central to the preparation of her earlier work *Unspoken Worlds*, co-edited with Nancy Falk (Falk and Gross xv). Gross, in discussing the collection of women's stories in that volume, notes that "the most obvious generalization that leaps from the [stories], which partially explains why this material has been so overlooked in androcentric scholarship, is the silence, the often nonverbal and almost always nontextual context of women's spirituality. (The word *unspoken* in the title derives from that fact)" (*Feminism* 81). Such comments on the unspoken spirituality of women implicitly allow scholars a relatively free rein in constructing the experiences of (the other) women as they will.[8] Indeed, for Gross, the collection of data necessarily involves repainting the entire picture concerning women's religious lives and their place in scholarly works (*Feminism* 76–85). But in her writing she implicates herself in a discourse on women that has a long Orientalist history. That is evident in her attempt to explain how the presentation of data may involve a paradigm shift from an androcentric to an androgynous representation of humanity. She dwells on the presentation of a particular type of statement: "'The Egyptians allow (or don't allow) women to...' The structure is so commonplace that even today many do not see what is wrong with it. But for both those who make such statements and... those who hear them without wincing, real Egyptians are men. Egyptian women are objects acted upon by real Egyptians...but are not themselves full Egyptians" (*Feminism* 18). Gross then proceeds to attempt a corrective to this statement: "Someone who understands the inadequacies of the androcentric model of humanity and the need for a more accurate, two sexed model of humanity would write that 'in Egyptian society, men do X and women do Y,' or perhaps, in some cases, she might write that 'Egyptian men allow Egyptian women to...,' thereby recognizing that Egyptian men have patriarchal control over the society but that Egyptian women are nevertheless Egyptian human beings, not a different species" (*Feminism* 20). That corrective is, however, not just about a representation of Egyptian women; it is also about the North American audience Gross addresses. She invites that audience to be in a position of thinking about saving Egyptian women from Egyptian men, or—in relation to a well-known phrase—asking white women to "save" brown women from brown men.[9] I will now turn to how that idea of "saving" permeates Gross's prescriptions for a feminist Buddhism and is embedded in particular conceptualizations of Buddhist practice.

Gross says that a biblical "prophetic voice" is missing in Buddhism, a spirit of self-criticism that she views as intrinsic to social transformation in religion. While she asserts that Buddhism itself does not lack a social ethic, she states that "Buddhists have generally not been willing to engage in social action" (*Patriarchy* 134). The fault, then, lies not with Buddhism, but rather with *Asian* Buddhists mired in a status quo. As a Western Buddhist, she herself claims "to use the prophetic voice as a Buddhist feminist"

(*Patriarchy* 134). Gross's thinking that a Buddhist feminism must emerge from among Western Buddhists rather than Asians has been widely criticized by scholars of Western and Asian origins (Cheng 5–6; Kawahashi 448; Koppedrayer 124; Kwok, "Gender" 26–28). Yet such thinking continues to inform her work in international forums and to influence others.[10] The very notion that Asian Buddhists need to engage a Buddhist feminism and yet are incapable of so doing attests to an Orientalist discourse that continues to pervade the scholarship on contemporary Buddhist nuns. Gross's articulation of a feminist Buddhism is disturbing on other grounds as well. First, it portrays a "Western" Buddhism which, like its foil, "Asian" Buddhism, is often represented as a somewhat undifferentiated unity. Second, it conflates textual idealizations and social realities. Third, it is based on the assumption of dichotomies, such as lay/monastic and private/public, that are of questionable relevance to Buddhist practice in general and the experiences of Buddhist women in particular.

Gross, in differentiating Western Buddhism from Asian Buddhism while drawing on various textual sources and Western practices, does not engage contemporary practices of women in the Asian societies she purports to discuss. That is very evident in her work *Buddhism after Patriarchy*, which is devoted to a textual Buddhism and a theoretical reconstruction based on it. That is also true for her comments on other Asian religions. For instance, half-way through her book *Feminism and Religion* she states that she has "thus far focused on feminist analysis of the *present* forms of religion" (149). However, a discussion of contemporary practices of the Asian religions she mentions is lacking in that book. Instead, she makes broad generalizations concerning certain religions—generalizations she bases on an analysis of texts—all the while putatively addressing a context that is more social and contemporary. For example, she proposes that "Christianity, Buddhism and Taoism...are less centered in the family and more concerned with the individual's spiritual well-being" (*Feminism* 92). The "individual's spiritual well-being" is a reference to the ideal religious life as represented in texts, yet it becomes part of a blanket statement about how those *religions* rather than religious *practitioners* are relatively less concerned with the family. Gross, by conflating textual ideals with social lives, has ignored family and kin networks that are intrinsic to the social engagement present in the everyday lives of contemporary practitioners. As she continues to explain, "These religions...also have monastic institutions in which women have participated, sometimes in great numbers. Thus women do have an alternative to their family roles in these religions"

(*Feminism* 92). Gross's work evokes three apparently self-evident dichotomies that I question: religion (the textual ideal) versus (the patriarchal/
oppressive) family, public versus private (a liberal distinction), and lay versus monastic. For example, by conflating those dichotomics, she clearly
intimates that an alternative to family roles—presumably that of wife and
mother, "which women *do* have" (92; emphasis added)—is the renunciant role outside the family. Such dichotomies may make some sense in
secular-liberal feminisms, but they need to be scrutinized afresh if we are
to attempt to begin understanding the particularities of the lived lives of
female renunciants who do not articulate themselves in such ways.

The public/private distinction draws on a feminist model that, as I detail
in the next chapter, has limited relevance for an analysis of Buddhist wom-
en's practices. The lay/monastic difference, which is hardly as clear-cut in
practice as some might suppose, is one that Gross develops in an attempt
to reconceptualize the meaning of sangha, typically translated as "monastic community." She focuses on concerns about the lay/monastic distinction in Buddhism in her chapter "Androgynous View: New Concerns in
Verbalizing the Dharma" in *Buddhism after Patriarchy*.[11] According to that
chapter, "Buddhism's institutional structure has stressed a dichotomy
between monastics and laypeople" (*Patriarchy* 271). She proceeds to suggest that "this focus on the monastic *sangha* as the true carrier of the religion has also been its greatest weakness. It has led to a relative lack of
attention to lay members" (*Patriarchy* 271).[12] While Gross mentions that
Buddhist practice in Asia and elsewhere may challenge that dichotomy,
she states that the dichotomy itself remains relevant. She suggests that the
very concept of sangha be rethought so that it is imbued "with the feminist values of community, nurturance, communication, relationship and
friendship" (*Patriarchy* 265). Here Gross has recommended a rejection
of a (somewhat dubious) lay/monastic dichotomy perceived as predominantly non-Western and revalorized it in terms of a Western Buddhist
feminism. Although Gross admits to Asian alternatives to this dichotomy,
she dismisses them. Subsequently she proposes that, rather than conventionally continuing to seek freedom *from* the world (again borrowing
from a questionable this-worldly/otherworldly dichotomy and hinting at
a private/public differentiation), "the feminist call is for nothing less than
finding freedom within the world, within domestic concerns, within emo-
tions, within sexuality, within parenthood, within career" (*Patriarchy* 278).
The call continues to find a grounding in an assumption about the presence of the sacred/profane and public/private distinctions that are well

known in the Western academy. It is unsurprising, then, that she comes to a conclusion that has disturbed many, claiming that reforming Buddhism requires a transformation that may ideally derive from the West: "Western Buddhism, in which the vast majority of Buddhists are both serious practitioners and lay people heavily involved in family and career concerns, may well be the most fertile ground for this development. Interestingly, Western Buddhism is also the only form of Buddhism subject to significant feminist influence and the most likely vanguard of Buddhism after patriarchy" (*Patriarchy* 271). Gross's message touts a Buddhism that speaks to Western interests and is couched in the kind of comparative and "world religions" framework that Fitzgerald and Masuzawa have critiqued. It resonates with what Mandair has referred to as the "repetition of the colonial event," in which the creation of a boundary between the West and the Rest involves "an innate ability to self-reference, even when the discourse is about the West's other" (Mandair 5). Gross indicates that while Asian Buddhism is in need of transformation (in terms of the feminist realization of a post-patriarchal Buddhism), the solution will probably have to come from the West. Gross's works should not be read as an analysis of Buddhism that is useful to Buddhist practitioners in Asian contexts.[13] In effect, Gross has found in Buddhist texts a formulation for the construction of (Western) Buddhist feminisms that has little significance for the realities of Buddhist practitioners in Asia. Such an adoption of Buddhist texts, while largely ignoring the voices of practicing Buddhists outside dominant Western contexts, is also found, albeit in a different way, in Tessa Bartholomeusz's study of Buddhist nuns in Sri Lanka, which I turn to next.

Renunciation and Its Freedoms: Inscribing Female Religiosity

Bartholomeusz's study of contemporary Buddhist nuns in Sri Lanka, like similar scholarship on early empirical studies of female renunciants, is to be commended for having lent a certain cachet to research in that area. When she began her work on those women, they were considered by some to be "unworthy" subjects of study.[14] In that sense, Bartholomeusz has accomplished for the study of contemporary Buddhist nuns a task comparable to that which scholars such as Rita Gross, Diana Paul and Frances Wilson, Miranda Shaw, Liz Wilson, Susan Murcott, and Arvind Sharma did for the textual and theoretical study in the field of women in

Buddhism in the 1980s and 1990s and that which Analayo, Elise DeVido, Ann Heirman, Anne Klein, Gisela Krey, and others have done more recently. Additionally, Bartholomeusz, as the author of the first major book-length publication on Theravada nuns that attempts to historically contextualize nuns in modernity, has broken new and difficult ground for both later scholars and practitioners to build on. My critical appraisal of the book *Women under the Bō Tree* needs to be seen, on the one hand, as a recognition of what Bartholomeusz, writing two decades ago in a particularly politically tense period in Sri Lanka, was able to accomplish and, on the other, as an attempt to indicate how her work repeats (to use Mandair's notion) the logic of a self-referential colonial discourse.[15] Whereas Gross uses Buddhist texts in her construction of a Buddhist feminism for the West, Bartholomeusz relies on texts to speak for the contemporary realities of female renunciants.

Textual models of *bhikkhunis* play a significant role in Bartholomeusz's engagement of nineteenth- and twentieth-century female renunciants ("lay nuns" in her terminology) in Sri Lanka.[16] Those models are extrapolated from two kinds of sources in Pali: Sri Lankan chronicles such as the *Dīpavaṃsa, Mahāvaṃsa,* and *Cūlavaṃsa,* which are generally used to portray historical events relevant to Buddhism in Sri Lanka, as well as canonical Buddhist sources deriving from India. Although Bartholomeusz claims to look at "Buddhism from the perspective of those women who have renounced the world" (11), a careful reading of her work indicates that the textual ideals she uses serve more to structure master narratives of discourse than to convey nuns' perspectives. There are two main discourses that inform her work. First, there is what she calls the "*Mahāvaṃsa* view of history," an idea she borrows from H. L. Seneviratne that suggests that, according to some, the *Mahavamsa* promotes Sri Lanka as the bastion of a pure and authentic form of Buddhism associated exclusively with the Sinhalese (Bartholomeusz 14). Second, there is a discourse about the "ancient *bhikkhunīs*" (to use Bartholomeusz's terminology) that falls under the rubric of the *Mahavamsa* view of history and includes the *bhikkhunis* of the Pali *Vinaya* texts. Whereas the latter is a reference to Indian *bhikkhunis* around the time of the Buddha, the "*Mahavamsa* view" spotlights the third-century B.C.E. story of the Indian *bhikkhuni* (previously a princess) Sanghamitta, who is recorded as having brought the *upasampada* to Sri Lanka and conferred it on the renunciant Anula (previously a queen) of Sri Lanka and her retinue of female renunciants. Bartholomeusz's discussion of the ancient *bhikkhunis,* like her account of the nuns' *Mahavamsa* view of history, takes on a life of its own when she describes it in terms of the *need* for the *bhikkhuni upasampada*. I will analyze the construction of each of those discourses in turn.

In her second chapter, "Nineteenth-Century Ceylon: The Emergence of the Lay Nun," Bartholomeusz situates the lay nun in a new "Protestant Buddhism" that centers on the "salvation" of the individual. The lay nun is also depicted as one who looks to the model of Anula in the chronicles:

> The lay nuns' vocation was conservative; its precedent was the post-canonical *Mahāvaṃsa* and *Dīpavaṃsa* story of Anulā who kept the ten precepts, renounced the world, and wore the ochre robe, even before entering the *sangha*. By setting themselves up in the roles of nuns, these pious laywomen...considered that their activities maintained and revived Buddhism." (43)[17]

That chapter indicates the presence of yellow-robed female renunciants in the nineteenth century. However, evidence that those nuns saw themselves as either following in the footsteps of Anula or of "reviving" Buddhism is lacking. That is the issue at stake in the depiction of the late nineteenth-century renunciant Sudharmachari, whom many view as a founding nun and who we are told "subscribed to the *Mahāvaṃsa* view of history" (95). Here Bartholomeusz, citing a source on the biography of Sudharmachari, attributes to her, as do her biographers, a memory of "Anulā and her retinue who...eagerly awaited the arrival of Bhikkhunī Saṅghamittā" (95). The master narrative that places Sudharmachari in relation to Anula is introduced by Sudharmachari's biographers and adopted by Bartholomeusz, yet it is not obvious that Sudharmachari herself saw Anula as a role model. In fact, Bartholomeusz reports that contemporary nuns who knew Sudharmachari said that she "did not intend to re-establish the order of nuns in Ceylon" (95). How then can Sudharmachari have seen herself in Anula, and what does it mean to claim that she supported a *Mahavamsa* view of history? I propose that Sudharmachari, as well as the late twentieth-century nuns Bartholomeusz interviewed, is placed in a narrative about ancient *bhikkhunis* to make sense of the absence of a *bhikkhuni* order since the late nineteenth century. However, as I will argue, making sense of that absence was of less concern to the nuns Bartholomeusz talks about than it was to Bartholomeusz herself.

The discussion of modern nuns in relation to the ancient *bhikkhunis* applies both to foreign nuns and to English- and Sinhalese-speaking

nuns. Two chapters focus on recounting how three foreign women came
to know the renowned ambassador of Buddhism Anagarika Dharmapala
through their work in the recently founded Theosophical Society. They
became central in the organization of late nineteenth-century institutions
for Buddhist women in Sri Lanka, such as the Sanghamitta School for Girls
and the Sanghamitta Upāsikārāmaya (hermitage for female devotees).
Those foreign women were the Australian Kate Pickett, who died within
two weeks of her arrival in the country, and two Americans: Miranda de
Souza Canavarro, who remained in the country for about three years, from
1897 to 1900, and Catherine Shearer, who was there for an even shorter
time. Canavarro and Shearer both adopted renunciant attire and collaborated with Dharmapala, who is cited as having been eager to establish a
bhikkhuni order at the time. What is interesting about Bartholomeusz's
narrative is the claim that Canavarro and Shearer were pivotal not only in
establishing a new nunnery but also in furthering Dharmapala's goal of
reviving the *bhikkhuni* order. The account about Canavarro is revealing.
We are told that while she did not distinguish between the eight or ten
precepts of the laity and the rules of the *bhikkhunis* and "eventually decided
on a modified Catholic habit" (62), she also appears to have claimed that
she and the other renunciants at her hermitage were akin to the *bhikkhunis* of the *Mahāvaṃsa* (74). As Bartholomeusz indicates in her cita-
tions of Dharmapala's doubts concerning Canavarro, the latter's model
of the *bhikkhuni* appears to have been of her own making. Yet, according
to Bartholomeusz, Canavarro (together with Dharmapala) is responsible
for having "re-established the tradition of female renunciation in Ceylon"
(65), and by challenging "the stereotype of the pious Buddhist woman as
wife and mother," she (and others) helped make "renunciation a respectable choice for Buddhist women in Ceylon" (82). Canavarro's notion of
being a nun, as Bartholomeusz herself notes, evidently differed from that
of the nuns of the Pali texts (68–70), yet Bartholomeusz affirms a distinct
connection between Canavarro and "the tradition of female renunciation."
In doing so, she falls prey to what Dorothy E. Smith refers to as *institutional capture*, in which the researcher "begins converting informants'
accounts of their experience into the terms of an institutional discourse
that constitutes people and their activities as the objects of…knowl-
edge.…In…these cases, institutional relations and the social organization of experience have slipped from view" (McCoy 110). Bartholomeusz,
in writing about Buddhist nuns, is reinscribing a narrative in which
Western women are given credit for having provided Sri Lankan nuns

with access to a respectable freedom of renunciation (set apart from the sphere of domesticity), and hence for having become pioneers on the Sri Lankan Buddhist scene.

Bartholomeusz's account of late nineteenth-century events in Chapter 4 seems tailored to promote a need for the re-establishment of the *bhikk-huni* order. That is also indicated in the chapters on the lay nuns in the early twentieth century as well as in Sri Lanka before its independence (Chapters 5 and 6) when she frames the nuns within efforts "to re-establish the tradition of female renunciation" (91) or to "revive a tradition" (117) that was lost.[18] Such a trope appears throughout Bartholomeusz's work and continues to pervade scholarly narratives on contemporary Buddhist nuns. Bartholomeusz presents it as a means of both providing continuity from one century to the next and framing accounts of the nuns she interviewed about a century after Shearer and Canavarro had been active in the country. Bartholomeusz implies that there is a difference between the textual image of the "ideal" of female renunciation and its "actual" state (13) in contemporary Buddhism, yet she uses that ideal to inform, mold, and speak for the actual. She explains her project accordingly.

> The account links the classical tradition of female renunciation immortalized in the texts with the living practice of contemporary lay nuns of Sri Lanka. In the process of this illustration, I highlight innovations and differences among the lay nuns and compare their vocation to that of the ancient *bhikkhunīs*. Though the lay nuns are not members of the *saṅgha*, they provide many of the functions of the defunct Theravādin order of nuns, albeit with important differences. (131)

Bartholomeusz indicates that among the nuns she interviewed at her main research site, "the majority would not accept entrance into the *saṅgha*, even if it were possible" (136), and that all the lay nuns she interviewed "agreed that if the nuns' lineage were reintroduced," their "power...[as renunciants] would be lost" (137).

How then are the twentieth-century nuns Bartholomeusz studied similar to the ancient *bhikkhunis*? The comparison of the so-called contemporary lay nuns with the "ancient order of nuns" (16) or the ancient *bhikkhunis* is apparently smooth and seamless, for "though there is not an officially sanctioned order of nuns in Sri Lanka today, there are women who set themselves up in the role of the ordained nun, the *bhikkhunī*,

without changing formal status" (3). Bartholomeusz states that contemporary lay nuns "set themselves up" as *bhikkhunis*. But did they? And if they
did consider themselves *bhikkhunis*, what did that mean? Were textual
notions of "the ancient *bhikkhunī*" the same as theirs? Or, like Canavarro,
did they understand the meaning of *bhikkhuni* differently? What did it
mean for the renunciants Bartholomeusz interviewed in the late 1980s
"to walk in the footsteps of the ancient *bhikkhunī*" (9)? I propose that the
continual elision between the world of the ancient *bhikkhuni* and that of
the subjects she interviewed promotes Bartholomeusz's broader agenda
of fitting contemporary renunciant practices into her teleological schema
of Buddhist revival and reform.[19]

The contemporary nuns who have been subjects of Bartholomeusz's
research do not typically consider themselves *bhikkhunis*, but because
they are often compared with ancient *bhikkhunis* in her narrative, they
are—without a *bhikkhuni upasampada*—implicitly lacking in "status"
and "rights." Hence, Bartholomeusz describes one nun who saw "continuity between her vocation and that of the ancient *bhikkhunī*...[yet]
argued forcefully...that lay nuns have no right to assume the privileges
of the members of the defunct order of nuns" (158). The postulation of
the *desirability* of the *bhikkhuni* ordination—which was rejected by most
Sinhalese-speaking nuns Bartholomeusz interviewed—later echoes in
another strand of her narrative when it is portrayed as being recognized
by Western renunciants. She infers that while a few nuns were in favor
of the *upasampada*, those who supported it were "mostly comprised [*sic*]
of western women; in fact, it is these women and the laity who keep the
issue alive" (169). While a footnote refers to the Sinhalese-speaking nun
Ambala Rohana Gnanashila Sil Mata, who favors the re-establishment of
the order, the next section, entitled "Western Women and the Path of the
Buddha," is devoted to Buddhist nuns from America, England, Germany,
and Australia—the "western nuns"—who for the most part believe that
the Sinhalese-speaking nuns are not following Buddhist renunciation as
they should (171). The uncritical acceptance of the idea that Sri Lankan
Buddhism needs to be resurrected by Westerners who know (or live) it
"better" than Sri Lankans resonates with a certain type of colonial knowledge production. That kind of thinking is reinforced in an account that
mentions how two German nuns were penalized in Sri Lanka for their
somewhat unusual efforts to bring about the *bhikkhuni upasampada*.
In contrast, two Sri Lankan women Bartholomeusz discusses in the
very next section are portrayed as failed renunciants. One of them, a

nun-turned-householder, is depicted as a woman who followed the example of a Western nun when she decided to renounce, yet she failed to continue the renunciant life because "her duty as a wife and mother weighed
heavily on her conscience" and because she was "discouraged" in her
progress in meditation. That lapsed renunciant is seen as an unsatisfied
householder who feels obliged to care for a sick spouse and "misses her
life of meditation" (176). The other Sri Lankan Bartholomeusz discusses
is a nun who "does not wish to see the re-establishment of the order of
nuns in Sri Lanka" (177). Although Bartholomeusz depicts renunciation
as freeing women from household responsibilities and implies that the
bhikkhuni status is desirable, she also intimates that there is no adequate
resolution of the supposed problem that Sri Lankan nuns must face. First,
the status of *bhikkhuni* is one to which mostly Western rather than Sri
Lankan nuns aspire. Second, Sri Lankan nuns are generally depicted as
unwilling to become *bhikkhunis* for fear of losing a certain "power" they
had obtained by becoming renunciants (137). She conclusively reinforces
the view that Sri Lankan nuns are in trouble, since they, "like the ancient
bhikkhunī saṅgha, . . . are the objects of ascetic misogyny" (179).

The conflation of modern lay nuns with their purported ancient "counterparts" occurs frequently throughout Bartholomeusz's work and has
effectively manufactured a certain homogenization of female renunciant
identities across time. According to Bartholomeusz, the female renunciants of the third century B.C.E. share with those of the twentieth century a
common bond—namely, difficulties that are unique to women: "Whether
they renounced lay life in the third century BCE or in the twentieth century CE, female renunciants—both lay and ordained—have faced hard-
ships unknown to men" (3). Bartholomeusz indicates that the *bhikkhunis*
of the third century included queens and women known for their "scholarly acumen" (3) and that many of the contemporary renunciants she
interviews are "from uneducated, farming families" (104), yet that contrast
does not detract from the comparison of female renunciants across social
boundaries—and centuries. The *bhikkhuni* of the past and the contemporary nun she talks about walk the same path. Bartholomeusz, in conducting her research with nuns, was mediating her interviews and framing
her writing with an essentialized, monolithic perspective of "the ancient
bhikkhuni." The images of modern nuns, often seen as little different from
those of the ancient *bhikkhuni,* involve a homogenization akin to what
Mohanty observes concerning Western feminist scholarship's narrative of
"the Third World Woman" as the "oppressed group." According to her,

"the application of the notion of women as a homogenous category to
women in the Third World colonizes and appropriates the pluralities of
the simultaneous location of different groups of women in social class and
ethnic frameworks" (39).[20] Mohanty warns of the pitfalls of constructing
categories such as "woman/women" as existing prior to specified social
and patriarchal structures in which women's lives are imbricated. She
indicates that one should instead consider how those structures and relationships are themselves foundational in producing categories of analysis
(27–28). Similarly, I propose that we be wary of constructing categories
such as "the ancient *bhikkhuni*" and the "the lay nun" without, for example, questioning the monastic and non-monastic structures in which those
categories are configured. In other words, *bhikkhunis* and nuns should
not be perceived as mere denizens within or without monastic structures
but rather as practitioners whose practices play out in the relations that
emerge from such structures. The definitions of who those women are
and what they do cannot be taken as self-evident. Bartholomeusz, by
inscribing master narratives on perceptions of female renunciants, holds
the renunciants and their everyday practices hostage to discourses not of
their making.

Bartholomeusz takes up the issue of *bhikkhuni* status again in her chapter entitled "The Sri Lankan *Bhikkhunī Saṅgha:* Trends and Reflections."
There she discusses the ordination of *sil matas* in the United States
and gives a separate account of *sil matas* who claim *bhikkhuni* status. In
both cases, Bartholomeusz implies that the *sil matas* are failed *bhikkhunis*. Those who travel to the United States for the ordination return to
Sri Lanka and continue their lives as novice nuns rather than as fully
ordained *bhikkhunis*. Their reasons for traveling to the United States
seem to center less on an enthusiasm for receiving the higher ordination than on a desire to travel abroad. Bartholomeusz visited a hermitage
where *sil matas* who claim to be *bhikkhunis* and follow the *Vinaya* are
viewed with suspicion by other *sil matas*. My concern with that narrative does not stem from a doubt about a claim as to whether those *sil
matas* could or could not be considered fully ordained *bhikkhunis*. Rather,
it derives from the implication that even though (in chapters 3 and 4
in particular) foreigners (in connection with Dharmapala) successfully
set the stage for the re-establishment of female renunciation, the Sri
Lankan elite and the female renunciants themselves were somehow
unable to follow through. Among the concluding remarks of the chapter
"The Sri Lankan *Bhikkhunī Saṅgha,*" Bartholomeusz indicates that the

contemporary female renunciants, though "subordinate" and in agreement that the re-establishment of the *bhikkhuni* order is "impossible," do not recognize their subordination (189–190). In other words, she implies that the Sinhalese-speaking female renunciants either are unaware of their subordination or are ambivalent about overcoming it, if not unwilling to overcome it. The inference that those nuns are essentially either ignorant or incapable of overcoming their subordination—which *is* recognized by others—is based on the assumption that to eliminate their subordinate (inferior) position, they (who are ignorant) need to be taught by enlightened (Western) others who can educate them so that they might seek a certain (feminist?) equality. Here the *capability* of recognizing and overcoming their subordination becomes superimposed on the conditions of the lives that nuns already live.[21] Like Gross, Bartholomeusz finds in Buddhist texts a way of framing the practitioners in her study that has little "meaning" for the practitioners' own lives; in so doing she produces a curative discourse about feminism and renunciation that sets norms for how practitioners should ideally practice. But those norms ultimately seek to *replace* the very lives that are to be improved. In other words, a moralist norm or ideal becomes a substitute or an alternative for the conditions of the nuns' lives. How easy it is to forget that one never lives one's life apart from the conditions in which one finds one's self. Norms—if there are such things—exist as part of the conditions in which people live, not as superimposed ideals that one can "choose" apart from those conditions.

Feminist Perspectives and Buddhist Nuns

Wei-Yi Cheng's work *Buddhist Nuns in Taiwan and Sri Lanka: A Critique of the Feminist Perspective* stems from a perceived dissonance between Western feminist discourses about Buddhism in relation to Cheng's own grounding as an "Asian Buddhist woman."[22] In effect, she questions whether Western feminist discourses on Buddhism have much relevance in understanding the contemporary experiences of Buddhist nuns in both Sri Lanka and Taiwan. Her ambitious study bridges the geographical and cultural divide between those places by interlacing narrative themes that play out in her analysis—namely, the themes of "feminist discourses," "empowerment," and "welfare." Her conclusions rely largely on extrapolations from surveys.[23] Cheng is evidently concerned about what a Western feminist discourse might mean for the study of religion as that discourse "may unintentionally set up imperial boundaries that homogenize differences among women" (6). Such a discourse is one she wishes to move away from. Thus, unlike the works of Gross and Bartholomeusz, Cheng's study is concerned about Orientalist representations of women in Buddhism. Nevertheless, a close reading of her work bears witness to a repetition of the very perspectives she seeks to critique.[24] While she is careful to avoid making generalizations about nuns and states that the diverse responses she has received prohibit easy conclusions in her comparative study, she persists in framing her work with reference to the very Western feminist discussions she wants to undermine. Additionally, she continues to adopt master narratives about Buddhist nuns that have been introduced by Western scholars and practitioners. Cheng, by placing her empirical study within such frameworks, fails to adequately question the rhetoric she adopts, and consequently falls short of focusing on concerns that seem central to the everyday lives of the renunciant subjects of her research. One such master narrative is related to her preoccupation with a Western feminist discourse and is tied into her conceptualization of empowerment, the *bhikkhuni* ordination, and the welfare of nuns. The second narrative concerns her portrayal of contemporary nuns whom she depicts both as counterparts of the ancient *bhikkhuni* (as does Bartholomeusz) and as practitioners of an authentic Theravada Buddhism. The first narrative is informed by scholars who assume a liberal feminism that suggests that renunciation and the higher ordination are acts that bear witness to feminist values, such as women's independence and self-reliance. That narrative is also associated with a discourse of development that construes "welfare" in a materialistic frame of reference. The second narrative assumes an unquestioned link between nuns of the present and nuns of the past and demonstrates an uncritical acceptance of the existence of a distinctive Theravada or Mahayana identity.

In her third chapter Cheng seeks to engage Buddhist nuns' opinions about selected textual topics that have dominated the discussion on Buddhist feminisms. Those topics focus on the suggestions that (1) women are subordinate to men, because they are born with an inferior karma; (2) women may not have the same potential as men to realize the ultimate goal (nirvana or arahantship for the Theravada nuns in Sri Lanka, and Buddhahood for the Mahayana nuns of Taiwan); and (3) the "Eight Special Rules" subordinate nuns to monks. In her fourth chapter Cheng addresses scholarly concerns about gender in Buddhism in relation to four topics in the experiences of contemporary nuns: (1) renunciation, (2) education, (3) the mixed-sex sangha (in Taiwan only), and (4) the *bhikkhuni* ordination (focusing on Sri Lanka).

All seven topics that her surveys and interviews address are spearheaded by comments from scholars of Buddhism whose arguments she seeks to assess in terms of views conveyed by contemporary nuns. Interestingly, several of those topics are selected and formulated in terminology used by Rita Gross. Gross, who has been a source of both inspiration and alienation for Cheng, continues to haunt the pages of Cheng's work (Cheng 9, 68–69, 198–199). The questions that Cheng raises were inspired by Gross, and they are for the most part irrelevant to the nuns she studies. One consequence is that Cheng wastes effort attempting to fit her narrative on nuns into a framework she herself acknowledges is removed from their own concerns. To her credit, Cheng articulates an awareness of her complicity in the narrative disjunction that she has produced. She states that many of the issues she raises in her study, such as those relating to the nature of "inferior karma" ascribed to women and those relating to women's ability to realize ultimate goals, are of little relevance: "Throughout my fieldwork, I often felt foolish for asking the hermetical questions (about women's karma and the ultimate goals). As much as these questions are often discussed by Western feminists (e.g., Gross 1993), it soon became apparent to me that these issues are trivial to the nuns" (80). At the end of the day, Cheng's findings remain inconclusive, and a sense of academic (and perhaps even personal) alienation echoes in her final chapter:

> Perhaps the biggest distortion of this research, however, is not what I have omitted, but the partial silencing of my research subjects.... My research subjects are partially silenced because I forced them to speak about issues raised by Western feminists, rather than beginning with their own agenda.... But if I had not asked the questions first, what would the nuns have said? What issues would they have indicated as the issues that matter most in their lives? (190)

What Cheng indicates is that her research represents nuns whose responses are constrained by her questions, whereas who they are and what is most important to *them* remain somewhat obscure. In her study Cheng has attempted to engage issues on which (Western) scholarship on Buddhism has centered, and she recognizes that there is a serious methodological problem. A main contribution of her book is that it bears witness to that problem.

Cheng, by examining the place of feminism and women's empowerment in Buddhism, seeks to assess the meaning of the "welfare" of Buddhist nuns. Throughout her work, empowerment is often framed by a liberal feminist conceptualization of the realization of potential in the public sphere (43–47, 200)—a conceptualization that I consider more in the next chapter. For Cheng, welfare is also connected to nuns' social status and the *bhikkhuni upasampada*, and (echoing previous scholarship on the subject) it is seen in terms of their securing "equality" or "equal rights" (103, 166–167, 174). Moreover, welfare is explained (in keeping with developmental discourses prevalent at the time) as access to material resources and education (16, 142, 115). Cheng's study of nuns' welfare, highlighted as a matter of the *bhikkhuni upasampada* and access to resources, is problematic—especially in the Sri Lankan context—because the questions she raises emerge from discourses that are at most peripheral to the everyday lives of those nuns. To better understand Cheng's work, I will take a closer look at two areas she considers important to the empowerment of nuns: the *bhikkhuni upasampada* and welfare seen in terms of access to resources.

Cheng notes that most householders cannot differentiate between *bhikkhunis* and nuns without the higher ordination (172). Nevertheless, she suggests that *bhikkhunis* seem empowered by their new ordination, since it enables them to participate in rituals that were previously performed only by monks (174).[25] While she characterizes the *bhikkhuni* ordination as a "feminist act" (173)—one that empowers nuns who accept it (185)—after further conversation with two *bhikkhunis*, she "found it difficult to determine the impact of the *bhikkhuni* status upon their lives" (51). Meanwhile, the higher ordination itself, which Cheng continues to perceive as empowering to Buddhist nuns, appears to be of little consequence to most householders. What is interesting is that Cheng does not make a clear case for the *bhikkhuni upasampada*'s being seen either as a "desirable" goal or as "feminist" by Sri Lankan nuns themselves. Additionally, in her conclusion she argues that the *bhikkhuni* ordination "marginalizes" nuns who reject it (185), whereas in terms of her conceptualization of welfare, the converse would hold true. Since the *bhikkhuni upasampada* remains unrecognized by the Sri Lankan state, it is the *bhikkhunis* who are barred from state resources that *sil matas* are allowed. In keeping with Gross's terminology of a "post-patriarchal" Buddhism, Cheng argues that there is a need for a "feminist transformation" that speaks to the "struggle of Buddhist women"—a transformation that is grounded in seeking equality and empowerment for women (201). Such enunciations (akin to those of Gross as well as other scholars) bear witness to Cheng's indebtedness to an institutional discourse of liberal feminism.[26]

Cheng shows more self-reflection in her discussion of welfare in relation to material resources in general (including educational resources) than she does in her examination of *bhikkhuni* ordination. Beginning with the assumption that the level of nuns' education is directly related to securing their welfare, Cheng conducts surveys to determine whether specific responses vary according to the educational level of her subjects. She focuses on whether obtaining a higher education has an impact on attitudes to (1) gender-related concepts in Buddhism, (2) material support, and (3) satisfaction with leading the life of a nun. Her surveys indicate that apart from attitudes to gender-related concepts, the educational level of nuns in both Taiwan and Sri Lanka has little if any influence on the material support the nuns receive or the satisfaction they express about their lives as renunciants. Her final assessment about the impact of promoting education for nuns suggests that unlike what most scholars have proposed, the impact is not in fact directly related to their realization of "empowerment." She concludes that although a higher level of education may result in enhancing the general "welfare" of nuns, it is ultimately "the broader socio-economic context" that has a greater influence on their welfare (148). She convincingly counters the scholarly perception that greater access to education necessarily makes a difference to nuns. Nevertheless, Cheng's discussion about welfare—defined in terms of the acquisition of material resources—is still questionable and becomes a matter of self-reflection. As a researcher, she indicates that her understanding of welfare differs from that of the nuns she studied: "I had worldly concerns in mind.... But the nuns usually gave me an answer related to their spiritual progress.... The fact that I am judging Buddhist nuns' welfare on the basis of worldly concerns may not truly reflect the interests of nuns" (127). She reiterates that thought a few times (142, 149) and proposes that the assumption that material comfort is important to an evaluation of nuns' welfare is based on Western feminist critiques (192). Cheng's discussion about the welfare of Buddhist nuns is useful in delineating tensions between the opinions of the nuns she studied and the overarching framework provided by scholars.[27] However, she does not explain how the very categorization of welfare in terms of empowerment and access to educational and material resources is part of a larger discourse of development and modernity in relation to so-called third-world countries. In other words, the difference between Cheng's thoughts on empowerment and those of the nuns is not simply one between Western feminist discourses and the realities she perceives among Buddhist nuns; it is also one between a discourse about third-world development and the disciplinary practices of nuns. It is the latter relationship that Cheng has yet to recognize and tease out in her research and writing about nuns. While she is clearly conversant with feminist critiques of Buddhism and the paradigms they suggest, she is less critical about other paradigms that are sometimes adopted by practitioners themselves. I now turn to such paradigms.

As mentioned earlier, Bartholomeusz's study assumes a supposed self-evident continuity between the *bhikkhunis* of the past and the contemporary nuns she discusses. Cheng adopts a similar approach. That is clear in her delineation of time lines for the "development of the Buddhist nuns' order in Sri Lanka" (20) as well as her attempt to continue and bring "up to date" 16) the work that Bartholomeusz began. Furthermore, Cheng, assuming an "equivalence" between nuns of different time periods, states that the "affluence of early Sri Lankan Buddhist nuns is a sharp contrast to the destitution and marginalization endured by their counterparts in the late twentieth century" (11). In addition, she embraces terminology used by a householder-practitioner to explain the new interest in the *bhikkhuni* ordinations, and in doing so she affirms a questionable conceptualization of a purist Theravada (and implicitly, Mahayana) Buddhism. The terminology one practitioner used to describe the emergence of *bhikkhuni* ordinations is that of "history unfolding" (Goonetilake qtd. in Cheng 32). It is that very terminology that Cheng, in her assumption of the historical continuity of the contemporary nuns with the *bhikkhunis* of the past, uses to describe the *bhikkhuni* ordination: "In the area of the reestablishment of the *bhikkhunī sangha*, history is unfolding in Sri Lanka" (17). That expression is reiterated several times in her work—for example, "History is indeed unfolding in Sri Lanka" (19). It is also used in relation to her own research: "The currently unfolding history of a Buddhist nuns' order in Sri Lanka might contribute to Sri Lankan nuns' friendly reception towards my research" (53). The question of "history," however, does not appear to have been an issue to the nuns of Cheng's study. In fact, one might argue that Cheng's notion of history is a Western, linear schema of temporal unfolding that, while adopted by some practitioners, is not very relevant to most practicing nuns who do not articulate themselves in such ways. That is not to propose that nuns have not *adopted* or will not adopt such a notion of "history unfolding." My point is that the (predominantly) Sinhalese-speaking *bhikkhunis* who were ordained in the late 1990s and the first few years of the new century did not for the most part see themselves as achieving a specific goal and as participants in an unfolding history.[28] What Cheng has expressed is an affirmation of a narrative that attempts to place Sri Lankan *bhikkhunis* in the framework of an ongoing timeless story. Hers is an account that—not unlike that of Bartholomeusz, in this sense—endeavors to connect the newly ordained *bhikkhunis* to early nuns such as Mahapajapati (the Buddha's foster mother/aunt) and Sanghamitta. While it goes without saying that contemporary nuns are familiar with versions of tales about those prominent *bhikkhunis*, it is not so clear that they are "struggling" for the *upasampada* in an effort to emulate them.

For Cheng, the so-called struggle of *bhikkhunis* is also about the preservation of a "Theravada identity" (34). The conceptualization of an authentic Theravada Buddhism, a notion that is promoted among some Buddhist practitioners from Sri Lanka, is the product of the partisan contestation of power and authority between Buddhists in which questions of what constitutes Buddhism and Buddhist identity become possible (Abeysekara, *Colors*). In other words, such a claim, far from being taken at face value, needs to be seen in the context of a particular matrix of power relations relative to time and place. Attempts to promote who may or may not define what is touted as an authentic Buddhism become possible in the matrix of such power relations. But Cheng, both in explaining how some *bhikkhunis* deny the validity of others' practices on the grounds that the others' ordination is "Mahayana" and in suggesting that for the former "the determination to preserve the Theravāda tradition [was] especially strong" (31), fails to adequately unpack what exactly the former meant by "Theravada." Taking for granted the rhetoric used by some *bhikkhunis*, Cheng affirms an incontrovertible Theravada identity that then becomes a scholarly affirmation of a specific partisan account appropriated by nuns associated with *one* organization—in this case, the Board of Sri Lanka *Bhikshuni* Order, based in Dambulla. Hence, she confirms that "the *bhikkhuni* ordination given by the Board of Sri Lanka *Bhikshuni* Order can claim to be *truly Theravāda* and Sri Lankan" (33; emphasis added). Cheng's adoption of an account provided by *some* informants, who are involved in a contest for the authorization of a "legitimate" Buddhism, precludes the possibility of a more nuanced analysis, which would involve questioning how and why *other* informants, who disagree with the Dambulla-based organization, appropriate Theravada in their own ways. Although it is clear that Cheng by no means sees "Theravada" as monolithic, she still assumes that it is a straightforward category of analysis, leaving unquestioned the relationship between informants who vie as claimants to an authentic Theravada.

Cheng's views on "Mahayana Buddhism" are somewhat similar to her understanding of Theravada in assuming that the category of Mahayana,

like Theravada, constitutes a self-explanatory set of doctrines and practices (albeit differing from one country to the next). Mahayana Buddhism
becomes important in her discussion about Sri Lankan nuns because
of their thoughts about it in relation to the higher ordination of *bhikkhunis* with which it is associated. Rather than locating perspectives on
Mahayana Buddhism as being centered on relations of power that might
determine how or why *sil matas* reject the *upasampada* in general—or
a particular transmission of it—Cheng seeks to provide a "correction"
to the attitudes on Mahayana among her Sri Lankan informants. Her
research—which conjectures that some Sri Lankans reject the *upasampada* because they associate it with an "accusation over the sanction of
sexual activities [granted] to Mahāyāna monks and nuns" in a mixed-sex
sangha—prompts her to "refute the misconception found among...Sri
Lankan informants regarding sexual activities in [the] Mahāyāna tradition"
(150). She goes to some trouble in explaining relations between monastic
communities involving a mixed-sex sangha in Taiwan in order "to make a
clear distinction between the mixed-sex sangha and sexual sanction" (154).
In other words, how and why some Sri Lankans are "incorrect" about
their assumptions concerning sexual activities among Mahayana monastics is depicted by her as a problem that needs to be resolved. In a similar
vein, Cheng states that one of the reasons for the aversion of Sri Lankan
informants to Mahayana is based on "ignorance" due to inadequate
"cross-tradition communication" (181). She argues that since Mahayana
Buddhism is not considered as "the authentic Buddhism" (180) by a Sri
Lankan informant and since attitudes to Mahayana Buddhism among Sri
Lankan practitioners are generally "misperceptions or generalizations"
(180), there is a problem that needs correction, and it is that need for correction that frames her narrative. In placing her (Sri Lankan) informants
in a position of ignorance that is in need of rectification about what "real
Buddhism" is, Cheng affirms the presence of a supposedly authentic
Mahayana Buddhism. In other words, she takes the rhetoric of nuns—
which is the product of specific conditions of power—as incontrovertible
assertions that differentiate Mahayana from Theravada. In doing so, she
allows herself merely to assess such assertions at face value. Hence, the
(supposedly incorrect) rhetoric of nuns comes to be equated with the *real*
state of nuns' existence and identity—a state that seems to need rectification. Had she not taken such rhetoric to be axiomatic, Cheng might have
set aside the apparent problem of rectification and focused more on the
conditions of nuns' lives.

In many ways, Cheng's views dovetail with those of Gross and Bartholomeusz who appropriate a liberal feminist discourse to analyze how practitioners presumably think about women's supposed status or role and the *bhikkhuni* ordination. Cheng's concern for the "welfare" of nuns evokes that general discourse while engaging a "first-world" and "third-world" concern in relation to women's access to resources and development. In adopting the opinions of her research subjects about what may figure as "authentic" Theravada or Mahayana Buddhism, she, like Bartholomeusz, is caught in what has been called *institutional capture*.[29] Most important, such an institutional capture preempts her thinking about the conditions that give rise to the debates between practitioners and the very emergence of such categories in the first place. Unlike Gross and Bartholomeusz, Cheng seems more self-critically aware, for she admits that some of the questions she raises may have little if any relevance to her research subjects. Nevertheless, her final work remains a result of research that relies on adopting the very feminist perspectives it seeks to critique.

Conclusion

In this chapter I have argued that grand narratives that are typically grounded in colonial and liberal feminist thinking continue to influence how scholars frame the question of gendered Buddhist practices and focus on an (ideal) consciousness that is not central to the subjects of study. That consciousness speaks, rather, to second- and third-wave feminists who seek meaning in seemingly universal categories. As mentioned (following Asad) in the introduction to this chapter, by misconstruing and focusing on such consciousness, one tends to downplay the centrality of the conditions in which people live and the kinds of possibilities those conditions might allow. By superimposing notions such as equality and human welfare on the representations of lived lives, one effectively produces a narrative of erasure—a narrative that simplifies or seeks to erase from view the conditions that inform the very living of such lives. And yet, it is by engaging with those conditions that one might most effectively ask what nuns can and cannot do.

If scholarly discourses on Buddhism as well as secular notions of feminism and freedom have proved inadequate in addressing questions concerning female renunciation in Buddhism, what options remain? How might we better understand and think about what some have considered a movement of female renunciants? I propose that we exercise caution when using narratives that may be less meaningful to the renunciant subjects than to the scholars talking about them. That is a difficult task. Rather than focusing on finding more-appropriate master narratives—whether from academia or from the reconstruction of written textual histories that may mean little to renunciants—I seek to understand the micropractices of everyday life and the microstructures of organizations, institutions, and relationships in order to think more carefully about how different frames, interests, and identities are constructed at different times and among different groups. What I am suggesting is a ground-up approach that is situated—as far as possible—less in the preoccupations of scholars and their scholarship and more in the articulation of the subjects themselves. For example, rather than focus on concerns of Western feminists, as does Cheng, or on *bhikkhuni* ordination as a "status" and an "identity" that some Buddhists may embrace, as does Bartholomeusz, I propose looking first at questions of central importance to the lives of renunciants without assuming that their lives are grounded in a self-evident rhetoric about their (emancipatory) "status." In doing so, one can better think about liberal notions of equality and subjectivity that tend to make their way into studies of lives that cannot be so easily translated. In other words, when questioning the relevance of the *bhikkhuni* ordination, one needs to ask, for example, How is *bhikkhuni* ordination "understood" by nuns? What does "*bhikkhuni*" mean to female renunciants and other interested practitioners? How is the process that has led to the introduction of the *bhikkhuni* ordination viewed by those who support it and contest it? What kinds of narratives emerge from renunciants who are, or are not, directly involved in *bhikkhuni upasampadas*? How do debates about the higher ordination relate, if at all, to renunciation itself? Rather than focusing on questions that tend to get scholars into trouble—questions such as those about the *status* of female renunciants, whether that of a *bhikkhuni*, a ten-precept mother (*dasa sil mātā/sil meheni/sil māniyō*), or a female devotee (*upāsikā*)—I suggest considering more carefully the kinds of practices that come to constitute the lives of those who renounce and how they come to do so. Here one can learn how some prevailing secular assumptions about the relation or difference between religion and politics are not helpful in thinking about renunciants.

2

Institutional Discourse and Everyday Practice

Introduction

Two prominent narratives have informed studies of female renunciants in Buddhism: a liberal feminist narrative and a colonial or an imperialistic narrative that is often related to it.[1] The dichotomous structures and binary oppositions scholars have typically used to aid understanding of Buddhist practice have lent themselves (albeit not always consistently) to representations of nuns' lives that invite liberal feminist interpretations. Not only do those interpretations remain at odds with the lives and practices of nuns who do not embrace such thinking, thereby producing a narrative disjunction, but they also echo a politics that seeks to improve lived lives with the intervention of the epistemic and economic ideology of modernity.

Scholars of Buddhism have used a variety of dichotomous structures to understand and represent lived practices of renunciation. As binary oppositions, they include such distinctions as lay (or householder or domestic)/monastic (or ordained), and a Weberian this-worldly (usually also samsaric)/otherworldly (usually also nibbanic/nirvanic). Such dichotomies also translate into a logic of female/male opposition that in turn coincides with a liberal feminist paradigm of a private/public or religious/secular distinction.[2] Even where that paradigm may not figure explicitly, scholarship on nuns remains embedded in a general liberal feminism such that it has become almost a normative moralist narrative—effectively, "a contemporary cultural text we inhabit, a discourse whose terms are 'ordinary' to a very contemporary 'us'" (W. Brown 142). By referring to that kind of thinking in studies of nuns, I suggest that it "will appear here as both a set of stories and a set of practices, as ideology *and* as discourse, as an obfuscating narrative *about* a particular social order

as well as a narrative *constitutive of* this social order and its subjects"
(W. Brown 142; emphasis in original). I argue that the implicit presence
of liberal feminist norms informing the scholarly narratives about nuns
forces us to think about renunciation as a putative expression of freedom
from the supposed subordination of the "household" life.

Narratives that represent female renunciation as something abnormal in life (that is, as a deviance from or a subordination to some other
life) always tend to present lived religious life and practice in terms of
notions of "resistance," "freedom," or "equality"—all pivotal values of the
public sphere. Seeking "correction" of this abnormality by way of Western
resources, such narratives produce a specific discourse. Homi Bhabha
says that the "subject" of colonial discourse is necessarily understood in
terms of otherness as well as abnormality, both of which are intrinsic to
understandings of power: "Colonial discourse produces the colonized
as a social reality which is at once an 'other' and yet entirely knowable
and visible....It employs a system of representation, a regime of truth,
that is structurally similar to realism" (*Location* 70–71). As he notes, the
"mode of representation of otherness" involves a "difference" in which
"non-satisfaction" (a lack or an abnormality) becomes present: "Cultural
otherness functions as the moment of presence in a theory of *différance.*
The 'destiny of non-satisfaction' is fulfilled in the recognition of otherness" ("Other Question" 89–90). The truth claims conveyed in narratives
about Buddhist nuns are supposedly based on the viewpoint of nuns themselves, a viewpoint that is consistently reiterated in studies of contemporary Buddhist nuns. Although the claim to realism is something that all
of us working with empirical data tend to make, questions arise when
"abnormalities" identified in academic narratives are unrecognized by the
subjects studied. For example, nuns do not always acknowledge—or they
simply reject—the perceived "need" to receive the *upasampada.* I argue
that frameworks that have been used in discussing female renunciation tend to center on binary oppositions that are grounded in a liberal
feminism. I suggest that avoiding the repetition of the colonial event, as
Mandair has advised (5), can help us better think about lives of female
(religious) figures without turning them into subjects who must speak
differently from the way they do.

I begin this chapter by first showing how the public/private distinction
cannot be used to adequately interpret the practice of female renunciation
in contemporary Buddhism. I propose that variations on the public/pri-
vate opposition are echoed in narratives on nuns and lend themselves to

placement in the framework of corresponding binary oppositions, such as lay/ordained and this-worldly/otherworldly. Second, I turn to select scholarly studies of female renunciants in Theravada and Tibetan Buddhist traditions in order to point out how they, to various extents, have been informed by this dichotomous structure and, in doing so, are complicit in reiterating a colonial narrative. Finally, on the basis of conversations with nuns, I argue that nuns' stories cannot be easily categorized in terms of such oppositions and that we need to reformulate how we set about understanding female renunciation in Buddhism.[3]

Public/Private and Other Dichotomies

Carole Pateman indicates that although the public/private dichotomy—as well as the valuation of equal rights, freedom, and autonomy—is central to both liberal theory and feminism, there is considerable variation in how that dichotomy is construed by liberals and feminists (118–140). She argues that because the public/private distinction has become a "a division *within* civil society…[it is] expressed in a number of different ways, not only private and public, but also, for example, 'society' and 'state,' or 'economy' and 'politics,' or 'freedom' and 'coercion' or 'social' and 'political'" (122; emphasis in original). The reason for that, she suggests, is that the seemingly universal ideal of the individual in civil society is, in fact, male. Comparable to what Pateman says about the private/public distinction as well as the assumption about the male identity of the individual in civil society, scholarly studies of female renunciation have appropriated variations of the public/private distinction in their categorization of lay/ordained, householder/monastic, female/male, domestic/religious, and so on. Often, the public sphere is associated with a freedom of renunciation that is seen ideally (in the sense of textual precedent) and practically (in terms of lived realities) as a male domain. Such studies depict female renunciation as a feminist act that produces "a social transformation of gender relations" (Butler 204), making possible a resistance to subordination, conventional familial norms, and the private sphere. Female renunciation ultimately allows women's entrance into the traditionally male sphere of public religion. In such accounts resistance and freedom become key words in understanding why nuns renounce, and those "liberational" concepts are privileged over other factors, such as practices that involve developing a better understanding of samsara or seeking nibbana. In fact, samsara, rather than being understood as something that women (whether renunciant or not) attempt to come to terms with in the *process* of *seeking* renunciation (whether within or without the household), is itself often identified with the private, domestic, and this-worldly. Those accounts conflate the meaning of seeking freedom from samsaric existence with seeking freedom from the private, domestic, and female. That is, the terms *samsara* and *nibbana* here become easily translatable into a dichotomous secular vocabulary that has no correspondence to the practiced lives of nuns.

Feminist freedom is generally associated with women's agency or ability to further the realization of their potential.[4] Such potential may be understood as a kind of social (educational, economic, etc.) advancement or as a religious self-realization. In mainstream liberal theory such potential is ideally actualized outside the private sphere—for example, in the educational system and in the area of career, which are usually outside the home. The private sphere of the household is viewed as the area in which women, tied to domestic chores and child care, are restricted. Feminist freedom—emerging as a "resistance" against the conventional family and established patriarchal norms—is seen in terms of its social embeddedness. Though nuns acknowledge the restrictions of living a conventional life within a family household as a daughter or a wife, they also understand and articulate such restrictions with reference to better understanding *dukkha*. Moreover, their purported resistance to the household (private?) life does not lead them to a total severance from family; thus, their lives blur the distinctions between private and public and secular and religious. In fact, it is not uncommon for a nun who encounters serious health issues that require extensive care to return home to live with family members (something that is unheard of among Buddhist monks who fall ill). As I argue below, nuns' less-than-total severance from family is often overlooked in scholarship on nuns even though the field research suggests that what nuns seek is a different social embeddedness in relation to their renunciant practice. The interdependence between nuns and the family unit does not fit the conventional notion of family in a renunciant setting. While it might appear that nuns, in leaving the private sphere for the sake of freedom in a public or religious sphere, are resisting conventional norms, their focus remains on another sense of freedom—if we can even use such a word—that is bound up with a religious self-realization in coming to terms with a life of *dukkha*. Their preoccupation with that self-realization involves a new type of social interdependence that cannot be equated with a liberal notion of freedom. The awareness of a need to fulfill a religious self-realization (or potential) is not characterized by entrance into a visibly identifiable renunciant life (marked, for example, by ordination). While female renunciants may appear to seek an individual freedom and autonomy away from the family or the private realm, the quest for a religious self-realization, being one that precedes their departure from the household life, cannot be understood as coincident with the socially identified renunciant life. In fact, the search for religious self-realization cannot be translated in terms of a renuciant's condition of social embeddedness. Nuns' external (social) renunciation may seem apparent in their religious attire, place of residence, and the nomenclature used for them, but the quest for nibbana itself cannot be so readily identified and measured.

Mahmood's argument "for uncoupling the notion of self-realization from that of the autonomous will" (14), which is also directly related to how agency should not be restricted to a "binary model of subordination and subversion" (14), may help us see how nuns' search for nibbana defies translation into social categories such as lay/ordained, this-worldly/otherworldly, and samsaric/nibbanic. The establishment of dichotomously opposed categories—which are often variations of the private/public distinction and vice versa and which are clearly incapable of subsuming religious self-realization (central to female renunciants)—have helped narrate female renunciation as a self-evident expression of freedom. Such narratives—which do not adequately address nuns' own understanding of *dukkha* and samsara (an understanding that is difficult if not impossible to translate)—effectively tell a story that avoids giving priority to how nuns in their capacity and "capability" as religious women think and engage in religious practices.[5] Here again we see that capability is not a "universal capability," in Nussbaum's or Kant's sense, but a product of the very lives nuns live.[6]

Mahmood contends that "liberal presuppositions have become naturalized in the scholarship of gender" (13); that naturalization, which Wendy Brown had already discussed some time ago, has yet to be fully acknowledged in empirical studies on religion. I propose that a naturalization of liberal presuppositions is prevalent in scholarship on Buddhist nuns and has become an institutional discourse that overlooks the centrality of religious intent and practice through which nuns' lives may be understood. By the term *institutional discourse* I mean what institutional ethnographers understand as: "any widely shared…authoritative way of knowing (measuring, naming, describing) states of affairs that render them actionable within institutional relations of purpose and accountability. . . . These are conceptual systems, forms of knowledge that carry institutional purposes and reflect a standpoint" (McCoy 118). The institutional discourse in which nuns' stories are narrated both inform and are informed by liberal presuppositions on, and feminist critiques of, public/private differences (and their variations). Such narratives—while making sense in terms of liberal notions of equality and individualism as well as of a feminist resistance to patriarchy, subordination in the private sphere, and so on—detract from a focus on the centrality of nuns' *religious* motivations for becoming renunciants and undermine the importance of their seeking nibbana as an end in itself. That is not to suggest that a conceptualization of renunciation as an "escape valve" is always opposed to one of renunciation as a means of addressing *dukkha*; the one might reinforce the other.

Dorothy Smith comments pointedly on the problem of addressing the relationship of discourse to lived lives, indicating that discourse may serve to "establish procedures for telling stories about people that isolate them from their own lives and the settings of their lives" (Smith, "Incorporating Texts" 77). Unlike Smith's subjects, Asian Buddhist nuns, who generally do not read and speak English, may not have access to most scholarly narratives about their life stories. Nevertheless, Smith's point about how scholarly narratives can alienate the subjects they supposedly describe is what I refer to here as a problem in liberal feminist narratives about nuns. Ultimately, as Smith notes, a text (i.e., the product of an institutional discourse) "formulates a process. People's doings are no longer just that but become interpretable as expressions or instances of a higher source of organization, independent of particular people" (Smith, "Incorporating Texts" 82). The telling of nuns' stories is often couched in a liberal and feminist sense about nuns' attempting to obtain access in such (public) areas as religion, education, and state recognition even though nuns themselves may remain indifferent to such attempts (and "temptations"). I now turn to select works on contemporary nuns and argue that dichotomous structures embedded in narratives about them fall in line with liberal feminist views on public/private distinctions.

Translating Renunciation

Renunciation appears to presuppose a dichotomy—a difference of attitude between attachment and detachment. Renunciation is not limited to the outward appearance of a renunciant who while mentally detached (or in the process of seeking detachment) from samsara, may live among those who are unlike herself. Nevertheless, the idea of renunciation in Buddhism, sometimes correlated with "monasticism," is often opposed to the idea of the attachment of the "laity." Although the monastic code of *Vinaya* texts appears to reinforce the distinction between those who are monastics and those who are not, the practice of renunciation itself is clearly not limited to those wearing the robes of a *bhikkhu* or a *bhikkhuni*, nor is it defined strictly in terms of precepts that practitioners observe.[7] Since the higher ordination of Buddhist nuns has not yet been fully recognized throughout the world and since Buddhist women practice renunciation without necessarily accepting the formal status of *bhikkhuni*, the question of what female renunciation is and how it may be identified in relation to the concept of *laity* has proved particularly difficult to answer. In fact, the practices of female Buddhist renunciants question the very conceptualization of "laity" in Buddhism. I propose that formulating a cogent language to talk about who nuns are and what they do is one of the biggest challenges we face in trying to understand female renunciation in Buddhism. I also argue that the uncritical scholarly affirmation of female renunciants within a framework of binary oppositions such as laity/non-laity, ordinand/non-ordinand, and sangha/non-sangha produces categories that belong to a misleading institutional discourse. So, it is necessary to revisit what exactly we mean when we use such categories and to rethink how they inform narratives about Buddhist nuns.

The complication of finding words in European languages that approximate terms for female renunciants in Asian languages is very real. Even though the term *nun* is often used for female renunciants in Buddhism—one that I too have reluctantly adopted—it is far from unproblematic. *Nun*, drawn from Catholicism, refers to a religious woman who remains celibate and has taken lay vows.[8] Unlike Catholic priests, Catholic nuns remain without a clerical ordination and thus cannot perform certain ritual services. In contrast, *bhikkhunis*, having been fully ordained, are not prohibited from performing important ritual services. In that sense they maybe more the (hypothetical) female equivalents of Catholic priests than nuns. It is perhaps for that reason that Bartholomeusz refers to the female renunciants in Sri Lanka as "lay nuns," since the expression conveys that they are not like priests in the Catholic sense (hence "nuns") and are also not *bhikkhunis* (hence "lay"). Her choice of nomenclature is confusing, however, when keeping in mind the notion of Catholic laity, for she states that Buddhist lay nuns have supposedly "exchanged their lay identity for monastic life" (3). The term *lay nun* is a tautology, since (Catholic) nuns are in fact lay.[9]

According to the *New Shorter Oxford English Dictionary* (OED), the term *lay* means "non-clerical; not in ecclesiastic orders," and a layperson may be described as "not professionally trained or qualified." More specifically, *lay brother, sister* refers to "a man, woman who has taken the habit and vows of a religious order, but is employed mostly in manual labour and is excused [from] other duties." Unlike the meaning of *lay* inferred there, Buddhist renunciants, or those seeking mental detachment from samsara, may or may not have a recognizable appearance (e.g., renunciant attire) that identifies their spiritual quest, and they may well be living in a conventional household. Alternatively, Buddhist renunciants may be living communally with other renunciants. Even as someone who has neither a novice (*samaneri*) ordination nor a full ordination, a Buddhist renunciant may have realized a higher "spiritual" training (in terms of meditation and detachment from samsara) or expertise in the *dharma* (Buddhist teachings) than a *bhikkhu* or *bhikkhuni*. Unlike a lay brother or sister in Catholicism, a Buddhist renunciant, who may have taken the responsibility of following a stricter moral code (*sila*) than Buddhist householders, does not have an obligation to follow the vows of a "religious order" in the manner of monks, nuns, or fully ordained clerics in Catholicism today.[10] In fact, Buddhist renunciants may also be householders—in the loose sense that they may live in a home that they own or rent.[11] The OED defines the term *laity* in opposition to *clergy*: "not in ecclesiastical orders as opp[osed] to the clergy" and states that "Christianity makes a sharper distinction than other faiths between the clergy and laity." The term *lay* or *laity,* though commonly used to help clarify the "status" of female renunciants in Buddhism, is clearly not easily adaptable for understanding the identity of Buddhist renunciants. The lay/clergy distinction in Catholicism cannot be seen as equivalent to a lay/monastic distinction in Buddhism, because the very concept of "laity" in Buddhism—assuming that there is one—is more fluid.

The terms *layman* and *pious layman* when used with reference to Buddhism are often a translation of the Pali word *upāsaka* or its female rendering, *upāsikā.* In the *Pali Text Society Dictionary* (PTSD) the term *upāsaka* is glossed as "a devout or faithful layman, a lay devotee." Rather than explaining that term in opposition to the notion of a *bhikkhu*, the PTSD derives it from the verb *upāsati*, which means "to sit close by," "to go after, attend, follow, serve, honor, worship." In other words, the *upasaka* or *upasika* is someone who is a devout religious practitioner. For much of the twentieth century *upasika* commonly referred to a female Buddhist renunciant who wore a saffron or brown robe and often lived communally with others like herself. A problem arises in affirming a clear-cut "lay" identity for female renunciants in Buddhism. Scholars typically place those renunciants—who are often neither fully ordained practitioners (*bhikkhuni*) nor "conventional" householder practitioners (*gihī* or *gihiyō*)—in an interstitial, anomalous, or ambiguous position within the lay-versus-ordained framework. Rather than being depicted as women whose practice might occupy a continuum where the householder or lay practitioner's identity merges somewhat imperceptibly into or overlaps the identity of a renunciant—and where the very categories of lay and ordained may be questioned—female renunciants are often portrayed as representing some unique category. The lay/monastic distinction, while more ambiguous in Buddhism than it may seem at first glance, fails to adequately translate differences in Buddhist (renunciant) practice.[12] In some instances scholars extend that distinction to fit an institutional discourse that echoes the variations of the public/private dichotomy to which Pateman refers. That distinction might be expressed in a number of forms, such as sacred versus profane (Gutschow 256; Havnevik 35),[13] Weber's world-renouncers versus others (Bartholomeusz 32, 82; Gutschow 174), domestic (private) versus religious (public) (Bartholomeusz 106–107; Gutschow 175), and lay/householder/domestic versus religious/renunciant/ordained (M. Falk x–xi, 28–29, 37, 67, 99, 186).[14] Accounts that use such dichotomies and consistently configure them within a lay/monastic frame of reference are questionable, particularly when applied to the contemporary practice of Buddhist nuns.[15] While relying on such dichotomies in their studies, some scholars (such as Gutschow, Havnevik, and Van Esterik) occasionally seek to go beyond them.

Penny Van Esterik, in her essay "Lay Women in Theravada Buddhism," acknowledges to some extent the kinds of questions I raise about the usefulness of binary oppositions for understanding female renunciation in Buddhism. A female renunciant in Thailand who is not a *bhikkhuni* is usually called a *mae chi* (variations include *mæchi, mae chee, māe chī, mae chii,* or *maechii* and *mae ji*), literally meaning "honored (or honorable) mother."[16] According to Van Esterik, "*Mæchi* do not present a complete contrast with either monks or other laywomen.... *Mæchi* are not members of a bounded category, but are continuous with the category labeled *upasika*. Yet, we cannot view *mæchi* as representing a legitimate intermediate category, for *mæchi* do not mediate between states" (57). Van Esterik's comments are those of a scholar who is attempting to explain the "place" of *mae chis* in order to translate it to others. What she notes here is the need to adopt commonly used terms in Thailand such as *upasika* to explain the meaning of *mae chi* as well as the difficulty in translating (and categorizing) *mae chi*. In a similar vein, Havnevik, in her book *Tibetan Buddhist Nuns*, mentions that a number of different terms are used for female renunciants in Tibetan Buddhism (44). Some of those terms, such as *ani* and *jomo*, are regionally specific, but they are also used for women who are married householders.[17] She indicates that the term *ani* cannot be strictly categorized: "The Tibetan *ani* denotes a woman who has taken the novice ordination. Nevertheless, in common usage the term *ani* is also used to include unordained women dressing and living like the ordained ones" (44). An informant she cites stated, "We call them all *anis* because it is impossible for us to know whether they have been ordained or not" (44). Havnevik proceeds to explain her own nomenclature for the female renunciants she discusses: "Since the term *ani* by some is considered impolite, I will generally use the English term nun" (44). The tension between what scholars perceive as a gray area in the study of female renunciants and the attempt to explain Buddhist renunciation in terms of social difference is clearly evident in Havnevik's study. Although she recognizes that tension, she proceeds to evade it in her narrative. On the one hand, she suggests that the lives of nuns may not be so strictly differentiated from the lives of householders, but on the other, she considers the lay/ordained distinction useful in contrasting householders and nuns.[18] Stating that the "gap in status between a pious laywoman and a nun may not be as great as the difference between a pious layman and a monk" (183), she indicates that there is *some* distinction between "laywoman" and "nun," but that it is unclear.[19] Havnevik, like the rest of us writing about female renunciants, understands the difficulty in using appropriate nomenclature for them—a difficulty that is hard to resolve, given that the language of translation is translation. The studies of Van Esterik and Havnevik provide good examples of the complexities in attempting to translate nuns' lives into a language that nuns themselves do not use.

Dichotomies, Imperialistic Discourses, and the "Needs" of Buddhist Nuns

Scholars (and some practitioners) writing narratives about female renunciants that are informed by a public/private distinction often appear tempted to articulate a need for resistance against the subordinate or inferior position of Buddhist nuns. While that idea of resistance may resonate with the pronouncements of a few English-speaking nuns,[20] it has little purchase among nuns who do not speak in those ways. For such nuns as the latter, the formulation of their identities in terms of who they are and what they do (an exercise which, as we know, is quite modern)[21] is of little interest. The logical development of those above-mentioned narratives culminates in recommending a means to overcome the reputed subordination of nuns—one such means being the higher ordination. Such narratives may promote the idea that certain nuns should lead an effort to "save" other nuns from a perceived subordination the latter may not know or recognize.

Studies on female renunciation that adopt the dichotomy of domestic (private) versus religious (public) enter (perhaps inadvertently) into a mode of thinking in which the former is viewed as undesirable and the latter as a sphere of potential and opportunity. In some studies female renunciation is seen as the most desirable, if not the *only*, option for women who choose to relinquish marriage, even though respectable employment is a possibility for them.[22] Sid Brown, for example, talks about the "oppressions" and "burden" of family life that may be relinquished in renunciation (13, 142). What is missing in her analysis is the recognition that even in renunciation Thai women remain well connected with family members; family responsibilities and family life are not forgotten.[23] Maintaining family connections is also important to the Tibetan nuns studied by Gutschow and Havnevik, some of whom may contribute labor to family fields or choose to live as renunciants *with* family members. According to Brown, the gendered identity of female renunciants involves a combination of "qualities of the ascetic role that are so admired in men in Thailand with those of the mother/nurturer role so admired in Thai women" (116). Yet, *mae chis* occupy a no-(wo)man's land in the public sphere, which ultimately situates them in a discourse of deprivation for they "lack many of the advantages of persons gone forth and also lack the advantages of laypeople" (26). Unfortunately, that understanding positions renunciant Thai women in a no-win situation: those living at home are oppressed, while those who renounce lack "opportunities."

The kind of situation presented in Brown's study of *mae chis* in Thailand has parallels in Bartholomeusz's discussion of *sil matas* in Sri Lanka. According to Bartholomeusz, the private/public divide happens in a few settings. It constitutes a difference between the "domestic" or "female sphere" and the "public religious arena" (107).[24] A layperson

who became a preacher in the late nineteenth century "found himself
or herself on the periphery of both the clerical and lay communities and
belonged to neither.... He or she occupied a 'marginal' position" (40). The
lay/monastic divide, while not considered by Bartholomeusz as absolute
for lay nuns (who are considered lay though acting in public as clerics),
allows for the creation of an interstice. Bartholomeusz's representation of
the situation of lay nuns in Sri Lanka resonates with Brown's depiction
of female renunciants who occupy a no-(wo)man's-land. Bartholomeusz's
subjects, like Brown's, are in a no-win situation: as women in Sri Lanka,
they are usually viewed either as lacking freedom and "choices," because
they are wives and mothers in the domestic arena, or as "inferior," because
they are not monks (Bartholomeusz 132, 190). Moreover, even though the
lay nuns are depicted in Bartholomeusz's narrative as possibly inferior
or subordinate to monks, they "find fulfillment in these roles" (190)!
Bartholomeusz concludes by wondering about possible transformations
in relation to the lay nuns' subordinate position but significantly reminds
us that for the nuns "these are no longer relevant matters. They have committed themselves to renunciation and have... turned their attentions
toward *nibbāna*" (190). Bartholomeusz's conclusion is telling: although
she asks readers to think about the supposedly (unfortunate) subordinate
or inferior position of nuns, a position she postulates as a potential problem, the Sinhalese-speaking nuns focus on concerns of daily routine and
ultimately nibbana (189–190). In a similar vein, Brown describes Kanittha,
an English-speaking *mae chi* who received her early education at a Catholic
convent school and has striven as a lawyer to facilitate reforms on behalf
of *mae chis* in Thailand. Brown reports that according to Kanittha, the
"biggest problem for *mae chi* in Thailand... is that 'they don't care. And
they don't think they have any problems'" (34). Here again we find a distinction between an individual who speaks in a certain mode and others
who differ. The question of the inferior or subordinate position, identified
by some practitioners and scholars alike, becomes a problem that must be
resolved.[25] Gutschow, for example, discusses the "subordination" and "inferiority" of Tibetan nuns vis-á-vis monks and asks "the question of where,
if any, resistance can emerge. How does a religion of self-effacement also
promote feminist questions about discrimination?" (187). She infers that
the resources for successfully assisting Tibetan nuns need to come from
the West (239–243).

Gutschow's description of Tibetan nuns' "poverty" and their reception
of "aid" from Western resources is suggestive of a discourse of deprivation

(86–87, 113–114). That narrative introduces a variety of questions about the politics of development projects in so called third-world countries that I raise later (in Chapter 5). Like Gutschow, albeit more explicitly, Havnevik sees the "inferior" situation of the Tibetan nuns as being both identified and resolved by Western nuns.[26] Ironically, even though Western women have seldom "found it possible to thoroughly adapt to the lifestyle, the diet, and the rigorous discipline" of Tibetan nuns living in India (191), Havnevik implies that the former are in the vanguard of transforming matters for the latter; since they "have acted as initiators, helping to bring about change in the situation of nuns in the Tibetan tradition" (190)! Those interpretations of nuns' "activities" in terms of their development, transformation, and entrance into the public sphere bespeak the language of opportunity and potential. I am not proposing that meditators and their seemingly otherworldly activities have no social relevance—a relevance to which previous studies bear witness (Bond, *Buddhist Revival*; Cook; Jordt, *Burma's*)—but rather that nuns' meditative and other practices cannot be limited to the language of opportunity in the public sphere. For nuns, opportunities and benefits in the public sphere are all too often conceptualized as being either legal and educational or related to a need for higher ordination.[27] What would perhaps be useful in assessing the opportunities for nuns (e.g., in the area of literacy and education), if one wants to do that, is not to compare nuns in relation to monks as scholars often do, but rather to look at them in relation to women who do not renounce.[28] Narratives such as those of Sid Brown and Bartholomeusz place female renunciants in a desperate, a subordinate, or an inferior situation and beg the question how, if at all, this "problem" might be overcome. The usual (colonialist) response to that question is to appeal to Western nuns and Western resources for assistance in "saving" Asian nuns from their purported predicament. Gutschow, for example, explains how Tsering Palmo, a Tibetan nun from Ladakh who hails from an elite background, finds assistance from Western organizations in her attempt to provide educational and other facilities for nuns in the area (236–243). That Palmo, a Ladakhi nun living in Ladakh, situates renunciants in such a discourse shows that such narratives are not peculiar to Westerners. In contrast to most Ladakhi nuns, nuns like Palmo typically speak English, have more formal education, and come from families that are more stable economically.[29] Echoing Palmo, Gutschow presents in her narrative the "problems" that nuns face and proposes a need to overcome "centuries of patriarchy" (250). She writes that "the global community of Buddhist feminists" have

sought reform in the areas of "ritual empowerment, reviving full ordination and increased education" (254). While Gutschow notes that it is
unclear whether the impetus for reform comes from "the East or the West"
(250), she suggests that such are the areas in which Tibetan nuns have
been afforded opportunities through the involvement of Western activists
and funding sources. She concludes that, ultimately, nuns who are not
"granted the material endowments, ritual patronage and respect historically reserved for monks" (256) cannot sustain their practice as nuns—
possibly entailing a "defeat for Buddhist monasticism" (256). The idea that
the current predicament in female renunciation is such that it requires
the *transformation* of Buddhist monasticism (through Western assistance)
is even more forcefully presented, with explicit Orientalist overtones, in
Monica Lindberg Falk's study, *Making Fields of Merit: Buddhist Female
Ascetics and Gendered Orders in Thailand.*

"Transcending the Lay Realm"?

Among recent studies on female renunciation, Monica Falk's work on
mae chis in Thailand integrates the public/private and male/female
dichotomies in perhaps the most consistent and self-evident manner.
Such oppositions undergird her own dichotomous distinctions between
the domestic and the religious and between the lay and the ordained.
Citing works by Charles Keyes and Andrea Whittaker about Thai women,
she agrees that those distinctions are informative in that "women reach
maturity in the secular realm by becoming mothers and lying by the fire,
and men reach maturity in the religious realm by being ordained as novice monks for a period of time"(7). She highlights other studies of Thai
women that also associate women with "fertility, nurturance and attachment and Thai men with otherworldly power and detachment" (33). Even
though women's participation in economic activity has led some scholars to ascribe a "high status" to women (32), for Falk "the" Thai woman
ideally "is expected to fulfill the role of wife and mother" (37). In other
words, the domestic, female, private domain is rendered distinct from
the religious, male, public domain.[30] Falk suggests that young women
who become *mae chis* in contemporary Thailand before marrying are
(considered) "deviant," since they do not follow "prescribed vocations
as wives and mothers" (100). She supposes that *mae chis* see their ordination as constituting "a clear break with the lay world"—as involving
entrance into a "new realm of life" (253). She thinks of their entry into

renunciation as an entry into a public, male, religious, ordained sphere, which involves the severance of family ties and which is essentially a feminist act that bespeaks renunciants' "autonomy" and opposition to "religious inferiority" (254).

Although Monica Falk recognizes that "the principal reasons for seeking ordination were to realize the basic Buddhist truths about suffering (*dukkha*), and to gain the opportunity to attain enlightenment (*nibbana*) through ordained practice" (55), the story she tells about female renunciants in Thailand bespeaks a liberal feminist orientation. The trouble with the dichotomization that pervades Falk's work is first that it is not as clear-cut as her narrative proposes and second, that it creates an interstitial space of female renunciation that is undesirable or deviant and therefore becomes the site of a problem calling for intervention and resolution. I will address each of those points in turn. In the first instance, it is evident from Monica Falk's own field research that the purported lay/ordained distinction is not as starkly defined as she implies.[31] The presence of different forms of renunciant practice in Thailand, for example, that of the *sikkhamats* (ten-precept renunciants); the widely differing living situations of individual *mae chis*; and the fact that the eight precepts which *mae chis* observe are also observed by householders, lay meditation leaders, *dhammacārinī* (female students or followers of the *dhamma* ["Teaching, Truth"]), and temporary renunciants (*chi phrāms*) also question that dichotomization of practice (16, 29, 37, 112, 120, 185, 215). Moreover, women who become *mae chis* do not leave family and "transcend the lay realm" (81–84, 96,102) in the manner Falk states, since they clearly continue to maintain family ties. Falk notes that ordination as a *mae chis* may take place with the support, or at the instigation, of family members (67–68, 72, 78, 90–91). In some instances relatives who encourage women to become *mae chis* are themselves already ordained as monks or as *mae chis* (68–69, 90). In one instance, a senior *mae chi* whose relatives lived with her at a *samnak chi* (hermitage) offered to assist another *mae chi* economically if the latter would help look after her relatives (91). Indeed, Falk's own research in Thailand indicates that *mae chis*, while living as renunciants outside the conventional familial household, do in fact maintain family relationships, thus undermining her claim that female renunciation involves "transcending the lay realm" (81). However, the structural dichotomies in Falk's narrative represent women's situation as so subordinate and undesirable that it casts doubt on the very possibility of equality between men and women in the public, religious sphere. That does not, however, prevent Falk from proposing a need for rectifying such inequality (244–245).

The lay/monastic distinction central to Falk's study (x) invites reflection on a perspective that recurs in general interpretations of female renunciation. Falk repeats the idea of the subordination of women (i.e., the issue of abnormality or non-satisfaction, in Bhabha's terms) vis-à-vis the purpose of renunciation. The implication is that renunciation gives women a desired escape from the private/domestic/lay realm and opens an avenue for their full participation in the public/male/religious sphere. In particular, that dichotomization places religious women in a position that, ipso facto, advances a need for them to struggle for freedom and equality. The struggle of female renunciants is presented both as a concomitant of the immurement of women in the private/domestic/lay realm and as a means for obtaining liberation by becoming *mae chis* (9). While renunciation allows entry into the public/ordained/male sphere of religion, some female renunciants in Thailand remain under the "control of the monks" (186). Even though a number of Thai renunciants Falk interviewed showed no interest in becoming *bhikkhunis*, Falk introduces liberal notions of equality and rights into her narrative and so establishes a need for the renunciants' full ordination (99–100). As renunciants, whether *mae chis* or *bhikkhunis*, Thai women, according to Falk, need to address their "subordinate position" in the religion (227).[32] Once again, the struggle is articulated in keeping with views on the desirability of obtaining equal opportunities and rights in the sphere of access to (1) education, (2) legal recognition of *mae chis*, and (3) the higher ordination. The female renunciants who appear in Falk's work as leaders in this struggle are all women who have graduate or post-graduate degrees or have studied or lived abroad (193–245). While those somewhat unrepresentative and activist *mae chis* share Falk's notion of the need to effect transformations in each of the three areas and have committed their lives to doing so, it is noteworthy that other *mae chis* do not appear to share their views. That is evident in the discussions Falk references in her work. The latter *mae chis* prioritize meditation—according to Falk, a "more lay-oriented activity" (194)—over the textual study of Buddhism (196); are ambivalent, if not suspicious, about attempts to promote their legal recognition (230); and appear to be uninterested in promoting the *bhikkhuni* ordination (10, 21, 30, 227). What appears to be central for these *mae chis* is their religious practice as renunciants (10, 248)—a practice that defies Falk's dichotomies. Ultimately, by employing a feminist perspective that reiterates binary oppositions such as lay/ordained, female/male, private/public, and domestic/religious, Falk claims that Thai women cannot, whatever they do, realize full equality as either lay or renunciant women. Such overtones resonate in her proposition that, given all the abnormalities present among Thai nuns, Buddhism itself "needs to be reformed" (245). For Falk, Thai Buddhism and Buddhist life come to need, as Asad would say, a "curative treatment."[33]

In the following pages, I take a closer look at how female renunciants in Sri Lanka understand and reflect on life and their decisions to become renunciants. They make one suspect the narratives above. In fact, nuns' renunciation of samsaric existence cannot be circumscribed by a framework of such binary oppositions. While the accounts to follow do constitute a narrative of sorts, I present them not to propose an alternative to a liberal feminist narrative (and its many dichotomies) that often informs accounts of nuns, nor to assert a uniquely "authentic" description of nuns' lives. Rather, I present them to highlight that liberalism's narratives limit interpretations of the lived lives of nuns.

Centering Dukkha and Living Life

Buddhi might be considered a nun who, at the time of our first conversations, stands apart from the other nuns I interview in this chapter.[34] She is relatively well traveled and knows some English. In fact, when she learned that I lived in the United States, she insisted on beginning the interview in English. We proceeded to do so. However, as it became clear to me that she was not entirely at ease speaking English, I posed one question to her in Sinhalese. She then switched to speaking in Sinhalese for the rest of the interview, though occasionally interjecting English words such as *stepmother* and *education* into her narrative. At first glance, Buddhi's account appears to correlate with a liberal notion of opportunities in the public sphere that presented themselves to young women in Sri Lanka during the 1980s.[35] Yet her story is not what it seems. Despite her use of a Sinhalese word (*avasthāva*) that could be translated as "opportunity," the notion of opportunity she conveyed was not identical to the liberal notion that connotes something inherently available to all. The latter notion also implies concepts of "rights" and "progress" in a career. According to the *Shorter Sinhalese-English Dictionary*, the Sinhalese word *avasthava* means "state, condition, situation, circumstance"; "stage, period, epoch"; or "season, time; occasion, opportunity." The emphasis in the word is on a particular timeliness of circumstance, and that is exactly how Buddhi talked about *avasthava*.

I first met Buddhi about seven years after her ordination as a *sil mata*. At that time she was living alone in a small hut (*kuṭi*) built for her on the grounds of her parental home. Her very living situation evoked an accommodation and cooperation with family members. Buddhi had worked at a garment factory before being invited to serve as a nanny to a family in the United States. She said that her decision to go to the United States was unexpected—it happened "suddenly." She spoke of that decision in relation to the opportunity (*avasthava*) it offered: "So I said yes. Who is there who would not want to go to America if asked, is that not so?" So she left her husband for a few years to work there; when she returned, she decided to remain in Sri Lanka. Buddhi's husband, an employee in a small business, had taken to drinking. After her return she worked as a seamstress employing a few other women. When one of her main clients left the area, however, she fell into debt. Her income was an important source of revenue for her (husband's) extended family, and as the family's needs increased, she fell further into debt:

> This was a question [*praṣna/prashna*], no? During that time when I was staying in the home of my husband, the people on my husband's side, we had to provide for them, his family and his younger sister's children and the many others—well, we had to look after them. I had to spend on them. The money that I had with me as well as the money that I had earned in America—that was lost...for my husband's matters.

The extended family that she catered to included her husband's father and stepmother, his brother, his divorced sister, and two other siblings who lived in one compound consisting of separate dwellings. She lived with her husband in his ancestral home, and she bore the financial responsibilities for the family both on a daily basis and on special occasions:

> All would come to our house, would they not? When mother [-in-law] and father[-in-law] were there, we had to look after them. So everyone would come there for any and every thing. My husband's older brother's child died. When he died, the funeral arrangements took place in our house—the merit making, the almsgiving, etc.; people came from everywhere. Then there were debts.

Acutely aware of the financial difficulties, she attempted to address them in the best way she knew. At the time, she was running errands on behalf of her sister-in-law's job search abroad, so she would carry her own passport with her for identification. It was while running such an errand that she chanced upon employment agents who asked her to find two young women who would be willing to work in the Middle East. Buddhi herself had no intention (*hita*) of working there, but she was at a loss as to what else to do. Her response to the employment agents and her subsequent decision did not arise from some grand plan but rather from her immediate situation:

> Then suddenly, suddenly, I thought, Now I have a big debt; There was no way of repaying it at that time. I [said], "Very well, I don't know that I can find other people, but here is my passport; if you like, you can send me," and I gave my passport right away. They saw that there was an American visa stamped there and that I had been to America, and they liked that a lot.... They quickly made the arrangements for me to go.... It was sudden.... It was like that also [when] I went to America—sudden—not that I had the hope [*balāporottuva*, "expectation"] or anything.

At that time she had a young baby, whom she left with her mother.

> Truly there was nothing else left that I could do at that time. I was happy for the opportunity [*avasthava*, "timely occasion"] I received, because I needed to repay debts, needed to bring up the child and secure [or preserve] our future. I did not have much hope [*balaporottuva*] for my husband. He would get together with friends and drink.... He would waste the money he made. It was necessary to see to his family. He would waste the money that he earned, and the money I earned was not enough.
>
> So I left. When I left... from the beginning our married life had not been successful. We had different ways of thinking. I tried very hard, I tried hard to make this [marriage] work. But [my husband] was in fact "uneducated." He had no wish to study, and he skipped school. After the death of his mother, he quarreled with his aunt and skipped school and left home and stayed with various aunts and uncles in different places. These questions [*prashna*] were already there. I had thought that he would love his wife a lot, because he did

not have a mother....That is why I wanted to marry; I married out
of compassion [sobbing].

I asked her if her husband had been abusive, and she assented somewhat
hesitantly:

> As time went on, that happened too, a little....It is like this: from
> the outside none of this was visible to anyone....All the questions
> [*prashna*] were within. From outside it was only his drinking. He
> was good to his friends and his relatives and his brothers and sister,
> very helpful in any way. But for me...[sobbing, unclear]. There were
> questions [*prashna*] like that....I had no encouragement; truly, fam-
> ily living [*pavul jīvitaya*] cannot go on like that, can it [sobbing]? So
> it was when things were like that that I left the country. He would
> scold me in the letters he sent. Then, even though I wrote letters
> later, he did not respond....Indeed, within the first two years, the
> debts were repaid. It is only after that that we saw some progress [in
> the marriage], so I went [back to Sri Lanka].

Leaving for work abroad gave Buddhi a temporary respite from her economic and marital difficulties. Her initial hope was that the marriage
could be salvaged. On her return to Sri Lanka, she accepted a job offer
and held the job until she eventually decided to become ordained as a
sil mata.

Buddhi's story may not be typical (if there is such a thing as a typical
story), as may be construed from reading some of the research on female
renunciation mentioned earlier. Buddhi had the ability to work outside the
home whether or not she became a wife and mother. She decided to do
such work in addition to embracing marriage and motherhood. Scholars
sometimes see renunciation as the only "option" for women who do not
wish to devote themselves to family life, but that was not the case here.
It would be easy to interpret Buddhi's account as a story of opposition to
a patriarchal family and the "double burden" she bore as housewife and
mother as well as wage earner—a story that resolved itself in a certain freedom from an abusive marriage and finally in her renunciation. That is not
the language in which she couched her story, however; she did not articulate it in terms of resistance and opposition to subordination. She saw
herself as someone having to face a number of questions (*prashna*) that
arose in specific circumstances at different times.[36] Her understanding

of how events in her life happened "suddenly" implies that she did not plan but rather dealt with events as they occurred. Buddhi had no qualms about working outside the home. What prompted her to renounce was the need to better understand *dukkha* and all that it involved. Buddhi spoke at length about her realization of the meaning of *dukkha* in the everyday lives of working people:

> We think that people have money. They have jobs. They live in foreign countries. And because of that they must be living in luxury. Internally, however, when we live together with them, we can see how much mental suffering [*mānasika dukak*] they must go through for this. They endure physical suffering [*kāyika dukak*] in order to earn.... Meanwhile, they have so many mental problems [*prashna*] and pain. When someone from a foreign country comes to Sri Lanka, we think, "They live abroad, how good it is for them, how much luxury they have." But I saw the suffering [*dukkha*] that they endured while earning money. In the same way, I saw that while earning money they were enduring many mental questions/concerns [*prashna*] [and] that very many different problems [*prashna*] arose for them. It was not just in our home; it was also in other homes and among friends.... I saw many questions/problems [*prashna*], so I became aware of very many things.

Buddhi's thinking on *dukkha* speaks to a continuum in the many events in her life, perhaps with a message to me about her understanding of life abroad. She spoke of renunciation primarily as a means of coming to terms with *dukkha*. The difficulties she had encountered helped her ponder the question of *dukkha*. Her understanding of its universality and of its presence in her story presented itself as another important moment in her life. In her case, that understanding led to a life of renunciation. Without centering *dukkha* as a part of life itself, Buddhi's renunciation makes little sense. I am not contending that her thinking about the meaning of *dukkha* was the only reason for her renunciation but rather that economic and family problems alone fail as explanations for her decision. Here it is essential to consider Buddhi's own description of the situations in which she found herself and of her actions.

Nuns' emphasis on *dukkha* and samsara has been interpreted by scholars as a major catalyst for women's taking on the renunciant life

(Bartholomeusz; Brown; Falk; Kusuma, *Dasasil*; Thamel). However, the analytical categories scholars have used to interpret female renunciation generally equate *dukkha* and samsara with the domestic or private realm, in opposition to the public realm. Understanding a life of *dukkha* and samsara defies such an interpretation. As far as Buddhi's story goes, *dukkha* was connected to conditions both in the home and in the workplace, without significant differentiation between the two.

The story of Dhamma, to which I turn next, is not unlike that of Buddhi in that Dhamma also renounced because of her realization of suffering and what she referred to as her *kalakirīma*[37] with life. Dhamma's account, like Buddhi's, attests to her potential to become a wage earner, but it is not a story of resistance; rather, it unfolds as a meditation on the question of *dukkha*. Whereas Buddhi spoke of how *dukkha* became a central theme in her life, Dhamma talked about her life's concerns in the "analytical" terms of *kalakirima* as well as *dukkha*. Both Buddhi's and Dhamma's families experienced economic hardship. One might suppose that such hardship led them to find an "escape" through renunciation, but that was not how either of them articulated their concerns and motives. Renunciation was not the only path open to them. Dhamma's realization of suffering came from her observations of sickness and death among those around her as well as from a concomitant acknowledgment of *kalakirima*. Dhamma had been in the robes of a *sil mata* for several years when I talked with her in the late 1990s. Dhamma's narrative, like Buddhi's, might be read in terms of resisting the role of wife and mother, especially when she explained that she did not want the household life after seeing the birth of twins in her family. As she mentioned, however, she was seen as a potential wage earner whose familial contribution was understood differently. She spoke of her decision to renounce in relation to addressing the concerns not exclusively of household life (*gihi jīvitaya*), but of life itself:

> Our family was at one time very rich, with many shops and trade, etc. Later the business went down. Our home became poor and the economic situation became troublesome.[38] During this time my older sisters [*akkas*] were all married and began to give birth to children. Meanwhile, I left school and helped with [their] babies. One day I was playing with my sister's sick child, who was about two and a half years old. That sick child while playing with me died....That was one *kalakirima*.

Dhamma proceeded to describe her pain (*vedanāva*) in observing the *dukkha* of an uncle who suffered from diabetes and had his legs amputated. That too, she said, was *kalakirima* for her. She also talked of the sufferings she observed when a sister gave birth in their home not to one child but (unexpectedly) to twins: "It was at that time that I thought that I did not want to have anything to do with this household life [*gihi jivitaya*]....I was about eighteen or nineteen at that time." One of her younger sisters was injured when a coconut fell on her head; she "went crazy" and never recovered. Dhamma described her as "very pretty—prettier than me." Ever since that incident, the sister had lived in suffering (*dukkha*), and Dhamma had observed it. Yet another attractive younger sister was diagnosed with a debilitating illness. Though the *kalakirima* Dhamma encountered as a young woman may seem to be a mode of being that relates to the matters of the domestic or private sphere, it cannot be confined to that, because what she was talking about was life itself. She emphasized that renunciation meant leaving a loving and supportive household:

> I had the hope [*bulaporottuva*, "expectation"] of studying, doing a job, and looking after my parents. However, after all those things, I did not consider staying at home....I told only my mother, and then it was with my mother's consent that I left secretly. The other people at home would not let me go, so I had to go secretly. My mother knew; the others did not. What I mean is that the others at home would not let me go; they loved me very much. Since they would not let me go, I left secretly....Those at home said that, because they loved me and I was clever, I could do a job and look after them.

Dhamma's story, like Buddhi's, indicates that the role of "wife and mother" was not the only alternative to that of renunciant. It is not uncommon for unmarried women in Sri Lanka to lead respectable lives in which they are welcomed and supported by extended-family members. Dhamma did not talk of familial pressure to get married, and it was clear that she was seen as a potential wage earner for her aging parents. Her own mother (and later, other relatives), supported her renunciation, again suggesting that her decision to become a *sil mata* was not driven by resistance to family members. One might at this point insist that it was resistance to family *life* that encouraged her to seek renunciation, especially because she associated *kalakirima* with events happening to family members. However, those events can more appropriately be understood as the catalyst that prompted her to universalize the meaning of *kalakirima* in life itself. That became clear as she listed the events as different *kalakirimas*.

Several other nuns talked about renunciation in relation to both *dukkha* and *kalakirima*; the lives they lived gave them a new awareness of the *everyday*. Still others spoke of having had the "thought" of renunciation at a very early age, perhaps even before having reflected deeply on difficult ideas such as *dukkha*. In some cases young girls would think of renouncing before they fully understood the differences between a *bhikkhu* and a *sil mata*. Sunita's decision to renounce, which I discuss next, is consistent with what I have often encountered in the stories of several other nuns. For those nuns, as for Sunita, the *initial* yearning (*āsāva*) for leading a life of renunciation did not occur in responses to experiences they had witnessed; it was just that—a yearning for a leading a life of renunciation. Nuns often spoke of having had a *thought* of renunciation because they either had observed the role model of a monk they knew or had come to know a female renunciant or because of the death of a family member. Again, the articulation of a yearning to become a nun points to something far more difficult to understand than the mere renunciation of domestic life. Sunita had thought about renunciation at a very young age, but she began to consider it more seriously after the death of her father when she was a young teenager:

My father's sister was a *sil māṇi* [ten precept nun]. We lost Father unexpectedly. Then our aunt-nun [*nända-māṇiyō*, literally "aunt-mother"] stayed at our home for about three months. I had a great yearning [*hari āsāvak*] to be ordained [*mahaṇavenna*], but no one at home liked me to do this. Since no one at home liked this, I kept this [wish] to myself and tried to study well.[39] At that time the *sil maniyos* had no proper place; they would collect something from somewhere and have *dāna*.... So, keeping this to myself, I thought I should study more, as it would be difficult to study once I had taken that path [of a *sil mani*]. I studied with that in mind and took my exams.

Then I would plead that I be ordained [*mahaṇavenna*], and I would weep about it, saying that I wanted to be ordained. But they would not allow me to be ordained. They said I should wait for my exam results, so I waited. I passed the exams well. Then they said that I should study for the higher exams. But I said no, I did not want just to study; I wanted to be ordained. Then one time when Nanda-maniyo came, I pleaded and I wept, I wept a lot. Then Mother also wept, asking me not to be ordained. Then I wept. And the whole family wept, saying that I should not be ordained. Then Mother [*amma*] said to the *maniyo*, "Take her and show her the hermitage [*aramaya*]. Let her stay for a month and come back."

Then I wept. I was also so sad to leave those people at home; I have never left home like that before. And I went and stayed at the *aramaya*. Then, after I had come to the *aramaya* itself, I had only the thought [*hita*] of being ordained. I had no thought of returning home; I just had the thought of being ordained. I waited a little while, and I told my mother, and she and the family certainly did not like the idea at all. But because the *maniyo* is the older sister of my father, she had some influence. Then,...after looking at an auspicious time, without telling my mother, she ordained me—yes,...without Mother knowing that she ordained me.

Q: Was that all right—not to get permission from Mother?
A: Well, Mother did not like it....She would not have it....Then the *maniyo* said that she has an influence, as she was my father's older sister. But then the *maniyo* did not like it either, because I could not do any work in the home; I could not cook or sew or do any of those things.
Q: Why not?
A: Because at home I am the "little one."...Then our *maniyo* said, "You cannot be ordained. This is the situation: at the hermitage I do all the sewing and cleaning and yard work. It is difficult even for me. How would you manage?" So Maniyo did not like to ordain me....I told her that I would do it all and that she should ordain me....And then after the ordination [*mahanavīma*] I sent a letter to Mother. Mother cried a lot and sent a letter saying, "You should consider your mother dead. Why did you do this?" Mother had much *dukkha*. Then, after about a month and a half, [we] went home with Maniyo. Then everyone at home cried....For about half an hour, no one at home spoke; everyone was weeping. It was like a funeral....Even people from the neighboring houses—they also stopped by....Then gradually things went better....People said, "Never mind. It is her wish."

Note here that the immediate family was not unhappy with Sunita's decision to renounce simply because it would prevent her from becoming a wife and mother. The concerns of the family appeared to center on the uncertainty and poverty that they associated with the lives of *sil matas* at the time, and that was probably why her mother encouraged her to visit a nuns' hermitage; she possibly hoped that after Sunita saw the hermitage, she would wish to return to the comforts of her own home. Sunita's position as the "baby" of the family, whereby she had not been groomed to do domestic work, ironically proved to be an obstacle to her ordination, thus calling into question the stereotypical portrayal of women as "wives and mothers" once again. Sunita had been encouraged to study instead, and perhaps she, like Buddhi and Dhamma, might have been seen as a potential wage earner for her family. Sunita evidently came from a very close-knit family; despite her yearning for ordination, she was sad to leave family members. Comparing the act of a young woman's renunciation to a funeral is not uncommon in Sri Lanka, as the act supposedly connotes a certain "death" and departure of a family member in a household. That connotation may seem to presuppose a division between the domestic life and the renunciant life, seeing both as autonomous modes of existence. However, Sunita's renunciation can hardly be understood as a complete departure and detachment from her family; she was, after all, ordained by her own aunt-nun. Nor can her ordination be seen as opposition to or freedom from (the oppression of) the duties of domestic life; she was never taught or expected to carry out such duties in the first place. Needless to say, in becoming a renunciant, she was largely entering unknown territory—certainly in relation to her material well-being. What Sunita's story does suggest is that the yearning for a life of renunciation cannot be placed simply within dichotomous structures that correlate with a grand narrative framework of secular-liberal discourses of freedom and emancipation. Sunita's renunciation centered on a yearning for leading a religious life; it cannot be seen as one choice among many available to her.

Conclusion

In this chapter I have argued that scholars writing about female renunciation have appropriated a particular set of dichotomous structures to interpret the world of Buddhist nuns and their practice of renunciation. I have considered some of the dichotomies that underpin select studies of nuns in Tibetan and Theravada traditions. I have argued that under close scrutiny it becomes clear that the use of such oppositions is misplaced. In fact, some scholars writing about Buddhist nuns recognize the shortcomings of the very oppositions that they nevertheless continue to employ. While they often claim to write from the viewpoint of nuns themselves, they frame their accounts with a discourse that is effectively unrecognizable to their subjects, thereby manufacturing a narrative disjunction.

The dichotomies that inform studies of Buddhist nuns generally continue to reflect notions of the public versus the private. Such thinking in turn informs the view that nuns' lives "need" intervention and assistance of various forms that can come only through access to Western ideas and resources, be they financial, educational, or otherwise. Narratives so informed—however benign the intentions of their authors—reproduce a specific "interpretation" of nuns' lives in which nuns are portrayed as indigents in need of assistance. Thus nuns become, if not the white woman's burden, at least the burden of those who are educated. Such narratives about nuns are both descriptive and prescriptive. It is essential to acknowledge the authorial complicity in such interpretations of nuns' lives if we are to interrupt future repetitions of such interpretations.

In presenting the accounts of three Sri Lankan nuns, I have not intended to provide an alternative narrative about nuns. Those Sri Lankan nuns have centered their renunciant lives on the difficult questions of *dukkha, kalakirima,* samsara, and nibbana as they go about being nuns in specific situations. Indeed, they speak of life's difficulties in terms of "questions" (*prashna*) that they face rather than as problems they need to overcome. Understanding lives of renunciation as being inseparable from such questions demands a different "interpretation"—one that cannot be subsumed under distinctions that lend themselves to interpretive codification in a ready-made paradigm. We need to recognize that if we are to go beyond liberal feminist constructions of nuns as agents whose lives await interpretation. Ultimately that recognition makes it possible to consider the *meaning* of such lives. Dorothy Smith's comments on the complexities of "interpretation" (in sociology) and on the question of meaning inherent in empirical research is helpful to rethinking our usual ways of framing female renunciants in Buddhism:

> The multiple perspectives of subjects, the multiple possible versions of the world arising in subjects' experience, create a problem for sociology only when our project is to establish a sociological version superseding theirs. It is a difficulty that arises largely from grounding sociology in "meaning," "interpretation," "common

understandings" and the like rather than in an ongoing coordering of actual activities accomplished in definite local historical settings. But when the latter is our ontology (the mode in which the social can be conceived as existing), then our business is to explore the ongoing socially ordered matrices differentiating experience and the extended social relations immanent in the everyday. (*Everyday World* 141)

3

Buddhism, Power, and Practice

Introduction

The Eight Revered Conditions (*aṭṭhagarudhammā* or *aṣṭaugurudharmāḥ*), sometimes translated as the Eight Chief Conditions or the Eight Chief Rules, which appear in many versions of the ordination account of the first *bhikkhunis*, are putative rules that appear to advocate the dependence of *bhikkhunis* on *bhikkhus* in early Buddhism.[1] They have been addressed in various ways by students and practitioners of Buddhism.[2] At one level, the Eight Conditions have received considerable attention in the field of Buddhism, because of the opportunities for intra- and inter-textual studies that they offer. At another level, the Conditions have assumed new significance in ongoing controversies centering on the recent *bhikkhuni* ordinations. A critical analysis of accounts on the Eight Conditions helps us understand how narratives can contribute to the construction of renunciant subjects through liberal notions of empowerment, autonomy, and freedom. Commenting on the power of narrative construction, Dorothy E. Smith notes that "our knowledge of contemporary society is to a large extent mediated to us by texts of various kinds. The result, an objectified world-in-common vested in texts, coordinates the acts, decisions, policies, and plans of actual subjects as the acts, decisions, policies, and plans of large-scale organizations" (*Conceptual Practices* 61). According to such thinking, we may see the world-in-common as one shared primarily by the author writing about Buddhism and Buddhist nuns and by the reader of the text. Additionally, we might liken some scholars of Buddhism to authors of the classic realist fiction that dominated European literature in the nineteenth century, a time that witnessed some of the defining scholarship in the field of Buddhism. Although on-site empirical research on Buddhism did not become popular until the latter part of the twentieth century, the early textual studies, which attempted to recreate ancient Buddhism in terms of how it might be realistically portrayed, were to influence empirical studies of Buddhism. In empirical work, the attempt to represent the *actuality* of Buddhist practice has remained a primary motive. However, only recently have scholars directed a critical focus on the authoring and reading of such narratives and on what those processes might mean for the construction of the (Buddhist) subject (Abeysekara, *Colors*; Almond; Ismail).

Although questions about the Conditions may be traced as far back as the early decades of the twentieth century, only in the last two decades have they occasioned serious debate. The recent higher ordinations of Theravada Buddhist nuns has brought a heightened awareness of the way the Conditions differentiate between male and female monastics.[3] Those who affirm the importance of the Conditions, although not necessarily condoning them, do so on the grounds that they are *Buddhavacana* (the word of the Buddha). Those who wish to question the significance of the Conditions do so mainly on the basis that they are not *Buddhavacana*. On one level there is the spectacle of debaters at loggerheads; on another there is a vista of common yet hotly contested ground, where narratives on the Conditions seek to construct the female renunciant as a subject who ultimately corresponds to a secular-liberal individual.

Since 1997 most women training for the higher ordination (*sāmaṇerīs*) in Sri Lanka are required to know and observe the Eight Conditions as a prerequisite for their *upasampada*. In my interviews with Sri Lankan nuns, I noticed that their acknowledgment of the Conditions was more nuanced and complex than many textual scholars have thought. Most interestingly, I noted a discrepancy between the way some monastics appeared to understand the practice of the Conditions and the way they "theorized" about them. I was left with the issues of how to reconcile the theory of the Conditions with the theory of their practice (past and present) as well as how to determine the relationship between their purported practice and their actual practice today. Did the Eight Conditions once ground and continue to support an oppressive monastic praxis? How is it possible that some nuns today claim to follow the Conditions and yet may not actually be doing so? Can one reconcile phallogocentric scholarly interpretations of the Conditions with contemporary *bhikkhunis'* understandings of them? How has the higher ordination of Theravada Buddhist nuns affected and been affected by interpretations of the Conditions? What, if anything, can we learn from contemporary understandings of the Conditions (both scholarly and monastic) in terms of interpreting past practice? Without more evidence than we have now, it is difficult, if not impossible, to reconstruct how the Conditions may have factored into early Buddhist life. Nevertheless, narratives of Buddhist practice tend to construct a textual ideology that conflates the world of authors and readers with that of the renunciant subjects as if the two groups share the same actualities. Current attitudes to the Conditions among monastics may point to the importance of rethinking narratives about early Buddhist life. That rethinking might question scholarly narratives of the Eight Conditions that overstate the hierarchal relationships between male and female members of the Buddhist monastic community. I argue that such narratives of Buddhist practice ultimately construct a textual ideology that unreflectively assumes that the authors and their readers as well as the renunciant subjects share common concerns.

I begin by looking at select scholarly interpretations of the Conditions and their significance. Although scholars may read the Conditions in a variety of ways, a fundamental divide opens up between readings that share the supposed ideology of the canonical account itself and others that question it. The difference between the former and the latter is a difference in assumptions relating to the canonical account of the first ordination of nuns. To use Catherine Belsey's terms, readings that support the ideology of the text see the text as "declarative" (conveying information) or as "imperative" (giving commands). However, readings that *contest* the ideology of the text provide an understanding of the text that is "interrogative" (raising questions) (Belsey 83–84). In the interrogative text, the "position of the 'author' inscribed in the text, if it can be located at all, is seen as questioning or as contradictory" (Belsey 84). Moreover, "the interrogative text refuses a single point of view, . . . but brings points of view into unresolved collision or contradiction. It therefore refuses the hierarchy of voices, . . . and no authorial or authoritative voice points to a single position which is the place of the coherence of meaning" (Belsey 85). My point here is that some scholars and practitioners view the Eight Conditions as a kind of interrogative text that lends itself to questions about its own interpretation (what the Conditions mean) and its applicability (how the Conditions work) in practice. Such a critical hermeneutic still creates a division between knowledge and practice. The lived monastic life is not reducible to such a division, however, as is shown by the ways the nuns interviewed for this chapter responded to questions about the Eight Conditions.

Discussions among practitioners, both in publications circulating within Sri Lanka and in my interviews with monastics, indicate alternative readings of the Conditions—readings that allow for the possibility of simultaneously affirming and denying them. Although many scholars interpret the Conditions as *rules* (whether in an imperative, a declarative, or an interrogative sense)—that is, as explicit moral *laws* that can be observed or transgressed—some monastics effectively depart from such a strict interpretation. As we will see, nuns who claim to observe the Conditions have different understandings of them. They observe them not in the narrow sense of observing rules but in the broader sense as *conditions* that make their identities as *bhikkhunis* possible.

The debate on the Eight Conditions in Sri Lanka, though not always sharing the hermeneutical spaces of Western scholarship, has similar interpretive tendencies. However, the author of Western scholarship cannot stand in the shoes (or sandals) of the Sri Lankan participant-debater. Moreover, the renunciant subject created by different debate-narratives remains apart from the lived lives of nuns. I question how the Conditions are theorized and suggest that contemporary practitioners' understandings of them may provide insights into how they might have been understood in early Buddhist life.[4] This chapter does not seek to provide a textual or philological interpretation of accounts of the Eight Conditions. Nor does it attempt to verify a particular representation of the practice of the Eight Conditions. Rather, it endeavors to understand how particular narratives of female renunciation are complicit in ideologies that are based on the liberal constructions of subjects and their agency.

The Eight Revered Conditions

The acceptance of the Eight Conditions first appears as a prerequisite for the higher ordination of Mahapajapati Gotami, the Buddha's adopted mother. *Garudhammā* has often been translated as "rules" (French: *règles*; German: *Regeln*) rather than "conditions," and *dhammā* is used to refer to monastic rules of the *Vinaya*. But the multivalent connotations and denotations of *dhamma* as "truth," "reality," "building block of reality," and "factor of existence" or simply "thing" perhaps provide more scope for the meaning of *garudhamma*. Several scholars have argued that the Eight Conditions lack the general format of *vinaya* injunctions, which were pronounced after specific practical problems were presented to the

Buddha. Translating *garudhamma* as "rule" can be misleading. Textual accounts generally point out that the Eight *dhammas* were *conditions* that permitted and identified the ordination of Mahapajapati Gotami. In the Pali account, each Condition is followed by a statement that the Condition is to be revered (*garukatvā*). The rendition Revered Conditions seems to convey the intended nuances of the text. Since this chapter focuses on the Pali and Theravada usage of *atthagarudhamma*, I refer to the term as the Eight Revered Conditions or the Eight Conditions.

The Pali account of the first renunciant(s) who accepted the Eight Conditions with the intention of becoming *bhikkhunis* is replete with inconsistencies that have generated diverse debates. The account, as is now well known, recounts how the Buddha repeatedly refuses the request of his stepmother, Mahapajapati Gotami, and five hundred women of the Sakyan clan to be ordained until Ananda intercedes. The Buddha does agree to ordain Mahapajapati, but only if she accepts the Eight Conditions. When Ananda gives the Buddha the news of her acceptance, the Buddha makes the controversial statement that the Buddhist dispensation will endure for only half its allotted time because women were allowed to enter the monastic order. He also states that the Conditions are laid down in advance "for the *bhikkhunis*" as a means of containment, just as a dam might be built to contain a body of water.[5] After the Buddha permits the higher ordination of *bhikkhunis* by *bhikkhus*, the recently ordained *bhikkhunis* claim that they have not in fact received the higher ordination.[6] The Buddha corrects them by saying that their acceptance of the Eight Conditions constituted the full ordination. The Eight Conditions are listed here:

1. A *bhikkhuni* who is fully ordained for a hundred years should greet a *bhikkhu* who is fully ordained but that day—for example, by respectful verbal greeting, rising up, greeting with palms together, and doing proper homage. This Condition is to be treated with respect, esteemed, revered, and honored and should not be surpassed lifelong.
2. A *bhikkhuni* should not spend the rainy season in a residential area devoid of *bhikkhus*. This Condition too is to be treated with respect... and should not be surpassed lifelong.
3. At the half-month a *bhikkhuni* should ask the *bhikkhusangha* about two things [*dhammā*]: the question of the [date of the] *uposatha* and the approach for the biweekly instruction [*ovāda*].[7] This Condition too is to be treated with respect... and should not be surpassed lifelong.

4. A *bhikkhuni* who has observed the rains' retreat should observe the *pavāraṇā* ceremony[8] in the dual sangha in three ways—namely, what has been seen, heard, or suspected. This Condition too is to be treated with respect...and should not be surpassed lifelong.

5. A *bhikkhuni* who has transgressed a *garudhamma*[9] should observe the fortnightly penance [*pakkhamānatta*] before the dual sangha. This Condition too is to be treated with respect...and should not be surpassed lifelong.

6. A female trainee who has trained in the observation of the six conditions [*dhammā*] for two rains' retreats should request full ordination from the dual sangha. This Condition too is to be treated with respect...and should not be surpassed lifelong.

7. A *bhikkhu* should not be reviled or verbally abused by a *bhikkhuni* in any way. This Condition too is to be treated with respect...and should not be surpassed lifelong.

8. From this day onward, for *bhikkhunis*, a certain manner of speaking to *bhikkhus* is forbidden, but for *bhikkhus* that manner of speaking to *bhikkhunis* is not forbidden. This Condition too is to be treated with respect...and should not be surpassed lifelong.

Reconstructions of Early Buddhist Lives and Ideological Complicity

In this section I question the work of select Western scholars whose reconstructions of the Eight Conditions in early Buddhism assume that they function as rules. Despite the scholars' differing stances, they consider the Conditions to be self-evident and inevitable adaptations of nuns to an androcentric monastic regime of early Buddhist life. The authority and authorship of the Conditions remain uncontested. Those scholars want to locate an intricate link between a unified author (the Buddha or later monk redactors) and a supposed declarative ideology of the text. Ironically, in treating the account of the Eight Conditions as either declarative or imperative or in accepting the Conditions as *Buddhavacana*, those scholars further reinforce particular interpretations of the Eight Conditions, creating a narrative about an essentially dependent and disempowered renunciant.

In her classic work *Women under Primitive Buddhism*, Horner devotes an entire chapter to the Eight Conditions, which she translates as the Eight Chief Rules. She considers them to be "precise and definite" (118) and states that because of them "the almswomen were not to be independent of the almsmen" (119). Although Horner in her general introduction criticizes the "monk-factor" and the possibility of "alterations" and "inconsistencies" (xx) in textual traditions, she does not offer a sustained criticism of the Eight Conditions.[10] It is striking that her explanation of the Conditions provides a relatively seamless account of the early nuns as depicted in numerous events that occurred sometime *after* the establishment of the *bhikkhuni* order. While she notes that the Eight Conditions differ from the *vinaya* stipulations in having not been occasioned by a recounting of a prior offense, she proceeds to explain the Conditions in the context of subsequent events. For example, she mentions that several of the Conditions correspond to later *vinaya* injunctions that incurred expiation (*pācittiya*), and she then discusses the situations that gave rise to those injunctions as a means of explaining the Conditions. That procedure makes little sense, however, because the Conditions were supposedly introduced *before* the establishment of *vinaya* regulations for *bhikkhunis*. Ultimately, Horner presents the Eight Conditions as rules that are consistent with later promulgations the Buddha made; that is, they appear to become part of a consistent and uniform text authored by a single subject. Consequently, for Horner the Conditions are declarative and imperative rules in that they constitute commands.

Wijayaratna, writing more than fifty years after Horner, provides a similar account of the Eight Conditions. He agrees that the Conditions appear to reflect the historical and social contexts of gender expectations. Furthermore, he affirms that the Conditions were established in order "to protect the Community of Nuns" (19). He does note, however, that Mahapajapati Gotami could not have observed many of the Conditions because the institutional structures that were a prerequisite for their observance were initially absent:

> The Eight Great Conditions were not commandments that had to be immediately executed; they were, rather, obligations imposed on an organization that would be set up in time. *The necessary conditions for fulfilling the rules were not present at the beginning. As for the Eight Great Conditions, they were meant for a Community of Nuns already well established, whereas the foundations of such a community were still being laid.* (Wijayaratna 31; emphasis added).

Although Wijayaratna, like Horner, assumes that the Eight Conditions were accepted as *Buddhavacana* among early Buddhist practitioners, he departs from her by noting some important practical problems regarding the Conditions' implementation. However, he does not elaborate on that point. By glossing over the question of how the Eight Conditions could have been laid down as a prerequisite for the ordination of the first *bhik-khuni* when the very means of observing the Conditions were absent,[11] Wijayaratna too produces a discourse about female renunciation and ordination in which the early *bhikkhunis* are perceived to have been subjects constrained by the "norm of the society of the day" (18).

Nancy Auer Falk, referring to the Conditions as the "eight special rules," concurs with that thinking in a liberal feminist vein. Although she appears to question the Conditions as *Buddhavacana*, she affirms that their authority is so rooted in Buddhist tradition that they have had a definite impact on monastic practice (N. Falk 162). She states that the Conditions were *"imposed* on the women as a price for allowing them to found their order. These provided that the women would be permanently *subordinated* to the men" (N. Falk 159; emphasis added). Falk's discussion of the Conditions has influenced subsequent research on Buddhist nuns.[12] Assuming that the Conditions were practiced as we find them in their "textual" form, she suggests that even though the rules stipulated that nuns remained subordinate to monks, because women of the time in India "had always been subordinated to men...nuns apparently did not find these rules oppressive" (N. Falk 160). Falk projects nuns' past subordination into the future and articulates the impact of that subordination with reference to a liberal discourse on equality and empowerment, asserting that the Conditions "meant that women would never be leaders in the life of the whole community or have any decisive voice in shaping its direction" (N. Falk 160). Unlike Falk and the seemingly modern author who recognizes their "subordination," the early nuns were ignorant of their own disadvantage. Indeed, they were so ignorant that they did not even know that the Conditions were "oppressive." Here Falk appeals to the sensitivities of the modern reader by creating a renunciant subject who is essentially devoid of agency. Like Horner, her presentation of the Conditions is couched, albeit resentfully, in a discourse of "negative" power—that is, one that is grounded in notions of (in)equality and (in)subordination. We still find that kind of conceptualization of power in the scholarly thinking about Buddhist practice. As Foucault has famously noted, power is not always negative; not only does it oppress or repress, but it also enables and obliges and even creates desires.[13] But in Falk's understanding, the early nuns were in a double bind: they had to succumb to the power of the monks, and they did not even recognize that power as oppressive. Ultimately, according to such logic, nuns have no way out of that predicament unless they simply adopt a Western logic of agency and *recognize* their oppression. That is why Falk, like Wijayaratna, raises some questions concerning the Conditions that remain unresolved.

Horner, Wijayaratna, and Falk all interpret the account of the Conditions critically. However, their interpretations of the Conditions themselves, whether as *Buddhavacana* or as a foundation for the ordination of nuns, border on a host of assumptions about history that I cannot take up here. My point is that they ignore the relation between the Eight Conditions and their practice within certain social relations. In other words, the previously stated understanding of the Conditions vis-à-vis a negative sense of power presupposes a distinction between "knowledge" and "practice," between a knowing subject and a practicing subject. More simply put, the early *bhikkhunis*, who lived their lives accepting the Eight Conditions, are not characterized as knowing subjects, since they either did not know or chose to ignore that they were oppressed.[14] If we set aside the liberal notion of power as subordination and oppression, we can better understand the monastic practices of nuns in relation to the Eight Conditions rather than affirming a distinction between a knowing subject and a practicing subject. The kind of discourse we find in the representations of the Eight Conditions by Horner, Wijayaratna, and Falk continues to this day, especially among those who emphasize the significance of the Conditions in defining monastic praxis, whether it be to affirm or to refute them.

Contesting Ideologies: Contemporary Reflections[15]

In this section I look at the contexts of select Western scholarly debates that explicitly question the coherence of the account of the Eight Conditions as well as its impact in Buddhist traditions. Such scholarship, which contests previous views on the Conditions, has unsurprisingly arisen only in the wake of renewed interest in studies on Buddhism and feminism.[16] That new approach has been spurred on by an enhanced late twentieth-century concern with global feminisms and the establishment of major international Buddhist women's organizations, which attempt to maintain grassroots contacts in predominantly Buddhist countries.[17] Such organizations have supported the reinstatement of the higher ordination for women of all Buddhist traditions.

Writing since the early 1990s as both a feminist and a Western Buddhist scholar-practitioner, Rita Gross has been well aware of the activities of the Sakyadhita International Association of Buddhist Women (*Patriarchy* 29). Referring to the Conditions as "special rules," Gross concurs with Nancy Falk in suggesting that the Conditions negatively affected the leadership of women in early Buddhism (*Patriarchy* 38). Although Gross ascribes a certain historicity to the impact of the Conditions, whose practice she infers was observable and observed, she departs from Falk in trying to show how and why the account of the Eight Conditions may not have been *Buddhavacana* (*Patriarchy* 38–39). With a self-avowed feminist reading of the Conditions, Gross speaks of an "agenda of maintaining male control over women" among practitioners who consider the Conditions authoritative (*Patriarchy* 39). Although she refers here to contemporary Buddhist practitioners, she may well have regarded that agenda as a bias within scholarship itself. Gross clearly wants to contest a perceived patriarchal consciousness in the textual account of the ordination. However, as we have already seen, she suggests that a transformation of gender relations cannot emerge from among Asian Buddhists (*Patriarchy* 133–135). Gross and Falk, despite using different approaches to the question of patriarchy, eventually attribute to Buddhists from Asia an inability to counter inegalitarian injunctions, simply because those Buddhists are ignorant and powerless. Once again, here knowledge and power become opposed to practice.

Alan Sponberg refers to the Conditions as an embodiment of "institutional androcentrism" (13), a term Gross echoes in referring to them as a form of "institutional subordination, not spiritual subordination" (*Patriarchy* 37). Sponberg, focusing his analysis on the Pali account of the ordination, refers to it as "a document of reconciliation, as a symbolic, mythologized expression of a compromise negotiated between several factions, including the nuns and their male supporters," suggesting that that account was "a later attempt to rationalize and legitimize post facto what had already become the status quo" (16). According to him, there was a need to address public concerns and "to deal with the social unacceptability of an autonomous group of women not under the direct regulation and control of some male authority" (17). Sponberg's investigation of the textual ordination account and the Eight Conditions is a serious scholarly attempt to contest the authority as well as the social impact of the text. Referencing several scholars, albeit primarily in his footnotes, and underscoring the need for more inter-textual and intra-textual study, he raises a number of issues concerning the chronology and historicity of the account and opens up doors for further research (Sponberg 32–33). In questioning the usual framing of the textual ordination account, Sponberg subverts the construction of the female renunciant as an unknowing and powerless subject. Ultimately in his account, even though the renunciant subject is not powerless, she can eventually recognize her own powerlessness. That is to say, for Sponberg, power becomes a matter of recognition. Thus, Sponberg does not depart far from Horner: the liberal liberation of the early nun then marks a transition from the unknowing subject to the knowing subject.

Around the same time that Gross and Sponberg were writing about the Eight Conditions in North America, Ute Husken, a German scholar, was also disputing the patriarchal ideology in the scholarly interpretations of the Conditions. Husken, addressing an academic audience, provides one of the first intra-textual studies in Western scholarship that critiques the Eight Conditions, which she too translates as "rules" (*Regeln*). Husken seemingly agrees with Horner concerning the editorial role of monks in transmitting the texts, and she refrains from critiquing Horner's presentation of the Conditions.[18] Although her writing appears to rely heavily on Horner in comparing the Conditions to later *vinaya* prescriptions, she differs from Horner in explicitly noting textual inconsistencies and raises important historical issues regarding their formulation (Husken 160, 164). She concludes that the large number of inconsistencies imply that the Conditions "did not represent an original conception, but rather the outcome of a later development" (170). She surmises (not unlike Gross and Sponberg) that because of changes that possibly occurred after the demise of the Buddha, members of the sangha may have attempted to find recourse in the Conditions as a means of strengthening the male monastic order. Thus, Husken's renunciant subject, though hardly the same as Gross's (unknowing) subject, is not unlike Sponbergs' (knowing) subject. As a scholar writing for a modern academic audience, she questions the historicity of textual records without portraying the female renunciant subject as either necessarily unknowing or powerless. In Husken's account we can see the "ignorant" and "powerless" female subject encountered in those previous narratives gradually becoming a knowing subject.

The scholars discussed in this section contest the coherence of the account involving the Eight Conditions by reading it interrogatively—clearly indicating, as Belsey states, that the text "refuses a single point of view but brings points of view into unresolved collision or contradiction"

(85). Although those scholars appear to share interpretive approaches in rejecting the notion that the Conditions represent an expression of *Buddhavacana*, their constructions of the renunciant subject vary but involve the same logic. While some scholars claim that the early *bhikkhunis* were powerless, others claim that they were not so powerless. Even though one may presume a difference in such scholarly understandings of the female subject, ultimately they both privilege the modern sense of a knowing subject. "Knowledge" (of nun's own supposed hidden power) is privileged over "practice" (subordination and oppression). In that view, a life of practice without knowledge is a life of disempowerment. But as I will try to suggest throughout this study, such a division between knowledge and practice is not present in life itself.[19]

Sri Lankan Conjunctures I: Theories of Monastic Practice

Now I want to focus on the writings on nuns that have originated within Sri Lankan Buddhist contexts—writings by scholars, practitioners, and scholar-practitioners whose works emerge primarily from those contexts. Although the focus of those works consider the account of the Eight Conditions interrogatively and may appear to echo opinions similar to those of scholars published in Western languages, they reflect a distinctive set of concerns and authorial voices. Most important, they create narratives that are typically grounded in the construction of a (dis)empowered renunciant subject—a notion with practical implications for renunciants themselves. The growing scholarly and public attention given to the text of the ordination account and the Eight Conditions (both in Western languages and in Sri Lanka) is relatively recent and is most likely tied to the increasing visibility of Ten-Precept mothers[20] in the 1980s and the emergence of Theravada *bhikkhuni* ordinations since the 1990s. I propose that scholarship on the Eight Conditions today may be usefully located within the context of their practice—or at least within that of the theory of their practice.[21]

My research of materials from the 1970s and 1980s suggests that the increased visibility of the *dasa sil matas* in Sri Lanka is necessarily interrelated with the creation of a narrative on the subject of the Theravada *bhikkhuni*. The renewed focus on both *sil matas* and *bhikkhunis* emanated from a variety of causes, ranging from burgeoning state activism, the mobilization of the mass media, and the institutionalization of *sil mata*

organizations to the publication of on-site scholarship. Writings emerging from Sri Lankan contexts, like the works of Western scholars, tend
to reiterate opinions of the Eight Conditions with reference to the same
binary opposition; that is, their debates center on whether the Conditions
can be validated as *Buddhavacana*. Consequently, such writings, like their
Western counterparts, tend to be about a subject who is defined in terms
of knowledge (in this case, a knowing subject), and they reproduce an
impasse in the conversation about the Conditions.

Dhammavihari, a scholar-monk, writing subsequent to the (Sarnath)
bhikkhuni upasampada of 1996, states that the Eight Conditions are "the
most vital issue in the founding of the *Bhikkhuni Sāsana* [dispensation of
bhikkhunis]" (41).[22] However, my research indicates that the first mention
of the Conditions in popular Sri Lankan sources appears in a 1934 article
by the prominent scholar G. P. Malalasekera, who uses the same frame
of reference as Horner and others adopted. He says that the Conditions
were "safeguards" that preserved the "supremacy of the male members of
the order" (47). Unlike some of the other scholars, however, Malalasekera
was writing from within a Theravada Buddhist context in Sri Lanka. As
George Bond notes, Malalasekera, in his capacity as president of the All
Ceylon Buddhist Congress and as a respected public spokesperson, was
a prominent participant in Buddhist activities during his time (*Buddhist
Revival* 78–85). Malalasekera's article proved seminal, having been refer-
enced in numerous publications that supported the *bhikkhuni upasampada*
(Dhammaloka 89; Gnanashila, *Sirilak* 109; D. A. Weeraratne, *Bhiksunī*
14–15; D. A. Weeraratne, *Buddhist* 18). More recently, it was published in
its entirety in the commemorative publication, the *Bodhgaya International
Full Ordination Ceremony*.

Media coverage of the possibility of "reviving" the *bhikkhuni* order in
the 1970s and early 1980s proved sporadic.[23] Although news items tended
to focus on the possibility of establishing a *bhikkhuni* ordination that was
"Theravada," there was little discussion of the Eight Conditions per se.[24]
The media's view of the *bhikkhuni* focused more on countering her perceived ritual subordination than on questioning the Conditions themselves. When television became more readily available in Sri Lanka in the
1980s, the *dasa sil matas* literally became more visible in the public eye,
prompting renewed interest in the *bhikkhuni* order.[25] In 1983 the government began collecting data on the *sil matas* and contributed, albeit mini-
mally, to funding their education. A few news items mentioned the Eight
Conditions.[26] However, until the publication by Urugamuve Vangisa Himi

that I discuss next, the popular focus remained on the appropriateness of reviving a Theravada *bhikkhuni* order without a pre-established lineage of Theravada nuns.[27] It is perhaps not insignificant that on-site interviews of *dasa sil matas* were first conducted by scholars in the 1980s. Although studies by Thamel, Bloss, and Kusuma (*Dasa Sil*) specifically addressed the contemporary contexts of the *sil matas*, Tessa Bartholomeusz and I began to think about questions of the relation between the canonical account of the Conditions and the contemporary lives of *sil matas*. How *sil matas* reflected on their lives and talked about them cannot be isolated from the conjunctures that were part of those lives and the questions that researchers asked of them.

The first scholarly study in Sri Lanka focusing on a discussion of the Eight Conditions was published in 1986, as part of a larger work written by a monk, Vangisa, who recounts the history of the establishment of the *bhikkhuni* order in India and Sri Lanka. The chapter devoted to the Eight Conditions uncovers a number of intra-textual inconsistencies concerning each of the Conditions and concludes that "it is difficult to accept the historicity of the *garudhammas*" (Vangisa 38). Most important for the ensuing debate of the 1990s, the author notes that if Mahapajapati Gotami did accept the Eight Conditions, observance of them was not requested of the five hundred Sakyan women accompanying her (Vangisa 38–39). Furthermore, he argues that even if Mahapajapati Gotami did accept the Eight Conditions, she may have accepted (as a knowing subject) a different set of the Conditions that were edited out of the *Cullavagga* and are unknown today (Vangisa 37). Vangisa's publication is important not only for its groundbreaking critique of the Conditions but also for its broader impact on Sri Lankan scholars and practitioners alike.

Since the publication of Vangisa's work, the debate in Sri Lankan circles has, like that of the Western scholarship discussed earlier, often focused on disputing the historical authorship and validity of the ordination account and the Eight Conditions. However, the Sri Lankan reflections on the Conditions are written from a somewhat different dialogical vantage point in which discourses on them form part of an ongoing debate about the subject of a *bhikkhuni* and the emerging ordinations of Theravada Buddhist women. That debate, in addition to invoking the perennial issue of whether the Conditions are *Buddhavacana*, has brought into clearer focus a more immediate concern that allows monastics to reject the Conditions even while accepting them as *Buddhavacana*. That controversy, highlighted in scholarly works by Vangisa and Kusuma, centers on the possiblity that observance of the Eight Conditions was intended for Mahapajapati Gotami alone, by virtue of her having been ordained by the Buddha. In contrast, her five hundred female companions were ordained by monks and, ipso facto, may not have been required to observe the same prescriptions. Arguments about the Conditions are developed in the 1993 commemorative volume dedicated to Sanghamitta, 2300 *Saṅghamittā Jayanti Saṅgrahaya*.[28] One essay by a monk who is well known for his support of the *bhikkhuni upasampada* identifies several textual inconsistencies and concludes that the traditional account of the Conditions is of doubtful historicity (Gnanarama 208). The other essay (by a *sil mata* who was to receive the *bhikkhuni* ordination several years later) suggests that they are a valid prescription for female renunciant practice and that after Mahapajapati Gotami received the Conditions from the Buddha, the five hundred Sakyan women approached the *bhikkhu* sangha for the ordination and also accepted the Conditions (Mitragnanissari 134). Those two articles assume the presence of nuns as knowing subjects and highlight questions at the core of the Sri Lankan debate concerning the Eight Conditions.

Another major publication in Sinhalese, *Nivan Maga*, which devotes itself to Buddhist women's religious freedom (*vimukti*), appeared in 1994. That work includes essays by Pearl Perera and Dhammaratana Himi that self-consciously enter the debate by discussing relevant Sinhalese publications on the Eight Conditions. The essay by Perera, a longtime proponent of the *bhikkhuni* ordination, is particularly significant in underlining the bipolar contours of the argument. Perera provides a list of references to academics and practitioners from Sri Lanka and elsewhere who she believes reject the idea that the Conditions are *Buddhavacana* (47–50). Proponents of that perspective, such as Saparamadu, Kodikara, and Rohana Gnanashila, have produced independent publications that include a rationale for the idea that Theravada *bhikkhunis* today need not observe the Conditions. The debate, which had been primarily textual and academic in most Western scholarship, came to have immediate practical implications, when monastics, such as Kusuma, Talalle Dhammaloka, Vakada Bhadra, and Panadure Vajira, became instrumental in promoting the image of the *bhikkhuni* (as a knowing subject) both in their writing and in their own participation in *bhikkhuni* ordination ceremonies.

The work of Kusuma, who writes as a leading *bhikkhuni* and a scholar-practitioner and who speaks to audiences throughout the world, brings a new dimension and practical context to reflections on female renunciation. Kusuma has disputed the validity of the Eight Conditions,

first in a transnational forum and later in a doctoral thesis. Speaking as
the first Sri Lankan *bhikkhuni* to receive the *upasampada*, in 1996, she
addressed activist scholars and practitioners at an international Sakyadhita
conference in 1998.[29] In her paper, which was subsequently published, she
provides several critiques of the Conditions. In one critique she argues,
as had others before her, that the Conditions did not conform to contexts
that generally gave rise to *vinaya* regulations ("Inaccuracies" 8). Most
important, she proposes what has been reiterated in ongoing debates in
Sri Lanka—namely, that the Eight Conditions, if applicable, may have
been relevant only to the ordination of Mahapajapati Gotami and not
to the other women who were ordained in her time ("Inaccuracies" 7).
In addition, Kusuma argues that the Conditions were unknown at the
time of the first establishment of the *bhikkhuni* sangha in Sri Lanka in
the third century B.C.E.; hence, she begins to speak to concerns that are
current in Sri Lanka. Noting the implications for *bhikkhunis* in contemporary Buddhism, she concludes that there "is clear evidence that the
garudhammas are not a *Vinaya* requirement, either as precept or as practice" ("Inaccuracies" 9).

By 1999 Kusuma had submitted a doctoral dissertation on the
Bhikkhuni Vinaya, which was subsequently translated, published, and
made available to the Sinhalese-reading public under the title of *Bhikkhunī
Vinaya*. Her dissertation, researched primarily in Germany under the auspices of Pali scholar Friedgard Lottermoser and submitted to a university in Sri Lanka, devotes a chapter to an intra-textual study of the Eight
Conditions. Contextualizing declarations made by the Buddha in general,
Kusuma indicates that there are no other circumstances in which considerations of gender alone become the basis for the establishment of a
rule ("Bhikkhunī Vinaya" 37–39; 61). Similarly, she argues that the apparent insistence on following certain Conditions "lifelong" ignores, among
other things, the event of the nun who disrobes ("Bhikkhunī Vinaya" 40).
Like Vangisa she asserts that chronological inconsistencies reflected in
the interface between the account of the Conditions and the establishment of *vinaya* injunctions involve a redundancy in the text: several of the
Conditions were similar to propositions that were purportedly established
after the first ordination of *bhikkhunis*. She further notes that the prereq-
uisites for observing some of the Conditions could not have predated the
introduction of the *bhikkhuni* sangha ("Bhikkhunī Vinaya" 46, 48, 53). In
a chapter that examines each Condition in detail and presents numerous
textual inconsistencies relating to each, Kusuma concludes that the Eight

Conditions could not logically have been *Buddhavacana* ("Bhikkhunī Vinaya"49, 53, and 65).

Interpretations of the ordination account and the Eight Conditions advanced by Sri Lankan and Western writers have a common frame of reference; they highlight *Buddhavacana* or "tradition" as the definitive criterion of validity. Yet Sri Lankan writers seem to be oriented more toward questions of religious praxis than toward abstract theorizing. The difference between the context of Western writings and that of Sri Lankan writings is primarily a difference of theory in practice. Western publications on the Eight Conditions are mainly written by and for an academic audience. There the construction of the subject of the *bhikkhuni*, though a matter of academic interest for a small audience, remains mostly theoretical. Publications circulating in Sri Lanka, however, whether in Sinhalese or in English, tend to be written for practitioners, for whom theorizing has a more immediate interest. The question remains as to how the debate on the authority of the Eight Conditions, as well as the construction of the renunciant subject (whether knowing or unknowing, powerful or powerless) plays out, if at all, among practicing monastics.

Sri Lankan Conjunctures II: Practices beyond Theory

In this section I interview nine Buddhist monastics and consider a variety of perspectives advanced by renunciants on the theory and practice of the Eight Conditions.[30] It is clear from her writings that Kusuma firmly rejects observance of the Conditions as a prerequisite for life as a female renunciant. It is noteworthy that unlike the nuns interviewed here, Kusuma is a scholar; she is bilingual and engages a cosmopolitan audience of scholars and practitioners. The nuns I interviewed in my research for this chapter speak about the Conditions differently from the way Kusuma writes about them. One may perhaps say that the responses of those nuns ranged from indifference to (or ignorance of) the Conditions to supposed observance (and knowledge) of them. Monks who supported the *bhikkhuni upasampada* were outspoken in their insistence on the relevance of the Conditions for *bhikkhunis* in the past and the present (Vajiragnana 46). One leading monk I interviewed argued in favor of the validity of the Conditions for *bhikkhunis* today by appealing to their supposed relevance for all *bhikkhunis* in the past. Although one might be tempted to think of monastics as knowing or unknowing subjects in terms of their responses to my questions about the Conditions, my research suggests something different. Some monastics today are positioned both to claim observance of the Conditions and to deny them to a certain extent in their practice. This does not mean that we need to establish a divide between knowledge and practice, but rather that a "reading" of the Conditions must be rooted in the lived practices of them.

The following exchange between *samaneri* Mitta (M) and me (Q) indicates a somewhat perfunctory attitude to the Conditions that is elusive because its significance does not figure in the way scholars assume it does in monastic life:

Q: Have you heard about the eight *garudhammas?*
M: I have heard of them.
Q: So you know what they are. Do you accept them?
M: Well, I can't say. What we are trying to do is to remove defilements [*kleśa*]. To say that this is wrong or that is wrong—we cannot say that.
Q: Do you accept them or not?
M: Whatever the case, well, our objective is nibbana.
Q: Do you accept them, or…?
M: I do not know, because I generally am not one who looks at books.

Samaneri Mitta claimed to neither accept nor reject the validity of the Conditions. Evidently, the Conditions had little significance for her understanding of monastic life, even as she awaited full ordination as a *bhikkhuni*. Another nun (a *bhikkhuni*) questioned the validity of the Conditions insofar as they had been prescribed only for Mahapajapati Gotami: "The *aṣṭagarudhammā* (Eight Conditions) were not preached to everyone; they were only preached by the Lord Buddha to one person," she said, echoing arguments made in publications available in Sri Lanka. For her the Conditions, though possibly *Buddhavacana*, were simply irrelevant. Three *bhikkhunis* with whom I spoke adamantly affirmed the relevance of the Conditions and acknowledged their observance of them. They insisted that the Conditions were a necessary condition of their *upasampada*. Most interestingly, however, they seemed to lack a detailed, "bookish" *knowledge* of what the Conditions denoted and were hesitant to *speak* about them. In other words, the nuns may have some "knowledge" about the Conditions, but they did not care to put it into words, even when asked to do so. The "absence" of such verbal knowledge cannot possibly be thought of as a sign of "disempowerment" and "subordination." The ways that knowledge does or does not figure as important have to be understood in terms of the conditions of monastic life itself. The following excerpt of my conversation with one of those *bhikkhunis* further complicates the question of knowledge about the Conditions:

B: We cannot stray from the *ashtagarudhamma*.
Q: You must accept them?
B: Without fail.
Q: Could you tell me what they are?
B: I cannot remember them now.

The *bhikkhuni* hesitated for some time and then went on to recite only six of the Conditions.[31] She stated that she had to observe them because the senior monk who had ordained her had requested that she do so or else lose her identity as an *upasampada bhikkhuni*.

A somewhat similar perspective was initially voiced by Soma, a senior *bhikkhuni* who had trained nuns for the *upasampada*. Over the course of an extended discussion with me on the Conditions, she articulated thoughts that were nuanced yet fraught with apparent contradictions. When asked if she accepted the Conditions, she assented: "Yes. Even if one does not accept them, the *Mahā Sangha* (male monastic establishment) expects one to adhere to them, because it [was] under the Buddha that the *garudhammā* were prescribed. The head monk says that one should not reject them; otherwise the *Maha Sangha* will not give permission for the *bhikṣunī śāsana* [dispensation of *bhikkhunis*] to exist." Notably, the head monk cited here, a staunch supporter of the *bhikkhuni upasampada*, appears to promote a presumed textual ground that affirms a certain type of relationship with *bhikkhunis*. However, his reason for doing so was not to ensure the "subordination" of *bhikkhunis* to *bhikkhus*, as some might suppose, but rather to affirm the subject of the *bhikkhuni* as a practical reality. That that monk did not attempt to reprove the *bhikkhunis* who had openly opposed the Eight Conditions and had been ordained under his tutelage represents a case in point.

Soma claimed to accept the Conditions, at least in theory, adding that they must be followed. Although she was well aware that the *Maha Sangha* was far from unified in its opinions on the *bhikkhuni upasampada*, she maintained that her identity and *bhikkhuni* status would be jeopardized were she not to accept the Conditions.[32] She corroborated that when she admitted to having learned the Conditions as a part of her training, but she somewhat amusedly confessed to not remembering them well.

We discussed the individual Conditions. She recalled the first one on her own and initially stated, "Yes, that needs to be accepted," but under her breath she added, "I do not understand what that *means* for *sīlaya* ['disciplinary practice; morality; virtue']." After we had talked about some of the other Conditions, she adverted again to the first Condition: "That is not a good one. That is the worst one. I think that really in fact as long as the *śāsanaya* ['dispensation'] is continuing in existence, that [condition] involves a *pavu* ['shame; sin'] for the *hamdurovō* ['monks']. [That] one who has much *sil* ['disciplinary practice; morality; virtue'] [must] worship another who has taken [precepts] just that day—is that not a sin?" Her initial insistence on the relevance of the Conditions was segueing into an interrogation of what they represented. One cannot of course ignore that such interrogation happens after someone like me continues to ask questions about them.

Soma had taught at a Buddhist Sunday school but was not a scholar-*bhikkhuni*. Although she was unfamiliar with the Sinhala publications on the topic and the research done by Kusuma, whose Sinhalese translation of the thesis had been published the previous year, Soma thought (like Kusuma) that the Conditions were a later interpolation. As she continued to muse on the first Condition, she became increasingly critical of it. "There is nothing in the *dhamma* that says that there is a male/female difference based on *sīlaya*, is there? If that is the case, that is patriarchy. If there is a difference in the *sīlaya* of male and female, then there is no equality, no? The Buddha gave the *upasampada* based on the equality of men and women, no?"[33] In addition, Soma stated that the observance of the first Condition was simply inappropriate, given the social context in which renunciants now lived: "Sometimes when one goes to worship young [*upasampada*] monks, they make a retreat. Well, we [senior *bhikkhunis*] are like adults [to them]; they get a little afraid; that is natural, is it not?" Her agitation regarding the practical observance of the first Condition was very clear. But note that she framed that agitation in terms of questions of discipline or morality (*sīlaya*), not in terms of some superimposed "theoretical" sense of subordination and inequality.

Turning her critical gaze to another *garudhamma*, she continued: "So, is it not possible for a female to criticize a monk? Can one who troubles a female not get criticized?...Just because he is a *bhikṣu* (bhikshu, fully ordained monk), no? Just think! As women we must consider our security. We cannot allow a reverend *bhikshu*[34] to do as he pleases without criticism. A monk is a male....In our society today, there are some sexual involvements, so that must be criticized. We cannot remain silent while they do anything they want to, can we? [Raising her voice] That is not right!"[35] We reconstructed the list of the Conditions together, as she was not confident in recalling the Conditions in their entirety. Although she affirmed the validity of the second, fourth, and fifth Conditions, she questioned the appropriateness of others on very practical grounds. She began to reflect on the third Condition, concerning the bi-weekly instruction *bhikkhus* were to give to *bhikkhunis*:

s: In the early times, it was good to get the *avvāda* (bi-weekly instruction). . . . These days, one cannot go to the temple every two weeks.
q: You do not get to go?
s: One can go, but then there will be more questions raised.
q: Because householders will think something?
s: Yes, stream-enterers. There are no stream-entering monks in the temples now. There are those who have the intention of becoming householders [*gihiyo*]. So if a female were to go to the temple on a regular basis, [the *bhikkhus*] would not stay in robes. It would be difficult. That is not appropriate.

Here Soma questioned the validity of the Conditions on the basis of what she saw as the declining morality of contemporary monks. She made little comment on the fourth Condition. She dismissed the sixth Condition, interpreting it as the requirement for women to observe six precepts for two years before the *upasampada*. "We take ten, not six," she said laughingly. That was clearly a reference to the irrelevance of the sixth Condition. (Typically, a woman who is about to be ordained as a *bhikkhuni* in Sri Lanka has already spent several years as a Ten-Precept mother). The Ten Precepts exact considerably more demands and a higher degree of renunciation than the six implied in the *garudhamma*.

In conclusion, Soma asserted that three of the Eight Conditions (the second, fourth, and fifth) were valid, but not the other five. Without prompting on my part, she raised the issue of the relevance of the Conditions for nuns today. She asserted that they were prescribed for Mahapajapati Gotami alone. "The other five hundred" women, she said, "were sent to the monks' temple. So why have these [Conditions] been given to us? They were not given to the other five hundred were they?" She was clearly aware of the popular controversy in Sri Lanka.[36] However, despite all her protestations, she insisted on proclaiming her allegiance to observation of the Conditions: "We have been told that the monks would be totally opposed if

we were to abandon the Eight Conditions. There will be the greatest acceptance [of the *bhikkhuni* order] in Sri Lanka if we have the eight *garudhammas*. It is, after all, an *upasampada* that was not given that we took."[37] For
Soma, the claimed, albeit questionable, observance of the Conditions is a
marker of her *upasampada* status and her newly found *bhikkhuni* identity.

My conversations with monastics indicated that attitudes to the
Conditions are more complex than interpretations of textual accounts
suggest. The apparent impasse created by the debate between scholars as
to whether the Conditions are *Buddhavacana* (a question that some have
translated into one about knowledge and practice) hardly occupies center
stage at this grassroots level. Here the argument for the Conditions is
based on a practical necessity and the conditions of lived lives—that is,
to further the acceptance of the *bhikkhuni upasampada* and comply with
requests made by senior supportive *bhikkhus*. Yet, when senior *bhikkhunis* who train others and claim adherence to the Conditions can simultaneously admit "ignorance" and rejection of them, there is a different
dynamic at work. Noncompliance with directives to follow the Conditions,
while arguably implied in ignorance and critiques of them, is not always
clear-cut or explicit. Furthermore, affirmation of the Conditions by some
senior monks is not necessarily reflected in practice by the monks themselves. Those monks claim to support certain *bhikkhunis*, notwithstanding
the latter's publications that openly reject the Conditions. Clearly some
bhikkhus' insistence on the *bhikkhunis'* acceptance of the Conditions is
concomitant with the monks' affirmation of the *bhikkhuni upasampada*.
That is probably because they see the acceptance of the Eight Conditions
as a gesture of compromise to (other) senior monks who reject the *bhikkhuni upasampada*. Monks who support the *bhikkhuni upasampada* must,
in other words, publicly affirm the Conditions in order to validate the subject of the *bhikkhuni* in the context of the heated debates about the higher
ordination. Meanwhile, the *bhikkhunis* who either reject the validity of the
Conditions or while claiming to uphold them, appear uncertain about
what they are effectively maintain that their subjectivity as *bhikkhunis* is
defined apart from adherence to the Eight Conditions. The (mis)practices
of the Eight Conditions indicate that the theory of the model implied by
the Conditions is not followed.[38] Clearly, the realities effectively represent
both acceptance and denial of the Conditions—what Pierre Bourdieu calls
"a logic which is not that of logic" (*Outline* 109). The Eight Conditions are
perhaps more revered in scholarly discourse than they are or ever were in
practice. That does not mean that they are insignificant, but rather that

their significance cannot be measured in terms of "knowledge" or by the liberal notions of equality and inequality.

Conclusion

The Eight Revered Conditions have been the focus of much debate between scholars and between practitioners because of the Conditions' association with the subordination of nuns to monks in early Buddhism. Those who, while noting certain textual inconsistencies, package the Eight Conditions as part of a coherent account of the first ordination are arguably complicit in reinforcing the very ideology suggested in the textual accounts. Others, however, openly interrogate that ideology. Whether the Conditions are *Buddhavacana* can, for the most part, be neither proven nor disproven. Yet both scholars and practitioners continue focusing on that question, which appears to have been given renewed attention in the context of recent Sri Lankan *bhikkhuni upasampadas*. Thinking about the debates on the Eight Conditions, which has tended to center on whether the Conditions are actually *Buddhavacana*, needs to focus on how the authors re-presenting the Conditions position themselves as subjects vis-à-vis their readers, as well as on how those authors construct renunciant subjects. Understanding the textual account of the Conditions as declarative or imperative, on the one hand, or as interrogative, on the other, helps us reflect more carefully about how interpretations of the Conditions create an epistemic (knowing or unknowing) renunciant subject.

This chapter has proposed new ways of thinking about scholarly perspectives on textual accounts of the Eight Conditions. Additionally, it has argued that practitioners, by articulating seemingly inconsistent understandings of the Eight Conditions and effectively contesting them, contribute to the construction of renunciant subjects who are characteristically invisible to the purview of recent scholarship. In contemporary practice there are *bhikkhunis* who question the relevance of the Eight Conditions in no uncertain terms. Some, in line with one perspective expressed in the debate between scholars, say that the Conditions are clearly not *Buddhavacana*. Others maintain the irrelevance or marginal relevance of the Conditions, on the rationale that the Conditions were meant to guide the practice of Mahapajapati Gotami alone. Still other practitioners, *bhikkhunis* in Sri Lanka, state that an acceptance of the Eight Conditions is essential to their identity as *bhikkhunis*. Those maintaining that idea are sometimes uncertain of what the Conditions are, thereby effectively defying the Conditions' authority in practice. Alternatively, they may question the applicability of individual Conditions despite an explicit acceptance of them. Finally, there are practitioners who simply say that they do not know what the Eight Conditions are, because their focus is on meditation alone.

Discussions with Buddhist practitioners today provide clues as to how scholars may overcome the apparent impasse in the debate on the authority of the Eight Conditions. Most important, such conversations highlight the complexities involved in the creation of an epistemic renunciant subject whose identity cannot be easily defined in terms of the affirmation or denial of the Conditions. Whereas some practitioners may articulate definite responses to questions about the Conditions, their practices speak differently.[39] Such (mis)practices of the Conditions might even have implications for how we rethink the subject of female renunciation in early Buddhism.

PART II

Identity

4

Invisible Nuns

Introduction

Studies on contemporary Buddhist nuns in many parts of the world demonstrate how and why they seem to occupy an "anomalous" or "liminal" position. They appear to conform neither to a cultural role model of wife and mother nor to that of fully ordained nun. However, their celibate life and their appearance seem to point to the embodiment of a religious ideal. Most studies define the putative liminal position of nuns by contrasting them with both householders and sangha (community of fully ordained monastics) without fully considering the practices of the "renunciant" (*pāvidi* or *pabbajjā*) person (Bartholomeusz 136–143; Bloss 22–24). An inquiry into how questions of the meanings of "renunciant" and "renunciation" emerge within the conditions of the lives that nuns live would be useful. Such an inquiry would acknowledge more-nuanced ways of understanding controversies about the supposedly ambiguous identity of nuns than the ways an analysis of the conventional householder/sangha distinction have acknowledged. Some householders (*gihiyo*) maintain that they respect individual nuns even more than they do some monks, yet others speak disparagingly of nuns for being "uneducated" and "ignorant" of Buddhism and for living "like beggars." Such divergent attitudes have led to public debates in newspapers and conferences centering on defining the religious identity of nuns. In this chapter I focus on three interrelated indicators that reflect perceptions on the renunciant status of nuns: (1) the Ten Training Precepts and their form as either "Renunciant" (*pavidi*) or "Householder" (*gihi*) *sīla* ("moral or disciplinary practices"), (2) the ascetic attire worn by nuns, and (3) the nomenclature used for nuns by householders and monks and by nuns themselves.[1] I situate those indicators with respect to precedents found in both canonical texts and contemporary Buddhist practice, as well as to the attitudes of practitioners who articulate opinions about the appropriateness of the *upasampada* for nuns, (i.e., in relation to their participation in a discourse of power).

The question of what renunciation of the *home* means cuts to the heart of defining asceticism in South Asian religions. The notion of "home" in Pali is inseparable from that of attachment (Collins, *Selfless* 170). Renouncing the home involves (1) leaving the home physically, (2) leaving the home mentally (i.e., leaving attachments), and (3) leaving the home ontologically (i.e., leaving samsara, the cycle of rebirth and redeath) (Collins, *Selfless* 167–171). These aspects of renunciation are helpful in understanding the debate on the appropriateness of considering nuns "renunciant" since contemporary female renunciation may involve any or all of these aspects. Nuns generally say that they are not householders (*gihiyo*), because they have renounced attachments that are usually associated with householders. They have taken on a life of piety and celibacy in place of living a conventional life as householders. It is not of course unusual for a nun (that is, a *sil mata* or an *upasika*) to live in the same building as her family or other householders rather than in community with other renunciants. Nevertheless, some practitioners would even argue that the term *renunciant* (*pavidi*) is more applicable to *sil matas* than it is to certain *bhikkhus*, who, despite their technically renunciant status, remain attached to the "world." However, since there is no clear evidence of textual or social-cultural precedent for determining the householder or renunciant status of nuns who are not *bhikkhunis*, there is room for controversy.

This chapter is based primarily on a consideration of the Training Precepts and on research I conducted between 1997 and 2002, a period of contestation and debate about *upasampada* rituals that were held for Sri Lankan nuns at the time. I conversed with five senior *bhikkhus* and thirteen Buddhist nuns. Those nuns practiced renunciation differently. They included two recently ordained *bhikkhunis* (previously they had been Ten-Precept nuns), eight Ten-Precept nuns, one *sāmaṇerī* (a novice nun or a woman who was observing the Ten Renunciant Training Precepts and undergoing further training for the *bhikkhuni* ordination),[2] one nun wearing white who observed only Five Precepts, as well as an Eight-Precept renunciant who has since become a *bhikkhuni*.[3] The reintroduction of the *upasampada* for Sri Lankan women was still in a fledgling state at the time of most of the interviews.

The 1980s and 1990s witnessed public debates on some of the most significant indicators of female renunciant identity, such as the nomenclature for nuns and their attire. As I argue in the following two chapters, the debates on how a *dasa sil mata* should be identified contributed to the eventual introduction of the *upasampada* of Sri Lankan *bhikkhunis*. While scholars and practitioners alike have defined female renunciation variously, the assumption of a clearly delineated female renunciant identity has remained elusive. In the summer of 1997, I learned of a nun who observed Five Training Precepts and wore white. She was known simply as Māṇiyō or "Mother." She lived about twenty-six kilometers from the city in a remote area that was accessible by vehicle via a difficult winding road. My aunt and a friend journeyed with me to her dwelling. Eventually we left the paved road and made our way on foot along a grassy path of uneven ground and hilly terrain overlooking green terraced rice paddies. Soon we came to a flight of stone steps that led to a house on one side and a gleaming white shrine-reliquary (*caitya* or *chaitya*) on the other. On one side of the *chaitya* was a *bō* tree[4] on which were tied several white strips of cloth (*paṇḍura*), each indicative of a request made of the gods, and on the other side was a small shrine to the deities (*devāle*). A board instructed visitors to worship at the *chaitya* before seeing Maniyo. Maniyo's daughter welcomed us at the house. After a brief conversation and an introduction to Maniyo's former husband, we were directed to her hut, or *kuṭi*, just above the *chaitya*.

Maniyo was a small soft-spoken woman. Her long gray hair was neatly tied back in a bun, and she wore an ankle-length white cloth (*redda*) with a long-sleeved blouse and a white sash over her shoulders.[5] Although she refused to entertain a taped interview until I had visited her at least three times, she allowed me to take notes of our conversation. At the time of our first (and last) meeting, Maniyo had been a Five-Precept nun for fourteen years. She renounced shortly after her only son, aged twenty-two, suddenly fell dead while working in the paddies. He had been poisoned inadvertently by regularly inhaling the pesticides he used in rice cultivation. After his death Maniyo fasted for seven days, taking only water. She then decided to commit her life to the religion (*jīvita pūja keruva*). Sick people consulted her for her healing powers and her ability to communicate with the gods. I asked her why, unlike most other *sil matas*, she observed the Five Training Precepts instead of the Ten. She said that diligently following the Five Training Precepts (which, according to her, included following a diet free of meat, fish, and addictive substances) effectively meant following the Ten Training Precepts.[6] Echoing what many *sil matas* had told me, she responded that she considered herself a renunciant (*pavidi*), because she was a renunciant "in mind." After a lengthy conversation on many personal matters (in which she offered words of advice for all), we concluded our visit and departed. Maniyo lived for another ten years and died prematurely in 2007, of the same type of cancer that had killed her former husband a few years earlier.

The presence of female renunciation has remained largely invisible to public attention for several decades, if not centuries. Women who have renounced marriage and lived lives of piety within households are women whose life stories have generally not been recorded. Gutschow, for example, notes that the *invisibility* of nuns in Tibet led scholars to assume that they did not exist (174). In a similar vein, Thamel suggests that in the late 1880s female renunciants in Sri Lanka who neither lived in communal dwellings nor wore the yellow robe, were also invisible (68). The renunciation of those women was both hidden and isolated, because they did not live in communities of renunciants and also perhaps did not contribute to a village community to the extent that even Maniyo did. Maniyo's renunciation shows how nuances in female renunciation defy a strict householder/monastic (or renunciant) dichotomy. Until the 1980s reporters and researchers showed little interest in documenting the lives of female renunciants. It is noteworthy that one of the first public records of female renunciants in Sri Lanka, appearing in 1894, refers to "nuns" but provides no details of their appearance, which was probably taken for granted at the time.[7] The prevalence of widely diverse forms of female renunciation in Sri Lanka—where women wore colored clothes or white, maintained long hair or shaved it, and adopted differing names of respect—cannot be ruled out.[8]

My own mother has childhood recollections of women who resembled the Five-Precept *maniyo* dating as far back as 1937. She recalls elderly women who, like Maniyo, wore a white cloth and jacket but had no white sash across their shoulders. Referred to as *upāsikāmmās* or ("devotee-mothers"), they lived with their families and often did odd jobs at the nearby temple built by her great-grandfather. My mother remembers some of them frequenting the house of her grandmother until the late 1940s. They would stop by in the evening and sit down to chat with her under the shade of the nam-nam tree of her southern coastal home. When I asked what had happened to them, my mother responded, "One by one they died off; ... now they are no more." Then thoughtfully she added, "Now they are *dasa sil māṇiyō* [Ten Training Precept mothers], ... but when I was a child, no one spoke of *dasa sil maniyos*."[9]

It may be no accident that the establishment of hermitages where communities of female renunciants lived together in the late nineteenth century coincided with initial attempts to better clarify who female renunciants were and what they could or should do. Even though such communities of nuns are known to have existed for more than a century, in recent decades we have witnessed some of the most controversial public attempts to define, renegotiate, and clarify female renunciant identities. Nevertheless, renunciant identities tend to defy clear definitions. The varied nomenclature used for female renunciants is also reflected in the term *dhammacārinī* (female "Truth-farer"/or female followers of the *dhamma*, or Buddhist teaching). Sri Lankan state officials in the 1980s and early '90s attempted to introduce that word to designate all female renunciants equally, including those observing the Eight and Ten Training Precepts, as well as those who wore white, yellow, or brown. However, the same term was used by a small group of English-speaking women from Colombo. Those women came together and formed an organization of *dhammacharinis*.[10] They lived with their families, and observed the Five Training Precepts or one of the two sets of the Eight Training Precepts.[11] They wore either white or the colored clothes associated with householders. When I first met the president of the *dhammacharini* organization, she followed the Eight Training Precepts and wore white. After a decade, however, she had shaved her head and accepted the *upasampada*. Today she wears the yellow robes of a fully ordained *bhikkhuni*.

What renunciation has meant for Buddhist women has varied widely, as have the external indicators of renunciant identity. Female renunciation in Buddhism defies facile categorization for a number of reasons, one of which is that the specific nomenclature used to address nuns, the training precepts they observe, and the attire that identifies them as renunciants tend to lack uniformity and seem to be subject to change. Not only do those apparent indicators of renunciation differ in how they are understood by renunciants, but they also vary when renunciants themselves find new ways of identifying who they are. Additionally, the Sinhalese terms for female renunciation carry nuances that do not lend themselves easily to translation into globalatinized idioms we have generally used when considering renunciation. Moreover, as I argue in this chapter, during the controversial years that saw the introduction of an *upasampada* for Theravada women, various persons attempted to redefine the "meaning" of renunciation to either support or reject such an *upasampada*. Further complexities emerge when it becomes clear that those participating in the debate on the *upasampada* often do so without being aware that the Ten Training Precepts observed by novice monks (and that may eventually lead to their *upasampada*) are in fact no different from the training precepts that some lineages of *dasa sil matas* have observed ever since the late nineteenth century.

The Ten Training Precepts

Most Buddhists would claim that they observe the Five Training Precepts; individuals who observe those alone would fall into the category of house-holder or male or female devotee (*upāsaka* or *upāsikā*), although the latter might also include Buddhists who observe additional training precepts. In general, someone who observes the Five or Eight Precepts is not consid-ered to be *pavidi*, or "renunciant," whereas someone who adopts the Ten Precepts is. The Eight Training Precepts are most commonly observed temporarily by householders, who often spend the full-moon (*pōya*) day at a temple, garbed in white and engaging in practices such as meditation, offering alms to the Buddha, and listening to Buddhist sermons (*baṇa*).

The distinction between renunciant and non-renunciant in the canoni-cal and non-canonical literature provides an interesting point of comparison with the contemporary representations of the distinction. In the canoni-cal literature there is a grouping of ten behavioral prescriptions known as teachings (*dhammā*) (A.II.253) or the ten teachings (*dasa dhammā*) (M.I.490).[12] That iteration of the ten *dhammas* differs from that of the Ten Training Precepts that *sil matas* generally observe.[13] Notably, these virtues that are prescribed for non-renunciants include abstention from miscon-duct in sexual activities rather than total celibacy. I have encountered only two canonical listings of Ten Training Precepts that approximate what is known today as the Ten Training Precepts, one of which is in the *Vinaya* ("Book of Monastic Discipline,") and the other in the *Khuddaka Pāṭha*.[14] The *Vinaya* refers to the training precepts as the Ten Training Precepts of the novices (Vin. I.83–84).

The wording of the *Vinaya* list of the Ten Training Precepts is almost identical to the wording of the list that monastics today know as the Ten Renunciant Disciplinary Practices or Moral Virtues (*pāvidi* or *pabbajjā dasasīla*).[15] The list, which is now commonly referred to as the Ten Householder Disciplinary Practices or Moral Virtues (*gahaṭṭha* or *gihi dasasīla*)[16] is basically the same list as the one in the *Khuddaka Pāṭha*. Yet there is no textual evidence in the canon indicating that householders fol-lowed the same ten *sila* that are known today as *dasa sila* (Ten Precepts).[17]

Nevertheless, nine of the ten Moral Virtues mentioned in the latter are recognized in a separate canonical list that refers to one who is considered a monk (*bhikkhu*) (D.I.63) or a renunciant (*pabbajito*) who is in the process of realizing enlightenment (M.I.267; M.I.179; M.I.345; M.II.162; M.II.226; M.III.33; A.II.208; A.V.204; Pu.58) or the Buddha himself (D.I.4). A commentary to a late canonical work indicates that devotees (*upasakas*) may once have observed either the Ten Householder Training Precepts or the Ten Renunciant Training Precepts that *sil matas* observe today (Smith, *Khuddaka* 35). Interestingly, according to the textual canon itself, several of the current Householder Training Precepts were observed only by ascetics or those close to realizing enlightenment. Most significantly, perhaps, many of the Householder Training Precepts that seem to define the lack of renunciant (*pavidi*) status of contemporary *sil matas* were once recommended for renunciants alone.

The Ten Training Precepts may be considered a modified version of the Eight Training Precepts. Today Buddhists might observe the Ten Training Precepts either temporarily, at the temple on a full-moon day, or at home. Occasionally they are observed on a more ongoing basis. The contemporary Ten Training Precepts fall into at least two different categories: the Householder Training Precepts and the Renunciant Training Precepts. The Ten Householder Training Precepts are as follows:

1. I undertake the training precept of refraining from taking life.
2. I undertake the training precept of refraining from taking what is not given.
3. I undertake the training precept to refrain from non-celibacy.
4. I undertake the training precept to refrain from speaking falsehood.
5. I undertake the training precept to refrain from alcoholic drinks and intoxicants—foundations for heedlessness.
6. I undertake the training precept to refrain from taking food at the wrong time.
7. I undertake the training precept to refrain from attending shows as well as dancing, singing, and musical events.
8. I undertake the training precept to refrain from the use of flowers, scents, and cosmetics and from finery and adornment.
9. I undertake the training precept to refrain from using high and large seats or beds.
10. I undertake the training precept to refrain from accepting gold and silver.[18]

Significant differences between the ten *gihi sila* and the ten *pavidi sila* have gone unrecognized by both scholars and practitioners (Copleston 471–472; Gombrich, "Temporary Ordination" 48–49; Gothoni 53). Those differences are intrinsically related to both perceptions and misperceptions of the appropriate attire and nomenclature for contemporary *sil matas*. Previous scholarship, such as that of Bloss, Kusuma, and Bartholomeusz, that has identified differences between the two types of Ten Training Precepts has tended to emphasize the sangha/laity opposition rather than considering the *meaning* of *pavidi* (Bartholomeusz 73–74, 157–159; Bloss 18; Kusuma, *Dasa Sil* 142–144).

Today young boys and men who undergo the novice initiation recite the Ten Renunciant Training Precepts, as do monks who receive the *upasampada*. A significant proportion of *sil matas* (about 10 percent, according to some informants at the time of research) also recite them at their ordination. Most *dasa sil matas*, however, observe the Ten Householder Training Precepts. The ritual differences between the Ten Renunciant Training Precepts and the Ten Householder Training Precepts are many.

First, the Ten Renunciant Training Precepts are usually recited as part of a monastic ritual in which one receives ordination as a novice or receives the *upasampada* as a full-fledged member of the sangha. Words and phrases mentioned in the monastic (renunciant) ordination ritual (*pabbajjā mahaṇavīma*) and excluded from the householder ordination ritual (*gihi mahaṇavīma*) are, according to some informants, central to the definition of renunciant status. In the initial request a novice makes for the ordination—"Having taken this robe [*kāsāva*], give me the renunciant ordination, Venerable Sir, for the sake of expelling all suffering and realizing nibbana"[19]—the word *renunciant* is pivotal. In one sense, the very idea of renunciation is implicit in the ordination ritual itself. (The *upasampada* is also considered a renunciant or *pavidi/pabbajja* ordination.) In that sense, *sil matas* or *maniyos* who do not have the *pavidi* ordination (in the Ten Training Precepts) might not be considered "renunciant," or *pavidi*. The debate, however, rests on a wider meaning of *renunciation* that is tied to contestations about the *bhikkhuni upasampadas* taking place at the turn of the century. Within Buddhism *renunciation* refers not just to a sociological state of "disassociation from the 'world' of inter-connected reproductive-kinship relations and obligations" but also to a state of being "without desire" (Collins, "Monasticism" 109). Hence, although the *sil matas* who have the householder ordination might not be considered renunciants in the sociological sense of "disassociation from the 'world,'" or *pavidi* (since have not formally undertaken the *pavidi* Ten Precepts), they may (while living within or without the household) still be called "renunciant," or *pavidi*, in that they seek to live a life without attachments.

Second, the recitation of the Three Refuges in the renunciant ordination ritual is unlike that which precedes the recitation of the Ten Householder Training Precepts.[20] In the observance of the former, there are two formulations of the Three Refuges, which differ in pronunciation and are both recited.[21] That difference in pronunciation, while perhaps appearing to be a technicality, marks, according to my interviewees, a crucial distinction of the ritual observed and the renunciant status of the participant (whether defined as renunciant or householder).

Third, when asking for the Ten Training Precepts, the ordinand specifically requests the administration of the Renunciant Training Precepts: "Venerable Sir, I request that you have compassion and please give me the Three Refuges and the teaching in the Ten Renunciant Training Precepts [*pabbajjā dasasīla*]."

Fourth, in the "renunciant" version of the ritual, the observance of the training precepts involves a single undertaking of all the training precepts as one "rule" rather than ten discrete rules. Thus, in the Pali the phrase "I undertake" is used only once after the tenth precept rather than ten times after each precept when the novice declares that he has "taken these Ten Renunciant Training Precepts."[22] That implies that if any one of the precepts is broken, the "rule" is violated, and all ten precepts are thereby transgressed. That is explained in a textual commentary to the *Khuddaka Pāṭha* and is recognized by the monks and nuns I interviewed.[23]

A fifth difference between the two types of the Ten Training Precepts, according to my interviewees, is that the Ten Renunciant Training Precepts, unlike the Householder Precepts, must be administered by a monk who has the *upasampada*. In the case of novice monks, that monk would be a preceptor who acts as a parent, teacher, and moral guide to the novice throughout his period of probation. Even though *sil matas* may receive either type of the Ten Training Precepts from a *bhikkhu*, the ordaining *bhikkhu* cannot serve the *sil matas* as a preceptor in the same way as he might serve a novice monk, because *bhikkhus* are barred from associating closely with members of the opposite sex. As a result, a newly ordained *sil mata* may not receive the typical guidance from which a novice monk might benefit. One *dasa sil mata*, emphasizing the relationship of moral discipline (*silaya*) to her renunciant status and nomenclature, explained to me that she observed neither the householder (*gihi*) nor the renunciant (*pavidi*) *dasa sila* but rather the "homeless Ten Moral Virtues" (*anagārika dasa sil*). (Her own ordination included a recitation similar to that of the Ten Renunciant Training Precepts, but substituting the phrase "homeless" for "renunciant.")

Finally, the renunciant ordination given to novice monks might be differentiated from both the renunciant and the householder ordination given to *sil matas*. *Sil matas*, unlike novice monks, do not train for examinations deemed necessary for the *upasampada* and formal entrance into the sangha.[24] Before receiving the *upasampada*, novice monks must pass an examination on Buddhist texts (Gothoni 135, 139). Some monks I interviewed were emphatic about the importance of this as a defining difference between *sil matas* and novice monks.

The woman who is generally recognized as the first "nun" from Sri Lanka and the founder of the Lady Blake Hermitage, Sudharmachari Upāsikā Māṇiyanvahanse or ("the venerable devotee-mother Sudharmachari") observed the Ten Renunciant Training Precepts.[25] According to a study by Kawanami, female Buddhist renunciants from Myanmar who do not have the *upasampada* (*thilāshin*; literally, "keepers of morality") today usually observe no more than the Eight Training Precepts. Those who adopt the Ten Training Precepts follow precepts that are a little different from the Ten Training Precepts listed earlier (Kawanami, "Religious Standing," 23–24).[26] Apparently, Sudharmachari followed the same Ten Training Precepts in Myanmar as those recognized by nuns from Myanmar, and then she undertook the Ten Renunciant Training Precepts in Sri Lanka, which were given to her by *bhikkhus* there.[27] Contemporary nuns in Sri Lanka who trace their lineage back to Sudharmachari practice the Ten Renunciant Training Precepts that are known in Sri Lanka.

Apart from some *bhikkhus* and *sil matas*, most Buddhists do not differentiate between the Renunciant Training Precepts and the Householder Training Precepts. Some *bhikkhus*, believing that *sil matas* observe the latter only, argue that *sil matas* are "householders" (*gihiyo*). I have not found canonical evidence of householders observing either of the two categories of Ten Training Precepts known today. The lack of canonical evidence relating to the *sil matas'* renunciant (*pavidi* or *pabbaja*) "status" fuels the debate on the matter. But ascertaining the renunciant status of nuns can be limited neither to assessing their status as *bhikkhunis* nor to considering their observance of a particular category of *dasa sila*. The controversy concerning the supposed status of the nuns has raised a range of questions that seem to focus on the pivotal question of whether the nuns are "household-ers" or "renunciants." Although *dasa sil matas* do not consider themselves either householders (*gihiyo*) or female devotees (*upasika*), other Buddhists sometimes disagree. Definitions of householder and renunciant status have also become central in debates concerning the attire and nomencla-ture appropriate to female Buddhist renunciants in Sri Lanka.

Ascetic Attire

Yellow or saffron robes are generally associated with asceticism in South Asian countries, and their specifications and use by Buddhist monastics is carefully regulated. Controversies concerning the use of the *authentic* attire associated with fully ordained members of the sangha are known in the canonical texts. The term *theyyasaŋgvāsaka* ("one who lives clan-destinely with the *bhikkhus*") (Rhys Davids and Stede 310) has been used to refer to those who wear the robes of monks by theft or undeservedly and need to be excluded from the sangha (Vin. I.86; I.135; I.168; I.320). In recent times there have been heated debates on the "rights" of *sil matas* to wear yellow robes. In order to understand the alternative positions framed by those debates, it is useful to discuss textual and historical precedents regarding types of attire Buddhist ascetics have worn.

The canonical literature makes several references to householders (*gihī*) who wear white (M.II.23; M.III. 261; A.I.73; A.III.384; A.III.297). It also mentions individuals who are both householders and devotees (*upasaka* and *upasika*) who wear white (M.I.491). Such persons are some-times referred to as *brahmacārī* (M.I.491), who might be understood to be celibate householders or householders who follow the Brahma (religious) path or both. The specific *sila* those individuals in white observed is not always clear. It is probable that householders who observed the five *sila* (or more than that) and *upasakas* who observed the eight or ten *sila* were included among those who wore white. Individuals referred to as *upasikas* who observed what are known today as the Five Training Precepts are also mentioned in the canon (A.III.203).

Today in Sri Lanka a male or female devotee is seen as one who gener-ally takes the Eight or Ten Householder Training Precepts, either at home or at a temple. Such a person usually wears white and does not shave his or her head. Copleston, writing in 1892, mentions women with shaved heads who took the Ten Training Precepts and wore white (Copleston 471–472). Shaving the head generally indicates a heightened degree of renunciation—at least outwardly—more than wearing white alone. As part of the *upasampada* ritual, a *sil mata* attired in yellow robes is expected to revert to white and reaffirm her renunciation before eventually accepting the yellow robes of the fully ordained monastic. In Sri Lanka, a renunciant in white is usually thought of differently from one wearing attire that is yellow, orange, or brown—colors that are used by *dasa sil matas*, and by *bhikkhus* and *bhikkhunis*, who are generally considered to practice a stricter form of renunciation.

Sudharmachari Upasika Maniyanvahanse, who returned to Sri Lanka in 1905 after her ordination, is said to have worn a white blouse and a yellow robe "to differentiate herself on the one hand from the *bhikkhunis* and on the other hand from the uninitiated, undisciplined women in white of which Copleston spoke" (Bloss 10–11).[28] Edith Blake wrote in 1914–1915 of one Buddhist nun who wore a "salmon-coloured robe" ("Buddhist Nun" 57) and of others who were attired "in a white robe, over which one of pale salmon colour was folded over the left shoulder" ("Sacred Bo Tree" 671).[29] According to one informant I spoke with in 1997, the color favored by Sudharmachari and the other nuns who observed the Ten Training Precepts at that time was not yellow (*kaha*), as suggested, but rather a brown (*guru*) color. It is possible that the first nuns in Sri Lanka wore white blouses with robes of a variety of colors, ranging from shades of yellow to salmon or brown. Several informants said that nuns did not begin wearing the complete yellow attire (i.e., the yellow blouse in addition to the yellow robe) until the mid- or late 1950s. Today most, if not all, *sil matas* who live in renunciant communities and observe the Ten Training Precepts wear attire that is completely yellow. One *sil mata* stated that Sri Lankan *maniyos* decided to uniformly adopt the full yellow attire in 1986, when the National Sil Mata Organization of Sri Lanka passed a resolution to that effect. According to her, "On that day, those who had worn brown, wore yellow; those who had worn [dark] red, wore yellow; even those who had worn the white blouse wore yellow."[30]

The main distinction between the attire of a fully ordained Theravada monk, or a novice monk or nun (a *samanera* or *samaneri* who is also "renunciant," or *pavidi*), and the attire of a *sil mata* who observes the Ten Householder (*gihi*) Training Precepts is that the robes of the former have been "cut into pieces" (*kaḍa kapala*); that is, the robes have been sewn together from separate pieces of cloth, as per *vinaya* regulations. From a distance, however, except for the long-sleeved blouse, the *sil matas'* yellow attire is hard to distinguish from that of a novice or a fully ordained monk.

The change from white to a combination of white and yellow or brown and eventually to complete yellow may be interpreted as evidence of how nuns have gradually distanced themselves from both the householder and the female devotee (*upasika*).[31] Nevertheless, the continued use of white or yellow renunciant attire by women who do not live in communities of renunciants suggests that renunciant practices defy the distinctions that we find in scholarly works about female ascetics.

Arguments about the appropriate color for *sil matas'* attire relate to the broader debate on the type of ordination the *sil matas* observe. Many who oppose the *sil matas'* wearing yellow robes mistakenly think that all *sil matas* take the Ten Householder Training Precepts and that they use the robes that are cut and sewn.[32] Not all *sil matas* take those precepts, however, and only one *dasa sil mata* I encountered (who had not had the *bhikkhuni* ordination) actually used the robes considered to be the prerogative of "renunciants." "According to the *dhamma*," one writer states, "it is the white attire that is suitable for the Mothers who have taken the Householder Precepts. If an ordained woman [*mehenak*] dresses in the robes that have been cut into pieces and sewn according to the *Vinaya*, she, realizing the status of '*theyyasaṃvāsaya*,' would be defeated by [*päräde*] the dispensation [*sasana*]."[33] According to that author, a *dasa sil mata* who wears the yellow robe has seriously transgressed a *vinaya* rule by wearing monastic attire that she should not.

The question of what the color for *sil matas'* robes should be was central to a conference of Buddhist prelates and scholars in which some argued that *sil matas* should don brown (*guru*) instead of yellow.[34] The debate has even extended to examining the etymology of the word *kaha*, used for "yellow."[35] One monk I interviewed strongly opposed both the *bhikkhuni* order and the *sil matas'* wearing yellow robes: "They have no right to wear the yellow color.... It is a great wrong that they are doing by wearing this color."[36] Some who support the *sil matas'* wearing yellow attire do so on the basis that anyone (including *sil matas*) has the right to wear yellow. Only one article I encountered in researching sources that were dated between 1980 and 1997 supports the *sil matas'* use of yellow attire. The writer, a *sil mata*, assumed that all *sil matas* had the status of female novices (*samaneris*) and were renunciant (*pavidi*) and therefore observed the Renunciant Training Precepts (Chandima 37). She points out that the *Vinaya* does not prohibit female novices from wearing yellow.

The controversy surrounding *sil matas'* attire has emerged in response to an increasing awareness of (and in some cases, resistance to) public perceptions of *sil matas'* enhanced social and religious status. It is evident that misunderstandings by the public—and by monastics— concerning the type of Ten Training Precepts taken by *sil matas* have also contributed to the debate. For example, contrary to common belief, not all *sil matas* take the Householder Training Precepts. That few *dasa sil matas* actually wear the robes recommended for fully ordained monastics in the *Vinaya* seems to be of little or no importance. Perhaps the most sensitive point is the perception that *sil matas* may be claiming a "right" to religious attire that they should not claim. Since householders are generally unaware of the technical differences in monastic attire, the appropriateness of the *sil matas'* robes remains a moot point that is necessarily connected to the *sil matas'* perceived renunciant status and the ongoing debates about the *upasampada*. Their controversial status is in turn intertwined with the question of defining an appropriate nomenclature for them.

The Question of Naming Nuns: Upasika, Maniyo, Meheni, *or* Sil Mata

A suitable nomenclature for nuns who practice the Ten Training Precepts has proved elusive for scholars as well as Buddhist practitioners in Sri Lanka. Although the term *maniyo* has been used loosely for such nuns, when applied to female renunciants, it has a wide range of connotations. I recall a woman known as Maniyo who would pay visits to the home of my maternal grandmother in the late 1960s. She had long hair and wore a white sari. That *maniyo* lived in her own home and paid monthly visits to residences in the capital city of Colombo, offering them her services, which included communicating with the gods by entering a trance state and conveying their blessings and protection. Her practice was perhaps not very unlike that of some of the women Gananath Obeyesekere discusses in *Medusa's Hair*. Today spoken Sinhalese refers to a *dasa sil mata* variously as Mother (*maniyo*) or its honorific, Venerable Mother (*maniyanvahanse*); Precept Mother (*sil mata*); or ordained woman (*meheni*) or its honorific, Venerable ordained woman (*meheninvahanse*). It is noteworthy that in Sinhalese the terms for "Venerable Mother" and "Venerable ordained woman" sound very similar and might therefore be confused or used interchangeably. Newspaper articles often refer to a Ten Precept nun as a Precept Mother (*sil mata* or *sil mäni*), sometimes preceded by the word *ten* (*dasa sil mata*; "Ten-Precept Mother").

Lack of a uniform nomenclature reflects the apparently ambiguous renunciant "status" of nuns. The first well-known nun in Sri Lanka— referred to as "devotee," as were other nuns of her time—was known as Sri Sudharmachari Upasika Maniyanvahanse or ("the Great Venerable Sudharmachari devotee-mother") and her disciples as *brahmacārī upāsikā* or "celibate female devotees" (Bartholomeusz 94–95). At that time, it was common to use the Sinhalese word for "devotee" (*upasika*) for a woman who took the Ten Training Precepts on a permanent basis (Bartholomeusz 94–102; Blake, "Buddhist Nun" 51–53). In the late nineteenth century and throughout most of the twentieth century, the residence of nuns was often referred to as an *upāsikārāmaya* (hermitage or residence of female devotees).[37] The term for "celibate female devotees," which was used for the disciples of the first nun, contrasts significantly with the term for "celibate homeless woman" (*anagārika brahmacārī*), used in a recent article arguing in favor of the renunciant (*pavidi*) status of nuns (Wijebandara 122). For want of better terms in English, scholars have referred to nuns as "Ten-Precept Mothers" or *Dasa Sil Matas* (Semmens), "lay nuns" (Bartholomeusz), and "nuns" (Gombrich and Obeyesekere 274–296; Tsomo, "Introduction" xxvi). None of those terms fully conveys the complex nuances of the Sinhalese nomenclature for nuns.

In the late 1980s, two individuals wrote to the newspapers to suggest that *sil matas* be designated as "homeless women" (*anagārinī, anagārikā*).[38] One of those individuals, a monk, argued that the word for "Mother" (*mātā*) was especially inappropriate when elders used it to refer to young women.[39] The second writer was a nun who ironically referred to herself as "Precept Mother" (*sil mata*). Although some *sil matas* I interviewed thought the designation "homeless man/woman" appropriately described the status of both *bhikkhus* and *sil matas*, all of them agreed that the distinctive use of that term for denoting a status of *dasa sil matas* alone was unsuitable.

The disputes about the use of the term "ordained woman" (*meheni*) are connected to the controversies centering on establishing a Theravada *bhikkhuni* lineage. According to some, *meheni* is a term that should only be used in reference to a woman with the *upasampada*, a *bhikkhuni* who is part of the sangha. One Buddhist householder I interviewed in 1997 said, "We say that there is no dispensation of fully ordained women (*meheni sasana*) in Lanka.... So we do not have any occasion to talk about *mehenis* now.... I myself do not use the reference '*meheni*.'... I do not use it because the reverend monks do not like it to be used." The term for "ordained" (*mahana*) is often used in conjunction with the "higher ordination," as in *mahana-upasampada*. Yet *sil matas* who talk about their ordination as nuns observing either the Householder or the Renunciant Training Precepts, refer to this as an "ordination" (*mahanavīma*). *Dasa sil matas* and householders tend to differ in their thinking about the appropriateness of the term *meheni* for a *dasa sil mata*.

I asked eight *sil matas* specifically about the appropriateness of using the term *meheni* for a *sil mata*. All but two of them insisted (with varying degrees of emphasis) that it was appropriate. One of the two dissenters insisted that the term "renunciant" (*pavidi*) was not appropriate for *sil matas*. A head nun (a *dasa sil mata*) whom I interviewed at length in 1997—and who belonged to a hermitage where, significantly, the *sil matas* practiced only the Ten Householder Training Precepts—also thought that the terms "ordained woman" (*meheni*) and "renunciant" (*pavidi*) for a *dasa sil mata* were inappropriate. She clearly defined the identity of the *sil matas* with reference to their initiation in the Ten Training Precepts ordination: "It is not right [*hari nǎ*] to call a *sil mata* an ordained woman [*meheni*], [because] she does not have the status of being ordained [*mahanakama*]." She supposed that being ordained referred to "one who is about to have *upasampada*." When I asked her if she then considered the novice monks to be ordained (*mahana*), she remarked, "Novice monks are 'ordained.' If the Precept Mothers were a part of the *Meheni Sasana*, then they would be considered ordained. At the moment, they have no ordained (*mahana*) status....The term 'meheni' can be used for *bhikkhunis*....The word 'ordained' (*mahana*) can only really be used for the *bhikkhus* and *bhikkhunis* who have the *upasampada*." When I suggested that by "ordained" (*mahana*) she meant the *upasampada*, she said that "in the ordination [*mahanavima*] the higher ordination [*upasampada*] is special. A novice monk is ordained [*mahana*] but does not have the higher ordination [*upasampada*]." She insisted that being "renunciant" (*pavidi*) meant that a person was "ordained" (*mahana*) and that when a woman is initiated into the Ten Precepts for the first time, "it is not right to call her an ordained woman [*meheni*], because...the 'status' or 'condition' of renunciation [*pävidikama*] is different from the Ten Precepts." She pointed out that at her hermitage, the *sil matas*, though they observed the Ten Precepts, did not live in the "condition of renunciation." She acknowledged that householders use the word "ordination" (*mahanavima*) in reference to *sil matas* but she also insisted that "there is no complete ordination (*mahanavima*) there."[40] That *sil mata*, like another who held a similar opinion of the use of "ordained," said that novice monks could be called "ordained" because the latter, unlike the *sil matas*, would generally proceed to the *upasampada* and then be included in the sangha. *Sil matas*, they argued, did not have access to the *upasampada*; therefore, they were not ordained (*mahana*). Those informants are possibly conversant with the notion of "*training* precept," which contextualizes the *sil matas* and novice monks as engaging in disciplinary practices in which the monks, unlike the *sil matas*, are *training* for an *upasampada* from the day they are ordained.

Although five *bhikkhus* I interviewed considered the use of the term *meheni* or ordained woman for a nun inappropriate, only one of them went so far as to state that *sil matas* were householders (*gihiyo*). Two monks explained their thinking on the meaning of "ordained woman." Like the head nun mentioned earlier, those monks said that the term referred directly to the ritual of higher ordination and that a Mother (*māṇi*) was not an ordained woman (*meheni*). According to them, an ordained woman (*meheni*) was renunciant (*pavidi*), and an ordained man was a *bhikkhu*.[41] Interestingly, those two monks, who fiercely opposed the introduction of a (Theravada) *bhikkhuni upasampada* for Sri Lankan renunciants, thinking (mistakenly) that no *dasa sil matas* practiced the Ten Renunciant Precepts, had just conceded to me that if women were to take the Ten Renunciant Precepts, they might be considered "renunciant." Those monks perhaps rejected the use of the term *meheni* for a *sil mata* because of its narrower meaning of "fully ordained *bhikkhuni*." One of them who opposed this usage and mentioned a preference for the term *upasika* to designate *sil matas* when questioned by me, nevertheless kept referring to them as *mehenis* throughout our conversation. He did not "correct" himself until after I pointed that usage out to him. How he seemed to *want* to conceptualize the *sil matas'* status differed from how he actually spoke about it.

Unlike the head nun mentioned earlier, five female renunciants who headed monasteries (including one who was training to be a *bhikkhuni*) suggested that *sil matas* be considered renunciant (*pavidi*). All the nuns I interviewed stated that the term "female devotee" (*upasika*) was not an appropriate designation for a *sil mata*; indeed, some of them vehemently opposed that usage. Two of the female renunciants objected strongly to the use of the word "Mother" (*maniyo*) for a *sil mata*, for that word had both mundane and secular connotations.[42] According to those two, neither "Precept Mother" nor "Mother" should be used for a *sil mata*, because those words did not convey the respect they thought a *sil mata* deserved. Some of the renunciants, though they recognized that the use of the terms "ordained woman" (*meheni*) and *bhikkhuni* for a *sil mata* were technically inconsistent with the *Vinaya*, argued in favor of using those terms. One *sil mata*, emphasizing that renunciation reflected a level of commitment to moral and disciplinary practice, noted that a *sil mata* who observed the Ten Training Precepts sincerely for a period of twenty years or more might be thought of as having received the *upasampada*. Two nuns, though they understood that *sil matas* did not technically belong to the sangha (when sangha refers strictly to those with the *upasampada*), argued that the term "sangha" had a moral significance, which might apply to *sil matas*. They even argued that *sil matas* who had a profound fear of samsara (*sasara bhaya*), might be considered both "renunciant" (*pavidi*) and *bhikkhuni*.

Conclusion

Buddhist nuns appear to represent an *innovative expression* of religious practice in a religious context where innovation can prove all too controversial. Contemporary *dasa sil matas* may trace their lineage back only to the end of the nineteenth century. As far as we know, the renunciant practices of Buddhist nuns in Sri Lanka who observe the Ten Training Precepts are relatively recent. *Bhikkhus* have an ordination that can purportedly be traced back to the time of the Buddha. The recent debates concerning the identities of *sil matas* appear symptomatic of a lack of textual and cultural precedent for identifying women who observe the Ten Training Precepts as either householders or renunciants. On a more fundamental level, however, the demand to articulate the meaning of female renunciant identity reflects the presence of a certain discursive space in which such identities become objects of representation.

Nuns and monks seem to represent variant ideals and ideas of renunciation that are rooted to different extents in traditions of monastic lineage, power, and social acceptability. The observance of the Ten Household Training Precepts would appear to exclude *sil matas* from renunciant status. Some *sil matas*, accurately citing canonical precedent, insist that regardless of the type of ordination they have, they may be considered renunciant or even *bhikkhuni* because of the sincerity of their renunciant intentions, prompted by a profound fear (*bhaya*) of samsara. It was apparent from my interviews that householders and nuns did not consider *sil matas* either householders (*gihiyo*) or *upasika*, although some monks did. According to householders, the nuns observed a renunciant practice that was more rigorous than that of householders. However, according to monks I interviewed, *sil matas*, unlike novice monks, did not (or should not) train for the *upasampada* and therefore their renunciant practice could not possibly measure up to that of either novices or fully ordained monks. Here asceticism and renunciation are defined in terms of training rather than "status." The monks disagreed on whether *sil matas* could be considered householders (either affirming that status or denying it), but they all said that they did not think of *sil matas* as renunciant (*pavidi*).

Obviously, a tension existed between *sil matas* who considered themselves renunciant in relation to householders and female devotees in general and monks who suggested that *sil matas* could not be seen as renunciants. But that tension was inextricably linked to the ways in which the nuns themselves were aware of and involved in the public debates about them that reached their height in Sri Lanka in the 1990s. The 1996 *upasampada* of Sri Lankan nuns in Sarnath, India, which occurred less than a year before my initial research for this chapter, had caused a nationwide stir among practitioners in Sri Lanka. Moreover, at the time of some of my interviews, the publicized plans to train *dasa sil matas* for the *upasampada* were already in full swing in Dambulla, Sri Lanka. My argument in this chapter is that the attempts to confirm or deny the renunciant "status" and "identity" of nuns speak not just to the apparent ambiguity inherent in female renunciation at the time, but also, at a different level, to practitioners' engagement in the ongoing debate on the *upasampada* of nuns—that is, an engagement in a discourse of power. I am not suggesting that the *upasampada* was or was not empowering in the different senses of that term, but rather that such claims about status and identity are inseparable from *claims* about power. Those who considered the *dasa sil matas* renunciants (*pavidi*) or "sangha" supported the *upasampada* of nuns. Those who opposed the designation of renunciant (*pavidi*) for *sil matas* opposed their *upasampada*. That some do and some do not regard nuns to be renunciant (*pavidi*) should be understood less as an assertion of *accuracy* about the objective social position of nuns and more as a specific statement about an informant's approval or disapproval of nuns' position in relation to the recent public debates about their supposedly changing status, as well as an assertion of the informant's authority in those debates. I have pointed out that the various Sinhalese terms used for nuns may be understood in relation to other aspects of renunciant indicators (e.g., questions of the training precepts and renunciant attire). Given such indicators, it is extremely problematic simply to look for explanations of nuns' identities in terms of their supposed meaning. Rather, I have argued that *meaning* of such indicators cannot be isolated from ongoing public debates about nuns.

The altering nomenclature used to designate who contemporary renunciants are in those debates speaks to the inappropriateness (or impossibility) of simply ascribing a particular status, identity, or role to the lives we want to understand. What takes place in such debates cannot be articulated in terms of what does or does not constitute the proper identity and status of nuns. That is why I have argued that the question about the supposed authentic status of nuns cannot be isolated from the contexts in which certain people—including Western scholars—begin to talk about nuns' so-called status. Worth considering is whether such notions of *authentic* identity are important in the lived lives of nuns. Perhaps it is only when we demand that those notions be translated into objects of representation that they become significant. To suggest that we think about why nuns' identities, practices, or discourses do not yield to globalatinized terms of representation is hardly to suggest that Buddhist practice is simply varied or that what Buddhists actually do is more "messy" than what they are supposed to do.[43]

5

Subjects of Renunciation

Introduction

Discourses construct objects and subjects of discourse. That is what we find in the liberal constructions of nuns as agents of resistance engaged in a movement or struggle for establishing *bhikkhuni* ordinations (Goonatilake 42–44; Mrozik).[1] Such discourse in turn constructs nuns as specific *subjects* of renunciation. The early conceptions of female renunciant practice as constituting a movement appear in the works of Lowell Bloss and Kusuma Devendra. Others have since appropriated Bloss's and Devendra's movement terminology without adequately theorizing the idea of a movement or discussing nuns' own articulation of such an idea (Cheng, *Buddhist Nuns*; M. Falk; Kabilsingh 45–54; LeVine and Gellner). That sort of common understanding of new religious phenomena—an understanding based on a hastily adopted notion of agency and subjectivity—deserves closer scrutiny.

Seeing Buddhist nuns as participants in a movement is misleading for at least two reasons. First, it assumes that a monolithic collective renunciant subject or agent exists who is easily available for representation across space and time. Second, it assumes that that agent lives a life of resistance. Some scholars have already begun to contest that relation between agency and resistance (Abeysekara, *Politics*; Asad, *Formations*; Scott). Such a view of agency quite simply masks an understanding of the lives nuns live and the conditions in which they find themselves. How nuns understand their lives is intrinsic to the very lives and practices they live; it is something that a notion of agency superimposed on such practices cannot capture.

I begin by discussing the usefulness as well as the pitfalls of social-movement theories for the study of Buddhist nuns. I then consider how the subject of the Buddhist nun has been constructed by researchers, development discourses, state officials, academics, and sometimes also the president and cabinet ministers. In the case of nuns who do not speak English, how they speak about themselves and their preoccupations, though not entirely incongruent with what others have said about them, is distinct from what others have said. The notion that female renunciation constitutes a movement for the restoration of the higher ordination is misplaced. If we had to consider female renunciation in Sri Lanka as constituting such a movement, we would need to regard it as beginning not as a protest against an institutionalized injustice but rather as a means of promoting the agendas of researchers and certain state officials. The researchers and state officials, and sometimes even the president and cabinet ministers—contributed, albeit differently, to the construction of renunciant subjects. They garnered "respectability" for those subjects in the spheres of government and the academic study of religion. Throughout the 1980s and the 1990s, *sil matas* hardly saw themselves as subjects who participated in a social movement of protest, as some have suggested. Thinking about the *construction* of such female renunciant subjects promotes better ways of comprehending the new visibility of *sil matas* and the interest in their *upasampada*. While movement theory may be of some usefulness in understanding the significance of modern female renunciation in Sri Lanka, it nonetheless detracts from the focus of nuns' lives of *renunciation* and tends to concentrate on their engagement in some type of collective activism and *protest*. As I have already argued, that is not to suggest that the practice of renunciation transcends the social. Rather, renunciant practice does not easily equate with a liberal juridical notion of social activism.

Movements and Their Subjects

Recent social-movement theory grew in response to particular political developments in the 1960s and 1970s, including civil rights, anti-war, and redefined feminist activism. It later came to fruition in the 1980s and 1990s with the development of third-wave feminisms, environmentalism, the dismantling of socialist regimes, and globalization. Movement theorists seek to determine a collective identity of individuals in a group that has coalesced in the face of a common set of grievances and that shares particular goals (Goodwin and Jasper 11–15). According to Calman, movements involve "a collective effort to seek change" (4). They are also "by their nature evangelical; they seek to convert" (Calman 5). Studies on social movements seek to plot their emergence and growth in terms of the relationship between "mobilizing structures," or the means through which collective action occurs; "framing processes," which involve a deliberate attempt to articulate and inspire action; and "political opportunities" that provide spaces for collective action (McAdam, McCarthy, and Zald). Social movements, we are told, coalesce around a bid for power that may take the form of protests against an established institution, such as the state, and may work either within national boundaries or beyond them. Generally, social-movement theorists attempt to assess movements with reference to their interrelation with macropolitical developments. Rather than focus on individuals, the theorists analyze the dynamics of a group and its goals. Foregrounding collective motivations and concomitantly downplaying individual subjectivities may help theorize how so-called movements occur. However, such broad delineations also introduce distortions. In particular, they ipso facto elide the very subjectivities of the stakeholders of the movement in question.

An example of the difficulties in identifying religious change with the movement of "movements" appears in Ingrid Jordt's work *Burma's Mass Lay Meditation Movement*. Jordt seeks to explain how a new "lay" interest in meditation contributed to effecting changes in what she refers to as the classical arrangement of relations between sangha, state, and laity. Even though she does not characterize the new lay activity as a protest against the junta-led state or as a movement "in search of a particular political solution" (158), she still describes it as an apparent social movement. She also maintains that the movement questions the sincerity of the government's actions and ultimately has a political impact (164–169).[2] Jordt attempts to describe the appearance of a new phenomenon that does not fit the category of a social movement as movement theorists have conventionally described it. For Jordt, the collective identity of the participants and their practices seems to constitute a movement. Yet the collective identity is diffuse, since the "millions" who participate in the movement eventually leave after a few years and follow divergent paths to lead "normal lives" as householders (159).[3] Moreover, the Buddhist participants understand their activity in terms of religious practice and Buddhist rhetoric—as activity that indirectly poses a challenge to the state. Jordt describes elements of what she terms the "meditation movement" in terms of "revitalization" and "millenarianism" (24–26). Nevertheless, she contends that the so-called meditation movement is neither primarily a "religious revitalization movement" nor a "millenarian movement" (206); rather, she sees it principally as a "means to accommodate" political developments (206).

Jordt's understanding of the term *movement* refers to the broader issues in the studies that use such terminology to make sense of apparently new social phenomena. To some extent, almost any newly visible religious phenomena might be termed a social movement, since the definition of a social movement is vague enough to be all-encompassing. One problem with the category of movement is that it begs the very naming of a collectivity. In doing so, it invites thinking about a pre-defined (named) social, religious, or political group that had its genesis at one point in time and space, has specific goals, and follows a trajectory that ends at a different point. A closer look at female renunciation indicates that such terminology is moot. *Sil matas'* lives are not imbricated in such a sense of social movement. A social-movement theorist might concur that as long as *sil matas* lived in isolation and "saw their situation as a function of individual deficiencies rather than features of a system" (McAdam, McCarthy, and Zald 9), they could not be seen as participants in a renunciant "movement."

The renunciation of Sri Lankan Buddhist nuns does not echo strains of organized protest. Central to the identification of female renunciation as a movement is the construction and representation of the *subject* of female renunciation. The subjects of social movements are typically viewed as protesting subjects. Glimmers of a collective identity of nuns may be present in a few nuns' articulations at certain points in time, but such a sense of identity was forged more in cooperation with state officials than in protest against the state. To be more specific, although the possibility of receiving the *upasampada* was attractive to some *sil matas*, the *upasampada* should be considered not as a "goal" for which *sil matas* themselves "struggled." It should rather be understood as something that happened several years after the idea of it had already been introduced in debates about the female renunciant subject. Situating the *upasampada* of *sil matas* in the trajectory of a female renunciant movement conceals the primacy of the renunciant everyday. By "the renunciant everyday" I mean the daily routines and rituals that define the disciplinary practices of those who live renunciant lives. The conceptualization of the *upasampada* as being the goal of some sort of movement also assumes a certain idea of "status" associated with a definition of *bhikkhuni*-hood that is far from clear-cut.[4]

Questions relating to female renunciation, which seem to have become more prominent in the latter decades of the twentieth century, can be considered in terms of how gender relations were being transformed throughout Sri Lanka as a whole. The 1976–1985 period marked by the UN Decade of Women instigated renewed concern for "women in development" (CENWOR, *Hidden Face*; CENWOR, *U.N. Decade*; Kiribamune and Samarasinghe). The open economic policy introduced by the newly elected president of Sri Lanka, J. R. Jayawardene, in 1977 ushered in an era of transnational capitalism and transformed attitudes to labor (Boserup). During that period and into the 1990s, governmental and non-governmental women's organizations in Sri Lanka grew in prominence as scholars in Western countries also began to address issues relating to the condition of women working in free-trade zones and the Middle East (Hewamanne; Gamburd; Lynch). New economic incentives, civil unrest, and war in the 1980s and 1990s affected the very structure of families throughout the country (Ruwanpura; de Alwis "Changing Role"; de Mel). The increased visibility of female renunciation and the debates concerning the *bhikkhuni* order also need to be seen in relation to the changing face of male-female relations at that time.[5] While a state of warfare continued, albeit intermittently in the north and east, and civil unrest resulted in serious human rights abuses throughout the nation, the ideas of femininity, masculinity, and "respectability" were reformulated and debated in different terms.[6] Cynthia Enloe has stated that

> patriarchal militaries need feminized military wives and feminized military prostitutes. Patriarchal corporations need feminized clerical workers and feminized assembly line workers. Every person who is pressed or lured into playing a feminized role must do so to make the masculinized people seem to be (to themselves as well as everyone else) the most wise, the most intellectual, the most rational, the most tough-minded, the most hard-headed. (*Curious Feminist* 6)

It should come as no surprise that at that time of re-articulation of gender, it was not just the *upasampada* of nuns, but the very concept of (female) renunciation that became a subject of debate.[7] What was at stake in such debates was, among other things, an attempt to determine what it meant to be a "respectable woman" (de Alwis, "Gender, Politics"). During the 1980s and 1990s—when shifting relations of power defining masculinity and femininity reworked how notions of family, religion, and nationality were authorized—*sil matas* were one of many subjects studied in the field of gender relations and hence cannot be considered in isolation. I now consider how the work of researchers contributed to the construction of the subject of female renunciation, a project that enhanced communications among the *sil matas* they studied.

Subjects of Research

Throughout the 1980s, state officials and researchers contacted and communicated with *sil matas*, an outreach that encouraged *sil matas* to think
about themselves as representative subjects in their own right. As subjects of the state, they were recognized as *sil matas*, having been registered
under their renunciant names and addresses and given national identity
cards. As subjects of academic research, they were *asked* to reflect on their
position as renunciants who were in material want and who lacked the
upasampada. Some researchers, in addition to facilitating *sil matas'* contacts with state officials, sought to "place" the contemporary *sil matas* in
the framework of early *bhikkhunis* mentioned in the texts (Bartholomeusz;
Bloss; Devendra, *Dasasil*; Nissan; Salgado, "Female Religiosity"). The
lengthy studies of *sil matas* conducted in the '80s included a historical
narrative of the textual origins of the *bhikkhuni* order, its establishment
and decline in Sri Lanka, as well as a discussion of select *vinaya* rules
pertaining to *bhikkhunis*. The contemporary state of *sil matas* was seen
in terms of a historical "evolution." Thamel, for example, focusing on
the "role" of contemporary *sil matas*, suggested that "it is necessary to
know the historical evolution of the *Bhikkhuni* Order in India" (42).[8] She
then stated that, in such an evolution, "the Dasa-sil Maniyo as an institution...practically replaced the *Bhikkhuni* Order" (65). She made those
claims in reference to one unusual group of *sil matas* (also studied later by
Bartholomeusz) who were considered *bhikkhunis* by a chief monk associated with them (61). However, she did not directly ask the *sil matas* about
their attitudes to the *bhikkhuni* order (62–65, 128–132). Other researchers
queried the *sil matas* on their thinking concerning the *bhikkhuni* order
and its possible reestablishment—matters that most *sil matas* had little
interest in addressing then. Academics, in conducting their research,
helped fashion the notion of a modern self-conscious subject struggling
to shape life in terms of the ancient ideals of a *bhikkhuni*. For example,
Bloss claims that the *sil matas* in general "are coming to see a close connection between themselves and the *bhikkhunis*" (9); this is even as Bloss
himself grants that most of the *sil matas* he interviewed would refuse to
accept the higher ordination (19)!

A few of the early researchers, such as Devendra, Bloss, and Thamel,
who had a common interest in enhancing the material condition of the
renunciants they interviewed, also became mediators between the *sil
matas* and state officials. Thamel, who studied nunneries in Kelaniya, a

region of southwestern Sri Lanka, sought to intervene in improving the relations between *sil matas* and the state:

> Some of [the *sil matas*] were completely *unaware* of the [Ministry of Cultural Affairs'] efforts to help them in their plight....Living as recluses, they had no communication with the outside world and the government agents did not even know where they lived. Some of the Dasa-sil Maniyos were informed of the registration system by me when I visited them to collect information. I have forwarded their names and addresses to the Ministry. (117; emphasis added)

What is interesting is that Thamel took it upon herself to assist in registering *sil matas* with the newly established Department of Buddhist Affairs (under the Ministry of Cultural Affairs), possibly with the aim of procuring aid from the state to mitigate their "plight." At that time most *sil matas*, whose existence had hitherto been of little interest to the state, responded to state communications with suspicion. The *sil matas* ignored the questionnaires that were sent to them, and most of them would not register their names and addresses with the ministry when asked to do so.[9] In the course of Bloss's and Devendra's research, conducted in the early and mid-1980s, the communications between *sil matas* and state officials were enhanced. Indeed, Rohana Gnanashila—then a *sil mata* but now a *bhikkhuni*—believes that the state programs to coordinate *sil matas'* affairs throughout the country were a direct result of meetings that Bloss and Devendra had held with officials from the Department of Buddhist Affairs.[10] Devendra told me that her associations with female renunciants, which had made her keenly sensitive to the *sil matas'* situation, dated back to childhood memories of her mother's sister, who had become a *sil mata*:

> She [my aunt] became a *sil mata*...maybe after about her thirtieth or fortieth year....She was a *sil mata* for about fifty years...and living in Anuradhapura. My mother built an *āśram* [hermitage] for her in Anuradhapura. She lived by herself, and she had one *gōlayā* [student]....I am the only one who visited them, because the family sort of discarded her because they said it was an insult....I felt very bad. I used to feel so sad, and I used to visit her....Even from my childhood days, nuns used to come to our house. My mother used to entertain Burmese nuns and the famous Mavichari.[11] She used

> to come to my house. And all these nuns are well known to my
> mother. They were in Katukale, Lady Blake Aramaya. They were in
> and out of the house. [My mother] used to be a regular visitor even
> at Sister Sudharma's at Biyagama.... She was very interested in the
> *dasa sil mata* movement, my mother.... She was known to Sister
> Sudharma and all these people.

Not only was Devendra well positioned to relate to the *sil matas* that she
and Bloss interviewed; she also had privileged access to Eardley Ratwatte,
the commissioner of Buddhist affairs, under whom the registration of the
sil matas was conducted.[12]

Conversations between researchers and *sil matas* often assumed a for-
mulaic character; it was common for different academics to ask similar
kinds of questions of the same *sil matas*. That contributed to the emergence of two new phenomena. First, researchers introduced a new kind of
relationship between themselves, the *sil matas*, and state officials. Second,
renunciants were *encouraged* to begin thinking of themselves not only as
subjects of renunciation but also as subjects seeking the status of *bhikkhunis*, even though the very idea of becoming *bhikkhunis*—according to
one Sri Lankan *bhikkhuni* ordained in Sarnath—was "unthinkable" then.
The subject of female renunciation was also construed from another
vantage point, articulated in a discourse of "third-world" deprivation and
development.

*Discourses of Deprivation, Development,
and the Suffering Subject*

Arturo Escobar in his article, "Discourse and Power in Development:
Michel Foucault and the Relevance of His Work to the Third World,"
seeks to show how the discourse of third-world development contributes
to Western domination and power over the third world. One question he
raises is useful in understanding female renunciation in Sri Lanka: "in
what ways are disciplinary and normalizing tendencies contributing to
the domination of the Third World?" (378).[13] He argues that new forms
of power and knowledge were produced in discourses of development
that introduced "truths" and "norms" in shaping the perception of particular polities as third-world countries. He points out strategic ways in
which the "deployment of development" played out in practice. Of particular interest is his postulation that the "creation of 'abnormalities' such

as the 'underdeveloped,' the 'malnourished,' and the 'illiterate'" required not just investigation and amelioration, but also intervention and control. The enterprise "constituted a whole political anatomy of the Third World which sought not so much to illuminate problems and possible solutions as to give them a visible reality amenable to specific treatments...[and which] resulted in the formation of a *field of intervention of power*" (387; emphasis in original). Connected to that enterprise was another strategy concerning how development was professionalized and how a type of knowledge was established that produced "a regime of truth and norms about development...[that] sought the formation of a *field of control of knowledge*" (387–388; emphasis in original). The latter strategy was related to "the establishment of economics as a 'positive,' 'objective' science...in which a specific economic rationality (based on certain institutions such as money, markets, banks, etc.) became dominant" (388). The ideas of deprivation and development informed much of the mainstream media's discourse on *sil matas* in the 1980s and 1990s in Sri Lanka.[14] The growing interest in female renunciation during that period was a byproduct of such discourse, in turn making possible the production of a regime of truth about *sil matas*.

As I have argued elsewhere, the discourse of deprivation that became prominent in the representation of *sil matas* has served to focus attention on the female renunciant who was putatively deprived of basic "necessities," such as housing, food, and education (Salgado, "Buddhist Nuns"). The female renunciant was someone whose situation needed to be treated and rectified, because hers was an "abnormal" and "underdeveloped" situation, especially from an underlying "first- world" perspective.[15] Sensitivity to that perspective was apparent among the government officials who began gathering information on *sil matas* in the 1980s with the goal of ameliorating their poverty. It was evident not just in my discussions with Department of Buddhist Affairs officials working with the *sil matas* at that time but also in media reports on the department's activities with Buddhist nuns.[16] Sri Lankan representatives of a broader liberal discourse on feminism and human rights co-opted the discourse of deprivation. That discourse was something that a few *sil matas* and non-monastic Buddhist practitioners began to emphasize, initially writing in newspapers and later in newsletters such as the *Meheṇi Udāva* (Dawn of the *Meheni*) and individual pamphlets. Those Buddhist practitioners tended, unlike the government officials, to assume that establishing the higher ordination for *sil matas* would prove that Buddhism was neither anti-feminist nor outdated. However, *sil matas* I interviewed in the 1980s and 1990s and who supported the *upasampada* seldom, if ever, adduced the promotion of "human rights" and "feminism" as relevant considerations in promoting their stance on the matter in their conversations with me.

Deploying the discourse of development in relation to *sil matas* elicited various responses to the question of ordination. Some opposed the higher ordination, and others supported it. What both supporters and detractors had in common was the desire to address the perceived impoverishment of the female Buddhist renunciants. That the material poverty of female renunciants may have differed little from that of their own homes was irrelevant. Female renunciants I interviewed came from a variety of rural and urban backgrounds and diverse economic conditions. Many of them lived in homes without flush toilets, running water, or electricity. *Sil matas* who joined established hermitages had facilities that were similar to those of their own homes. What became prevalent in the discourses concerning *sil matas* of that period was the fashioning of a subject in the mold of an impoverished female renunciant of Buddhist piety whose necessities had been neglected. I am not denying that there were no *sil matas* who were "in need" or "impoverished." But then the question of need was hardly interrogated. From whose viewpoint was "need" regulated? With whom were the "indigent" *sil matas* compared? At the time, the media's discourses identifying the *sil matas'* deprivation encouraged *sil matas* and their supporters to launch appeals for the *sil matas'* material welfare.[17] That the "renunciation" of female renunciants was one of several paths women followed and that it entailed what might be considered a voluntary poverty (in material terms, not perhaps unlike that of their own homes) were beside the point. The *sil matas'* focus on piety served to further attract the social conscience of Buddhists who recognized that the responsibility for the welfare of the female renunciants lay with them. The increased attention to female renunciants in recent decades may have been due more to the proliferation of the rhetoric of development, along with the enhanced visibility of women's issues at the time. It was not, as some may have claimed, a resurgence of female Buddhist piety but the increased *public* attention to the subject of the renunciant that made the "deprivation" of the *sil matas* visible.[18]

On the one hand, throughout the period numerous articles were written to inform the public of the deplorable poverty of *sil matas*.[19] Those articles focused on addressing needs such as food and lodging—needs typically ascribed to "less-developed" nations in general.[20]

Prospects for the alleviation of *sil matas'* poverty were sometimes linked to the possibility of their obtaining the higher ordination.[21] On the other hand, there emerged a concern as to whether female renunciants should wear yellow robes and who might in fact "qualify" as a *dasa sil mata*.[22] The discourse of deprivation was intrinsically linked to the creation of the subject of the nun, which, as it was debated and redefined, gave rise to the notion of the (Theravada) *bhikkhuni*. Such a discourse, with its emphasis on the suffering subject of the female renunciant, produced a distinctively post-independence and postcolonial idea of the Buddhist nun.

Dipesh Chakrabarty argues that the universalization of the suffering subject essentially speaks to the construction of the conveniently distant yet empathetic individual of modernity:

> The capacity to notice and document suffering (even if it be one's own suffering) from the position of a generalized and necessarily disembodied observer is what marks the beginnings of the modern self. The self has to be generalizable in principle; in other words, it should be such that it signifies a position available for occupation by anybody with proper training. (119)

Chakrabarty, who discusses the modern subject of the Bengali widow, notes that Bengali narratives of modernity identify a different mode of subjectivity—one involving kinship, family, and *interiority*—one that cannot be generalized and hence defies easy translation into European intellectual traditions. Although the modern citizen-subject may exist in the public sphere, he states that "this single subject breaks up, on examination, into multiple ways of being human, which make it impossible for us to reduce this moment to any summary narrative of transition from a pre-modern stage to modernity" (148). We find in the postcolonial Sri Lankan state an intervention to translate women into a similar subject of suffering. For example, the 1978 Sri Lankan constitution, understanding women as state subjects, thought of them as being "vulnerable and [in] need [of] the protection of an activist state" (Wickramasinghe 177). The idea of the female renunciant as a suffering subject worthy of state sponsorship and the material welfare of private individuals had its precedent in the way the postcolonial state began to objectify and normalize a certain female subjectivity.[23] While scholars, activists, and others began to invest themselves in the "welfare" of the *sil matas*, the state helped authorize the subject of the suffering *sil mata* in keeping with the generalized constitutional idea of the woman as a state subject.

Subjects of the State

The state helped create the subject of female renunciation in two ways. First, in defining nuns as a collectively identified category and in raising funds for their welfare and their education, the state began to authorize who should and could be considered a female renunciant. Second, the state helped construct an infrastructure that would become the basis of national and district organizations of *sil matas*. From the 1970s to the mid-'80s, key government figures specifically promoted the *bhikkhuni* ordination. However, the state's view of the *sil matas* changed as media debates about the ordination became increasingly virulent. The state subsequently sidestepped the question of the *upasampada* and focused instead on promoting the idea of a respectable and uncontroversial renunciant subject that was *not* a *bhikkhuni*. However, state involvement in the organization of *sil matas* continued.[24] Ironically, that involvement later led to the planning of the first *bhikkhuni* ordinations in Sri Lanka that took place at the turn of the century.[25]

In 1974 several national newspapers highlighted the government's interest in the "revival" of the *bhikkhuni upasampada*. In one article, then-president William Gopallawa, having returned from China, spoke of possibly reestablishing a Sri Lankan *bhikkhuni* order with the assistance of Chinese *bhikkhunis*: "If at a time when there was not a single upasampada (ordained) bhikkhu in Ceylon, it was possible to reestablish ordination with assistance from Siam, I do not think it will be such a difficult task to reestablish the order of bhikkhunis here" ("Govt. Will Help to Revive"). A leading monk of the Asgiriya Nikaya—a sect that now officially opposes the *bhikkhuni* ordination—was cited as saying that it was "fitting for independent Sri Lanka to once again attempt to re-establish the Bhikkhuni Sasana" ("Govt. Will Help to Revive").The occasion for the statement was laying the foundation stone for a nunnery (*upasikaramaya*) and training center in Madiwela, Kotte. A few years earlier, the All Ceylon Dasa Silmata Saṇgamaya (All Ceylon Dasa Silmata Society or Association), which was to later have its center at Madiwela, articulated an interest in introducing the *bhikkhuni sasana*.[26] Associations between the Madiwela center and the efforts to bring about a *bhikkhuni upasampada* with state support continued well into the mid-1980s.[27] Today Madiwela itself, though serving as a training center for *sil matas*, is known for its opposition to the *upasampada*.[28] The two governments that became most involved in working with the *sil matas* during the period were those of President J. R. Jayawardene and his successor, President Premadasa.[29] However, the Jayawardene and Premadasa administrations did not adopt a consistent state policy of support for the *bhikkhuni sasana*.

In 1981 the Buddhist Congress, an independent organization closely connected with the state, proclaimed an interest in improving the "well-being" of *sil matas*.[30] The intention of the Buddhist Congress was to eventually hold an all-island conference and provide the *sil matas* with suitable education. The state also began conducting surveys, cataloguing the names and whereabouts of the *sil matas* throughout the island, and organizing and sponsoring classes to educate them.[31] At the time there were two senior government officials who were working independently—and initially in different capacities—to begin interactions with female renunciants. They were Eardley Ratwatte, who was the first commissioner of Buddhist affairs, and Abhaya Weerakoon, who was to succeed him. Devendra had several meetings with both officials in her attempt to draw attention to the perceived needs of the *sil matas*. While Ratwatte launched a campaign to reach out to *sil matas* nationally and organize them in the Colombo district, Weerakoon, the additional government agent of a *kacceri* (regional office of the central government) in Kurunegala, attempted to bring *sil matas* in the area together.[32] In 1985, when Weerakoon became commissioner at the Buddhist Affairs Department, he discovered that his predecessor had initiated for *sil matas* in the Colombo district a project with intentions similar to his own; since 1983 those *sil matas* had been meeting monthly. However, as he explained in an interview with me, Weerakoon wished to take things a step further:

> [Ratwatte] had got the nuns of the Colombo district to meet once a month at the John De Silva Memorial Theater for about 2–3 hours to have discussion. They would have a sermon on a particular day of the month and a class...on Pali, English, and Health once a week or so....This was not enough; I did not think that was what the *sil matas* wanted....The monthly meetings involved a sermon by a priest; [they were] not really meetings. A sermon by a priest is something you could do anywhere; there was no real point to it,...no *association* as such.

After conferring with *sil matas* he knew, Weerakoon planned the establishment of district-wide organizations of *sil matas* to ensure that the *sil matas* won the support of the monks. Consequently, many of the monthly meetings in the various districts, which began in 1985–1986, were held at temples with the permission of the monks residing there. Weerakoon used the state network of *kacceris* to contact *sil matas* throughout the electoral districts and received a positive response from the *sil matas*: "We worked slowly and surely to avoid island-wide failure," he told me. By 1986 many of the *sil matas* had already been issued identity cards, and the government had made a financial commitment to sponsoring their education (Salgado, "Buddhist Nuns"). Between 1986 and 1988, district-wide associations of *sil matas* (*sil mata saŋgamayas*) emerged with separate meetings of *dasa sil matas* held in different districts, each of which had elected a representative secretary and president (Salgado, "Buddhist Nuns" 49). In 1986 "members from district committees in the island met in Colombo and chose from among themselves an electoral committee that in turn appointed the first-ever national organization of *sil matas* in Sri Lanka. Thus, the *Sil Mātā Jātika Maṇḍalaya* (SMJM), or the National Sil Mata Organization, was founded in 1986" (Salgado, "Buddhist Nuns" 50).[33]

Creating an association with and of *sil matas* had been a main goal of Weerakoon. By the end of his tenure, it was clear that *sil matas* who had never before interacted with one another were now communicating at the district and national levels. Those incipient relationships laid a foundation for the district and national organizations of *sil matas* and *bhikkhunis* that has continued to this day. Throughout the 1980s, *sil matas* had begun to interact more among themselves and with government representatives and monks and to develop communicative and administrative skills that would prove invaluable.[34] *Sil matas* elected as district and national representatives were among the first to be ordained as *bhikkhunis*, under the auspices of the Dambulla temple, a few years later. Weerakoon indicated that there was a deliberate effort to work in a non-threatening fashion with the monks. His goal of building a real "association" of *sil matas* appeared to have been met.

Social-movement theorists seek to explain collective action in terms of networks, through which a kind of mobilization may take place (Tarrow 135–136). One might say that the kinds of research that early scholars such as Devendra undertook among *sil matas* helped advance the mobilization of *sil matas* by creating what Charles Tilly and others refer to as "netness" (McCarthy 143). Within such "netness," female renunciants were becoming aware of themselves as having a commonality and being state subjects.

However, theirs was still a very loose collective that did not culminate in any mass protest movement. Unlike the insurgent activists assumed to constitute social movements, *sil matas* worked with the state. The relations between the *sil matas* and the state were governed by constraints and conditions. One of the conditions of the state-sponsored meetings to promote the welfare of the *sil matas* was that discussion of the *bhikkhuni upasampada* was prohibited. Moreover, as one *sil mata* (of about four *sil matas* I knew to favor the *bhikkhuni upasampada* in the mid-1990s) put it, *sil matas* did not collectively request state support for the idea, simply because many of them did *not* want it.[35] Although the associations of *sil matas* that were formed then may have looked like they were the nodes of some incipient movement, they did not strive to establish a *bhikkhuni upasampada*. To suggest that *sil matas* constituted a collective seeking the *upasampada* not only misconstrues them as subjects of a movement but also overstates the extent to which the *upasampada* was a common goal among the *sil matas*. In 1995 I discussed with Weerakoon, then recently retired from his official position, his opinion on the *bhikkhuni sasana*. The *upasampada*, he said, was a divisive issue the state sought to avoid: "The *bhikkhuni* issue was basically left up to them. If we were involved in this, we would have created a split within the [government] office itself, and this would have disrupted our work for the *sil matas*." Weerakoon noted that the state's relations with *sil matas* were based on a model of accommodation and cooperation. Within such a model, the idea of a female renunciant subject who was respectable to the male monastic establishment and deserving of state assistance remained central to the state's vision of the *sil matas'* future welfare.[36]

The main purpose of state registration of *sil matas*, as Weerakoon put it, was to identify who was "really a *dasa sil mātā*" (Bartholomeusz 149).[37] While the *sil matas'* renunciant identity as potential *bhikkhunis* continued to be debated among academics and male monastics, officials in the Department of Buddhist Affairs recognized female renunciants as subjects worthy of state support. Raising funds for the *sil matas* was coordinated with attempts to regulate who that renunciant could or should be.[38] A number of different governmental documents were drawn up in the attempt to define the female renunciant.[39] While that attempt may appear to have aimed at forging a "framework to create uniformity among the lay nuns" (Bartholomeusz 149), what was significant was the state's authorization of a particular representation of the female renunciant subject. The endeavors to identify and authorize the subject of the female renunciant for state matters, which had begun with the registration of *sil matas* in the early '80s, continued well into the next decade.

The question of identifying the renunciant subject remained contested throughout the 1980s and 1990s. Apart from a lack of consensus between the state officials and the *sil matas* concerning the objectives of the regulatory documents for determining female monastic identity, the general relations between the two groups point to the ways in which such a contestation lay in the shifting nomenclature of the renunciants.[40] Whereas a 1988 state document called them *dasa sil matas*, a later state document referred to them as *dhammacārinīs* (dhammacharinis or female followers of the *dhamma*, or Buddhist teaching) who should belong to a *Dhammacharini Institute* (*Dhammacārinī Saŋsthāva*) and follow the rules in the *Cariyā Dhamma Paddhatiya*, or Dharmic Code of Conduct.[41] That document, entitled *Dhammacārinī Saŋsthāva* ("Institute of *Dhammacharinis*"),which came to my attention in 1995, comprises fourteen points, one of which states that "a woman who leads a celibate (*brahmacāriyā*), homeless (*anagārikā*) life based on the model of the *bhikshuni*...is considered a *dhammacharini*. Hence, every single *sil mata* is a *dhammacharini*."[42] A 1989 newspaper report had also outlined a code of conduct for all *sil matas*, or "*dhammacharinis*."[43] Apart from one recommendation that was also in the 1988 document[44] and the expectation that all renunciants, or "*dhammacharinis*," be registered, that report outlined a number of new guidelines. It stipulated that all *dhammacharini* activities be regulated "at the national level by the national board, and at the district level by the district board." That report reaffirmed the state authorization of renunciants, and made a new proposal: to extend the category of female renunciation to include *all* renunciant women—that is, *sil matas*, *dasa sil matas*, and even the white-clad *upasikas*—under the common label of *dhammacharini*. What was significant was the state's assumption that the distinction between a person leading a householder's life and a renunciant, though difficult to distinguish in practice, needed state recognition.[45] The state's regulation, control, and patronage of female renunciants involved, ipso facto, the construction of a definable subject of the state.

The idea of a "renunciant subject" was not a matter of concern for *sil matas* until state interventions made it necessary for *sil matas* themselves to take up the idea.[46] *Sil matas* on the national committee officially representing all *sil matas* in the nation complied with state officials in coming to a consensus on requests for recognition they would make of the state. Yet those requests indicated that *sil matas*' understanding of themselves (in terms of what was important to their lives) differed from the state's understanding of them. Their focus was on how they and their institutions should receive certain benefits already accorded to male monastics. In April 1995 *sil matas* who had official representation on the national organization of *sil matas* submitted to state officials (for the second time) a document entitled "*Sil Mata Cariyāpaddhati*" (*Sil Mata* Codes of Conduct). The ten-point document, which met with no response from state officials, differed in its overall focus from the 1989 document issued by the Department of Buddhist Affairs. Referring to renunciants as *sil matas*, it made a number of requests.⁴⁷ The *sil matas* sought not so much a "status" in reference to a higher ordination as a "recognition" comparable to that of monks. For example, the *sil matas* requested that they be reserved a front seat on public buses.⁴⁸ That was a "privilege" already enjoyed by Buddhist monks. The very possibility of the *sil matas* requesting such a "privilege" existed in the modern state's construction of a respectable cleric that could be recognized as such in official terms. That is not to say that *sil matas* had not enjoyed a certain reverence among Buddhists, but rather that a new type of reverence had emerged—one that had to be recognized officially. That new sense of reverence had to become meaningful in the construction of the respectable renunciant subject who was tied to ideas of rights and a modern state. I am not suggesting that *sil matas* were fighting for certain rights but rather that they were being asked to think of themselves in a way that was meaningful to the modern state's construction of the modern renunciant subject. The new idea of official reverence that they were asked to think about was not the kind of reverence that had existed between monastic and non-monastic practitioners of Buddhism—a reverence that had *preceded* the state's recognition of it. That idea did not completely undermine conceptions of hierarchy in the ways *sil matas* were given reverence in Buddhist practice. However, it did take over (without necessarily overtaking) and authorize previous meanings of reverence.

The question of *bhikkhuni upasampada* that the state had entertained intermittently receded into the background in the wake of the raging debates about it. In the early 1990s a few *sil matas* who sat on the executive committee of the SMJM enunciated an interest in the *bhikkhuni upasampada* in the hope that it might enhance their recognition as renunciants worthy of state assistance.⁴⁹ However, a lack of consensus among *sil matas* at large—and state officials' evasion of the question—precluded its official discussion between the SMJM (as a representative body) and the state. As subjects of the state and as "respectable" renunciants, *sil matas* were not in a position to take up the question of the *upasampada*. At the time, the context of the debates about female monastic identity and the constraints that marked them could not be understood in terms of a movement in which nuns as agents aiming to introduce the *upasampada* struggled to resist the power of the state or to contest the hierarchy of a male monastic establishment.[50] The associations of *sil matas* that the state organized, coinciding with the emergence of public debates about the *bhikkhuni upasampada*, tell us about the kinds of lives *sil matas* lived and the conditions in which they lived. Liberal conceptions of political life interpreted in terms of such norms as resistance can hardly help one understand such lives.

Becoming Sil Matas, *Becoming* Bhikkhunis

The idea of receiving the *upasampada* was remote from the purview of most *sil matas* until the mid- to late 1990s. In fact, the very term *bhikkhuni* was not clearly differentiated from *sil mata* until very recently. Even a decade after the 1996 ordination of *bhikkhunis* in Sarnath, the distinction remained vague for many Sri Lankans. One *dasa sil mata*, Sumana Maniyo, whom I first interviewed in 1984, suggested that perhaps the first *sil mata* was a *bhikkhuni*. While she admitted that she knew nothing of the first *dasa sil mata*, her tentative suggestion indicated that she did not perceive a significant difference between a renunciant who was a *sil mata* and one who was a *bhikkhuni*. She went on to tell me that she called herself a *bhikkhuni* or a *srāvaka* ("listener" or "disciple"). Those were not names used for her by folks who visited her hermitage. Most likely, the "role" of "*bhikkhuni*" was simply one with which she wished to identify when pressed. Her own understanding of *bhikkhunis* was derived from depictions of *bhikkhunis* she had learned about in classical Sinhalese literature and Pali texts. Ten years later, Sumana, having become more conversant with some of the controversies surrounding the *bhikkhuni upasampada*, was even more ambivalent about becoming a *bhikkhuni* herself. Soon after that, however, she received the *upasampada*! Sumana's seemingly changing attitudes to the subject of the female renunciant vis-à-vis higher ordination clearly lack an idea of struggle waged against male monastic dominance.

In the mid-1990s I discussed the matter with another nun, Nanda Maniyo. Like Sumana, she initially said that there was no difference between a *bhikkhuni* and a senior *dasa sil mata*. Citing the authority of her *guru maniyo* or "teacher-nun", she claimed that a *dasa sil mata* who had renounced for a period of twenty years could, by virtue of her renunciation, be considered a *bhikkhuni*. In other words, with over two decades of a life of renunciation, she could consider herself a *bhikkhuni*. Shortly after Nanda's *upasampada* as a *bhikkhuni* in the late '90s, I reminded her of our previous conversation only to find that she had revised her thinking on who might become a *bhikkhuni*:

Q: I recall that in earlier times, *Meheninvahanse*, you told me...there was no *upasampada*....When I asked about the *bhikshuni* status, you told me that your *guru maniyo* had told you that a *sil maniyo* who had observed *sil* well for twenty years was like a *bhikshuni*.

N: [Laughing] Yes, at that time we were unable to take the *upasampada*. If a *sil maniyo* observed *dasa sil* for twenty years without breaking the vows, she is like a *bhikshuni* observing *sil*....Once we have the *upasampada* and we do the *vinaya karmaya* [acts of disciplinary rules] for the *upasampada*, then with the *upasampada* there is a different *nītiya* ["rule" or "law"].

Q: So [what you are saying is that] now that the *upasampada* is present in Lanka, your earlier thinking has changed somewhat?

N: It has changed a lot, very much....

Q: So when one says *"bhikshuni,"* it must refer to one with an *upasampada*?

N: Yes, it must.

Q: It cannot just be one who observes *sil* well?

N: No, it cannot, it cannot.

Of course, what had ensued between our earlier and later conversations was the introduction of the *upasampada* for *sil matas*. Both Sumana and Nanda, for whom the ideas of *bhikkhuni* and *sil mata* had been at the outset very similar, had since become *bhikkhunis* and altered their thinking accordingly. Perhaps at a different level, one cannot rule out that such change in thinking was the product of the idea of the *bhikkhuni* that emerged in the conjunctures in which researchers, state officials, and media outlets debated it. The conversation with Nanda Bhikkhuni indicated that after her *upasampada*, she no longer thought, as she had when a *sil mata*, that a *dasa sil mata* of twenty years' standing could qualify as a *bhikkhuni*. Her earlier understanding of *sila* did not relate specifically to observing *vinaya* rules, which are prescribed for fully ordained monastics. Clearly that was not Nanda's understanding after her *upasampada*. She explained that the main change for her as a *bhikkhuni* involved the *social* acceptance of her role as a female renunciant who could now perform the duties previously restricted to the fully ordained monk.[51] By emphasizing her new ritual activities as a *bhikkhuni*, she reaffirmed that becoming a *bhikkhuni* was not primarily a matter of assuming a nibbanic path.[52] The question of whether the *upasampada* helps or enables one to realize nibbana is one that has been debated publicly in the media and remains contested among contemporary monastics. What is important here is that the affirmation of *sila* was not central to either Sumana's or Nanda's decision to become *bhikkhunis*. As *dasa sil matas*, they had seen no difference between their *sila* and that of a *bhikkhuni*. In the ten to fifteen years between our earlier and later conversations they had both received the *bhikkhuni upasampada*. However, neither of them had *sought* to receive it. As they noted in conversations with me, they had simply accepted the invitation to receive it when it was offered. Their actions were not the result of a protest nor or of some resistance movement but rather seemed to reflect the convergence of ideas that led to the formation of the subject of the *bhikkhuni*.[53] Sumana and Nanda, like several other *sil matas* who received the *upasampada* at the turn of the century, were not engaged in a struggle for the legitimation of their status as *bhikkhunis*.

Meheṇi Udāva (*Dawn of the Meheni*)

In 1958 the now highly profiled *sil mata* Sudharma Maniyo of Biyagama wrote a letter to the newspapers, insisting that the restoration of the *bhik-khuni* order was unnecessary.[54] Rohana Meheni, who is celebrated as a longtime advocate of the *bhikkhuni upasampada*, quickly countered her. Rohana then discontinued her public communications on the topic until the 1980s, when she heard a monk who opposed the *bhikkhuni upasampada* deliver a radio sermon.[55] Rohana responded by initiating a correspondence with the monk. My intention here is not to explain how Rohana eventually became a *bhikkhuni* but rather to consider how the idea of the *bhikkhuni* emerged in recent times. Rohana's engagement with the idea of *bhikkhuni* ordination continued in her interviews with Bloss and Devendra and in the newspaper articles she wrote.[56] A six-year stint as the president of a district organization associated with the SMJM encouraged her to articulate her opinions on the perceived needs of *sil matas*. Her thoughts on the *bhikk-huni* question as well as the needs of *sil matas* were disseminated through readings of her poetry on the radio in the late 1980s and the launching of a newsletter, *Meheṇi Udāva* in 1989. Her poems recited on the radio were advertised as having been authored by several named *sil matas*. Similarly, the works published in *Meheṇi Udāva*, although ostensibly those of several different *sil matas*, were in fact composed only by her and two others. Without any compunction, she later acknowledged in an interview with me that she had used the names of *sil matas* she knew in order to "show to society that it was not just I who was voicing this." Her writings attracted the attention of intellectuals, activists, and detractors who assumed that her opinions were representative of larger numbers of *sil matas* than was in fact the case.

Although the first issue of the *Meheṇi Udāva* was privately funded and was representative of very few *sil matas*, in the English-language media, that publication came to be hailed as the *Journal of the Buddhist Nuns Association*, representing the nuns of an entire electoral district.[57] The change in funding and editorial authority after the first issue of the newsletter evidences how the subject of the *bhikkhuni* had gained center stage.[58] Whereas the first issue, authored by Rohana and a few other *sil matas* she knew, had included short essays and poems about general topics on Buddhism and nuns, later issues clearly centered on promoting the *upasampada*.[59] The first issue had received the attention of academics who generally supported the *bhikkhuni upasampada*; those academics then contributed to the later issues, thereby changing the newsletter's tenor and purpose.[60] The later issues, which attempted to lay the groundwork for *bhikkhuni* ordination, were authored predominantly by senior university lecturers and proponents of the *bhikkhuni* ordination, and they included longer writings that were more organized and deliberate. The annual *Meheṇi Udāva* prompted the establishment of a monthly newsletter with a similar name. It was sponsored by Kumar Piyasena, the owner of a printing press, who was a vocal supporter of the *bhikkhuni* ordination.

Piyasena became the editor of the monthly newsletter named *Sirilaŋkā Meheṇi Udāva* (Sri Lanka Dawn of the Meheni), published by the Samasta Lankā Janōpakāra Bauddha Saŋgamaya (All-Lanka Buddhist Association for Community Service). The first issue, dated October 1991, included an acknowledgment of the work of Rohana.[61] In a 1995 interview, Piyasena told me that two thousand copies of that issue had been printed, most of which had gone to *sil matas'* hermitages.[62] According to Rohana, there was "no connection" between her annual *Meheṇi Udāva* and Piyasena's monthly newsletter. She was informed by an academic that Piyasena had in fact reprinted pieces in his newsletter that had already appeared in hers.[63] Piyasena was familiar with the debate on the *bhikkhuni sasana* in the media and was well connected with a few intellectuals who wished to see a *bhikkhuni upasampada* established in Sri Lanka. The publications of the Janopakara Sangamaya made possible the creation of the first widely disseminated Sinhalese writings that unequivocally supported the *bhikkhuni upasampada* in a consistent manner.[64] The subject of the female renunciant as a respectable *bhikkhuni* became the focus of the intellectuals writing articles for the newsletter. According to Piyasena, by 1995 the thirty-seven-member advisory committee of the Sangamaya, including university professors and monks, had made plans to erect a building in India for ordaining and housing nuns if they could not do so in Sri Lanka. The ordination was to take place in 1996 or 1997. The Sangamaya sent out applications for higher ordination, but, according to one *sil mata* who received an application, "no one bothered with it." The ideal of the *bhikkhuni* that the advisory committee and the newsletter had promoted was not one to which *sil matas* themselves aspired. With Piyasena's unexpected death in 1997, the group's attempts to make the *upasampada* available to *sil matas* came to a standstill.

Shortly after Piyasena's death, an individual whom I shall call "the Professor" spoke of yet another public endeavor by academics to train and ordain *bhikkhunis*. The Professor himself helped establish an organization whose board included well-known university professors of religion from the United States. He and other Sri Lankan activists sought to encourage the recognition of *sil matas* and initiate classes for those living in the area. The classes continued for a few years with financial help from sources from both within Sri Lanka and abroad, but the initial goals of provision for a formal education and the creation of an organization of *sil matas* were never realized. The Professor had been one of several academic contributors to the debate on the *bhikkhuni upasampada*:

> I thought that this was an "anti-women campaign," and I did not like that. I was working for the cause of the *maniyos*, so I thought if I could help them that would be good. But then it became a political issue . . . that the *meheninvahanses* should or should not be given the *upasampada*. . . . I thought to myself, "That is not right . . . they should be given this," and in order for that to be, I did a lot of work there and thought that they should have sufficient education. . . . But

in the end...well...what a shame; "*pavu anē*," they have no understanding.... They would come and go for the classes and... We got
maniyos from different places for these classes.... It was a very
rag-tag thing. Basically I was very naive.... So those classes were
very successful at first. But at the end, what happened was this: it
became to clear to me that, however much they studied, they were
not very inclined (*nämburu*) to study.... Apart from one or two of
them, the others would just go for the classes, as though they were
tuition classes, and, apart from going to those classes, there was
no clear articulation here with our classes. So in the end it sort of
fizzled out.... What I think is that these people [*maniyos*]—they
have no sense of basic direction. I tried to get an intelligent group
together and do something with it, but it was clear to me that this
was not possible. Later I saw that they were "lost causes" and that
they could not do anything on their own. They would do it with
the support of... males, with the support of others, and that was
about it.

On a more optimistic note, the Professor added that "it was not such a
disappointment," because one *sil mata* who had entered the training program and later received the *upasampada* (outside the country) remained
"very promising." My point is not that the Professor did or did not achieve
his goals but that, for the most part, the *maniyos* known to the Professor
had no interest in becoming *bhikkhunis*.

Conclusion

Sri Lankan women who received the higher ordination did so provided
that it would not interfere with cultivating their everyday renunciant
practices.[65] That the Professor knew *sil matas* who were less interested
in a higher ordination than he was suggests that the resistant subject
that is sometimes assumed was absent. Although the print media had
helped construct the subject of the *bhikkhuni*, that subject was not readily
embraced by most *sil matas*, who viewed the debates with indifference or
suspicion. If one were to seek exemplars of a resistant subject among *sil
matas*, one might focus on the few *sil matas* who accepted the plans of
the monk Inamaluwe Sumangala of Dambulla. The most senior *sil matas*
who first began training for the *upasampada* were among those who had

served on the executive committee of the SMJM and who were impa-
tient with the state's reluctance to address their requests. Some of them
believed that receiving the *upasampada* might oblige the state to grant
them the privileges already enjoyed by male clergy. They did not begin
training in order to either resist or be equal to the monks in any sense of
organizing a collective protest or in order to affirm some liberal notion of
rights. They just accepted the *upasampada* when the conditions leading
to it met their approval. Several of those *sil matas* had already declined the
invitation to be ordained at Sarnath in 1996. They did, however, accept
training for the *upasampada* at Dambulla, which involved less disruption
of their renunciant everyday. What is interesting is that the *sil matas* who
accepted the Dambulla training for the mentioned reason later sought
to dismiss the Sarnath ordination and promote their own at Dambulla
on the basis of its "authenticity."[66] One such renunciant rationalized her
plans to be ordained at Dambulla accordingly. I discussed the matter with
her in 1997, before plans for her ordination (eventually in Bodhgaya)
were finalized. She first spoke about the ordination attempts made by
Piyasena and his Association:

They have not been able to do anything, really. A householder cannot do this; it must be requested by a *sil maniyo*. Until this time,
a *sil maniyo* has not requested this.... There was no connection
with the organization.... Now in Lanka, the Sangamaya—the new
one, the Samasta Lankā Kantā Saŋgvidhānaya [All Lanka Women's
Organization]—they are also asking for this. The Janopakara
Sangamaya [Kumar Piyasena's Association] is also asking for
this. But these did not include *sil maniyos*. The first one that has
involved the *sil maniyos* is this [Dambulla] one.... The Janopakara
Sangamaya is planning to go to Kandy with fifty *sil matas* to give
them the *upasampada* there. They sent me an application form too.
I did not respond.... It is supposed to be in August...but I don't
think that it is going to take place; there is no one who is interested.
They are once again training...at the Parama Dhammachaitya
Pirivena [a monastic center of study near Colombo] for an *upasampada* [of women]. Yes, there are several organizations, but not one
of them is meaningful [*sārthaka*]. Ours is meaningful....[67] Ours
is of all Lanka,...and after this [training], all will be ready for the
upasampada.

While clearly endorsing the *bhikkhuni upasampada* that she was about to receive, she made light of what she saw as misguided attempts to ordain *sil matas* elsewhere: "Some are going to Varanasi [Sarnath], and others to Bodhgaya [laughing] and who knows where the Kanta Samitiya [Women's' Organization] is taking their *upasampadas!*" What is important to note here is that there were several putative attempts to provide the *bhikkhuni upasampada* for *sil matas*, but they were not, according to her, "meaningful," because they did not suit what the *sil matas* themselves wanted. Clearly, the visions of organizations and individuals who wished to assist the *sil matas* in ways they saw fit, whether by invoking discourses of deprivation, human rights, and feminism, or by upholding a religious heritage, rarely harmonized with *sil matas'* understanding of themselves.

The 1980s and 1990s marked the emergence of multiple debates that centered on the subject of female renunciation. Those debates dovetailed with the debates about *bhikkhuni* ordination. However, many senior *sil maniyos* who were either selected or given the "opportunity" to receive *bhikkhuni* ordination did not find such programs convenient or meaningful. Indeed, as some of the *sil matas* put it quite bluntly, they could not bother about such programs, because they simply interfered with taking care of temple duties or "work" (*väda*)! The priority for the *sil matas*, then, was not obtaining the higher ordination, as some think, but living a life of taking care of everyday "duties" specific to living the life of a renunciant. In seeking to fulfill their duties, nuns were hardly involved as agents in a political struggle attempting to receive higher ordination. Indeed, the idea of the *bhikkhuni* was a product of the very conditions and constraints of the duties in which they worked with the state, developing administrative and organizational abilities and furthering communications among themselves. While many of the *sil matas* rejected the idea of the *upasampada* and have continued to work with the state, a few *sil matas* (believing that the *upasampada* might provide them with access to state and ritual privileges that they would not otherwise have) left the state-sponsored organizations of nuns and joined new efforts that sought to promote higher ordination. One of those efforts, led by the controversial monk Inamaluwe Sumangala, attracted a few senior *sil matas* who were already well established in their home hermitages. However, *sil matas* who trained for the higher ordination in Dambulla did so after first ensuring that the conditions of training did not interfere with the everyday management of their hermitages. What is consistently evident among the *sil matas* who initially trained in Dambulla is not just that they were willing to accept *bhikkhuni* ordination but that they did so (having rejected other such "opportunities") on terms that suited their lives. The very possibility of the idea of *bhikkhuni* ordination, marked by the networks of debates in the 1980s–1990s, did not and could not take precedence over *sil matas*' own concerns with leading a life of renunciation. Taking care of temple duties was part of such a life.

Becoming Bhikkhunis, *Becoming Theravada*

Introduction

In introductory texts on Buddhism, "Theravada" characteristically denotes an "early" Buddhism that is associated with Pali texts and practiced in specific countries (e.g., in Sri Lanka, Thailand, and Myanmar).[1] Theravada Buddhism is essentially differentiated from Mahayana in terms of divergences in specific doctrines and practices. Such differences similarly surface in discussions of Buddhism in Sri Lanka, where Theravada is often contrasted to Mahayana. When I refer to Theravada in general throughout this book, and for want of a clearer terminology, I also do so in that broad sense. Nevertheless, with reference to contemporary practices, what "Theravada" connotes is not so easy to determine.[2] Gombrich and Obeyesekere, in their book *Buddhism Transformed,* provide definitions of different expressions of Buddhism (Sinhalese Buddhism, Protestant Buddhism, etc.) and identify Theravada Buddhism as one that is connected with a specific textual tradition and monastic and religious practices (3).[3] They describe it as a doctrinal and ethical Buddhism imbued with a specific soteriology (242, 274, 422). Heinz Bechert, whose work *Buddhismus, Staat und Gesellshaft in den Ländern des Theravāda Buddhismus* has become a classic in defining the history of Theravada Buddhism, suggests that the "ordination tradition" is a central marker of Theravada (vol.1, 43). Gombrich and Obeyesekere, however, consider the Theravada/Mahayana distinction in terms of differences in "doctrinal currents" rather than "monastic traditions" (274); they suggest that the distinction lies in various interpretations of the doctrine (*dhamma*) rather than in ordination lineages and monastic rules (of the *Vinaya*).[4] Most often, in keeping with our textbook understanding of Theravada (with which Bechert's work would agree), they view Sri Lankan Buddhism *in comparison with* Buddhisms of other countries. According to them Theravada in Sri Lanka is either distinct from Mahayana (and other schools) or similar to a Buddhism found elsewhere, as in Thailand or Myanmar (254, 289, 302, 340, 350).[5] The historical identification of Theravada as a distinct form of Buddhism is a large question that I do not have the space to fully address here.[6] But how Theravada is defined has figured prominently in debates about recent *bhikkhuni* ordinations of Sri Lankan nuns, so it is only appropriate to ask what monastics themselves mean by "Theravada."

The question of the Theravada identity of *bhikkhuni* ordinations was a conspicuous feature of debates in Sri Lanka throughout the 1980s and into the 1990s.[7] At that time opponents of the *bhikkhuni* ordination vigorously disputed its validity, claiming that because the *bhikkhuni* ordination lineage in Sri Lanka had been discontinued centuries ago, there were no Theravada *bhikkhunis* who could perform the *upasampada* ritual according to the Pali (Theravada) *Vinaya*. Supporters of the ordination suggested that despite the cessation of the *bhikkhuni* ordinations in Sri Lanka, it was possible to conduct a valid Theravada ordination of Sri Lankan *bhikkhunis* with the assistance of *bhikkhunis* from East Asia. They argued that because the fifth century ordination of *bhikkhunis* in China had involved the participation of *bhikkhunis* from Sri Lanka and was directly related to the Dharmaguptaka ordination lineage in China (and other East Asian countries, such as Korea and Taiwan), the Dharmaguptaka lineage was de facto Theravada. Consequently, East Asian monastics ordained in the Dharmaguptaka lineage could effectively provide the uninterrupted line of succession necessary to perform a valid *upasampada* of Theravada nuns from Sri Lanka.[8] As one *bhikkhuni* from Taiwan who was involved in promoting the *upasampada* of Sri Lankan nuns asserted, "We received the lineage from Sri Lanka.... It is our intention to return [to Sri Lanka] what the Sri Lankan nuns have given to China." It was that argument about the continuity of an East Asian *bhikkhuni* lineage that was first used to support an ordination of Sri Lankan *bhikkhunis* in Sarnath, India (henceforth called the "Sarnath group"), in December 1996 and later of Sri Lankan *bhikkhunis* in Bodhgaya, India (henceforth, called the "Bodhgaya-Dambulla group"),[9] in February 1998. The former ordination involved the participation of Mahayana sangha members from Korea, and the latter, the participation of Mahayana sangha members from Taiwan. Some monks and nuns in Sri Lanka have disputed the "Theravada" character of those ordinations. Among other things, they suggest that introducing Mahayana monastics into an ordination ritual of Theravada nuns is detrimental to the practice of Theravada Buddhism in Sri Lanka.[10]

My discussion about Theravada identity is indebted to Ananda Abeysekara's *Colors of the Robe: Religion, Identity, and Difference*. Abeysekara suggests that "the questions of what it means to be Buddhist and the answers to them are made possible and centrally visible by altering conjunctures of discourses and debates" (17). In other words, what seems to "define"—conjunctures that make things "visible" hardly define any *thing*— and an identity such as "Buddhist" or "non-Buddhist" should not be taken as self-evident. Rather, we should attempt to understand how particular competing debates seek to make authoritative *claims* about what can or cannot count as Theravada Buddhism. It is easy to miss the import of what is being said here. On the one hand, the conjunctures producing those debates render the *determination* of what constitutes Buddhism questionable. That is what Abeysekara says when he argues that "particular authoritative narratives that contend to represent Buddhism cannot be taken as readily available ethnographic examples of the relation between religion and society because *they are to be found in those altering ideological conjunctures*" (25; emphasis added) Yet, if one seeks "empirical examples," one can find in Abeysekara's discussion how Buddhist householders come to debate and evaluate differently the conduct of two "rival" monks who have supposedly violated the same monastic rule concerning celibacy in particular networks of power (52–56). The supporters of one monk ignore his infraction—even when pressed—and continue to provide for him; but they condemn the rival monk for the very "same" offense. Again, this is not a matter of focusing on people holding "different" opinions that *change* but "conjunctures"—that name for the networks of power— producing them, making questionable the idea of some objective reality of a "Buddhism" that can *change*. One should not, of course, consider those views hypocritical on the part of the monks' supporters; to do so would be to mistake one assumed reality against another desired reality. As Abeysekara contends, what is important to note here is that "debates and disputes are not self-evident ethnographic examples that enable us [to have] any privileged disciplinary access to Buddhism, monasticism, and difference" (64). The argument about what constitutes a "good monk" within such conjunctures extends to other seemingly incontrovertible categories, such as Buddhism versus non-Buddhism and Theravada versus Mahayana. If we think of those categories in the way Abeysekara suggests, we can begin to dispense with certain assumptions with which we usually approach them. Again, Abeysekara's general argument helps us understand not only how discourse and power authorize particular competing claims about religious identity but also why such debates which are taken by scholars (and others) to constitute some reality find recourse in liberal modes of analysis of religious life and are grounded in certain moral norms of identity. The pitfalls of such liberal assumptions are many. In the previous chapters, I have attempted to show that liberal narratives about nuns rely on precisely such analyses of nuns' lives. Those narratives risk privileging (as accurate and authentic) one claim over another, thereby presuming that some claim (as opposed to another) ultimately constitutes an incontrovertible normative truth about nuns' lives. Now, broadly put, according to Abeysekara's argument, the affirmation of the category of Theravada identity, for example, is not centrally about whether one follows Pali texts, even though texts may be cited to make such an assertion about Theravada. Rather, that affirmation is about a claim to an identity that is made possible by those conjunctures—and one which can mislead us into thinking about an identity that is *separable* from the conjunctures themselves.

I follow Abeysekara's argument by assuming that the category of Theravada in contemporary Sri Lanka is contestable and involves a claim to its authorization in the context of competing debates as described earlier. Closer to the argument of this book, it is in terms of the relation between conjunctures and the claims they produce that one may want to understand what it means for a nun to become a "Theravada" *bhikkhuni*. I suggest that the recent *bhikkhuni* ordinations have introduced new questions about monastic precedence or seniority and that those are generally inseparable from claims to Theravada identity and power. That does not mean—again, following Abeysekara—that Theravada as such does not "exist." Rather, the question of "Theravada" and how it comes into "view" tends not to figure into everyday life *apart from* the competing claims and debates about it. To think otherwise is to make the mistake of separating such claims (discourse) from power. Nevertheless, scholars of Theravada Buddhism still persist in separating "discourse" from "power," thereby seeking to determine an authentic identity in terms of a "difference between what is *done* and what is *said*, and between what is actual and what is 'rhetoric'" (Abeysekara, "Buddhism, Power, Modernity" 496). Ultimately, such a difference implies that "power" (i.e., as something political) remains apart from or external to an "authentic" life (and religion) itself.

Questions of Monastic Seniority and Power

In August 1997, when I visited the *bhikkhuni* training center in Dambulla, I took a group picture of the twenty-six nuns who were training there for the *bhikkhuni upasampada*. The photographer in me suggested that the taller nuns stand behind the shorter ones and that some nuns move to the flanks so as to ensure a photogenic group portrait. The nuns, however, seemed to be either deaf to my requests or simply unwilling to comply. Eventually, one of their teachers (an ex-monk) indicated that the nuns were probably reluctant to move because of considerations of monastic seniority that would be upset if they did so. Without further ado, I quickly snapped the photo. That incident, seemingly trivial at the time, is one on which I have often reflected. To what extent is the image that scholars want to produce of nuns an image that they themselves would subscribe to? To what extent is the image that nuns create one that scholars accept at face value? In this case, the nuns' perspectives on their proper "placement" (according to seniority) did not fit with the image I attempted to construe. Whereas I was concerned with the aesthetics of a picture, their attention was focused on appropriate physical positioning in terms of seniority. Such a recognition of seniority is significant in the everyday interrelations of nuns. Processing in line from one place to another, sitting down to partake of alms that are served by practitioners according to the seniority of renunciants, greeting each other, and welcoming guests to the hermitage and engaging in other public functions involve observing proper precedence.[11] The placement in line of seniority is recognized in everyday activities when junior nuns (*poḍi mǎṇiyōs*) defer to nuns senior to them.

Such seniority is well understood among monastics themselves and is generally clear-cut. It is typically determined by the date and time of ordination; for example, a nun would be considered senior to another if her ordination preceded that of the other by even a minute. Monastic precedence is meticulously observed by *sil matas*. The same proved true at the *bhikkhuni* training center I visited at Dambulla.[12] Such precedence, which has been countered by new attempts at authorizing seniority among *sil matas* and recently ordained *bhikkhunis*, is my focus in the following pages. The emergence of *upasampada* training for *sil matas*—who had already accepted a certain precedence that had been established in their *sil mata* ordinations—introduced complications that would upset the usual order of seniority: junior *sil matas* received the *upasampada* before more-senior *sil matas* (who may even have been their teachers or ordaining *sil matas*). This chapter considers how nuns articulate their own understanding of monastic precedence concerning seniority. I focus on the meaning of monastic precedence and seniority in some detail, not just to delineate how the *bhikkhuni* ordinations have introduced apparent confusion into the everyday lives of some nuns but also to point out how claims to Theravada authenticity are embedded in the question of monastic precedence.

I first met Citta when she was a junior *sil mata* in 1984. I have maintained contact with her hermitage over the years and visited it intermittently. After conferring with the other nuns at the hermitage, as well as with their householding supporters, Citta decided to train for the *upasampada*. She eventually received the higher ordination in Sri Lanka from Sarnath-group monastics. When I met Citta, about five months after her *bhikkhuni* ordination, she was the only *bhikkhuni* at the hermitage, where three *sil matas* and one *samaneri* (novice *bhikkhuni*) also resided. The elderly head nun had no plans to receive the *upasampada*. Since she was unwell, she had handed over the daily management of the hermitage to a younger *sil mata* who acted as the de facto head nun. Citta's *bhikkhuni* ordination introduced complications in monastic seniority because all but one of the four nuns living with Citta *bhikkhuni* (including the *samaneri*) had received their *sil mata* ordinations before her. *Sil mata* ordination seniority made Citta junior to all but one nun at the hermitage and fourth in line in terms of her precedence in partaking in communal activities, such as processing in line, partaking of alms (*dana*), leading religious practices, and receiving salutations from householders. However, her *bhikkhuni* ordination set her apart from the *sil matas* and allowed her to formally participate in rituals with other *bhikkhunis* that were denied to other nuns at her hermitage. Citta's ritual seniority as the only resident *bhikkhuni* was compromised by her continuing to live in community with *sil matas*.

Citta sought to respect the seniority established by the *sil mata* ordination precedence. Interactions between the nuns and householders proved to be difficult. Householders had considered inviting her exclusively to say *pirit* for them, on the grounds that she was the only *bhikkhuni* at the hermitage. However, she rejected their suggestion for the same reason. When the nuns are invited to perform ritual services at homes, Bhikkhuni Citta avoids attending: "It is because the head nun has to go in front that I do not go. There is no problem [*prashna*], is there, if I just step away and stand apart? The majority in this *aramaya* are *manis* [*sil matas*]. If I were to be the foremost person, it would be difficult to get things done." Citta felt that the only way to deal with the difficult situation was to exclude herself from religious activities with the other nuns outside the hermitage. Her sensitivity toward her fellow nuns extended to her interrelations with them within the hermitage. She told me that she thought the seniority determined by the *sil mata* ordinations was more important than her new "status" as a *bhikkhuni*, and if she were to claim seniority as the first (and only) *bhikkhuni* at the hermitage, it would be "hurtful" (*ridenava*) for the other nuns living with her, so she insisted on maintaining the *sil mata* seniority. When alms food was served at the hermitage, Bhikkhuni Citta stood aside while the others were served first, according to *sil mata* ordination seniority. Somewhat laughingly she explained that even though she was served later, she received the food in her alms bowl *before* the more senior *sil matas* sat down to eat. That way, she explained, she was "neither ahead nor in the middle."

As my accompanying family members and I prepared to leave Citta's *aramaya*—in some confusion about how monastic seniority really worked with her—I was unaware that we were about to confront a further imbroglio. Usually, when leaving this hermitage, we had paid our respects to the senior-most nun first and later to the junior nuns, according to seniority. The nuns would stand in a row in order of seniority, and we would bow to them in turn, greeting them individually, according to their placement in the line. That day, however, after expressing our intentions to leave, something different happened. Citta Bhikkhuni and the only *samaneri* there continued a prolonged conversation with us as we waited for the elderly head nun to emerge from her room. Earlier we had been told that the acting head nun—junior to the actual head nun but senior in *sil mata* ordination to both Citta and the *samaneri*—was feeling unwell and could not see us off. Dusk settled, and the "farewell" conversation with Citta and the *samaneri* continued for what seemed like more than half an hour, or at least an unusually long time. The elderly head nun appeared to be taking longer than usual to come and see us off. When she eventually appeared, Citta and the *samaneri* moved some distance away from us. As usual, we first paid our respects to the head nun. However, because the other two nuns had moved aside, we were obliged to walk several yards to take our leave of them. That was awkward. We left that hermitage as we had left no other hermitage. Of course, it was not until we had parted company that I realized something of the importance of what had happened about the way monastic seniority works among nuns. Citta Bhikkhuni and the *samaneri* had wanted to see us off without the head nun's being present so as to skirt the complicated question of determining monastic seniority in that situation. Note again that when the head nun came to see us off, Citta and the *samaneri*—the two "junior" nuns who were "senior" to the head nun by virtue of their *bhikkhuni* and *samaneri* ordination—moved away from us, hence allowing us to bow farewell to the head nun first. As I realized later, they did so not simply out of respect for the head nun. In distancing themselves a few yards from us and the head nun, the *bhikkhuni* and the *samaneri* avoided having to acknowledge that they were in any way "junior" to the head nun, who was still a *sil mata* and neither a *bhikkhuni* nor a *samaneri*. The way they stood apart from us allowed us to simply respect the head nun without having to "decide" to whom we would first bow farewell. Obviously, the questions of monastic precedence and seniority among nuns are complicated, and this incident refers only to the way one *bhikkhuni* and one *samaneri* sought to deal with those questions so as not to disrupt monastic practice and living in nunneries. Such questions of seniority are important to being a nun. However, they are not "problems" that nuns seek to resolve but rather "questions" that they both face and evade in their daily lives.

Nuns' interactions with visitors are generally well choreographed. The situation of monastic precedence I encountered at Citta's *aramaya*, which I had visited multiple times, was wholly new to me. A few years later I encountered a situation at another *aramaya*, where a comparable question of monastic precedence or seniority arose. I had known the head nun of that hermitage, Padma, since the mid-1980s. She had ordained several *sil matas*, but she usually lived alone. She and some of her student nuns had received their higher ordinations from the Bodhgaya-Dambulla group of nuns, albeit at different times. One of her *gōlayās* (student nuns)[13] had received the *upasampada* before she had. Even though Padma's *golaya* did not live with her, she visited her often. Padma recounted how those visits raised new questions (*prashna*):

> This question has arisen. Now the *golaya* has one year [of *bhikkhuni* ordination] seniority over me. But I cannot offer reverence to her, because I am the *guruverya* [teacher, mentor]. . . . She cannot worship me . . . because she is senior by one year [of *bhikkhuni* ordination]. This is a big question. . . . She cannot worship me, since she is the *guruverya* [according to the higher ordination], and I cannot worship her, because she is the *golaya* [junior according to her *sil mata* ordination]. Nevertheless, she is the one who helps me out here.

Again, such accounts may make one think that questions produce problems. However, immediately following what she had said, Padma detailed how her *bhikkhuni-golaya* would visit and clean the hermitage and so on. The *golaya*'s cleaning of the hermitage pointed to the way both nuns sidestepped the question of seniority. In such seemingly simple tasks as cleaning the hermitage, the nuns went beyond the question of monastic precedence and seniority (or power) and attended to their everyday routines at a temple. The monastic duties of the *golaya* cleaning the temple set aside the issue of seniority, which obviously could not (nor perhaps needed to) be solved. Problems do exist, but the conditions in which the nuns live render them as questions to be faced rather than problems to be solved.

A few years after my discussion with Padma, I (unknowingly at the time) became a party to the questions Padma had noted. On this occasion, I arrived at the *aramaya* as arranged, accompanied by my family members. A dog's loud barking at the *aramaya* announced our arrival. We waited an unusually long time as the dog barked incessantly. Finally, the head nun, Padma Bhikkhuni, appeared and came out to greet us. After some conversation we were joined by the *bhikkhuni-golaya*, mentioned earlier, whom Padma had once ordained as a *sil mata*. Clearly our arrival produced a quandary concerning which *bhikkhuni* should precede the other in receiving us as we entered the *aramaya*. There was probably a short interchange between the two *bhikkhunis* as to how we should be welcomed. If the *bhikkhunis* appeared together, we would pay our respects first to Padma, whom we knew, and then to her *golaya*, whom we had not planned to meet anyway, because she was not resident there. Proceeding thus, however, would have violated the precedence of *bhikkhuni* seniority. Following customary practice, we would have become a party to the seeming confusion about monastic seniority. During the course of the day, the *golaya* remained in the background while I conversed with Padma. She joined the conversation intermittently and occasionally left to attend to other duties. At the end of the day, my family members and I prepared to leave—this time with the two *bhikkhunis* we were visiting, having offered them a ride. My family members went ahead to the vehicle, parked some distance away at the bottom of a hill, while I waited for the *bhikkhunis* at the hermitage. Once again, the wait seemed interminable. Eventually the *bhikkhunis* appeared, ready to leave. They walked in single file, with the elderly Padma following the lead of her much younger pupil, while neighbors looked on. My family members had wondered why I was taking

forever to leave the hermitage. Only later did I realize that once again we
had encountered a complication about monastic seniority. Our departure
had likely been delayed because the two *bhikkhunis* had taken some time
to decide on an appropriate single-file precedence that they would observe
as they walked (with me following) from the *aramaya* to the vehicle.

The questions of seniority presented by the newly introduced *bhikkhuni* vis-à-vis the *sil matas* are those that nuns face and live with. Citta
Bhikkhuni had decided to withdraw from certain communal activities
while avoiding others that might complicate the lives of the nuns living
together at her hermitage. In so doing, she had mostly relinquished her
seniority as a *bhikkhuni*. Padma Bhikkhuni, had, on the contrary, decided
to observe *bhikkhuni* seniority in giving precedence to her student, who
had received the *upasampada* before her. Padma's situation was somewhat
different from Citta's, because Padma lived alone and did not need to
address the question of seniority every day. However, because Padma had
regular contact with the *golayas* who visited her and frequently participated
with them in specific rituals for *bhikkhunis* mentioned in the *Vinaya*, she
was obliged to acknowledge their seniority as *bhikkhunis* when processing in line and so on. Neither Padma nor Citta (whose ordinations had
different origins, one associated with the Bodhgaya-Dambulla group and
the other with the Sarnath group) were training nuns for the *bhikkhuni*
ordination. Neither attempted to *represent* herself as a *bhikkhuni*, whose
seniority in the hermitage was implicated in a debate about the meaning of Theravada authenticity. However, other nuns I have met—both *sil
matas* and *bhikkhunis*—who are involved in educating and training junior
nuns for ordinations (as either *sil matas* or *bhikkhunis*), define monastic
seniority with reference to the question of the Theravada authenticity of
bhikkhuni ordinations of Sri Lankan nuns.

That definition of seniority was clearly evident in conversation with a
head nun, a *sil mata* who ran an educational center for other *sil matas*, and
one of her student *sil matas*. Echoing views of senior monks who asserted
that it was impossible to establish an authentic Theravada ordination, she
opposed the *upasampada* of nuns, citing the loss of a Theravada *bhikkhuni*
lineage and the absence of the necessary quorum of Theravada *bhikkhunis*.
The two *sil matas* proceeded to object to the *bhikkhuni* ordinations that
had recently occurred in India and Dambulla. They suggested that the
ordinations had been conducted in a "Mahayana" manner and that some
monastics had made money from the ordinations. Those *sil matas* also
voiced concerns about the confusion the new ordinations had introduced

regarding monastic seniority. They explained that elderly and senior *guru maniyo* were usually unwilling to undergo the rigorous *bhikkhuni* training program, which was more suited to young nuns. According to them, the junior *sil matas* under their tutelage might have fewer qualms about undergoing a demanding training program. The junior nuns, however, out of loyalty to their teachers, whose seniority they respected, were also usually unwilling to embark on the training program. They were hesitant to train as *bhikkhunis*, realizing that confusion concerning monastic precedence might ensue, for their potential ordination as *bhikkhunis* would effectively render them senior to their teachers, with whom they lived. The two *sil matas* with whom I discussed the issue were well aware of the complications introduced by the *bhikkhuni* ordinations and described situations in which elderly *sil matas* who had many more years in the renunciant life (as *sil matas*) were obligated to recognize the seniority of their younger student nuns who had become *bhikkhunis*. *Sil matas* who realize that their ordination as *bhikkhunis* would bring confusion into their everyday lives also tend to criticize the *bhikkhuni* ordinations as being "Mahayana" and thus inappropriate for Sri Lankan renunciants. For them Theravada invalidity is another name for difficult questions of monastic seniority at an everyday level. The same questions, however, have been evaded by *bhikkhunis* who promote the Theravada identity of the *bhikkhuni* ordinations.

Bhikkhuni Sama, a vigorous proponent of the Theravada authenticity of the Bodhgaya-Dambulla group's *bhikkhuni* ordinations, sought to overlook their effects on complicating certain relations of monastic seniority among *bhikkhunis* she knew. Sama (one of several *bhikkhunis* with whom I have spoken about this) waxed on about how unified the *bhikkhunis* with whom she had trained at Dambulla were. She emphasized that because all those *bhikkhunis* lived either with other *bhikkhunis* or with *samaneris* whom they were training, there were no "questions" about monastic seniority. However, when I referred to a disruption of monastic seniority that had occurred within a Bodhgaya-Dambulla hermitage known to her, she conceded that there had indeed been some concerns at that hermitage:

Q: So several of them [junior nuns] would like to be *samanera*?[14]
S: Yes.
Q: That is, they would like to take the *pabbajja dasa silaya* [Ten Renunciant Precepts]?

s: Yes.... Another thing is that all those who are at a *bhikkhuni aramaya*
    are becoming *mahana* [ordained] as *samaneras*.

q: So there are many *samaneras* at *aramayas*?

s: Yes. Now, at a *bhikshuni aramaya all* of them are *samaneras*. They are all
    samaneras. The *golaya* of a *bhikshuni* is not a *sil mata* anymore.

q: Now, at the *aramaya* of Bhikkhuni Vimala?

s: Yes. [She laughs and lowers her voice.] Yes. There is a question [*prashna*]
    there, is there not? Vimala Meheninvahanse is a *bhikshuni*, and the
    others—they do not wish to be *samaneras*.

q: Why?

s: That is the question [*prashna*] there, is that not so? Vimala
    Mehninvahanse finds it difficult to control them, does she not?

q: Why?

s: They have come from different places.

Sama proceeded to give reasons why Vimala Bhikkhuni was unable to
influence the junior nuns with whom she lived—reasons I was in no
position to confirm or deny. What is important is that Sama, in wishing to elaborate on the efficacy of the *samanera* and *bhikkhuni* ordinations (probably bearing in mind an expectation that my research would
be made public), preferred to evade the very real questions some nuns
faced because of their new *bhikkhuni* ordinations. She was attempting
to validate the living situations of *bhikkhunis* and their junior nuns in
which seniority was well defined. She (as well as other *bhikkhunis*) considered *sil matas* who wear robes different from those of *bhikkhunis*, observe
a distinctive disciplinary practice, and are barred from rituals open to
fully ordained nuns to be *gihī* ("householders"). However, she thought of
samaneras, who wear the same robes as *bhikkhunis* and are often seen as
bhikkhunis-in-training, as being *pavidi* ("renunciant") and more like fully
ordained nuns. Since *vinaya* rules restrict *bhikkhunis* from living, eating,
and, sleeping with householders, hermitages in which both *bhikkhunis*
and *sil matas* dwell face some complicated situations that would be absent
in *aramayas* where all renunciants had received the same type of ordination. Because I was already aware of Vimala's situation and knew that
Sama interacted frequently with her, I was in a position to question Sama's
idealized portrayal of harmonious renunciant hermitages. In the course
of our conversations, Sama attempted to assure me that the higher ordination of nuns with which she was involved was distinctively Theravada
and that its implementation had provided orderly living situations for

bhikkhunis. She tried to correlate lived realities with *vinaya* practices. My point is not that her attempt to claim an idealized view of renunciant life marked a difference between precept and practice or between what was said and what was; rather, it is that her claim was part of a narrative that sought to authorize the distinctiveness of the Theravada *bhikkhuni* ordinations at Dambulla, to which she was connected, as opposed to the Sarnath-group ordinations, whose validity she consistently opposed in our conversations. She clearly preferred not to publicly acknowledge any discord within the hermitage of a Bodhgaya-Dambulla *bhikkhuni.* Meanwhile, her initial insistence that all junior nuns who lived with *bhikkhunis* wished to be *samaneras* was an attempt to assure me that the ongoing Dambulla *bhikkhuni* ordinations were more authentic than the others that Sri Lankan nuns had received, because they accorded well with the Pali *Vinaya* and Theravada protocol.

The emergence of new lines of seniority, and of female renunciants' understanding of the extent to which those lines are authoritative bears on another related dispute between nuns—that concerning the validity of *bhikkhuni* ordinations as Theravada—which I take up later in this chapter. For now, however, I will turn to assessing how the significance of a Theravada identity for *bhikkhuni* ordinations became central to monks engaged in missions outside Sri Lanka. Sri Lankan monks, both those residing in the country and those living abroad, were among the first to support the *bhikkhuni* ordinations of Sri Lankan nuns. The articulations of what Theravada meant in the transnational context were different, albeit related, to the claim to Theravada authenticity in Sri Lanka itself. The uniquely Theravada identity of *bhikkhuni* ordinations was clearly promoted in an attempt to further foreign missions. Indeed, establishing what constitutes Theravada became important for Sri Lankans' acceptance of recent *bhikkhuni* ordination rituals, including the one that eventually took place in Sarnath, India. That ritual has been hailed by some as the first "successful" Theravada *bhikkhuni* ordination in recent times and as the precursor of all subsequent Theravada ordinations.

Missionary Differences and International Representations

The 1988 ordination of Sri Lankan nuns in Los Angeles was conducted with the intention of propagating Buddhism in America and defining a Theravada Buddhism that was clearly differentiated from Mahayana.

According to a letter written by Walpola Piyananda, a monk officiating at
the Los Angeles ordination,

> Strong criticism is being made against the Theravada form of
> Buddhism because of the denial of women into the order. Some
> female devotees have abandoned Theravada temples and joined
> Mahayana temples and entered the *Bhikkhuni* Order. This num-
> ber is ever on the rise... If we are going to continue the spread of
> Theravada in this country [America], we need to reexamine our
> position on the ordination of women. (qtd. in Bartholomeusz 187)

Promoting the higher ordination of Theravada women was primarily
about ensuring the success of Theravada missionary efforts in America.[15]
Sri Lankan *sil matas* who received the higher ordination in Los Angeles—a
ceremony that was conducted by both Theravada and Mahayana monastics—eventually returned to Sri Lanka. They did not continue their practices as *bhikkhunis*, because of a number of factors, including a lack of
support from other monastics as well as householders. Theirs was not an
ordination they sought out or struggled for; rather, it was about meeting
the needs of a Theravada Buddhist mission in America that faced new
questions. While those *bhikkhunis* from Sri Lanka effectively disappeared
from the gaze of the public, the event of the ordination reaffirmed the
need to clarify what higher ordination meant and whether it was ritually
valid for "Theravada" Buddhist women—fueling a debate that persisted in
the mainstream media over the following years.

Piyananda was once again involved with a higher ordination of Sri
Lankan nuns, this time conducted in December 1996 at Sarnath, India. A
main organizer of this ordination was Mapalagama Vipulasara, who was
the joint general secretary of the World Buddhist Sangha Council (WBSC),
the president of the Maha Bodhi Society of India, and the president of the
Sri Lanka Buddhist Congress.[16] In an interview published in the papers he
mentioned that the writings of Anagarika Dharmapala motivated him to
support the *bhikkhuni* ordinations:

> I read many books and a lot of writings of our Anagarika Dharmapala,
> the Founder of the Maha Bodhi movement. Anagarika Dharmapala
> maintained fine records in his diaries. He has written down every-
> thing that he considered important for the development of the sasana
> [Buddhist dispensation]. In his 1897 Diary, Anagarika Dharmapala has

written that Buddhists should utilise the services of Dasa Sil Matas and Bhikkhunis to propagate the Dhamma to spread the Buddhist way of life all over the world. That day, I made a prarthana [firm resolve] that in 1997, that is one hundred years after Anagarika Dharmapala made that record, suitable steps will be taken to provide an opportunity for Dasa Sil Matas to spread the message of the Maha Bodhi.[17]

The Sarnath ordination, like that conducted in the United States the previous decade, was arranged with the publicized intention of promoting Theravada Buddhism. But when the time came for staging the higher ordination in Sarnath, questions arose about the availability of potential ordinands. Steps were taken to select the most suitable candidates. The Sri Lankan organizers relied on the government infrastructure of national and district *sil mata* organizations to communicate with nuns throughout the country and invite applications for the *upasampada*. Of the twenty *sil matas* who were eventually chosen to train, only ten were willing to make the journey to India. One condition of the ordination was that the *sil matas* would leave Sri Lanka for at least three years, during two of which they would do missionary work in India. That stipulation allowed for maintaining the continuity of *bhikkhuni* training, but, more important for the *sil matas*, it meant leaving their home hermitages. Among the organizers initially selected for training for the Sarnath *upasampada* were senior *sil matas* who had honed their skills in leadership and administration while working in district and national *sil mata* organizations for a decade or more. Those were also head *sil matas* who ran the hermitages in which they lived. Unwilling to abandon their hermitages and the communities they served, they refused to leave the country.

The ten female renunciants who eventually agreed to accept *bhikkhuni* training in Sarnath were ones who (1) would and could leave their home hermitages and families, (2) would commit to participating in missionary work in India, and (3) would accept potentially prolonged absences from managing the duties of their hermitages (assuming they lived in community with others). Such training was not an option for some of the senior-most *sil matas* who were initially selected, but it was a possibility for *sil matas* who lived alone or whose performance of services at a hermitage was not considered indispensable. The ordination at Sarnath was an event of global proportions that, according to Kusuma's report, sparked opposition from senior (Mahanayaka) *bhikkhus* from Sri Lanka and evoked concern among the Korean monastics who were organizing the ordination. The Sri

Lankan *bhikkhus* who agreed to preside at the ordination did so with the assurance that the Korean *bhikkhunis* who were to ordain Sri Lankan nuns belonged to a lineage that derived from the Dharmaguptaka lineage (a lineage not significantly different from that of the Sri Lankan nuns who had ordained Chinese *bhikkhunis* in the fifth century c.e.). Kusuma Devendra was assigned the task of verifying the connections between the Korean ordination lineage and that of the Dharmaguptaka in order to ascertain its "Theravada" character. For the foreign missions, "Theravada" was another name for a Sri Lankan Buddhism of international stature, a Buddhism seen as having to embrace the full participation of women if it was to be successful.

While Sri Lankan monks and Korean monastics, as well as interested householding practitioners, laid plans for an international ordination, the Theravada *bhikkhuni* remained but an ideal. Some questioned the suitability of the *sil matas* who had agreed to the conditions of the training program and the ordination. Vipulasara worried that in this pool of *sil matas*, there was no renunciant adequately equipped for the task; in fact, he was concerned about the qualifications of the *sil matas* who were preparing to train at Sarnath. The idealized Theravada *bhikkhuni*, largely the creation of controversy and dissent, was not a figure that the *sil matas* themselves readily embraced.[18] This resulted in a crisis that may have scotched the plans to ordain Sri Lankan *bhikkhunis* at Sarnath. Kusuma Devendra, who had not originally intended to join the *sil matas* in receiving the ordination and was already in Korea researching the lineage transmission in an attempt to verify the suitability of the Korean ordination lineage for Sri Lankan nuns, was suddenly asked to step forward as a prospective *bhikkhuni*. I cite from her published account of what occurred:

At this point, Ven. Vipulasara telephoned me from Sri Lanka and conveyed the facts. The Koreans were alarmed and some even doubted the pure intentions of Bhikkhu Vipulasara. Bhikkhu Vipulasara told me that he felt the nuns selected were not up to the standard required for ordination, because their language skills and knowledge were inadequate. "It is an international responsibility," he said. In the face of all this, he invited me to join the nuns and take a leadership role as the first *bhikkhuni*. Otherwise, he said, he would be constrained to abandon the whole project! I was caught between two worlds and had hardly any time to think. I replied, "Venerable sir, please do not abandon the project. Even at the risk of my life, I will be willing. There will never be another chance." So by the time Ven. Vipulasara hung up the receiver, we had decided to go ahead with the ordination. This was how I decided to become a *bhikkhuni*.[19]

It is possible that Vipulasara had premonitions that the renunciants selected for ordination would be unable to fulfill their commitments. I have heard a variety of stories concerning the newly ordained *bhikkhunis*, some of which may lack credibility. Whatever the case, it appears that of the ten *bhikkhunis* who were ordained in Sarnath in 1996, at least four reneged on contracts and returned to Sri Lanka before their agreed-to time in Sarnath was over. One *bhikkhuni* who happened to win a visa lottery granting her permanent residence in the United States eventually relocated there, and another chose to renounce her Sarnath ordination and was later re-ordained in Dambulla. Bhikkhuni Kusuma, the most senior of the ten who were ordained, continues to travel globally, providing religious instruction. Within Sri Lanka little is known about the other seven *bhikkhunis* ordained in Sarnath. The renunciants who were ordained there were in a position to accept the terms of *bhikkhuni* training and ordination not only because they were eligible to do so but also because they were willing to reside outside Sri Lanka. Additionally, as was evident in my conversations with them soon after their *upasampada*, they were not, as some have suggested, renunciants who had "struggled" to become *bhikkhunis*.[20] That fact ties into the argument in Chapter 5—namely that *sil matas* were not leaders in a social movement that promoted ordination (if one can even consider the *bhikkhuni* ordination as a movement). The first *bhikkhunis* ordained in Sarnath did not *strive* to become *bhikkhunis*. Another important point about the Sarnath ordination is that the very idea of Theravada had a distinct meaning in the context of an international setting, a meaning that was congruent with the goals of Sri Lankan Buddhist missions abroad. Next, I will discuss how and why the idea of Theravada authenticity nevertheless had significance for monastics living in Sri Lanka. That particular idea of Theravada authenticity emerged from among competing narratives that eventually questioned the Theravada identity of the 1996 Sarnath ordination.

Ensuring Theravada

A few months after the higher ordination of Sri Lankan nuns in Sarnath in 1996, Inamaluwe Sumangala, the head monk of the Dambulla temple outlined plans for training and ordaining *bhikkhunis* in Sri Lanka. It is important to understand his plans to train nuns for the *upasampada* in light of his ongoing attempts to establish a unique place for the Dambulla temple as a center independent of the Asgiriya chapter based in Kandy. A few years earlier, Sumangala had challenged the authority of the Asgiriya monks, who until then had been accepted as the owners of the Dambulla temple (Abeysekara, *Colors* 190–192). On becoming the head monk of the Dambulla temple, Sumangala defied senior Asgiriya monks by denying the prevailing relationship between the monks affiliated with Dambulla and those from Asgiriya. Whereas the Asgiriya monks permitted only a restricted caste-based ordination, Sumangala, who questioned that, began ordaining monks regardless of caste distinctions. Championing the cause of the *upasampada* of *bhikkhunis* helped him further undermine the authority of the Asgiriya monks. The head monks of the Asgiriya and related Malwatte sects strongly opposed a *bhikkhuni* ordination of Sri Lankan nuns, and Sumangala's endorsement of the *bhikkhuni upasampada* positioned him to challenge them once again. Interestingly, Sumangala had not been a player in the heated public disputes of the 1980s and early 1990s about the ordination of women. It was not until about the time of the Sarnath ordination that he joined the debates.

After Sumangala organized an initial meeting in March 1997 and inaugurated the Sri Lanka Bhikkhuni Re-awakening Organization (SLBRO), he planned to begin training *sil matas* at a center near Dambulla (Salgado "Unity"). When I visited the center in August 1997, he intended to ordain *bhikkhunis* in the Dambulla area itself. But as details of the 1998 Bodhgaya International Full Ordination Ceremony (organized by the Foguangshan monastery in Taiwan) unfolded, his plans changed.[21] Sumangala made arrangements for ten senior nuns training in Dambulla to be ordained at Bodhgaya, together with ten *sil matas* associated with Sarvodaya.[22] Once the *bhikkhunis* trained in Dambulla had received the *upasampada* in Bodhgaya and had begun ordaining other Sri Lankan nuns in Dambulla, the Bodhgaya-Dambulla *bhikkhunis* made public claims to an exclusive Theravada identity, thereby rejecting the prior 1996 Sarnath ordination as Theravada. By claiming a unique Theravada identity, the Bodhgaya-Dambulla group was asserting its seniority over the *bhikkhunis* ordained in Sarnath in 1996. It is important to note that Sri Lankan monks (including Mapalagama Vipulasara) who had ordained *sil matas* at Sarnath in 1996, at Bodhgaya in 1998, in Sri Lanka itself (in Dambulla, Galkissa, and Anuradhapura), and in Taiwan were drawn from the same pool of monks who, initially at least, worked together. The Bodhgaya-Dambulla *bhikkhu-nis'* claim to the unique Theravada identity of their ordinations is part of a competing narrative about where, how, and by whom Sri Lankan nuns should be ordained. It is also important to understand that claim in terms of Sumangala's contestation of the authority of the Asgiriya and Malwatte monks who denied the possibility of a Theravada *bhikkhuni upasampada* and who disapproved of Sumangala's recently established ordinations of "low caste" monks. Interestingly, in his criticisms of the *bhikkhuni* ordinations associated with the Sarnath group (i.e., the ordinations conducted in Sarnath, Taiwan, and Sri Lanka excepting Dambulla), Sumangala was not just promoting the idea of centralizing *bhikkhuni* ordinations and validating only those associated with the nuns under his tutelage. A few years earlier (in connection with the new ordinations of monks he had inaugurated), he had criticized the very principle of centralized ordinations that he was now espousing. "What Sumangala finds astonishing," notes Abeysekara, "is that…Sri Lankan monks…have confined ordination to certain central locations monopolized by a few privileged monks. He wants to deprivilege this centralized practice. He maintains that such centralization obstructs one of the purposes of the higher ordination intended by the Buddha" (*Colors* 181). Rather than conclude that Sumangala either was being insincere or had changed his attitude regarding the centralization of monastic authority, one needs to understand Sumangala's promotion of the unique Theravada authenticity of *bhikkhuni* ordinations under his tutelage in relation to his separation from the Asgiriya temple and its caste-based ordinations of monks. As Abeysekara argues, that separation was necessarily related to Sumangala's reconceptualization of the sacred antiquity and independence of the Dambulla temple (*Colors* 187–194). I suggest that in ordaining *bhikkhunis*, Sumangala was making "possible the relation between tradition [in this case, Theravada] and difference [Mahayana] to be authoritatively argued in centrally visible ways" (*Colors* 200).

The Sri Lankan nuns ordained at Sarnath in 1996 took the Bodhisattva vow and were ordained in Korean-style monastic attire rather than in Sri Lankan robes. The Sarnath ordination may have served to confirm the criticisms of monks who had argued against the validity of a Theravada ordination lineage of Sri Lankan nuns, but it also drew strong criticism from Sri Lankan nuns (*sil matas* and Bodhgaya-Dambulla *bhikkhunis*) themselves, who referred to the Korean monastic attire as "trousers." That Sri Lankan monks who had presided at the ceremony donated their own monastic robes to the new *bhikkhunis* appeared to be irrelevant. Some of the *sil matas* who had trained for the *bhikkhuni* ordination in Dambulla and were later ordained in Bodhgaya witnessed the Sarnath ordination. They went to great pains to dismiss the Sarnath ordination, even before they themselves had received the higher ordination. The potential for a rift between *bhikkhunis* ordained in Sarnath in 1996 and those to be ordained later by Sumangala was evident several months *before* the Bodhgaya ordination.[23] In 1997 one *bhikkhuni*, in keeping with Sumangala's rhetoric, explained to me that the Dambulla training program for *bhikkhunis* was uniquely Theravada: "It is the Theravada *upasampada* of Lanka that we are trying to establish, not the Mahayana. This [Theravada *upasampada*] is [found] nowhere else in the world." Even though it was decided later that her own ordination would be conducted in Bodhgaya—by [Mahayana] Taiwanese monastics—after she had been ordained, she continued to emphasize the Theravada character of her ordination in her conversations with me. She explained that the Sri Lankan *samaneris* with whom she had received the *upasampada* in Bodhgaya agreed to accepting that *upasampada* on the condition that it would include procedures that were specifically "Theravada."[24] Theravada "authenticity" was then ensured by a "second" ordination, in which the Sri Lankan *bhikkhunis*, subsequent to their international Bodhgaya ordination with Taiwanese monastics, traveled to Sarnath and said the Pali *pāṭimokkha* (confessional recitation of *vinaya* rules) in the presence of Sri Lankan (Theravada) monks. Notable here is that *bhikkhunis* from Sri Lanka who had already been ordained at Sarnath in 1996 participated in the 1998 ordination rituals (in Bodhgaya and Sarnath) of nuns from Sri Lanka. The 1998 rituals included an international ceremony at Bodhgaya as well as a brief ceremony in Sarnath conducted by Sri Lankan monks. The Sri Lankan monks at Bodhgaya asked a Sri Lankan *bhikkhuni* (ordained at Sarnath in 1996) to translate the training instructions and explanations of ritual procedures from English into Sinhalese. They also asked her to perform the ordination of the *sil matas*. According to that *bhikkhuni*,

> All the monks were together, and this particular monk [Sumangala] knows.... He was witness to the fact that... I was the one that asked the questions and gave the ordination.... The monks were only observers. They were not asking questions. They said, "You ask the questions," and they gave me permission to conduct the ordination in their presence.... The Sri Lankan monks did not perform the ordination. They said, "You perform the ordination on our behalf." They were observers. I had to do it.

The monks remained silent as she queried the ordinands in Pali and conducted the ordination ritual.[25] The *bhikkhunis* who had just been ordained in Bodhgaya then traveled to Sarnath to participate in a second ritual that would affirm that their ordination was "authentically" Theravada. At Sarnath, after some dispute between Vipulasara and Sumangala over whether the Sri Lankan *bhikkhunis* who had previously been ordained in Sarnath in 1996 should participate in that second ritual, those *bhikkhunis* established their seniority by processing in line ahead of the *bhikkhunis* who had just accepted the ordination at Bodhgaya. Their seniority was further affirmed when they presented themselves as witnesses at the second, "Theravada" ordination of the *bhikkhunis* who had just accepted the international ordination at Bodhgaya.

The Sri Lankan *bhikkhunis* ordained in Sarnath in 1996 assisted with the training and ordination of the Dambulla-based nuns who became *bhikkhunis* in Bodhgaya (and Sarnath) in 1998. Without the participation and support of the former, the ordination of the latter would not have transpired as it did. But if the *bhikkhunis* ordained in Bodhgaya in 1998 wished to claim the foremost place among *bhikkhunis* in Sri Lanka, they needed to refuse to acknowledge the contributions to their own ordinations of the 1996 Sarnath group and to stigmatize as Mahayana both the Sarnath ordination and subsequent ones at which the Sarnath *bhikkhunis* officiated. And that is exactly what they did.[26] Although some monastics have touted Theravada authenticity as the defining difference between Bodhgaya-Dambulla monastics' ordinations and those associated more directly with the monastics who had participated in the 1996 Sarnath ordination, the difference is less a question of Theravada authenticity than one of claims to monastic seniority. The discussions that follow suggest that what is at stake is not, as some might assume, a debate about the "purity" of a Theravada *bhikkhuni* lineage but rather a contestation of who could validly make what claims about *bhikkhuni* ordinations. One cannot begin to understand what constitutes "Theravada" without recognizing the meaning of such contestations.

The Mahayana Difference

The case for a valid Theravada ordination of nuns was made once again in an announcement of the first Dambulla ordination of *bhikkhunis* in March 1998. That announcement, prominently displayed and taking up an entire half page of a national Sinhalese-language newspaper, presented the arguments of two well-known head monks: Inamaluwe Sumangala and Talalle Dhammaloka.[27] It also listed ten senior monks who would be participating in the ceremony, including monastics from India, the United States, Malaysia, England, and Sri Lanka. Mapalagama Vipulasara and Walpola Piyananda, who had participated in the 1996 Sarnath ordination, were among them. The ten *bhikkhunis* who had trained in Dambulla and received their *upasampada* in Bodhgaya returned to Dambulla and conferred the *upasampada* on nuns training there. That event was well publicized in the Sri Lankan media and was considered a first in Theravada Buddhism, for it celebrated "the beginning of the Bhikkhuni order in Sri Lanka again after nearly eight centuries."[28] It was presented on the front pages of national newspapers in dramatic and colorful photos of nuns in processional.[29] Within a month of the Dambulla ordination, the leading monks of three Nikayas met at the Asgiriya temple and announced their disapproval of the ordination in a letter to the president of the country, thereby contributing to a new public discussion about the issue.[30] Significantly, the Asgiriya monks led the concerted resistance to the Dambulla ordination of Sri Lankan nuns. The previous ordination, at Sarnath, had not resulted in such a unified opposition. The opposition to the Dambulla ordinations was likely part of an ongoing contestation for monastic precedence between Inamaluwe Sumangala and the Asgiriya monastics.

The Dambulla monastics continued to promote the Theravada authenticity of the Dambulla ordinations. A short publication entitled *Higher Ordination and Bhikkhuni Order in Sri Lanka* presented their argument.[31] That booklet was authored by Bhadra, a Sri Lankan *bhikkhuni*, who, perhaps not coincidentally, had originally accepted the *upasampada* in Sarnath in 1996. Unable to remain in Sarnath to complete her training, she returned to Sri Lanka, began working closely with Sumangala, and was reordained at Dambulla. In her booklet the Mahayana-Theravada difference is presented in black and white. According to her, all ordinations of Sri Lankan *bhikkhunis* except for those at Bodhgaya and Dambulla had been unacceptable because of their association with Mahayana. Of the Los Angeles ordination and its Taiwanese Mahayana connections she states, "Those nuns were ordained by bhikkhunis of Taiwan. But they were not accept[ed] as bhikkhunis in Sri Lanka, because Taiwan is a Mahayana Country" (25). In fact, the reasons for the Sri Lankan nuns' discontinuation of *bhikkhuni* practice after the Los Angeles ordination varied; the link to "Mahayana" was only one of many factors.[32] Bhadra continues to describe the 1996

Sarnath ordination as one that was "also received from Mahayana," as a direct result of which "all the other nuns in Sri Lanka held a meeting and discussed about the situation. Several Maha Theros [senior monks] from various districts came forward to support them to re-establish the Higher Ordination according to the Theravada Tradition" (26). She admits that the 1998 *bhikkhuni* ordination in Bodhgaya took place "in the presence of both Theravada and Mahayana bhikkhu[s] [and] bhikkhunis" (27). But adding that there was a second ordination "in the presence of Sri Lankan Bhikkhus," she reasserts a distinctively *Theravada* character of the Bodhgaya-Dambulla group *bhikkhunis* in stating that when they returned to Sri Lanka, they "succeeded in re-establishing the Theravada Bhikkhuni Order in Sri Lanka after nine hundred years" (27). By saying that the Sri Lankan *bhikkhunis* ordained in Los Angeles, Sarnath, and, more recently, in Taiwan "were not being accepted as Theravada bhikkhunis" (29), she undermines the ordinations of those *bhikkhunis* and ultimately promotes the Bodhgaya-Dambulla group *bhikkhunis* as the only authentic Theravada *bhikkhunis* from Sri Lanka.

I raised the Theravada-versus-Mahayana question with Sumangala. According to him, the 1996 Sarnath ordination was a "Korean" and "Mahayana" ordination. But he maintained that the ordination of Sri Lankan nuns by Taiwanese *bhikkhunis* in Bodhgaya was valid. He indicated that the latter ordination had originally derived from one officiated by Sri Lankan *bhikkhunis*, because "Devassara, a *bhikshuni* [*bhikk-huni*] . . . went from Lanka to China and took the *bhikshuni* order there."[33] Nevertheless, he was clearly disturbed by the ordination of Sri Lankan *bhikkhunis* in Taiwan that had occurred in 2000. He suggested that that ordination was done for the "wrong reasons" and was upset that he had not been consulted about it at the outset. In an attempt to deny the validity of the ordination of the *bhikkhunis* in Sarnath and Taiwan as well as that of the *bhikkhunis* whom they later ordained at different temples in Sri Lanka (i.e., outside Dambulla), he advised the Bodhgaya-Dambulla *bhikkhunis* against participating in *vinaya* acts (*vinaya karmaya*)[34] with them.[35]

I asked Sumangala to comment on his advice to the Bodhgaya-Dambulla group *bhikkhunis*. He said that because the ordination of Sri Lankan *bhikkhunis* in Taiwan had been orchestrated to make money for the sponsors rather than to promote the welfare of the religion, he was not prepared to recognize it. He associated the organization of the *bhikkhuni upasampada* of Sri Lankan nuns in Taiwan with Sakyadhita, particularly with two (non-monastic) Sakyadhita members: Kumari and Sunita.[36] Unsurprisingly, he had nothing positive to say about them or Sakyadhita:[37]

q: You have forbidden the Dambulla *bhikshunis* to do *vinaya karmaya* with the other *bhikshunis*, is that correct?

s: What do you mean by the "other *bhikshunis*"?

q: I mean…the group from Kaoutaramaya [in Sri Lanka], that it is not good to do it with them. Have you said this?

s: Yes, I have.…Now in the *Vinaya* it says that you should do the *vinaya* acts with those members of the sangha with whom you reside [*samāna samvāsika saŋghayā*]. Now the Kaoutaramaya *upasampada* that the Sakyadhita organization has done is a serious wrong [*barapatala vāradak*].

q: A wrong? What have they done?

s: That means they have…, even while *bhikshunis* were being ordained here [in Dambulla], taken *bhikshunis* to China [Taiwan] and given them the ordination there.…It is at that point that they did the wrong. What is the wrong? Even while there was an ongoing and established program for the *bhikshunis* in Lanka, they created a different group (*tavat kaṇḍāyamak ēgollaŋ nirmāṇaya keruvā*). The Sakyadhita organization found the money for this from Foguangshan. They did that work with the expectation of receiving money. I have seen this.…I have told this to them before, and I tell it to them today—that they should not do bad work like this for money. They have done a great wrong in doing that; they have done the greatest damage to the program, the *bhikkhuni shasanaya* program, in doing that. Now because of that there are two groups [*kaṇḍāyamas*].…They did it; that means it is Sakyadhita that has done this. Sakyadhita has had no connection at all with our [organization]. What they wanted to do was to show off to the world that they have a *bhikkhuni* (*vādapiḷiveḷa*) program—to get an income from abroad. That is how I saw that that is not a good idea. But this work that we are doing is not being done with the expectation of money from anyone. This is done out of sincerity [*saddhāven*]; that is, our work is for the sake of the Buddhist dispensation—to bestow [on women] the proper status that the Buddha gave them in the dispensation. They had one objective, and we had another.

q: So it appears that there are two branches [*śākhā*]?

s: There are two branches. Two branches came to be.

q: That could become two sects [*nikāyas*]?

s: That could in the future become two sects. Sakyadhita needs to take the responsibility for that—Kumari and the other one…

Q: Sunita?

S: Sunita needs to take the responsibility for that.

Q: Do you think that those *bhikshunis*—those who belong to that lineage [*paramparāva*]—do you think that they are not really *bhikshunis*, or what do you think of them?

S: I need to clarify that a little more. Now those at Kaoutaramaya— those *dasa sil matas* who were at Kaoutaramaya—if they had wanted to be ordained, then Sakyadhita had the duty to discuss this with us and then form some sort of program here. Without doing anything like that, they wanted to obtain the funding from Foguangshan and somehow take anyone to go and get the *upasampada*. That was like a contract. That is not something that they did for the sake of the religion but for the sake of money. You see, they wanted somehow to take some [nuns]—that is, some twenty or so in number—and show them off and then fulfill the contract and get the money. . . . That is wrong. They had the opportunity of. . . . When they were doing this the [*bhikkhuni* training] program had already begun at Dambulla. . . . They came to Dambulla and have seen this; they know what is being done here. The Dambulla *bhikshunis* were doing this [ordination] already. . . . If we had gone there and talked and then said that it was not possible, then . . .

Q: What do you mean "say it was not possible?"

S: If we had said that it was not possible to. . . . If they had made a request of us [for the ordination] and we had rejected it . . .

Q: That conversation never took place?

S: That conversation did not take place. We did not even know that they were doing something like this. They did this secretly [*horeŋ*][38]. . . . We did not know that there was something like this taking place! That is why I think that they should be called not the Kaoutaramaya Nikaya, but the Sakyadhita Nikaya [laughing]. . . . Otherwise, we could call it the Sunita Nikaya. That is very wrong work. Now for that reason it is difficult to join these [Dambulla] people with those [other nuns]. Why? Because we went with the [Sri Lankan] monks from Lanka to Bodhgaya and to Sarnath, and, having gotten together with the monks without any issues, we are continuing our work with the registration of the *bhikkhunis*. Now it is difficult to get those people together with these people because the *bhikshunis* from here were not connected with that [Taiwan *upasampada*]. So, in the future it is possible that two sects can come about.

Clearly, Sumangala, in dismissing the Taiwan ordination of Sri Lankan *bhikkhunis* as having been done for the "wrong reasons," saw in that ordination a rival to ordinations being conducted in Dambulla. The accusation of insincerely performing actions in the name of religion while focusing on monetary profit is not, of course, new. In fact, *sil matas* who refused to be ordained as *bhikkhunis* accused Sumangala himself of seeking financial gain from foreign countries for ordaining *bhikkhunis*. Sumangala expressed a sense of betrayal; he felt that because he had an ongoing program of *bhikkhuni* ordinations, the prerogative to ordain *bhikkhunis* lay with the program at Dambulla. In our conversation he affirmed that the two groups—the one associated with *bhikkhunis* from Sarnath and Taiwan and the other with the Bodhgaya-Dambulla *bhikkhunis*—were and should remain distinct, because only the Bodhgaya-Dambulla group was authentic.[39]

Sri Lankan monastics aware of Sumangala's attempt to dismiss the Sarnath ordination were among those who organized ordinations for Sri Lankan nuns at different centers in Sri Lanka as well as in Taiwan. One such monk, who had initially worked with Sumangala and later distanced himself from him, described the Dambulla ordinations as *deśiya*, or something that belongs to the country. Disputing Sumangala's claim that only the Dambulla ordinations were Theravada, he explained Sumangala's stance in terms of party politics:

Let's say I think of starting a Theravada *pakṣaya* [party]....Let us imagine that I have broken off...and that I start a separate party. I want to develop this party....So what would I do? I will attack the other party....It means that I will argue against it and find fault with it. And I develop [my own] party. That is all that I think is happening—nothing else....I [referring to Sumangala] want to give people the idea that the Theravada *bhikshuni shasanaya* that I started and that is from Dambulla is the Theravada *bhikshuni shasanaya* that is spreading throughout Lanka....That is a wrong idea, no? I [referring to himself] say it is wrong....It is I, after all, who gave the training and the *upasampada* to both [i.e., the *bhikkhunis* ordained at Sarnath and those ordained at Bodhgaya] [laughing wholeheartedly]. This is the reason; there is no other reason. It is just that they want to have people think that it is only from one place in the world, Dambulla, that the Theravada *bhikshuni* is being trained....That is an incorrect idea.

The monk recognized that Sumangala "did not want to accept that they [the Sri Lankan nuns ordained at Sarnath] had the *upasampada* in the Theravada way." He was displeased with Sumangala's attempt to dismiss the Sarnath ordination. To challenge Sumangala's claim, the monk described how he himself had brought together Sri Lankan *bhikkhunis* ordained at Sarnath (i.e., connected to Korean monastics) with the Sri Lankan *bhikkhunis* ordained at Bodhgaya (by Taiwanese monastics) in an ordination in Taiwan that also included Taiwanese monastics who had officiated at the Bodhgaya ordination. Because the Bodhgaya ordinations, with which the Dambulla *bhikkhunis* were connected, had been conducted by Mahayana monastics from Taiwan, the monk hoped that by orchestrating another ordination that involved nuns ordained by *both* Korean and Taiwanese monastics, he could undermine the claims of the monastics centered in Dambulla. Subsequently he, together with other monastics, continued to organize and officiate at other ordinations in Sri Lanka in which Sri Lankan *bhikkhunis* who had been ordained in Sarnath (in 1996) and in Taiwan (in 2000) participated. In doing so, he attempted to consolidate the connection between the Sarnath and Bodhgaya ordinations.

Asserting the Theravada authenticity of the ordinations they sponsored and labeling all other ordinations of Sri Lankan *bhikkhunis* as Mayahana gave Dambulla monastics an important means of dismissing the Sri Lankan *bhikkhuni* ordinations that they had not organized. Bhadra voiced misgivings about the "Mahayana" character of some ordinations, and Sumangala, though acknowledging those misgivings, did not mention them to me in our discussion about the Taiwan ordination. Although the question of Theravada (and Buddhist) authenticity has been debated publicly among high-ranking monks and politicians in Sri Lanka for some time, the meaning of "Mahayana" itself (apart from its differences from Theravada) is not so clearly established among Sri Lankans. The next section looks at how Sinhalese-speaking nuns understand the apparent division between groups of recently ordained *bhikkhunis* and how that apparent division is tied to their articulation about the meaning of Theravada and the *bhikkhuni* ordinations that took place at the turn of the century. The point here is not just to show that there are different views on what is meant by Theravada and Mahayana but to highlight that claims about Theravada and Mahayana are inseparable from discursive strategies (to use Abeysekara's terminology) that underline competing narratives about who may authorize a form of Buddhism as "authentic."

Sri Lankan Nuns and the Authorization
of Theravada

While the Bodhgaya-Dambulla *bhikkhunis* cast doubt on the Theravada validity of the ordinations of Sri Lankan nuns in Sarnath in 1996 and later in Taiwan (by *bhikkhunis* ordained in 1996 in Sarnath), and while Sumangala also raised questions about the ordination in Taiwan, yet another rivalry emerged in the contestation about Theravada authenticity. Despite the Mahayana/Theravada distinctions, ostensibly centering on the *bhikkhuni* ordinations, this rivalry concerned a dispute between a teacher (*guru*) nun and her two pupils (*golayas*). Some of the female renunciants involved in the rivalry were associated with the Bodhgaya-Dambulla group in question, whereas others were closely connected to the *bhikkhunis* ordained in Sarnath (who ordained *bhikkhunis* in Taiwan and at Kaoutaramaya).

The rivalry centers on a *sil mata* from Kaoutaramaya, Seelavatie Maniyo, and two junior *sil matas* under her tutelage. Apparently, Seelavatie fell out with the two *golayas*.[40] While Seelavatie remained a *sil mata* (for some time), the *golayas* went on to receive the *bhikkhuni* training and *upasampada* in Dambulla and Bodhgaya. The position of her *golayas* as two of the senior-most *bhikkhunis* from Sri Lanka was established early. Although Dambulla organized *bhikkhuni upasampadas* on a regular basis, Seelavatie, their *guru maniyo*, decided not to be ordained there. Had she been ordained there, she would have had to pay obeisance to the two "junior" nuns with whom she had had a disagreement. But later Seelavatie, together with other *sil matas* from Sri Lanka, was invited to receive the *upasampada* in Taiwan. Accepting the ordination from Taiwan enabled her to become a *bhikkhuni* without having to recognize the seniority of the two "junior" *golayas*.[41] *Sil matas* mention that incident as an instance of the difficulties that confront the new *bhikkhunis* and a good example of why *sil matas* should reject the *upasampada*. Bodhgaya-Dambulla group *bhikkhunis* argue that since Seelavatie received the *upasampada* after her younger pupils, she should pay obeisance to them. Seelavatie herself was reluctant to talk about the matter with me in greater detail. What is of importance here is that what appears to be a grand narrative including Theravada/Mahayana, Sri Lankan/Taiwanese, or "correct"/"incorrect" distinctions in ritual procedures that may make sense of the different ordinations detracts from what is happening among female renunciants in their everyday lives. Whereas Sumangala sought to undermine a Sakyadhita-Taiwan ordination on the grounds of insincerity and Bhadra's booklet positions the *bhikkhuni* ordinations within the context of a Theravada-versus-Mahayana debate, the rivalry was articulated differently by some Sinhalese-speaking nuns.

I asked a group of nuns (referred to by the letters A–E) who had connections with the Sarnath-group *bhikkhunis* to reflect on the different ordinations being conducted for Sri Lankan *bhikkhunis*. Although they knew that ordinations were taking place in Dambulla and that the Dambulla *bhikkhunis* did not participate with them in rituals, they were uncertain as to why. Because they were still nuns in training, they discussed among themselves how they should address my questions and decided to respond collectively as a group. While aware of the rift between Seelavatie and her *golayas*, they appeared to be unclear about its origins. The putative "Mahayana" character of an ordination did not seem to be an issue to them, as is apparent in an interview with me about *upasampadas* that Sarnath *bhikkhunis* had conferred on *bhikkhunis* at Kushtanagara and Kaoutaramaya. (Both were centers in Sri Lanka where nuns had received the *upasampada*).

A: I think there is one [ordination] in Dambulla, and there is one in Kushtanagara.

Q: Are they the same?

A: [Hesitating] Kushtanagara and Dambulla...No...from what I have heard, the one in Dambulla is different....Is it to do with the Siam Nikaya and the Burma Nikaya?

Q: No, there are no Nikayas [involved].

A: No, we do not know, really...

B: [Referring to the *guru-golaya* rift] It has to do with the teacher, and now there is a separation.

A: But...we do not know for sure; we are just saying what we think ....[They talk among themselves.]

C: The nuns from Kaoutaramaya come here....They cannot go to Dambulla; it is too far, is it not?

After more discussion among themselves, one nun volunteered, "If one does it properly, really there is just one *upasampada*....It is people who make the difference [in the *upasampada*]. According to the rules, it is just one....In Lanka it is one way, and in other countries it is different."

D: The *upasampada* is one, but they [at Dambulla] are creating a division....They say that they have the Theravada *upasampada* and that the other one is Mahayana...but theirs was a little Mahayana too, is that

not so? The *bhikshunis* at the first *upasampadas* were Mahayana...so I
do not know which is right.

E: Well, that is so, since the countries are different. But if we look at this,
it is really the [one] *dharma* of the Buddha that allows one to realize
nibbana.

The question of difference that I raised was likely one that the nuns had not
been asked to discuss previously. It was evident that they were attempting
to think it through while responding to me, continually conferring among
themselves so as to provide me with the "correct" response. Eventually, they
rejoined that the *dharma* of the Buddha is one, and whether an *upasampada* was Mahayana or Theravada made no difference to the realization
of nibbana. Theirs was a response I have commonly encountered among
monastics not primarily associated with the ordinations at Dambulla.
Such monastics note in general that a Theravada/Mayahana difference did
not exist during the time of the Buddha and argue that such distinctions
are not important in the first place. Thus they skirt the question about the
Theravada identity of the ordinations.

A senior officiating *bhikkhuni* associated with the Bodhgaya-Dambulla
group nuns and much in tune with Sumangala, insisted on recognizing a
distinction between the Sarnath group and the Bodhgaya-Dambulla group
bhikkhunis and their *upasampadas*. Notably, this Bodhgaya-Dambulla group
bhikkhuni, like the nuns associated with the Sarnath group (see the preceding interview), was unclear about the specifics of the Mahayana difference.
Our conversation centered on the ordination of certain Sri Lankan *bhikkhunis* we knew in common. Because those *bhikkhunis* were not ordained at
Dambulla, the Bodhgaya-Dambulla group *bhikkhuni* attempted to dismiss
their ordination as Mahayana. Interestingly, although she had no doubts
that their ordination was "not Theravada," she was unsure about the specific country in which their ordination took place:

R: They [some of the Sri Lankan nuns in question] have been ordained
once. Once—that means only the Korean *bhikshunis* got together
and ordained them. They have not been ordained by the Lankan
bhikshunvahanses.

Q: Where did they go for the *upasampada*?

R: They went...to Korea.

Q: To Korea?

R: [Thoughtfully] Korea means Taiwan, no?

Q: Korea is one country, and Taiwan is another.[42]

R: I think it was Taiwan.

Q: Taiwan?

R: [Pondering my suggestion and then decisively] It is Korean *bhikshu-nis* who did [the ordination] in Taiwan. There are Korean *bhikshunis* in Taiwan. They [the Sri Lankan nuns] did it there and came. There were no Lankan monks at all who went there.

Upon my furthur questioning, she agreed that some Sri Lankan monks had taken part in the ordinations but that this did not constitute the required quorum needed to conduct an authentic Theravada ordination ceremony. The main thrust of her argument was that the Sri Lankan *bhikkhunis* ordained in Taiwan could not be considered Theravada, because the stated condition had not been met and because the ordination was "Korean"—an argument that she used in opposing the Sarnath ordination. Interestingly, she attempted to discredit the ordination because of its putative "Korean" and "non-Theravada" character, even though members of the Taiwanese sangha, rather than Korean monastics, had organized it. Having difficulty in explaining some details about the event, this *bhikkhuni* suggested that "Korean *bhikshunis* in Taiwan" had conducted the ordination.[43] Another point that arose in our conversation (only a part of which appears above) was her conflation of "Theravada" with "Lanka" and "Mahayana" with "Korea" or "Taiwan." What this Bodhgaya-Dambulla *bhikkhuni* wanted to make clear to me was that the Mahayana ordination in Taiwan had been quite different from the ordinations in Dambulla. She emphasized unequivocally that the ordination in Taiwan was "not Theravada." But she herself, like the junior nuns (A–E) mentioned earlier, was uncertain about what exactly made it "different." This *bhikkhuni* attempted to discredit the Taiwan ordination on the grounds that it was Korean or Mahayana and therefore could be viewed as inauthentic and inappropriate for a Sri Lankan.

Both the Sarnath and the Bodhgaya-Dambulla group *bhikkhunis* acknowledge the presence of a dispute between the Kaoutaramaya *bhikkhuni* and the two *golayas* who became senior to her with their *bhikkhuni* ordination, and both groups recognize the existence of contesting narratives about the idea of Theravada among *bhikkhunis*. Those narratives, which in some ways resemble those emerging from the disputes between the head monks at the Dambulla and Asgiriya temples, are framed in terms of competing claims to a supposedly authentic Buddhism. Common to both disputes about Theravada authenticity are central questions of monastic seniority and power.[44]

Concluding Remarks

In this chapter I have sought to understand what it means for Sri Lankan nuns to become *bhikkhunis* and identify themselves as "Theravada." I have argued that the meanings of Theravada are rooted in the debates about monastic seniority and power in which they occur. Sinhalese-speaking nuns without access to the globalatinized vocabulary used by scholars and other nuns to discuss the identity of nuns have different assumptions about what is and is not "Mahayana." Understanding contemporary nuns' views of Mahayana is important not, as scholars such as Cheng think, for affirming that they are or are not "accurate" but for suggesting that their views are embedded in an ongoing debate about the meaning of monastic seniority and power. It would be a mistake to assume that the so-called internationalization or globalization of the higher ordination of nuns has equivalent meanings for Buddhist monastics around the world. As a whole, what Theravada means to scholars, monks, and nuns can differ, and Theravada can become a buzzword for claims to monastic seniority and power—whether of monks or of nuns—both outside and inside Sri Lanka.

Outside Sri Lanka, monks supporting Theravada missions center their concerns about monastic precedence on promoting an egalitarian and distinctively Theravada Buddhism, a Buddhism that is as accepting of nuns as Mahayana. Within Sri Lanka, monks and nuns assert the Theravada character of ordinations to either sanction or undermine contesting narratives. *Sil matas* who reject the *bhikkhuni* ordination do so echoing the concern with Theravada authenticity while focusing on a potential confusion of monastic seniority among nuns. Such confusion has already been borne out in the everyday interrelations of nuns. *Sil matas* and monks who deny the possibility of a valid Theravada *bhikkhuni upasampada* are among those who also oppose the authority of influential monks such as Sumangala. Some senior *bhikkhunis* who affirm the authenticity of their ordination as Theravada and deny that of other *bhikkhunis* are simultaneously contestants in a *guru-golaya* or "teacher-student" rift; such rifts are connected with disputes about who has seniority and proper precedence. Meanwhile, Sumangala and senior *bhikkhunis* ordained at Dambulla champion the cause of the Theravada ordination of *bhikkhunis* and reject the validity of the *bhikkhuni* ordinations in Sarnath, Taiwan, and Sri Lankan centers other than Dambulla on the grounds that such ordinations are "Mahayana." Nevertheless, several nuns I interviewed—including both those associated with the Bodhgaya-Dambulla ordination and those associated with the Sarnath ordination—though granting that differences may exist between those ordinations, are uncertain about what those differences are. Again, this chapter has not been concerned with assessing which ordinations are most authentic or most appropriate for Sri Lankan *bhikkhunis*. Rather, it has attempted to show that, in order to better understand the questions surrounding the ordination debates in Sri Lanka, one must go beyond the assumption that the category of Theravada is self-evident.

PART III

Empowerment

Renunciation and "Empowerment"

Introduction

Scholarly framing of nuns' reputed stories of freedom in renunciation are limited by their embeddedness in liberal ideas about empowerment. Saba Mahmood, in her study of Muslim women and practices of piety in Egypt, has critiqued liberalist concepts of freedom and power that are grounded in notions of resistance and agency (1–39). One of the questions she raises about how we may think about notions of resistance and power helps us reflect on scholarly stories of Buddhist nuns. She asks, "Does the category of resistance impose a teleology of progressive politics on the analytics of power—a teleology that makes it hard for us to see and understand forms of being and action that are not necessarily encapsulated by the narrative of subversion and reinscription of norms?" (9). Proponents of liberal feminism would expect nuns to desire autonomy in renouncing family, own their residences, and seek the higher ordination—all to enhance female renunciants' "forms of being and action" in terms of ("third-world") female resistance and struggle. That is how scholars tend to think about the so-called empowerment of Buddhist nuns. Scholars have yet to consider how nuns themselves understand such notions in relation to their renunciant everyday. Here I focus primarily on *sil matas'* understanding of the ownership of residence and land and argue that the practices of empowerment—if such a term is even applicable to nuns—may be seen as an altered terrain of power relations that both inform and are informed by practices of renunciation that do not correspond to a liberal feminist paradigm.

As Iris Marion Young says, "Empowerment is like democracy: everyone is for it, but rarely do people mean the same thing by it" (89). Liberal feminist meanings of empowerment cannot simply be equated with a notion of nuns' renunciation. In effect, the praxis of Buddhist nuns whose lives are not governed by modern notions of sovereign selfhood defies interpretation in the idiom of liberal feminism. Nuns, rather than attempting to affirm a putative selfhood, seek to embody practices focusing on the *renunciation* of self. Moreover, they realize religious fulfillment in the immediacy of the concrete actions that define their everyday renunciant lives. They are hardly subjects aspiring to liberal ideals of freedom and equality. For them, what is central is the realization of renunciant practice—namely, the cultivation of *sila* ("moral or disciplinary practice"), which becomes possible within a network of redefined family relationships and the observance of monastic duties.

Empowerment, an ideal that social scientists and feminists in particular esteem as a democratic virtue, has multiple connotations. According to the *New Shorter Oxford English Dictionary*, to "empower" means, among other things, to "invest formally with power; authorize, license (a person to *do*)" or to "endow with the ability or power required for a purpose or task; enable, permit." Those two senses inform the general idea of empowerment. The first sense is congruent with Max Weber's understanding of power that is officially sanctioned by a state or a bureaucracy; the second sense, more fluid and nuanced, suggests that an empowering potential can come from without, perhaps independently of state or bureaucratic investiture. But both definitions dovetail in assuming that empowerment derives not so much from within the individual in question but from without. Thus, one may say that because the "status" of contemporary female renunciants is such that the Sri Lankan state or bureaucracy or the monastic establishment as a whole does not officially accept the *bhikkhuni upasampada*, it enables scholars to contrast that status with some other power that may intervene to enable and empower nuns to seek liberation. However, the kind of female monastic empowerment that concerns me in this chapter does not come from without; rather, it arises from the concomitant renunciation of selfhood, marriage, and property—that is, from the very practice of *sila*. Liberal feminisms, in their eagerness to translate the forms of being and action of "third-world" women's lives into ready-made secular and juridical concepts, have neglected to think of such practices of religious fulfillment.

Grounding Renunciant Practice

Studies on female renunciation tend to define it with reference to the renunciant's severing her ties with family, without an understanding of the ways in which family relationships and networks may continue to inform her everyday practice. Such studies speak of nuns in terms of how their cultivation of Buddhist practice affords them autonomy apart from the household, which is characteristically viewed as a patriarchal unit in which women live lives of oppression. Although there has been considerable discussion of the importance of autonomy in feminist literature, I suggest that the autonomy associated with female renunciation, rather than involving a total severance of family ties, is more like what some feminists have identified as "relational autonomy," in which kin relationships are redefined (Friedman 55–58). Marilyn Friedman suggests that in relational autonomy it is possible "that relationships of certain sorts are necessary for the realization of autonomy, whereas relationships of certain other sorts can be irrelevant or positively detrimental to it" (56).¹ It is common in studies of Buddhist nuns for the household or the family to serve as a handy trope for the putatively unchanging patriarchal unit that typifies the Asian community in which it exists. I argue that the discourse on female renunciants and their supposedly oppressive families encodes the perennial objectification of the female renunciant as the "non-Western" other in need of succor. I am not implying that nuns' decisions to renounce are necessarily unrelated to familial concerns. But I propose that if one does see in "family" a reason for women to renounce, it is necessary to review how one thinks about gender and its positionality in broader terms. The family, ipso facto, need not represent an unchanging male-dominated unit. Rather, it more aptly represents a nexus of dynamic power relations whose vulnerability to social transformations affects women variously and may encourage some of them to lead a life of renunciation.

Inferring that women living in predominantly Buddhist countries have suffered oppression in the way that Western women have ignores both the significance of the extended family and the participation of Asian women as wage-earners. Additionally, by neglecting the various far-reaching forms of colonial politics that have affected Asian women's lives, one lacks a macro-level understanding of the ways distinctive social and political factors may prompt women to seek an alternative to living and working in the household as Western women might. For instance, Ashis Nandy, in his discussion of the rise of *sati* (literally, the "good wife" but also the "widow who is immolated") in eighteenth- and early nineteenth-century Bengal, affirms the need to address wide-scale social changes that were taking place at the time. He suggests that although *sati* "may have involved Hindu traditions…it was not a manifestation of hard-core Hindu orthodoxy" (8). Furthermore, he suggests that *sati* became more prevalent because of significant political and economic developments that diminished the power of widows within the extended family during the time of British colonial rule. I point out the necessity of entertaining a parallel between female renunciation in Buddhism and *sati* but not because those phenomena are similar in that both involve women's engaging in specific religious practices. I do so, rather, to suggest that the emergence of female renunciation in nineteenth-century Sri Lanka (assuming that it began then) and the emergence of *sati* in India (both of which involved a radical shift in women's economic and familial relations) are related to various factors that produced widespread political changes at a particular time in colonial history.[2] Hence, just as new land-settlement policies and economic and social relations may have encouraged the rise in *sati* throughout Bengal, I want to suggest that in Sri Lanka, transformations in the newly introduced capitalist economy, which coincided with land reforms and legal changes to definitions of marriage and the rights of inheritance, contributed to women's increased interest in renunciation.[3] Whereas at the time, *sati* was arguably "not a manifestation of hard-core Hindu orthodoxy" but rather a ritual that "became a battleground between the old and the new, the indigenous and the imported, and the Brahmanic and the folk" (Nandy 2), the emerging popularity of female renunciation in Sri Lanka since the late nineteenth century was arguably not primarily a manifestation of a Buddhist revivalism, contrary to what some have suggested. A consideration of the public emergence and popularity of female renunciation in predominantly Buddhist countries should also involve an assessment of the legal and social factors that have impacted women. In Sri Lanka, although individuals such as Anagarika Dharmapala and G. P. Malalasekera (who are often thought to have been the architects of Buddhist reform and revival) advanced the ideal of female renunciation, the public emergence of nuns in the late nineteenth and early twentieth centuries was largely a result of other dynamics.[4] Scholars often interpret in the rhetoric of practitioners promoting the idea of female renunciation an articulation about Buddhist reform or revival, but the emergence of female renunciation was more likely a result of extensive legal and economic changes rooted in material transformations engendered by colonial encounters.

In *Gender Transformation, Power and Resistance among Women in Sri Lanka: The Fish Don't Talk about the Water*, Carla Risseeuw shows that women in Sri Lanka during pre-colonial and early colonial times were economically significant as landowners and workers and had considerable authority within the family unit. Others have indicated how family networks in Sri Lanka have been inseparable from prevailing notions of land tenure (Grossholtz; Leach; Obeyesekere, *Land Tenure*). With the imposition and implementation of colonial legislation and the erosion of their power within the family, women became increasingly marginalized and dispossessed. Pursuing a life of renunciation would provide a woman with the possibility of maintaining some independence and decision-making authority within the family in the realization of a religious goal.[5] As renunciants "within the family," women could assume a new kind of authority that affirmed re-defined relations of power with immediate family and extended kin. Renunciation then provided a certain freedom and fulfillment at a time when women's situation within the family unit was being transformed. I am not suggesting that women turned to religion as an "opiate" in times of trouble. Female renunciants often cite a consistent and unsurprising reason for their renunciation: they renounce to overcome the *dukkha* of samsara.[6] For them, renunciation is after all about advancing their practice of *sila*. But the progressive erosion of women's authority within the family as income-earners and as landholders likely rendered a life of renunciation attractive for some. Risseeuw's study makes clear that the nineteenth and twentieth centuries saw significant changes in gender relations—changes that adversely impacted the power of women in new ways (125–128). It was probably no coincidence that female renunciants in Sri Lanka seem to have first appeared *publicly* in the late nineteenth century, a time when women were being increasingly excluded from what had been a relatively privileged position within the family. Rather than endure the difficult familial circumstances that Risseeuw documents, a woman could effectively renounce land and property and thereby avoid conflicts between competing family members. Moreover, she might also enjoy the economic support of her family while being revered as a *religieuse* in her community.[7]

Risseeuw, who studies transformations in gender and power that occurred in Sri Lanka during the British colonial period, analyzes changes wrought in the areas of marriage and property throughout the nineteenth and twentieth centuries. She speaks of significant developments during this time in terms of "gender transformation": "Through macro-economic and social change, women and men find themselves in changed positions vis-à-vis each other both in society at large and at the micro-level of family and interpersonal relationships" (14). Risseeuw shows that marriage was defined more fluidly before the introduction of colonial legislation (17).[8] At the time, polyandry and polygamy co-existed (sometimes simultaneously) with monogamous unions. Colonial authorities, informed by Victorian ethics and the British norm of the male-headed household, misunderstood the Sri Lankan woman's centrality in the family structure and her involvement in the labor force, which may have resulted in inaccuracies in census data (94–97). Although marriage customs varied from one part of the country to another, the system of marriage known as *binna* allowed women considerable access to property as well as influence within the extended family. As laws were made to narrow and define concepts of marriage, adultery, and divorce—gradually circumscribing women's power—women's access to land ownership also became more restricted. Risseeuw points out that during the nineteenth century, "women's relatively independent position in marriage, provided by her life-long access to land and property and the right to divorce was to shift to that of a legal and economic dependent.... Her position became one which was at best secure but which lacked economic potential, because even as a widow her right to land and property was curtailed" (71–72).

In one area of Sri Lanka, Risseeuw notes, "changes in marriage laws occurred during the same period, at times separated by only one or two years from the mutations made in the laws of the ownership of land" (44). She shows that as land came to be seen as a marketable commodity in the new capitalist economy of the nineteenth century, and as communal land ownership was curtailed and more restrictive marriage legislation became effective, women's access to landed property diminished, and they enjoyed less economic security than before (49–53). She indicates that the decline in women's access to land and property, together with the new legislation on marriage, affected relations within the family. But she notes that without further research, it is difficult to explain how women addressed those issues and "the question of how women responded to their decrease in decision-making powers and property rights has to remain unanswered" (58). Writing in the 1980s, Risseeuw comments that among Sinhalese peasants, the scarcity of land that was evident in the later part of British rule "was, and remains to this day, the greatest source of conflict at village level" (126). The nuns we encounter in this chapter are renunciants who, in seeking a tract on which to establish a hermitage, confront fierce competition for land that can undermine their very practice as renunciants.

The Sri Lankan nuns whom I have interviewed since the 1980s articulate a deep devotion to their religious practices and clearly privilege them over any preoccupation with the ownership of land and property. In that respect, they are perhaps not unlike their predecessors in the late nineteenth and early twentieth centuries. They have sought a life that involves venturing into unfamiliar territory to pursue a religious goal. For them the land on which they live and practice is not a marketable commodity. Rather, it provides them with a place where they can engage in religious services, perhaps a means of growing food for sustenance, and a physical nexus for maintaining relations with family and a community that supports them. For the nuns with whom I conversed in the 1980's and 1990's, the very prospect of inhabiting land apart from renunciant practice was unthinkable; moreover, they did not see the capitalist "ownership" of property as an end in itself. Ownership, with its acquisitive connotations of selfhood, is after all what they had professedly renounced. For nuns, taking up residence in a particular neighborhood is invariably associated with their relationships to donors of the area who often initially invited them to live there. The support from householders may bear associations with what Pierre Bourdieu refers to as "symbolic power," because of how nuns lead their renunciant lives in specific places (*Language*). Female renunciants who are identified with a relatively continuous space on which to live are more readily available to provide necessary services and receive donations. The ways nuns relate to their land differs from the ways monks who come from well-endowed temples relate to theirs. Among monks, temple properties are sometimes handed down from a head monk to a male relative who is chosen to ordain for the very purpose of claiming a monastic inheritance. While a tradition of pupilage (*śiṣyānuśiṣyaparamparāva*) maintains a certain lineage among monks, a tradition of kinship (*ñātiśiṣyaparamparāva*) further consolidates the succession of monks to an inheritance.[9] That is not to suggest that all monks belong to wealthy temples. Monks too may lack suitable housing and adequate *dāna* (alms), but they tend to be better provided for than female renunciants. Often nuns are invited to take up residence at a small one- or two-room abode, because such a dwelling, while potentially acceptable to a nun, is considered unfit for a monk.

The nuns encountered in this chapter have faced various difficulties in the course of occupying places of residence. Although one might understand nuns to be empowered in the act of finding a suitable abode, it is important to note that for them, "settling down" does not center on land ownership in itself but rather on its very renunciation. In fact, those nuns speak neither of feminist freedom nor of autonomy from a male-dominated family. They do not privilege the ownership of private property. Their settling down is rooted instead in the very landlessness that constitutes their renunciation, paradoxically often "grounded" in the same kinds of kinship and village networks they supposedly renounced. Whereas a feminist perspective might emphasize nuns' independence from family relations, and a modern liberal discourse would typically affirm the inviolability of private property, I argue that nuns pursue their practice while remaining connected to family and land and in tandem with distinctive ways of thinking about them.

Some scholars see nuns' endeavors to take up a life of renunciation away from the conventional household as an ability to overcome a struggle of some sort. Nuns' attitudes to land and their attempts to maintain their places of residence may be seen as expressions of resistance and struggle that tie in with Bourdieu's conceptualization of symbolic capital. But that interpretation would be misleading at best because it would imply that nuns have a desire to proactively exert some kind of control. Bourdieu, describing the tension between the Weberian notions of the "priest" and the "prophet," explains this as a "struggle for the monopoly over the legitimate exercise of religious power over the laity and over the administration of the goods of salvation" (qtd. in Engler 447). In other words, earning symbolic power is also about competing for control. According to Steven Engler, "Bourdieu relativized Weber's conceptual distinction, suggesting that this tension between orthodoxy and heterodoxy, between established and innovative authority, plays itself out in every context where humans struggle for control over some form of capital, whether economic, cultural, artistic, or religious. These arenas of struggle constitute separate 'fields'" (446). A correlation of priest (or established "church") with Buddhist monk and of prophet with Buddhist nun would be questionable. In particular, the priest-prophet analogy would not reflect *gendered* relations of power. Furthermore, the notion of struggle that Bourdieu uses suggests a deliberate, conscious contestation for power.[10] In contemporary Buddhist monasticism what often happens is a perceived *erosion* of such symbolic power among monks who may begin to resent an alteration in social equilibrium caused by the apparent incursions of nuns into the scene. Nuns, on the other hand, pursuing a renunciant life from a position of relative "weakness" (in that they are at first often unknown or quite new to a neighborhood or do not share the privileges that monks typically enjoy), attempt to find a space in which they may live their lives. They do not *aim* to threaten the social position of monks (or of anyone else). In that sense, the male monastic response to the new situation effected by the presence of nuns is quite different from that of nuns who are attempting to find a niche for their practices. Rather than conceptualize nuns' relation to monks essentially as a struggle for power, I suggest that nuns are engaged in something more akin to a tactical maneuver of holding their own in the ongoing effort to pursue religious practices. Nuns, contrary to waging a struggle to overcome opposition and seeking a "victory" over those who challenge them—although they may *appear* to be doing such—engage in certain activities in order to maintain their existing renunciant practices. They are generally not strategists—if strategy is about "the calculation (or manipulation) of power relationships.... [that] postulates a *place* that can be delimited as its *own* and serve as the base from which relations with an exteriority composed of targets or threats...can be managed"(de Certeau 35–36; emphasis in original). Unlike some monks and others who challenge nuns and might be strategists in that they distinguish their own place of power in particular situations, nuns use tactics that lack a panoptic vision and overall strategic planning. A tactic "takes advantage of 'opportunities' and depends on them, being without any base where it could stockpile its winnings.... What it wins it cannot keep.... It must vigilantly make use of the cracks that particular conjunctions open in the surveillance of the proprietary powers. It poaches in them. It creates surprises in them. It can be where it is least expected" (de Certeau 37). Although de Certeau's initial definition of *tactics* relies, as does Bourdieu's ideas of "fields," on a notion of struggle, he introduces a difference of perspective between the weak and the strong where "a tactic is determined by the *absence of power* just as strategy is organized by the postulation of power" (38; emphasis in original). In other words, tactics center on a mode of survival, whereas strategy centers on a perspective of power. We may say that female renunciants live by acting in a manner akin to the tactics mentioned by de Certeau. Their actions, which are congruent with their capacity to lead renunciant lives, constitute a certain mode of authority, even though nuns themselves may not articulate it as such. Those actions are precisely what allow nuns to lead the life of abnegation that they seek. I now turn to consider how nuns' renunciation is tied to the very land on which they live. Here I will point out how the language of liberalism and the capitalist ownership of property remain dissonant with nuns' renunciant practice.

The "Disappearance" of a Nun

My very first conversation with a *sil mata* occurred with a nun named Metta Maniyo in December 1983. Metta, born of a farming family, received ordination in the Ten Precepts after the death of her husband.

At the time of our conversations, she was still in touch with her two adult children, one of whom she regularly visited for short periods of time. Aged sixty at the time, she lived with an *upasika* in a two-room dwelling that was just able to accommodate a bed, a chair, a mat for sleeping on the floor, a cooking area for a small kerosene stove, and space for a few items of kitchenware. There was no running water or electricity at this abode, which had barely enough space to accommodate the two renunciants living there. About fourteen years prior to our first meeting, Metta had been invited to live there by a householder, Ranjan Weerasinghe. She built the shelter and a *mal āsana* (place for offering flowers) near a large *bo* tree. I visited her several times between 1983 and 1986. After Weerasinghe died, Metta continued to live in the dwelling, believing that her residence there would bring merit to Weerasinghe in his next rebirth. She stayed on for several years, despite having suffered some harassment from non-Buddhist neighbors who wished her to move so they could build a thoroughfare from the road to their garage. Her appeal to the police temporarily stalled their activities. A few months later, a high-ranking army official connected by marriage to the Weerasinghe family collaborated with her neighbors and attempted to force her to move once again. That time, she was confronted by drunken rowdies who began to attack and destroy her dwelling. She told me that her appeals to the police were of little avail, because the neighbors wished to avoid a clash with the army official.

At the time of our interviews, Metta was supported by family members and householders living in the vicinity. She took no interest in the higher ordination and focused on leading a life devoted to religious practice. She kept in close contact with a nearby temple as well as with the teacher-monk who had originally ordained her. As with several other nuns I came to know, legally owning the land on which she lived had not occurred to her; her immediate concern was to pursue a life of renunciation. After leaving the country in 1986, I returned a few years later and observed that her hermitage door was padlocked from the outside, something she would do when she left temporarily. She still appeared to live there. During my subsequent visits in the early and mid-'90s, I noticed that she must have left the place. The door had been sealed shut from the outside with a wooden plank nailed to it, and years later the two-room dwelling was torn down. Today there is no a trace of a hermitage. The *bo* tree remains, as does the *mal āsanaya* (place for offering flowers), but the nun has disappeared; she lives elsewhere or is deceased.

Metta's account remains a largely untold story; it is one of the few that I have been unable to pursue in the course of my interactions with nuns in the past decades. It is clear that Metta intended to lead a renunciant life despite the obstacles in her path. She accepted the invitation to live at the abode with the thought of generating merit for a deceased person. Despite its location in a premier residential area of the city, her space had "value" for her only insofar as it grounded her religious practice; that was where she found fulfillment, at least for a time. Although some neighbors who opposed her wanted her space for their personal use, she was determined—as she had explained to me—to remain there out of loyalty to the memory of a donor she hardly knew. That memory, a sort of existential "mooring," was intrinsic to her practice as a nun.

My conversations with Metta led me to think that the challenge of finding and maintaining a suitable dwelling likely faced other nuns as well. That was confirmed not just by nuns whom I encountered throughout my research but also by government officials who worked closely with them. According to one such official, the biggest obstacle *sil matas* faced had to do with "the question of a dwelling place and leading their lives in a suitable environment without troubles." Invariably I found that nuns took up residence (usually with an invitation from a potential donor) in spaces or dwellings that were viewed as uninhabitable by others (including monks). As nuns gained support from householders who contributed to developing the hermitages, they often faced challenges either from male monastics or from householders who subsequently laid claim to their much-improved land. The nuns generally had no legal ownership of the land on which they lived. Rather, their connection to the land was also a connection to the network of supporters who lived in their neighborhood. Hence, their "claim" to the land was at best moral. But when others attempted to appropriate their land, their claims could become untenable. Having come across recurrent instances of that situation, I began to question how nuns themselves related to the land they occupied. Nuns tend not to focus on acquiring land; they simply occupy it as they further their religious practice. Rather than pursue potential avenues of what in modern discourse may be considered rights and opportunities, most nuns clearly accord importance to a certain kind of freedom (if we can even use that word) to lead a life of renunciation away from familial responsibilities but not necessarily by severing all family relationships. Evidently, what is most meaningful for nuns is their cultivation of renunciant practice.

Bourdieu's discussion of symbolic capital can partly explain the power relations between nuns and monks in disputes over land. As is well known, his notion of symbolic capital draws on Mauss's interpretations of gift giving. According to Bourdieu, gift giving in certain societies differs from a contractual exchange in that it concerns a "good-faith economy" (*Outline* 172–173),[11] where a gift may be understood not as expressing monetary value but rather as expressing a confidence that the receiver will reciprocate in kind whenever possible. Giving ensures symbolic capital as a form of credit or a guarantee of reciprocation (181). Such "a law of exchanges means that the closer the individuals or groups are in the genealogy, the easier it is to make agreements, the more frequent they are, and the more completely they are entrusted to good faith" (173). Nuns move to new places and build support amid a community, to which they become close and which grounds their specific practice. In doing so, they enter into economies of good relations, in which symbolic capital seems to become the all-important medium of exchange.[12] Some neighboring monks who recognize actual or potential destabilization of their sources of support approach the nun-householder relationship with trepidation and thus urge nuns to leave the land on which they live so the monks can maintain (or acquire) for themselves the patronage of a neighborhood that would otherwise provide sustenance to nuns. Whereas monks may find in the presence of nuns a potential attenuation of such symbolic power that they either have received or may yet receive, their livelihood as renunciants is generally not threatened. That notion of symbolic power may be understood to apply to nuns in terms of the reciprocation for their religious services by supportive householders who donate their labor to construct buildings for the nuns and provide them with other material needs. In one sense, nuns are empowered when they receive what they need to continue their cultivation of *sila*. The freedom of nuns involves the ability both to engage in tactics that defy those who seek to jeopardize their religious practice and to sustain the practice itself. Such freedom, grounded in specific concrete instances of lives nuns live within a network of connections, does not convert to a universal normative category of female liberation from some oppressive power. More specifically, the very disruption of Metta's life, as difficult as it may have been, can be seen to have been part of the life of renunciation she lived. Had one intervened to empower her (in a liberal sense of the word), enabling her to fight for her "rights" to stay on the property (granting that she was not conversant about such matters), she would have been involved in a life she had after all renounced. That is how renunciation becomes freedom in the world of the nuns I studied.

Practices of Freedom

According to Saba Mahmood, freedom and agency need to be seen apart from the narrow binary opposition of "subordination and subversion." The question she asks in relation to Muslim women and their subjectivities is, "How do we analyze operations of power that construct different kinds of bodies, knowledges, and subjectivities whose trajectories do not follow the entelechy of liberal politics?" (14). Here she is interested in part in understanding how power, far from being opposed to religious practice, in fact makes such practice possible. I suggest considering the idea of empowerment of nuns in terms of their ongoing relationships with others as they pursue their renunciant practices. Those practices are inseparable from power relations involving family members, donors and supporters, and critics and adversaries. Such relations, though seemingly oppressive at times, ground the very renunciant lives they embody and live. Recall Foucault's remark that power is not opposed to freedom but rather power and freedom make each other possible (Abeysekara, *Politics* 188–189).

The story of Nanda and her many peregrinations provides clues about how we might reflect on a certain sense of empowerment among nuns.[13] It is a narrative about the freedom to practice renunciation as she saw fit. That freedom involved sustaining connections with family members while maintaining a mode of detachment from her places of residence. For her, what was important was not that she led an autonomous life away from family and householders but that she could engage in practices of *sila*. Nanda had wanted to be ordained as a *maniyo* when she was about five years old, even though she, like others, did not distinguish between a *bhikkhu* and a *sil maniyo* at that age.[14] She came from a large devout family of five brothers and four sisters, none of whom was happy when she began to train as a Ten-Precept nun at the age of seventeen. A cousin and an aunt paid the rent for her to live in a house with her *guru maniyo*, and she continued to remain there after her ordination (in the Ten Precepts) a few years later. After the demise of the *guru maniyo*, she relocated to an abandoned temple in a remote, nearly inaccessible area of the country. She was later invited to stay in a house with a female doctor. But because she preferred to live with monastics, she eventually accepted the land offer of a local government official who encouraged her to move to another area with the *podi maniyos* then under her tutelage. Although some of that land was owned by the official, the adjoining parcel belonged to her own sister. It was there in the early 1980s that I first met Nanda. Her tiny hilltop hermitage could only be reached after a walk of some distance across rice paddies. Since there was no plumbing at that hermitage, the nuns would carry water in buckets from a well at the bottom of the hill. At that time Nanda was still in close contact with her family members and was not interested in owning the land on which she lived. Her sister's daughter was one of her *golayas*, and because her own sister owned some of the land on which the hermitage was built, she and her *golayas* could purchase the land for a nominal price. But Nanda insisted that the deed not be made in her name: "I have no use for land," she told me. "My intention is to remove the suffering of samsara and realize nibbana." The land was deeded jointly to the *podi maniyos*. Nanda proceeded to develop her hermitage on the remote and rocky terrain where she lived. Her relatives helped her clear the jungle surrounding the hermitage and make it more habitable. Neighboring householders who had volunteered to help contributed less than had been promised, because, according to Nanda, a nearby monk, Tissa, objected to their supporting her. Nevertheless, she established a Buddhist Sunday school that was well attended—that is, until Tissa made it clear that the children should be attending his school instead. Afterward the number of children attending her school declined.

Nanda was willing to continue living where she was, despite the difficulties she encountered there. Eventually another, more spacious piece of land became available to her. At first, she was unwilling to move, despite the entreaties of her *podi maniyos*. "Why does one want so much land and property...? What we have here is enough," she told them. Her *podi maniyos* thought she was crazy. Nanda believed that Tissa was having someone recite *vas kavi* (black magic) to force her to leave the area. She felt that Tissa was jealous of what she was doing. Eventually she left to live on the new parcel of land, located in a less remote area. The possibility of having additional space to live in and more land on which to grow her own food without having to face the animosity of an interfering monk appealed to her: "One must have a place until one's last days... a small place where one can plant something.... I thought, 'If I could give the [other] place then to the monk, I would.'" For Nanda what was important was the freedom to pursue the life of renunciation and conduct religious services without hindrances. Although she had effectively purchased the land on which she and her *golayas* had lived and she had developed it with the support of family and community members, the monk's persistent antagonism finally persuaded her to move. She understood that the monk's opposition to her being there arose not because he considered her hermitage a marketable commodity but rather because he viewed her as a threat to what might be seen as his symbolic authority in the community. She refused to sell the land and hermitage that had been developed under her auspices, because, she said, "this would mean that I would be commercializing [vikuṇanava] the sasana [Buddhist dispensation]." In other words, her symbolic power (if one can call it that), grounded as it was in the land on which she lived, defied understanding in terms of a capitalist language of ownership and landholding. Moreover, in keeping both with her renunciant vocation and whatever influence she had earned in the neighborhood, Nanda wished to deflect the ill will of the neighboring monk: "That monk came with a householder and requested that I not give the aramaya (up there) to any other monks without his permission. The monk [the one who had been supposedly reciting vas kavi] asked me for the aramaya. Then, I signed over the aramaya to the monk and said he could do what he wants with it. Yes, it is to that monk that I eventually wrote the aramaya."

Nanda relocated to the new parcel of land in 1988. Since then she has repaired the dilapidated buildings, built a shrine reliquary (caitya or chaitya), and begun a Buddhist Sunday school with help from a government official as well as from individuals in the neighborhood. She has communicated with several other nuns in the area and participated in the government meetings for sil matas since their inception in 1983, once serving as a district representative of the National Sil Mata Organization. Nanda's story about her search for a renunciant life away from the household did not exclude her family. Her relations with her kin remained close, and her own niece was among the golayas she trained. In fact, family members were among her strongest supporters. Nanda's account indicates something important about the practices of empowerment and freedom among nuns: supported by her family, she found freedom in forsaking her own land for the sake of the practice of renunciation and sila. She signed it over to the very monk who opposed her. Needless to say, Nanda's story, much like that of Metta, does not square with liberal notions of freedom and equality. Indeed, her very "sacrifice" of such "rights" (if she was even aware of such rights in the first place) was paradoxically synonymous with her understanding of freedom. Freedom involved living a religious life centering on the symbolic power of Buddhist renunciation and the maintenance of an economy of religious relations with her supporters.

Economies of Relations between Nuns and Supporters

For nuns, living their renunciant everyday requires maintaining good relations with their supporters. Such relations enable nuns to lead a renunciant life, which might perhaps be translated into economic capital only when it is mediated through religious practice. With some risk, one may see such relations in terms of what Bourdieu calls an economy of "good faith"—exchanges built on the confidence that each contribution will be reciprocated over time. Although that economy may not characteristically involve a monetary exchange, it may possibly be translated into economic terms, for the "symbolic capital, which in the form of prestige and renown...is readily convertible back into economic capital, is perhaps *the most valuable form of accumulation*" (*Outline* 179; emphasis in original). The householders in a nunnery's neighborhood are often its main supporters; they donate their services, not only providing nuns with everyday necessities such as food, water, and transport but also helping build and repair their residences. But legal issues involving property ownership by nuns can complicate such relations. For example, nuns tend to avoid obtaining a deed to the land on which they live (something I often encouraged them to do), because holding a deed can change their relationships with neighbors and potentially compromise good relations with their donors. That tendency was evident in the accounts of the nuns Mettika and Sama Maniyo. Mettika had lived for decades at a hermitage that had been supported for generations by one family. The original donor members of that family had "given" the land to her *guru maniyo* without a title deed. The hermitage land shrank as the original donors died and parcels of land were reclaimed by later generations of their family for their own use. Because she had close ties to members of the donor family, who were also members of her own extended family and still her supporters, she had avoided obtaining a land deed from them. Attempting to obtain and possess one would have entailed entering into a type of contractual relationship that she deemed inappropriate. Whereas Mettika recognized the pitfalls of potentially relying on a legally binding contract at the expense of maintaining good relations with her lay supporters, the monks who encouraged Sama to leave her hermitage may have been more worried about losing symbolic capital.

Sama was a *maniyo* I first met in the early 1990s. Through much of that decade she was an active member of both the district and national *sil mata* organizations. Sama's relationship to the land on which she has lived has changed over time, partly perhaps because of my questioning her about it. Early in her life as a *sil mata*, she seemed indifferent to owning the land on which she lived, but as she grew older she began to think differently. When Sama was first ordained as a *sil mata*, she lived in a small community of twelve nuns in abandoned caves associated with a historic royal temple (*Rāja Mahā Vihāraya*). The monks who owned the temple helped her *guru maniyo* make the place habitable. They and neighboring householders welcomed the nuns' move to the area. The land on which the *sil matas* lived was leased land, which was to revert eventually to the temple. Sama recalled that it was not considered imperative that the *sil matas* leave their hermitage when the lease expired, but they nevertheless decided to do so. First, her *guru maniyo* departed to her hometown, leaving behind the junior *maniyos* to make their own decisions. "At that time [of the change in the lease]," Sama recalled, "I could have either stayed or left, is that not so? The head monk said that it was a good place.... But we knew that at some time we would be asked to leave.... So before we were asked to leave...we left." "But [the monk] did not tell you to leave?" I asked. Sama replied with the following account:

> It was in our minds that in the future we would be told to leave. So before that, we left happily, having given over the land together with all our things...all the things that we had had for sixteen years—that is, apart from the things in my room (the clothes, the cupboard, the bed)—apart from those things, we gave everything over. Then after that we made an offering of the place to the monks.... The head monk said that we should make an offering of it to the [monks there]. Then five [monks] came, and we did a *sāŋghika pūjā* [offering to the sangha] for that. At first, all we had had was a rock. It was we who had really constructed buildings and made that into a temple. Then, after about sixteen years, together with our *guru maniyo* and various [other] people working on it, this became a sizable temple.

In a somewhat amused manner she went on to describe the fanfare that took place when the offering was made to the monks:

> When I was getting ready to go [away] the monks said, "You cannot do that; you need to offer this as a *sanghika* offering."...So I offered it in a public procession [*perahära*]. It was [the monk's] own land. It was *his own* temple. Thinking that I might be angry, he

said that I could not just leave like that. I said that I just wanted
to leave, having handed it over to him. He said, "You cannot just
hand it over like that. You need to do a *perahera* and make an offering of it." So we did the *perahera* and made the offering to five
monks [laughing]....Then there was a celebration and a formal
offering of merit, and then the monk sent me here [to her current
hermitage]—in his own vehicle!

Sama's decision to leave the land belonging to the historic temple came
at about the time that a householder invited her to reside in a makeshift
hut that had been abandoned by another *maniyo* on a more remote hilltop. Nevertheless, the monks considered it necessary for the departing
sil matas to publicly demonstrate their willingness to leave the area. That
would benefit the monks insofar as the donors who had assisted the *sil
matas* for well over a decade would not be irritated by the monks who were
about to relocate there. Moreover, the monks would be ensured of the continued support of the householders in the neighborhood. In that instance,
the technical "legality" of the land's status was not in dispute; the land
clearly reverted to the monks. Yet legal title to the land was not enough.
Missing from the monks' mandate to use the land was the symbolic power
of the *goduragama* (literally "village-fodder," referring to the area from
which a monastic may obtain support). The concept of *goduragama* does
not fit neatly into a modern legal notion of rights. It is a notion of support defined by space—one in which householders provide regular donations to particular temples in a certain proximity to them. In practice that
means that monastics who dwell in temples outside a given *goduragama*
are not to perform religious services for householders associated with that
goduragama without the permission of the chief incumbent of the temple
in that *goduragama*. In that sense, one may say that Buddhist monastics
"earn" their livelihood through the religious example they set and the reputation they gain over time. The nuns were well liked and respected in the
area. The monks, averse to being viewed as responsible for the *maniyos'*
leaving, wished to maintain their own good reputation and continued support. They wanted neighbors and supporters to see them as recipients of
a donation from the departing *maniyos*, even though the *maniyos'* hermitage and the land on which it rested had legally been theirs and had
never legally been the *maniyos'* to give. The unmistakable recognition of
the monks' position in terms of the reassertion of their authority in the
goduragama involved staging a public ceremony in which the apparent

symbolic capital of the *maniyos* was essentially transferred to the monks who had owned the land in the first place.

When I initially discussed the matter with Sama, she was unclear about the status of the land of the new hermitage where she had eventually taken up residence together with a *podi maniyo* whom she had decided to train. At first she had not been particularly interested in learning more about the land on which she lived, and she had assumed that the state would simply grant her a deed. After further conversations, during which I persuaded her of the importance of securing a title for the land and asked her to consider the future interests of the *podi maniyo* living with her, Sama began to look into the matter. At the time of writing, I discovered that she, having visited both the offices of the Ministry of Buddha Sasana and the land registry in Colombo, had learned that the land on which her hermitage was built included three discrete parcels. The hermitage included two separate buildings, an exterior worship area by a *bo* tree, and a separate outdoor shrine. The exterior worship areas, one of which lay beside a big black rock, had been built on land belonging to a neighboring villager who owned an adjoining part of a bordering coconut estate. Unknown to Sama at the time, that piece of hermitage land had apparently been sold to yet another individual. A building used as a worship and meeting place stood on a second parcel of land that had been part of an unused pathway leading to a stream; that is, it was common land that legally belonged to the village. Finally, the buildings that included the living area of the nuns rested on state-owned land designated as "leased land." Apparently, it was Sama's duty to pay a monthly rent on that land (a duty she had been unaware of and was not in a position to honor). With some frustration Sama recounted her conversation with the land registrar:

> They [the land registry] said that either I should buy the land or else I should pay for it [as a lease]....To take money!...For this black rock! What is the income from this? We do not look at this for income; it is a *pūjanīya* [sacred] place....As long as I am here it is OK. But after that, once everything is built up, someone else could come and push [the *podi maniyo*] away, could they not? For that reason I should pay a lease.

Sama clearly wanted to remain outside the purview of monetary exchanges. Her interest was in maintaining a sacred area and cultivating her renunciant practice. Yet (partly at my instigation) she would consider protecting the future of her hermitage and the livelihood of her *podi maniyo*, though she still did not value her land as a monetary asset per se.

Mettika Maniyo's thoughts on her hermitage resonated with Sama's. Mettika, a *bhikkhuni* at the time of writing, lives in a hermitage on a steep hill. For several decades since its founding, the hermitage had no access to water, so the nuns would have to walk some distance downhill to wash and to fetch their water from the nearest well. At one time, when plans were initiated for constructing a road up the hill, monks living in the vicinity sought to prevent it. But their opposition was short-lived. Because the monks' temple also lacked water and they were unwilling to remain there, they soon abandoned their own temple. When I first met Mettika, she had no interest in obtaining the deed for the hermitage land that donors had offered to her *guru maniyo*. By the time of this writing (after several conversations I had had with her over the years), Mettika's hermitage had a secure deed, which was granted decades after the hermitage was founded by her *guru maniyo*, Nuwara, in 1953. Now the hermitage includes several brick structures, such as a dormitory with space for a dozen nuns, an audience hall for receiving *dana* and conducting discussions, as well as a *chaitya*, a *budugē*, and a *pōyagē*.[15] Mettika is currently constructing additional structures for worship in the area.

When Nuwara founded the hermitage, it had only two small huts. The Perera family, who originally gave the land to Nuwara, was distantly related to both Nuwara and Mettika. Their initial donation of land was never formalized legally. According to Mettika, Nuwara was happy to accept the offer and live there with her *podi maniyos*, and she was never concerned with formalizing the transfer of the deed. Mettika recalled that Nuwara had said, "If it is donated land, just donate it." When Mettika told me how the acreage originally offered to the hermitage shrank as the land was appropriated by later generations of the Perera family, she commented on the thoughts of her teacher nun: "Our *guru maniyo* did not think ahead, then, did she?"

As time passed, members of the Perera family decided to deed the land to Mettika in her name. But, although she was fully aware of the consequences of her own teacher's actions (perhaps in keeping with the Buddhist idea of *anatta* [no-self or no-soul]), Mettika hesitated to accept the deed in her name. "When [Perera] was going to write it to my name, I refused.... Yes, I refused, [partly] because I had not trained any *golayas*." Mettika, a modest and somewhat retiring nun, felt uncomfortable accepting property in her name, so she suggested that the land be deeded to another *maniyo* at the hermitage. The Pereras did not initially agree, but later they were prepared to compromise by giving the land to yet a third *maniyo* from the same hermitage. Negotiations on deeding the land ground to a sudden halt, however. When I asked Mettika why she did not probe the matter further, she said, "We do not encourage them after all [to write the deed], really.... I am not happy to ask them. If they are giving [the land], they should just give it." Mettika assured me that because the Pereras were a respected family in the area and also were distantly related to her, she had no concerns about the security of the land on which the hermitage was built. In the late '90s I came to believe that Mettika, like her *guru maniyo* before her, had no wish to formalize a contractual relationship with her donors. In conversation with her at the time, she suggested that such formalization would indicate a lack of trust in her relationship with the Pereras, her main donors. Perhaps as a result of my insistence, the Pereras finally deeded the land to Mettika and her lineage of nuns.

My interviews with the head nuns Mettika and Sama suggested that their lives of renunciation centered on running a hermitage, engaging in meditation, and providing social and religious services. Like Nanda, neither of those nuns thought of the land on which they dwelled as anything more than a space where they could live their renunciant lives. Such a "renunciant space" enables nuns to build networks of support in the neighborhood and ensure the security of a kind of symbolic capital. Note, however, that nuns neither *intend* to compete with others (householders or monks) for land nor strive to engage in some kind of struggle to compete with other monastics for symbolic power, *because* their renunciant lives rely on symbolic capital. For Mettika, Sama, and Nanda, obtaining legal ownership of land was not a concern, let alone a priority. Sumana Maniyo, to whom I turn next, understood the question of land somewhat differently. Sumana, unlike most nuns, was willing to appear in court to safeguard the interests of her nunnery. Although some might consider her to be competing for symbolic capital, a nuanced reading of the account below indicates differently.

Rites/"Rights" of Renunciation

Sumana is the only Sri Lankan nun I have known to use the terminology of rights (*ayitivāsikam*) vis-à-vis her land. But her notion of land ownership is more akin to that of the other nuns I have interviewed than it is to a liberal postulate of individual rights and private property. Sumana is one of the few nuns who has attempted to retain ownership of hermitage lands by defending her claims in court. At one time she was involved in five different court cases centering on different parcels of hermitage lands. Although one might be inclined to think of Sumana's attempt to retain her lands as an instance of how nuns employ secular ideas of rights, such thinking fails to account for the way her ritual practice is tied to her land. Unlike other nuns, such as Nanda and Mettika, her religious duties are inseparable from the precise physical location of her practice. Sumana resides near a pilgrimage center known for its shrines to gods (*devālayas*). She asserts that the gods inspired her to move there and claim parcels of land in the area. Her widespread reputation for healing the sick with the assistance of deities is rooted in the land on which she lives. According to the nuns living at her hermitage, visitors to the place are special individuals whose good karma has enabled them to go to the sacred land on which it is built. They also say that although Sumana is capable of healing the sick from afar, her healing is most effective for people who visit the hermitage itself.

When Sumana left her family to renounce as a nun, her youngest child was seven years old. Informants have given me different explanations for Sumana's decision to leave her husband and become a *sil mata*. Some claim that she left her husband because he had had an extra-marital affair. Another informant told me that she renounced in order to come to terms with the assassination of her brother, a JVP (Janatha Vimukti Peramuna [People's Liberation Front]) sympathizer.[16] Sumana herself maintained that she had left her family at the instigation of a god who directed her to meditate in a remote jungle. Relatives who had known her shortly before she had left her family indicated that her ability to communicate with the deities was unquestionable. According to them, those communications gave her special powers to know things that others could not. Reflecting on her departure, Sumana told me: "I thought that I had nothing, wanted nothing.... Then I came here and spent about three months meditating and cut my hair and wore the robes." Directed by a god, she sat under a *bo* tree in the forest and continued her meditation.

In time, Sumana attracted the attention of donors from distant areas of the country. Word of her healing powers spread as she ordained *podi maniyos* and continued to care for the sick. Supporters made a clearing in the jungle and erected buildings. Donors continued to contribute to the hermitage, and by the 1980s they had installed electricity and a pipeline for tap water. Despite that support, she faced difficulties during her early years at the hermitage. Neighboring monks and householders who collaborated with them caused her the most trouble. Prompted by a monk, a number of men began to vandalize the newly erected buildings of her hermitage. At that point a deity directed her to leave with her *golayas* and take up residence at an abandoned temple site deeper in the jungle. Soon thereafter a monk in the vicinity of her second (jungle) hermitage laid claim to the land there and lodged a court case against her. Sumana, determined to follow the instructions of the deity who had guided her there, refused to move. According to her and her *maniyos*, late one evening, eight men incited by the monk arrived at her new jungle abode and threatened to physically attack them. The men, who were clad only in loincloths, fled when a leopard miraculously appeared. One of them hastily draped himself in a nun's yellow robes that were hanging out to air, and then ran off with the others.[17] That was not the last time that individuals threatened to physically attack the *maniyos* or their renunciant abode. Sumana refused to relocate in response to the monk's threats and his litigation, which continued for almost twenty years. Her engagement with that litigation necessitated the payment of hefty lawyer's fees and long and difficult journeys to attend court hearings. While attending to the court case, Sumana returned to her original hermitage and continued to manage the second one for the *podi maniyos* who lived there. Upon later losing the court case to the monk and his pupils, she and her *golayas* eventually moved out. In time, a god directed her to start a branch hermitage in yet a third jungle area that was less remote. She built a new place to live and worship there while continuing to manage the original hermitage. Throughout the late 1980s and the 1990s Sumana's *golayas* resided at different hermitage sites under her direction. During that time she also reconnected with her then adult children, who have become her main supporters.

By the early 1990s donors had constructed more buildings at Sumana's original hermitage. These included several shrines, a wall surrounding the *bo* tree, additional dwellings for nuns, and huts to house visitors who sought assistance from Sumana. But during the post-election violence in 1994, the hermitage suffered a setback when villagers destroyed several buildings. Claiming that hermitage lands included a section of public land belonging to the village—namely, an old road that had fallen into desuetude—the villagers dug a pathway through her land, marking the place of the old road and thereby bisecting the hermitage. More court cases ensued. Sumana told me that she was aging (she was in her mid-seventies by then) and was tired of going to court. When I last visited her (about twenty-six years after my first visit), her original hermitage had changed drastically. Fewer nuns lived there. A new road had replaced the rough pathway that the villagers had once created and claimed, and the hermitage had been subdivided into three sections—each inhabited by at least one of the four nuns then residing at the hermitage and each surrounded by a high wall with gates that were locked every evening. Although the nuns slept separately in different buildings, they assembled when making daily offerings and performing religious services. In the evening they retired to their respective buildings and used cell phones to communicate when necessary. Unlike in previous years, the hermitage was now kept under lock and key. It was impossible to enter without prior notification.

Sumana, in explaining the difficulties she encountered, often compared her meager parcels of land with the extensive lands belonging to neighboring monks. Having come from a family that had been deeply involved in the JVP uprising during the early 1970s, she was familiar with a discourse of rights and equality. In addition, such a discourse had entered into the numerous legal battles she had fought. Nevertheless, she maintained that her claims to land ownership were based on the divine instructions she had received. Living on the land meant living her renunciant practice—communicating with the gods and curing the sick. Because many of her donors came from afar, the nuns at her hermitage recognized the need for land where they could grow their own food. As one of her *podi maniyos* told me in the mid-'90s, "It is important to have some land…to eat…especially when the *guru maniyo* is no more. What if someday we do not receive alms? We cannot rely on receiving alms all the time."

Religious fulfillment for Sumana and her *golayas* meant leading a renunciant life at a specific place defined by its connections with the gods. Sumana, like several other nuns I have known since the 1980s, emphasized cultivating meditative practices to the exclusion of acquiring a formal education. According to her, the latter detracts from the former. She actively discouraged her *podi maniyos* from engaging in the government-sponsored training for *sil matas* that began in the early 1980s, the kind of training that some might consider empowering in a secular sense. Although one might interpret Sumana's religious fulfillment in terms of a discourse of equality with male monastics and her supposedly acquiring ownership rights to property, we should note how she actually centered on a certain type of renunciant practice that was inseparable from the land on which she lived.[18]

Conclusion

Liberal juridical notions of freedom vis-à-vis female (renunciant) subjectivity conjure a teleology of emancipation based on oppositions such as freedom/domination, resistance/compliance, and autonomy/submission. Some have criticized such emancipatory frameworks as precluding understanding of how power relations produce and authorize religious subjectivity (Scott 70–90; Mahmood 148–152). One may argue that modern female renunciation among Sri Lankan Buddhists emerged because of transformations effected by colonial legislation—transformations that in one sense resulted in the increasing disinheritance and disempowerment of women. But it is not helpful to understand the lives of contemporary Buddhist nuns with reference to such oppositions alone. The constraints of *religious* practices in which nuns find themselves renouncing make—and "empower" (for want of a better word)—the lives they live. Those practices cannot be easily separated from power relations that involve, for example, questions of land ownership and family relationships. In turn, the idea of the higher ordination, perceived in terms of the status and recognition it supposedly affords, does not, as some think, take center stage in the world of such religious practices. By becoming renunciants, not only have women relinquished responsibilities that they might otherwise have assumed as householders, but they have turned the tables by rendering kinfolk morally responsible to them in new ways. In such networks of power, a nun's relations with a former spouse are typically attenuated if not severed, and relations with parents, children, extended family, and friends are altered so as to provide support to her as a renunciant who has renounced conventional family relations. That support, usually understood as generating positive karma and merit for donors, may either be given consistently throughout a renunciant's lifetime or become available when illness and old age prevent a nun's active participation in the everyday life of her renunciant community. Hence, nuns find themselves using "tactics" that enable them to lead the lives that make them female renunciants—lives that secular notions of empowerment, connected with ideas of rights and land ownership, fail to grasp.

The scholarly story of nuns' so called status has been based on a capitalist notion of "improving" the lives of "non-Western" women. Although Nanda, Mettika, Sama, and Sumana were to receive the *bhikkhuni* ordination in time, none of them talked to me about it as a means of resisting patriarchy or affirming rights of some kind. Sri Lankan nuns who do not articulate a liberal discourse are generally not interested in meanings of status vis-à-vis identities—meanings on which scholars tend to focus. Researchers seeking to find meaning in the lives of female renunciants must often find ways not just to understand but also to represent nuns' lives so as to empower the researchers' own pursuits. As Young herself acknowledges, empowerment is an idea that everybody in a democracy supports, yet "rarely do people mean the same thing by it," so one may pause to think of it not as a ready-made idea that corresponds to some life "out there" but in terms of what may be present in the lives of those who do not use such an idiom to describe the world in which they find themselves living. The lives of such individuals may shatter assumptions about the very conceptual moralistic divisions in terms of which the story of women's empowerment continues to be told.

8

Global Empowerment and the Renunciant Everyday

Introduction

In December 1988 five *sil matas* from Sri Lanka received a "Mahayana" higher ordination as *bhikṣuṇīs* (*bhikshunis*) at the Hsi Lai Temple in Los Angeles (Bartholomeusz 182). That event has since been remembered as a defining moment in the subsequent higher ordination of the Theravada *bhikkhuni*.[1] Yet what happened on that day was fraught with incongruity. The Sri Lankan *bhikshunis* returned home and discarded their *bhikshuni* robes, only to assume their previous attire—namely, the robes of Ten-Precept nuns. Those newly ordained *bhikshunis* continued to live their renunciant everyday as *sil matas* rather than as *bhikshunis*. In effect, their *bhikshuni* ordination made little difference to how they lived their renunciant lives.[2] Of greatest interest in this chapter is not so much how and why their ordination took place, or why they continued to live as *sil matas* rather than as *bhikshunis*, but rather that that *bhikshuni* ordination can still be touted as an inaugural event in the making of a certain kind of nun. The ideal of the higher ordained nun, framed with reference to liberal notions of equality and freedom, speaks to a global or transnational sisterhood of Buddhist nuns that has come to shape perceptions of female renunciants over the past several decades.[3] However, transnational ideals of renunciant sisterhood are the product of a Western project, with which nuns who do not speak in globalatinized ways have little concern.[4] The transnational debates about the *bhikkhuni* ordination have invoked comparisons between nuns in the Tibetan and Theravada lineages. Accordingly, I engage renunciants from those distinct lineages in order to better understand their own thinking about the higher ordination. Asian Tibetan *anis* who do not subscribe to Western ideals of nuns, like the *sil matas* encountered in the last chapter, focus more on cultivating their everyday renunciant practice than in pursuing the question of the higher ordination. In contrast, nuns who espouse a liberal politics tend to participate consistently in transnational networks that promote the higher ordination of nuns who belong to lineages in which the ordination is not yet recognized.

Academic and popular literature on the subject of female renunciants often assumes that recent debate on the higher ordination began in 1987 with the founding conference of the Sakyadhita International Association of Buddhist Women (SIABW) in Bodhgaya, India, and its subsequent conferences (Jutima; Le Vine and Gellner 178–181; Tsomo, *Bridging Worlds* 4–9). Although that assumption may be disputed, because other, less-publicized discussions were held on the subject earlier,[5] the SIABW conferences linked female renunciants' empowerment to their access to the higher ordination. At the inaugural conference, members decided that SIABW should focus on the "fostering of an international Buddhist sisterhood" and would "assist women who wish to obtain ordination and [to]...work towards establishing full ordination for Buddhist women in countries where it is not currently available" ("First International Conference" 36). Mavis Fenn and Kay Kopperdrayer, in their research article "Sakyadhita: A Transnational Gathering Place for Buddhist Women," assess that conference and note that participants sought to "continue to promote the empowerment of Buddhist women" (49). The global discourses that SIABW has nurtured have continued to enjoy widespread publicity through the organization's transnational conferences (held approximately every two years), book-length publications, and, since the popularization of cyberspace webs of communication, new forms of interaction. The electronic communications available through access to such resources as Web sites, Facebook, Twitter, and blogs are reinforced at transnational conferences such as the International Congress on Buddhist Women's Role in the Sangha: Bhikshuni Vinaya and Ordination Lineages (ICBW) held in 2007 in Hamburg, Germany, and also serve to perpetuate a debate whose terminology is couched in a discourse promoting equality, rights, and global sisterhood. On the one hand, differences between Buddhist practitioners are celebrated in the name of multiculturalism and pluralism. On the other, the identity of *the* female renunciant in Buddhism is universalized and her supposed empowerment is conceptualized in terms of her acquiring access to the higher ordination and material resources.[6] Recognition of the new discursive space centering on the higher ordination helps us understand how the *need* for a specific type of empowerment of female renunciants, while not recognized universally by Buddhist nuns, has become a universalized shibboleth.

It would be inappropriate to maintain a strict (and arguably Orientalist) distinction between Western, Anglo, or European monastics and Eastern or Asian monastics in the ways they think about the higher ordination of nuns.[7] Buddhist monastics of Asian descent have established missions outside their countries of origin and those of European, Australian, or African descent may likewise live anywhere in the world. What seems most noteworthy in debates about the higher ordination is the language in which notions of rights and equality are couched. Such language might be used by monastics anywhere, although, at the time of writing, it seems to be most commonly employed by those of Western origin. In transnational forums about the higher ordination, such language has typically emphasized the construction of an idealized female renunciant, who, though enjoying the ideal status of *bhikkhuni*-hood, is essentially disembodied. By the disembodiment of the *bhikkhuni* ideal I do not mean an apparently abstract ideal, such as the liberal citizen, which *in fact* has a distinct male identity (Hekman 6). Rather, I refer to a vision of an idealized female renunciant whose identity is informed by Buddhist textual precedents and hence to a vision that conceals the renunciant everyday of contemporary nuns who do not speak in such a manner.[8] Although this disembodied *bhikkhuni* may appear "different" according to the various textual traditions through which she is construed, she effectively represents a homogenous ideal that evokes the egalitarian vision of a sisterhood among Buddhist nuns across the globe. It is the effective erasure of the lived life of renunciants—that is, their renunciant everyday—that permits the creation of an ideal that can, at least theoretically, be instantiated by *all* nuns.

Engaging Renunciant Sisterhood

In her work, Chandra T. Mohanty critiques the characterization of women's condition as globally homogenous. She states that such a characterization can involve an "assumption of women as a unified group on the basis of secondary sociological universals. What binds women together is an ahistorical notion of the sameness of their oppression and, consequently, the sameness of their struggles" (112).[9] Mohanty's comments are relevant to understanding the debates about the higher ordination that pervade transnational conferences, which assume a homogeneity of perspective in defining the putative "struggles" of nuns in terms of an idea of empowerment and a global feminism. Mohanty indicates that global feminism reflects biases rooted in the middle-class origins of its foremost exponents: "Universal sisterhood, defined as the transcendence of the 'male' world, thus ends up being a middle-class, psychologized notion that effectively erases material and ideological power differences within and among groups of women, especially between First and Third World women" (116). Practitioners acknowledge the material differences between Buddhist women in the transnational spaces that serve as a venue for promoting their so-called empowerment, and those differences are necessarily embedded in a developmental discourse that reifies a first-world/ third-world difference within which the image of the impoverished and indigent Asian nun is depicted. Transnational venues effectively serve to perpetuate economic differences.[10] The liberal feminism that dominates such venues portrays female renunciants as exemplars of a global sisterhood of nuns while ignoring other important distinctions. That assertion of an apparent homogeneity among nuns cannot be easily separated from the need to affirm some kind of equality and justice as the shared ideals of a global sisterhood. As Wendy Brown notes, "in liberalism, injustice occurs when those considered the same are treated differently; but ontological difference is a problem outside the purview of justice" (153).[11] Liberal feminist rhetoric places nuns in a position of having to seek gender equality in the higher ordination. Because equality is intrinsically "desirable," the higher ordination *must* be supported, as if by law. Meanwhile, renunciants who ignore the putative issue at hand or contest its desirability are, ipso facto, "uneducated," "incorrect," or simply "dumb."

As Foucault and others have indicated, concepts of power correlate with specific notions of subjectivity and identity. The subjectivity of the fully ordained *bhikkhuni* becomes distinguishable against the backdrop of the renunciant who has not received the full ordination. The distinction between the fully ordained nun and one who has received a different ordination (in that it is not a *bhikkhuni* ordination, as in the case of *sil matas* in Sri Lanka, *mae chis* in Thailand, and *thilashins* in Myanmar) surfaces particularly in transnational forums promoting the *bhikkhuni* ideal. Espousing the full ordination becomes a struggle in liberalism's overarching advocacy of a subject defined in terms of its claim to human rights and equality. In such a definition, we know how power, equated with oppression, comes to be seen as something external to a seemingly essential human quality like equality. Aurelia Armstrong, interpreting

Slavoj Zizek's work, discusses a relationship between subjectivity, power, and colonial domination which is relevant to understanding the discourse about *bhikkhuni* ordination. Armstrong points out that for Zizek, the notion of struggle against domination entails the reification of a specific (national or oppressed) identity vis-à-vis the oppressor. That identity (produced by oppression) and the resistance that accompanies it become possible only because they "are in fact generated by the situation of oppression" (20). In this case, of the *bhikkhuni*, the liberating identity that is sought in terms of the *upasampada*, accompanied by the purported struggle to realize it, is shaped by a dynamic of oppression or inequality. The very postulation of that dynamic reinforces a politics of domination. Hence, for those seeking the higher ordination, the category of the *unordained* nun becomes a desideratum, as if necessitated and mandated by some (unquestionable and unexplainable) *law*.[12] That category provides a platform from which the higher ordination can be desired and sought. In an ironic way, that category also comes to serve as a tool of domination—further reifying the distinction between those who seek the *upasampada* and those who, for whatever reason, do not, will not, or cannot. As Asad notes, here what we see is the "intrusiveness" of Western power that involves the "reshaping of the social spaces in which distinctive kinds of struggle now take place" ("Comment" 37).[13] It is perhaps not coincidental that the female renunciants most vocal in promoting the higher ordination tend to be those who have already received it (albeit not necessarily from their particular lineage or school of Buddhism).[14] The presumption about a *need* for the higher ordination to gain equality is anchored in a (colonial) discourse that affirms not only an "otherness" but also a certain unquestioned relationship between equality and inequality. In other words, the liberal logic that feminists use to think of universal equality is already subsumed under a "difference." Many seem to ignore this logic when they appeal to equality vis-à-vis nuns' identity. Equality as some think of it—as an autonomous universal human quality to be achieved—is not possible. We find this problem precisely in the correlation feminist scholars construct between choice and higher ordination. That is, nuns must make a choice to gain higher ordination as a way of gaining equality. There is something attractive yet deceptive in this correlation between choice and equality. This is what Abeysekara notes when he says "We may not all be equal, but we become equal in our *ability* to choose! Better yet, *inequality becomes equality in choice!*" ("Sri Lanka" 228; emphasis in original).

The emergence of transnational networks supporting the higher ordination has effectively blurred perceptions of distinctions between nuns hailing from Theravada and Tibetan lineages.[15] In fact, the predominant scholars and practitioners participating in such networks often understand the traditions as equivalent and comparable.[16] Although considering "Tibetan" and "Theravada" as discrete lineages proves problematic in principle, because each incorporates different monastic lineages and disciplinary practices, the comparison of the two has tended to dominate recent transnational discussions about the higher ordination. In fact, what is most often meant by "Tibetan" Buddhism in such contexts is predominantly a Buddhism of the *dGe-lugs-pa* sect, headed by the Dalai Lama, whereas "Theravada" refers more generally to a Buddhism associated with the authority of Pali texts. Despite the vastly divergent histories of those seemingly discrete and identifiable lineages, "Theravada" and "Tibetan" are, for purposes of rhetoric promoting the higher ordination, basically "comparable" and *equivalent* lineages. They are considered separate because they are grounded in different textual and ritual practices, yet equivalent, because they have supposedly shared comparable challenges in promoting the full ordination for women. The seemingly innocuous equivalence of the Theravada and Tibetan lineages has been explicitly recognized by SIABW. Here, there is purportedly little that all nuns, seen as equal inheritors of the legacy of the founding *bhikkhuni* and foster mother/aunt of the Buddha, Mahapajapati Gotami, do not share. The cultural legerdemain of translating difference into corresponding equivalences emerges as a trope in an ongoing liberal feminist chronicle of liberation.[17]

Tibetan and Theravada Buddhism constitute distinctive textual and historical traditions and reflect divergent slants on state power as well as monastic authority. First, the religious specificities and state infrastructure that shape certain deliberations on the higher ordination of Tibetan nuns differ from those in which Theravada nuns engage. Many Tibetan monastics of Asian origin, unlike most Theravada renunciants from Asia, live in exile. Such Tibetan monastics, though living in exile in various countries, acknowledge the political and religious authority of the Dalai Lama and thus have a central figure to whom they may turn.[18] Those who do not acknowledge the Dalai Lama as their main religious authority tend to look to the authority of another leader. On the other hand, Theravada monastics involved in the ordination discussions belong to more-diversified and decentralized ordination lineages. Second, Tibetan Buddhists, like Theravada Buddhists, might find precedent for the higher ordination of nuns in their (Mūlasarvāstivādin) *vinaya* texts, but, unlike Theravada Buddhists, they cannot make a claim to a *historical* lineage of fully ordained nuns (*dge slong mas* or *gelongmas*). Moreover, since the establishment of the leadership of the Dalai Lama arose relatively late in the history of Buddhism, and that leadership is absent in canonical texts, there are added (and different) complications in relation to the question of the higher ordination of nuns in Tibetan Buddhism. As the Dalai Lama himself once observed, there was no Dalai Lama present when *bhikkhunis* were first ordained (Bstan -'dzin-rgya-mtsho, "Comments").Whereas Theravada nuns might differ from one another in understanding their histories (for example, practitioners in Sri Lanka, unlike those in Thailand, may boast a seemingly long and continuous history of *bhikkhunis* in their country), Tibetan nuns, who simply do not have a comparable history, do not have comparable narratives.

Scholarship on contemporary Buddhist nuns of Tibetan and Theravada lineages—in keeping with the goals of practitioners participating in transnational discussions—often introduces a textual narrative of the higher ordination as a backdrop to the story of contemporary nuns (Bartholomeusz; Cheng, *Buddhist Nuns*; Gutschow; Havnevik). In so doing, such scholarship sets the stage for a seemingly normative but effectively strange incongruity between the apparent egalitarianism pronounced by the Buddha and the purported subordination of nuns today. Such studies, being somewhat oblivious to how the histories of contemporary nuns may not resonate with the narratives about Mahapajapati Gotami, tend to perpetrate a static view of unchanging textual pasts while also reinforcing ways in which the modern impoverished (usually Asian) nun is defined vis-à-vis a struggle against male domination, within both the contemporary family unit and Buddhist monastic structures. More important, that approach tends to rely on an inadequate understanding of how the lived lives of contemporary female renunciants correlate with their putative counterparts in texts. I suggest that texts not be considered readily available for the translation of the lives of nuns in terms of desired ideals from which subjects have fallen. Edward Said argued long ago that the idea that "the modern Orientals were degraded remnants of a former greatness" (233) and that the static depiction of the Orientals' past intrinsic to the construction of a panoptic vision of the Orient were concomitant with the apparent superiority of scientific specialization and the ability to generalize broadly on all "Orientals" (233–239). Transnational forums about Buddhist nuns have become heir to that kind of thinking.

Discourse and "Empowerment"

Discourses about the supposed empowerment of Buddhist nuns postulate a collective identity for all female Buddhist renunciants who desire (or at least *should* desire) higher ordination.[19] That kind of discourse, which emerges from transnational forums, may have been produced with the best of intentions, but it has an underlying universalist "civilizational" mission in which the language of human rights, egalitarianism, and Buddhist "equivalence" renders some female renunciants—those who do not have, or do not wish to take, the higher ordination—less equal than others.[20] Importing the idiom of rights and equality provides prescriptions for living a renunciant "life" that cannot otherwise be lived on its own terms.[21] Practitioners who are unprepared—in so many senses—to embody discourses couched in such an idiom become, by such standards, renunciants with nothing to say.[22]

Karma Lekshe Tsomo, an American-born nun of Tibetan Buddhist lineage and a founding figure of SIABW, articulates that idiom in the preface to *Sisters in Solitude*: "Despite serious educational and economic disadvantages, Buddhist women in Asia, both lay and ordained, are becoming increasingly aware of their spiritual and social worth. In this fertile climate of awakening feminist consciousness, fostered through continual networking, publications, discussion and conferences, the potential exists for reinstituting an order of fully ordained nuns in all Buddhist countries"(xi). Among other things, Tsomo, who assumes that a "feminist consciousness" is increasingly prevalent among "Buddhist women in Asia," suggests the *desirability* of the goal of establishing the higher ordination "in all Buddhist countries." Moreover, the "fully ordained nuns," who implicitly transcend the "educational and economic disadvantages" that Asian women face, represent liberalism's disembodied ideal, which speaks to the "spiritual and social worth" of *all* women and is recognized by those who gain access to the seemingly boundless transnational spaces of "continual networking, publications, discussion and conferences." That same ideal purportedly facilitates the "correct" way of thinking about renunciants (and women) in Buddhism. In other words, Asian Buddhist women depicted as having limited access to educational and economic resources are once again in need of succor.

We find that kind of rhetoric in the work of other participants in SIABW conferences—among them, Thea Mohr, who has published a book about SIABW: *Weibliche Identität und Leerheit: Eine ideengischichtliche*

Rekonstruktion der Buddhisthischen Frauenbewegung Sakyadhītā International.
In a 2004 publication of the collected papers of the seventh Sakyadhita
conference (Taiwan, 2002), Mohr asserts that "the focus of these [SIABW]
gatherings of Western and Asian women is the demand for freedom—
freedom based on the achievements of both traditions" ("Sakyadhita"
22). She proceeds to explain that "secular self-determination consciousness characterizes Western Buddhists, whereas sacred self-determination
consciousness marks the Buddhist traditions" ("Sakyadhita" 22). The way
she distinguishes contemporary "Western Buddhists" from "the Buddhist
traditions" is significant. According to Mohr's study, the former express a
feminism that "developed in opposition to canonical [Greek and Christian]
texts" (23). That legacy, she claims, has resulted in a "self-determined consciousness in the West…which is consciously or subconsciously present in all Western women" (23), whereas the "sacred self-determination
consciousness" of Asians Buddhists is rooted in ideas such as "no-self
(*anātman*) and emptiness (*śūnyatā*)" (24). Most important, according
to Mohr, those Buddhist concepts and the texts that articulate them are
perceived as resources that aid Western Buddhist women in finding an
alternative identity, whereas the present situation of Asian women is such
that "the details of the teachings seem to be difficult to study, because the
administration of Buddhist knowledge and teachings is in the hands of
androcratic/male authorities" (24). In other words, a yoking of Buddhist
pasts and doctrines with secular Western feminism promotes the realization of modern liberal ideals for Western Buddhists, whereas in Asia,
women engaging the same Buddhist doctrines are limited by an institutional patriarchy. Setting aside the problematic of the seemingly clear-cut
distinction between sacred and secular implicit in Mohr's work,[23] my
main concern here is that the analytical categories she uses assume an
appropriation and commodification of a bygone Buddhist past that can
best be recovered with the assistance of *Western* Buddhists, and (implicitly) on their terms. Because male dominance pervades societies in Asia
today—unlike those of the West, where women have been successful in
challenging it—and the egalitarianism of the Buddha has essentially been
forgotten:

in order to obtain proper access to the contents and meanings of the
[Buddhist] teachings, Asian Buddhist women might make use of
the achievements of the West. The successful resistance of Western
women to patriarchal infringement and androcratic exertion of

power may provide inspiration for Asian women to succeed in their
demands for the transmission of teachings. (24)

In other words, the West can learn from Buddhism an "emancipation that
can be helpful for achieving personal integration" (25). Additionally, "the
mutual questioning and analysis of each other's traditions" at Sakyadhita
conferences is useful (25). But that "mutual questioning," though it
erases differences between Buddhist renunciants in the name of a global
sisterhood, is grounded in these self-same differences. Mohr's account,
attempting to affirm specific norms, suggests that the re-establishment
of the nuns' order in Buddhism is considered a "basic human right" for
"traditional female Buddhists" (26).[24] Her account reinforces the ideology of a new type of Western Buddhist imperialism. Mohr goes on to
claim that the SIABW conferences "are part of a global women's movement that is inspiring discussions of gender democracy in both Asia
and the West" (28), and she suggests that the power to do that lies in
the hands of "women from Western cultural backgrounds...*who can
reevaluate the Buddhist teachings,*" in contrast to "women from traditional
Buddhist backgrounds *who are challenged to transmit the teachings*" (28;
emphasis added). Although women of Western cultural backgrounds are
privileged in their access to Buddhist teachings, other Buddhist women
remain challenged and in need of assistance. Such thinking about
Buddhism was also clearly evident in the film *Women and the Buddha
Potential* (directed by Babeth VanLoo) and dominated the ICBW held in
Hamburg in 2007.

The first ICBW was organized by the Studienstiftung für Buddhismus
(Foundation for Buddhist Studies) in cooperation with the Asia-Africa
Institute of the University of Hamburg and enjoyed the sponsorship of
several institutions, based largely in Germany. Jampa Tsedroen (Carola
Roloff), a German-born Tibetan Buddhist nun, played a key role in organizing the congress. Tsedroen was also involved in the Vinaya Research
Committee, established in 1987 in the wake of the first Sakyadhita conference, which addressed, among other things, the possibility of promoting the higher ordination for Tibetan nuns.[25] The congress was held in
response to the Dalai Lama's recommendation that the question of the
higher ordination for Tibetan Buddhist nuns be part of a global discussion: "We Tibetans alone can't decide this. Rather, it should be decided in
collaboration with Buddhists from all over the world" ("Background and
Objectives"). The congress literature stated that a main objective was "to

elicit a statement from His Holiness the Dalai Lama declaring *that and how* the Bhikshuni lineage *will* be established in the Tibetan tradition"[26] (emphasis added). Such a declamation is perhaps surprising, given that only a few months earlier, the Dalai Lama, speaking at Smith College in Massachusetts, had demurred in giving an opinion on the *appropriateness* of the establishment of such a lineage, saying that he did not have the "authority" or the "right" to support a particular stance on it and that it was "out of [his] control" (Bstan-'dzin-rgya-mtsho, "Comments"). *That* the ordination was desirable was not an issue for the organizers of the conference; it was assumed to be such. *How* it was to be implemented was their focus. In keeping with the recommendations made by the Dalai Lama, monastics, practitioners, and scholars of Buddhist monasticism from around the world were invited to participate, present formal papers, and lead discussions about female renunciant histories, contemporary practices, and ordination lineages in different Buddhist traditions.

At the ICBW in Hamburg, organizers and many participants hoped to achieve a consensus on how best to implement the higher ordination of Tibetan nuns, in accord with suitable Tibetan monastic regulations from among the various alternatives that had been forwarded.[27] A discussion took place on the evening of the second day of the conference, which preceded the final day's session that the Dalai Lama attended. What follows in the next few pages includes my direct observations and an analysis of what transpired that evening. The discussion focused on the possibility of having Tibetan monks following the Mulasarvastivadin (Tibetan) *Vinaya* officiate at a higher ordination of Tibetan nuns in a "single ordination ceremony" or, alternatively, having *bhikkhunis* ordained in the Dharmaguptaka lineage associated with China also participate in what would be a "dual ordination ceremony." Although the latter ordination would involve a certain "mixing" of lineages that have noticeably different rules and procedures, it would include the participation of *bhikkhunis*. That dual ordination seemed preferable to some monastics. The burning issue throughout the session became not so much which of the options for ordination was preferable but whether the higher ordination was desirable at all. In the course of the evening, the very rationale of the conference itself was questioned. What was most remarkable about the session was the yawning divide evident between Tibetan nuns of Asian origin who were not governed by globalatinized ways of speaking and other Buddhist monastic practitioners who were. The latter were mostly of Western origin. The former were effectively denied a voice. At that session the issue of translation became central both literally and metaphorically. Whereas some of the other congress sessions had been simultaneously translated into multiple languages, the proceedings of that evening were not.

The question of "voice" became central at the evening session. At the conclusion one Western Tibetan nun stated that the congress had gone to much trouble to "unsilence the voices of the [Asian] Tibetan nuns." Her comment—spoken to end the session by having the Asian Tibetan nuns come to a clear consensus—assumed that the question of the higher ordination was a concern of those Tibetan nuns. It also implied that the organizers of the conference *could* "unsilence" them. Paradoxically, that evening the voices of non-English-speaking Asian monastics who were Tibetan Buddhists could be heard by English speakers only when conference participants volunteered to translate.[28] During that session Tibetan nuns of Asian origin stated their misgivings about the very idiom in which the higher ordination was being spoken; they raised questions about the intentions of the organizers of the conference. Diverging concerns about the conference—voiced by Tibetan renunciants of Asian origin, on the one hand, and by participants of Western origin, on the other—seemed grounded in the latter's focus on how best to implement the higher ordination for Tibetan nuns, and the former's questioning of the very "need" for the ordination. One Asian Tibetan nun suggested at the outset that discussion about ordination be more geared toward practice of the *dharma* and service to humanity than to addressing concerns about rights, discrimination, and subordination or a lack thereof. Another Asian Tibetan nun voiced the same concerns, objecting to the proceedings' focus on the meaning of "equality and inequality" rather than on concerns about lineage. A woman of Western origin (who was not robed in monastic attire) retorted that the Tibetan nuns did not appreciate the "opportunity" being presented to them at the conference, noting that many people had spent a lot of money to attend and that the Tibetan nuns should not just "throw it away." She voiced frustration that the Asian Tibetan nuns were temporizing. Implying that their approval of the higher ordination was even more necessary because of the financial outlay for the conference, she attempted to pressure the nuns into forming a consensus and approving a higher ordination. The response from an Asian Tibetan nun was telling. She argued that the Tibetan nuns from Asia were concerned more about the contemplation of the teaching and receiving alms and training on a regular basis than about who was bringing the ordination to them and from where. She added that the worry of Tibetan nuns was more fundamental:

adequate food and access to a basic training. "We are not ready yet," she said. She was met with a reiteration of the suggestion that the nuns not "throw it away." The proceedings that evening were dampened by dissatisfaction, if not acrimony. *Vinaya* scholars and some Tibetan monastics seemed to agree that the best option for implementing the ordination was to promote a single ordination procedure conferred on nuns by Tibetan monks alone—that is, an ordination in the Mulasarvastivadin lineage rather than a dual ordination including monastics of the Dharmaguptaka lineage.[29] An individual of Tibetan origin affirmed this saying: "It is not that we do not like Dharmagupta[ka], but we like Mulasarvastivadin better." By that statement, the individual was perhaps indicating a sensitivity to the deeper political divide concerning the Tibetans' relationship with China. The Dharmaguptaka lineage is associated with *bhikkhunis* residing in China and is often referred to as the "Chinese lineage." It is self-evident to some that Asian Tibetan monastics living in exile might prefer to avoid associating with the Chinese lineage. However, for others, the debate about ordination lineages (which focused on differences in *vinaya* regulations and practices) simply ignored the question of political tensions between China and Tibet.

During the session, several individuals attempted to persuade Asian Tibetan nuns to support the higher ordination. A Western Tibetan monastic reminded everyone that it was the Dalai Lama himself who wanted Western nuns to make the question of the higher ordination a focus of international attention. A Tibetan nun of Western origin implored the dissenting nuns to support the "right" to the higher ordination, even though they themselves demurred.[30] A Tibetan monk of Western origin noted that because there was a fundamental divide between "East and West," even though the Western Tibetan nuns might want Asian Tibetan nuns to have the higher ordination, they should "not impose it on them if it was unsuitable." Echoing those words, a Western Buddhist nun suggested that the focus on gender was misplaced, and another observed that Asian Tibetan nuns "recoil from the language of human rights" and that the higher ordination was not about "demands" but rather (following the wording in ordination rituals) about requests to be "raised up" out of compassion.[31] An Asian Tibetan monk addressed the audience at length in Tibetan. That speech was followed by laughter when a volunteer translator, having taken the microphone, hesitated and then rendered the protracted speech into English. What seemed evident in the English translation was that the Asian Tibetan monk was trying to reconcile the articulations of the Tibetan nuns of Western origin with those of Tibetan nuns of Asian origin. Addressing the Asian Tibetan nuns, he implored them to agree to the idea of the higher ordination in order to make available to other Tibetan nuns a "choice" so that the Dalai Lama and senior Tibetan monastics could come to a consensus about the matter.[32] A silence ensued. Eventually, a scholar of Western origin (obviously trying to draw things to a hurried conclusion) asserted—much to my amazement—that it was quite evident that everyone there did support the *bhikkhuni* ordination in the Mulasarvastavadin tradition (rather than the dual ordination). There was then a short discussion of how a summary statement would be presented to the Dalai Lama the following day and a peremptory attempt to take a vote in support of the higher ordination with a show of hands. At that point, several Asian Tibetan nuns "voted" by leaving the conference hall. A moderator quickly declared the evening session closed.

The deliberations that evening appeared to have surprised as well as discomfited many participants. Some thought that the Asian Tibetan nuns who spoke out that evening had not been officially delegated to do so.[33] The dissension expressed by Asian Tibetan monastics at the Thursday evening session had been met with both alarm and condescension when a scholar of Western origin remarked, "Even though it is not part of the program, it is very interesting to hear the Tibetan nuns speak. Tibetan nuns are saying different things."[34] The scholar added that it seemed "reasonable" that some nuns should want to take ordination and not others. Those words were greeted with loud applause from the participants, as though it were a good thing (after all) that Tibetan nuns, who were not "officially" on the program, spoke freely, and that there was no need for them to seek the higher ordination if they did not want it. However, when those words were translated into Tibetan, they were met with silence.[35]

Transnational forums geared toward instituting the higher ordination of Tibetan nuns are not new. The Dalai Lama has "personally" stated that "if an authentic *bhikshuni* lineage [such as the Chinese lineage] could be established within the Tibetan tradition, this would truly be something to be welcomed" (Bstan-'dzin-rgya-mtsho, "Opening Speech" 44). Not only has he supported researching the question of the higher ordination of Tibetan nuns, but he has also not discouraged those who wish to do so from receiving the higher ordination from outside their own lineage. Nevertheless, the Hamburg conference broke new ground by focusing on the higher ordination while also ostensibly including the participation of Asian Tibetan nuns for the first time in a public setting.

But the predominant language of the conference had little relevance to the practice of those nuns. Western Tibetan monastics who sought the ordination wished to include Asian Tibetan nuns on whose heritage they drew; the support of those nuns could not be excluded. Nevertheless, it was. Earlier in the conference, an Asian Tibetan nun had conveyed to me with some dismay that in her country of residence (in Asia) the Tibetan nuns did not even know about the ICBW. Her point was that the Tibetan nuns with whom she associated had more immediate concerns. The difference between the predominantly Western Tibetan nuns who had spoken in a globalatinized idiom and Asian nuns who did not was affirmed in the comments of another Asian nun (also living in Asia), who told me that it was hard to understand why some Tibetan nuns of Western origin were stumping so hard for the ordination in the Tibetan lineage, because many of them had already received the higher ordination in another Buddhist tradition.[36]

The following day's session featured a panel comprised of select Buddhist monastics from different lineages. The members of the panel, including monastics of both Asian and Western origin, suggested procedures to implement the higher ordination for women in Tibetan Buddhism. But the Dalai Lama, much to the dismay of many present that day, demurred from (or evaded) making the firm commitment to the higher ordination that the conference organizers were expecting. What is most important for the purposes of this study is not the Dalai Lama's position on the higher ordination nor whether he was pronouncing a clear decision about it. What is of note are the relations of power involved in the proceedings of the formal and informal sessions at the conference, and, in particular, the language that guided the conversations about the higher ordinations, as well as the cultural translation (or lack thereof) that ensued.[37] In the English idiom, there appears to have been a focus on furthering gender equality among Buddhist monastics. Yet the conversations were embedded in a problematic cultural translation of the issues—a translation that ignored the asymmetrical relations of power among the renunciants involved.

Although the congress focused on promoting the higher ordination of nuns in Tibetan lineages, it is noteworthy that only one Asian Tibetan nun formally presented a paper supporting the higher ordination. Moreover, the voices of dissenting Asian Tibetan nuns were not even heard (for whatever reason) until the late evening session prior to the final day, when the Dalai Lama was to be present. Additionally, when those Asian Tibetan nuns did speak, many other participants did not (or would not) hear them. The capacity to organize, sponsor, and hold the international congress in Hamburg, as well as the authority to give and select paper presentations, lay in the hands of a select few. As is well known, the determination of panels and paper presenters at conferences is hardly arbitrary. On one level, the focus on "roles" and representations of Tibetan monastic identity that dominated the conference, coupled with the reluctance of Asian Tibetan monastics to engage those ideas, indicates participants' differing attitudes to the meaning of renunciant practice.[38] On another level, the reticence of the Asian nuns suggests a flat refusal to traffic in a particular cultural translation of their renunciant lives. To claim that the nuns were being "unsilenced" assumes not only that they needed to speak on their own behalf but also that they should speak in the idiom that prevailed at the congress. But when the Asian Tibetan nuns were put in the position of speaking about the ordination, they spoke of other concerns.[39] The tensions that emerged at the congress underscored the existence of deep divisions between practitioners (and scholars). Those tensions, also present among Tibetan and Theravada nuns in other transnational spaces, are discussed next.

Tibetan Transnationalisms, Theravada Ordinations, and the Renunciant Everyday

Although some Tibetan nuns of Western origin talk about the introduction of a higher ordination for Tibetan nuns in the language of equality and freedom, Asian Tibetan nuns I have conversed with speak about it differently. In the late 1990s I discussed the question of the higher ordination with Tibetan *anis* from Nepal who were visiting the United States. They claimed that the Dalai Lama did not favor establishing the higher ordination, so they had little interest in it. About ten years later, I interviewed Tibetan *anis* living in India about the higher ordination. They evinced a similar dearth of enthusiasm, suggesting that if their (male) teachers favored the higher ordination, they would be willing to receive it. One of them said that the matter had caused considerable "fighting" among Tibetan monastics—a dispute in which she wanted no part. In fact, the *anis* treated the question with disdain and levity; it was not something that they wished to pursue seriously.[40]

Some of the Tibetan nuns I interviewed lived at a nunnery established as part of a transnational project to "revive" Buddhism in Mongolia. Mongolia, a formerly communist country, was undergoing significant changes in political infrastructure in the early 1990s that transformed the government's attitude to established religion.[41] The nunnery I visited in Mongolia publicly evoked the restoration of (Tibetan) Buddhism in Mongolia to the outside world—a Buddhism that some now perceive as dangerously moribund. Interestingly, the non-Mongolian Asian *anis* I interviewed who were living at the nunnery had not sought to leave their home hermitages in Asia; their senior male teachers had "decided" for them. Their positioning in a global or transnational program did little (if anything) to allow them to make and effectively carry out their own decisions. They went to Mongolia to fulfill a religious mission in training, teaching, and propagating a certain form of Tibetan Buddhism in a country that had only recently permitted the presence of foreign religious missions.[42] They shared with the Tibetan *anis* from Nepal who had visited the United States some years previously their position as representatives of Tibetan Buddhism in transnational spaces. Their religious practices and renunciant lives had, to some extent, become an export commodity. Their interest in the higher ordination was ambiguous, if not tinged with both amusement and rancor.[43]

The Theravada nuns whose interviews are included in the following pages had access to transnational engagements similar to those that the Asian Tibetan nuns had. Nevertheless, some of them viewed the higher ordination differently from the Asian Tibetan nuns. Jenti, an Asian Theravada *bhikkhuni* residing in Nepal, had received the higher ordination on two different occasions. In contrast to the Asian Tibetan *anis* I interviewed, she considered the higher ordination essential and *necessary* to her transnational identity. Jenti had been invited to take the full ordination on three different occasions by Korean, Taiwanese, and mainland Chinese monastics. Because she felt that her knowledge about the Korean lineage was inadequate, she did not seriously consider being ordained in Korea. In 1997, when apprised of the international ordination in Bodhgaya (see Chapter 6), she officially accepted the invitation to be ordained there with about seventeen other nuns from Nepal. At the time, she had no thought of receiving multiple ordinations. Not long after the nuns in Nepal accepted the invitation (around October 1997), they were invited to receive the higher ordination in mainland China. Because the Chinese invitation prioritized the recruitment of nuns like Jenti, who had passed a high-level Buddhist examination, she was considered eligible and her name was given to the organizers. After a forty-five-day training period in China, she was ordained there in late 1997.

At the time of Jenti's first ordination (in China), she was aware that she would receive another, higher ordination arranged by Taiwanese monastics in Bodhgaya. Her ordination in Bodhgaya took place in February 1998, a few months after her ordination in China.[44] When asked why she was ordained twice, she stated, "In this [the Nepalese Bodhgaya] group, the older nuns were not educated. If only they went [for the higher ordination], there would be problems. But in China, they had only selected the well-educated nuns." The "problems" (akin to those experienced by the Sri Lankan nuns mentioned in Chapter 6) related both to nuns' worry about complications involved in maintaining monastic seniority and to their concern about long-term prospects of a *bhikkhuni* lineage in Nepal,which lay in the hands of younger *bhikkhunis*. Introducing the higher ordination first to young nuns who were junior (in years of renunciation) than their older teacher-nuns meant that the latter, as non-*bhikkhunis*, would effectively become (ritually) junior to their students and have to show deference to them. Whereas young, highly educated Nepalese nuns received the higher ordination in China, according to Jenti, the Bodhgaya ordination was planned to ensure the seniority of the elderly nuns, even though they had less formal education than their younger students. Jenti, aware of such problems and of the delicate diplomacy involved in responding appropriately to the invitation to the international ordination at Bodhgaya, had no compunctions about receiving the ordination twice.

The multiple invitations that the Nepalese nuns received attest to, among other things, the international competition for influence between lineage traditions and temples. That competition is reminiscent of what a Sri Lankan monk told me as we viewed a video of the 1996 Sarnath ordination of Sri Lankan nuns (organized by Korean monastics): "So many people have so many agendas. The Koreans might want to say that it is *they* who [first] ordained the Theravada nuns." It is necessary to understand that such competition at the transnational level is associated with defining how certain kinds of recognition and identity are interpreted, forged, and appropriated by the monastics who participate in higher-ordination rituals for Buddhist nuns. Most important, individuals and organizations orchestrating transnational or international ordination ceremonies may understand them differently from the ordinands. Such a divergence cannot be delineated simply in terms of a putative Western/Asian opposition, nor does it instantiate global/local differences.[45] Indeed, Asian monastics who seek international spaces in which to conduct ordinations, as do Western monastics, are often in competition among themselves.[46] Rather, the divergence reflects the ideas of female renunciants who articulate the need for the higher ordination in globalatinized terms and want recognition beyond the boundaries of their home countries versus the ideas of those who do not. For some nuns who live outside Asian countries— whether of Asian or non-Asian origin—such international recognition abets their "role" as representatives of Buddhism from Buddhist countries. But for other nuns of Asian origin who live in Asian countries the higher ordination may be understood quite differently.

In contrast to the Tibetan nuns of Asian origin discussed earlier, Jenti believed that obtaining the higher ordination "legitimated" Buddhist nuns' position as full monastics in global or transnational spaces. She described an encounter that took place during a visit she made to the United States shortly after a senior Nepalese nun with whom she was traveling had received the higher ordination (she herself had not received it yet):

J: We went to the American Theravadin monastery, and they asked Dhammavati Guruma if she was fully ordained or not, and when she said that she was fully ordained in California in that Hsi Lai temple, [the Theravadin monk] respected her as a fully ordained monk, but I said I am not fully ordained; then they treated me like…an *upasika*….So very different…[dejectedly]

Q: So, you felt a need…

J: Yes, like insulted. In Taiwan also, they will ask, "Are you fully ordained or not?" If I am not fully ordained, they keep me [behind]. So, I feel very insulted.

Jenti explained that although the higher ordination was essential to enhancing her renunciant identity outside Nepal, it was irrelevant within Nepal itself:

J: if we are not ordained, we are not qualified as a full nun internationally.

Q: It is an international thing?

J: Yes.

Q: So, what difference does it make for you in Nepal?

J: No difference in Nepal.[47]

Comparing the position on the higher ordination taken by Jenti, a Theravada *bhikkhuni*, with that of the Asian Tibetan nuns is not as simple as one may assume. The Asian Tibetan nuns whom I encountered in different countries, though they were active in transnational projects, acknowledged the need to execute the wishes of their male teachers (and ultimately, of the Dalai Lama), none of whom were training them for a higher ordination. They responded to the very idea of introducing a higher ordination for Tibetan nuns with resentment or ridicule. On the other hand, Jenti, who had visited the United States as a nun without the higher ordination and had felt "insulted," saw a *need* for the higher ordination outside Nepal. Whereas Jenti wanted a certain kind of recognition that was accorded to recipients of an already established, transnationally accepted higher ordination, the Asian Tibetan nuns I met in transnational forums were more focused on cultivating their everyday renunciant practice at their home hermitages. That is not to say that Jenti was unconcerned about her renunciant practice, but rather that the question of the higher ordination, which interested her, was simply irrelevant to the Asian Tibetan nuns I interviewed, whose priorities lay elsewhere.

It would be facile to think that the new Theravada *bhikkhuni* ordinations taking place throughout the world instantiate a global sisterhood of nuns. It is important to note, in keeping with the view of Anna Tsing, that meanings of the global are varied and that globalization cannot simply be understood as some "transcultural historical process" (469). What the higher ordination means for Asian Theravada nuns inhabiting transnational spaces is not uniform; it often remains related to the reception of the higher ordination both within those spaces *and* in their home countries. Mutta, a Theravada nun from Myanmar, who, like Jenti, participated in SIABW conferences, differed from her in believing that the *upasampada* was unnecessary. She refrained from suggesting that the higher ordination was unacceptable to the government of Myanmar and indicated, using another Asian country as her example, that the question of the higher ordination had caused significant turmoil among monastics in the country and had detracted from addressing more immediate social and religious concerns.[48] Meanwhile, Isidasi, another Asian nun with origins in Myanmar, who had received the higher ordination in Sri Lanka and had similar access to transnational conferences, supported the higher ordination. Isidasi was an American citizen living in a remote area of the United States where she could continue her religious practices as a *bhikkhuni* without needing to address the prohibitions imposed by the government of Myanmar (unless she visited there). Her isolated living situation was comparable to that of Tissa, a nun of Asian origin also living in the United States. Tissa received the higher ordination after having spent several years as a Zen monastic. But she too—notwithstanding an online interface she had with monastics that eventually led to her own *upasampada*—lived apart from other nuns. Although connected with a nearby Theravada temple that was geographically situated in a predominantly non-Buddhist community, she was, at the time of our conversations, the only monastic living in the annex of a house belonging to family members who provided for her. Tissa and Isidasi were living renunciant lives markedly different from those of the Sri Lankan nuns described in the preceding chapters. The practice of Vasetthi, an American Theravada nun who, like Tissa and Isidasi, had access to transnational forums, also diverged from that of the Sri Lankan nuns mentioned above. Like Tissa, Vasetthi had previously received ordination in a non-Theravada lineage. After she became a Theravada *bhikkhuni*, she proceeded to wear the robes of nuns from a different Buddhist lineage. That is, she had no compunctions about alternately wearing the maroon robes associated with Tibetan nuns and the brown and saffron robes worn by Theravada nuns—a practice that would be *unthinkable* among Theravada nuns living in Buddhist communities. Eventually, she met some Theravada *bhikkhunis* from Sri Lanka who convinced her of her "mistake"; they told her that, as a Theravada nun, she should not wear maroon robes. For Vasetthi, assuming the maroon colors of Tibetan nuns' robes was not so much a choice as something she had done because she lacked grounding in the practice of the Sri Lankan Theravada nuns. In other words, her appropriation of the maroon robes was governed by her not having lived the life of a Theravada nun (in Sri Lanka) rather than by her lacking access to freedom of choice or knowledge concerning attire. Although the Sri Lankan nuns may have corrected her for her "ignorance," their correction of her "mistake" was effectively their way of asserting their authority over her by pointing out that she was not practicing properly as a Theravada nun. What was appropriate for her became possible in the most rigorous manner when the Sri Lankan nuns literally put her in her place. The question of proper attire hence becomes a question about power and discourse.

But discourse has its limits. Although modernity seems to suggest that one has endless choices, in so-called traditional communities such choices are unavailable, if not unthinkable; there are limits that cannot be transcended. In fact, one's limits do not so much circumscribe one's "selfhood" as give meaning and substance to it. It is within such limits that what is or is not appropriate becomes self-evident. The question of apparent choices was present in how another renunciant, Anopama, decided to become a Theravada nun. Anopama, a *bhikkhuni* of Western origin, had considered being ordained in other Buddhist traditions before her Theravada ordination. She commented on her decision to accept the invitation to receive the *upasampada* in Sri Lanka: "I didn't have any preferences between the traditions." But because one of her teachers had been ordained as a Theravada monastic, "that became a comfortable place." That kind of *decision*, about which Buddhist tradition to be ordained in, would be considered inappropriate in Sri Lanka and other Asian countries because of the way discourses define "correct" Buddhist practice and the limits of the everyday renunciation of nuns living there.[49] That is not to say that nuns' lives lack a liberal notion of freedom, which *should* therefore be present, but rather that such notions of freedom and choice are simply not relevant to their renunciant everyday. It is in this sense that they are unthinkable.

Conclusion

In this chapter I have argued that focusing on transnational discussions of the higher ordination is essential to understanding how one thinks about contemporary female renunciation in Buddhism. It allows one to rethink supposedly apparent divergences between "East" and "West." Moreover, such a focus underscores the dominant character of liberal discourses in the consideration of transnational contexts of renunciant lives. Most important, it foregrounds the practice of Asian nuns who do not speak in globalatinized voices and whose everyday renunciation differs from that of nuns who do. I am not suggesting that one can always clearly differentiate between the renunciant everyday of those Asian nuns and that of other nuns who participate regularly in transnational forums. To do so would be problematic, if not inaccurate.[50] Nor am I suggesting that "Western" necessarily implies transnational and "non-Western," Asian, because there are Asian nuns who engage in transnational activities and have come to embrace a globalatinized idiom. What I have proposed is both the need to become more attuned to the difficulty, if not impossibility, of affirming a uniform attitude to the higher ordination that is based on whether nuns are of "Western" or "non-Western" origin and the need to reconsider what empowerment means and how, why, and for whom the higher ordination of nuns might be considered empowering or not.

It is important to note that the higher ordination may have little recognition in the communities of some Asian countries, such as Sri Lanka and Nepal, where *bhikkhunis* are often indistinguishable from nuns without the higher ordination. Yet, this ordination is celebrated in transnational venues, where it is considered as somehow empowering for all Buddhist nuns. But nuns participating in such venues do not always understand it to be universally empowering. One Theravada nun living in Myanmar, who has participated in transnational forums and refused to accept the higher ordination, critiqued another, well-known Theravada *bhikkhuni* of Asian origin, noting that the latter, though independently wealthy and thus worry-free about the finances of running a hermitage as a *bhikkhuni* in her own country, had little or no following among other monastics living there. Her point was that the higher ordination basically denoted a certain status and privilege for those who could afford it and wanted the title of *bhikkhuni*, but it meant little to the Asian community in which the *bhikkhuni* lived.

I have argued in this chapter that the renunciant lives of Theravada nuns are not easily comparable to those of Tibetan Buddhist nuns, insofar as the higher ordination within a Tibetan monastic lineage is historically and currently unavailable to Tibetan Buddhist nuns. To introduce the question of the higher ordination in conversations with Tibetan nuns is to focus too narrowly on ordination ritual procedures and rules and to introduce some kind of problem that has little meaning for the nuns' everyday practice. Moreover, to compare the higher ordinations of Buddhist nuns of Theravada and Tibetan persuasions flies in the face of inveterate differences.[51] I have also proposed that transnational projects, aiming to find commonality in an ideological unity and a global sisterhood, are grounded in rhetoric about notions of rights and equality; their image of an idealized *bhikkhuni* tends to displace the lived experiences and voices of nuns whose primary concerns as renunciants lie elsewhere. That kind of rhetoric contributes to the perpetuation of a certain way of thinking in which renunciation is effectively configured to the vanishing point of a Western teleological project. The analysis of such a project, as Asad notes, engages "the question of precisely how (in what times, places, ways) the West's powers have enabled the translation of certain concepts of justice, reason, and the good life into the practices of dominated ('developing,' 'modernizing') societies and how incomplete or unsuccessful translations have come to be seen as evidence of *failure* on the part of entire societies and not as indications of other kinds of history" ("Comment" 38; emphasis in original). The narratives of contemporary Asian nuns have yet to be appreciated on their own terms, aside from their situatedness within dominant Western projects.

Notes

1. Derrida invokes an argument about "Latin" or Anglo-American senses of religion that scholars read into the religious. Those senses are often read into the lives of Buddhist nuns. When I make a distinction between nuns who do not speak a globalatinized idiom and those who do, it is with Derrida's point in mind. For more on such senses of religion, see Mandair.

2. I use the term *female renunciants* to include women and girls who have decided to renounce the conventional practices of household life to focus on religious practices. They may or may not live with family members. By *nuns* I mean female renunciants who have generally, but not necessarily, accepted an ordination, wear renunciant attire, and may or may not live in community with other nuns. Nuns may include novice nuns or *sāmaṇerīs* and may or may not have received the full ordination (*upasampadā*) as *bhikkhunīs*. In other words, in this study, female renunciants include nuns, and nuns may include *bhikkhunis*, but both *female renunciants* and *nuns* refer also to those who are not *bhikkhunis*. I use the term *monastic* to include nuns as well as *bhikkhus* (monks who have the full ordination) and novice monks or *sāmaṇeras*. Note that throughout this work I only use diacritics for the first or occasional use of a foreign term.

3. Although "everyday" is in the singular, the daily practices to which I refer are multiple, and may differ from one nunnery to the next, so the "renunciant everyday" has a plural connotation. Some of the everyday concerns of nuns might differ little from those of householders (*gihiyō*), rendering a householder/renunciant distinction inadequate. Nevertheless, we may say that the conditions and constraints under which renunciants generally live are different from those under which conventional householders live.

4. In his article "Un-translatability," Abeysekara develops Asad's argument about life in terms of life's untranslatability.

5. See Gunawardene's thinking about the ending of the *bhikkhuni* order at the time (39). Whereas some scholars think the order ended around the tenth or

eleventh century in Sri Lanka, Gananath Obeysekere (in a personal communication) has cautioned against drawing inferences about the order from the absence of references to nuns in texts that male monastics wrote from their perspective. He has also indicated that future studies of inscriptions and Sinhalese literature may help in better dating the end of that order more precisely.

6. *Sasana* is commonly translated as "order." More broadly, it means "message" or "teaching." Gombrich suggests that *sasana* refers to the "institutionalization" of the Buddha's teachings and concerns Buddhism as a "historical phenomenon" (*How Buddhism Began*, 4–6).

7. When I use the terms *colonial(ist)*, *imperial(ist)*, and *Oriental(ist)* in relation to how they generate particular discourses, I use them interchangeably, although I am aware that each of these terms has its own distinctive connotations and genealogy. For more about the origins and use of these terms, see R. Young 15–43 and McLeod 6–8.

8. In the study of religion, for example, there are numerous works focusing on how religions have been molded by colonial administrators, scholars, and Christian missionaries (Almond; Cohn; Inden; Pennington). Other works question the very concept of religion as a discrete category with universal significance (Abeysekara, *Politics;* Fitzgerald; Masuzawa; Mandair).

9. Spivak's essay first appeared in 1988, in *Marxism and the Interpretation of Culture*. An abbreviated version of the essay was published in Ashcroft et al. A version of the 1988 essay appeared in 1999 in *Critique of Postcolonial*. The 1999 version and the original essay were later published in a volume of collected articles reflecting on the idea of subaltern speech, edited by Rosalind Morris.

10. For a useful essay on the question of "authenticity" and "tradition" in association with "Asian Buddhism," see the thoughtful article by Natalie Quli.

11. Note that while critiquing secular notions of empowerment, I still use the term *empowerment,* but do so to convey a meaning very different from that which connotes liberal ideas of freedom and power (see Chapter 7). Renunciants' lives lack significance without assumptions of everyday renunciant practices, yet narratives about renunciants seek to create meaning in their lives through recourse to often universalized paradigms about empowerment.

12. The term *sila* has connotations specific to Buddhist contexts. It often refers to specific *sikkhāpadas* or Training Precepts which may be five, eight, or ten in number. But by suggesting that it be translated as "disciplinary practices," I am likening the cultivation of *sila* to the cultivation of disciplinary practices mentioned by Talal Asad in which rituals and other activities that involve "programs for forming or reforming moral dispositions" (*Genealogies* 130) are "the product of varying disciplined performers who discourse with one another in historically determinate ways" (*Genealogies* 131). Whereas Asad focuses on the cultivation of obedience in medieval Christian monasticism, my work centers on that of

renunciant dispositions and the engagement of specific practices understood by the Pali term *sila* ("morality"; "virtue"; "precepts") for Buddhist nuns.

13. By the term *Sinhalese-speaking nuns*, I do not necessarily mean simply nuns who speak Sinhalese as opposed to English, but rather nuns who find themselves living in particular conditions that make possible the embodying of the Sinhalese language in their daily practice.

14. Attempting to identify precisely who the subaltern is would be misleading, if not mistaken, since the idea of the subaltern cannot be separated from ideas of subaltern representation. As Spivak notes, the subaltern in her essay "was not a 'true' subaltern" ("Can the Subaltern Speak?" [R.C. Morris] 64).

15. As Spivak points out, "it is important to acknowledge our complicity in the muting" of the subaltern ("Can the Subaltern Speak?" [R.C. Morris] 64).

16. In her article, "Defining Women's Bodies," Carol Anderson explains that "normative bodies are those that are sexed according to a heterosexual two-sex system." Only women who claim to have normative bodies may accept the higher ordination.

17. The idea of nuns' being beyond gender has also been noted by Lori Meeks in her study of premodern Japanese nuns. According to the sources Meeks studied, such nuns evaded questions of gender by assuming an "indirect approach [that] allowed them to 'talk past' the dominant discourses" of priests at the time (265).

18. All references to Cheng in Chapter 1 are to her book, *Buddhist Nuns*.

19. This chapter is a revised version of my article "Eight Revered Conditions."

20. This chapter is a revised version of my article "Religious Identities."

21. By "conjunctures" and "contingent conjunctures," I have in mind the idea of contingent conjunctures that Abeysekara introduces in his work *Colors*, when he refers to "a period of a few years, if not months or days, in which competing narratives and debates conjoin (and converge) to make centrally visible particular authoritative knowledges about what can and cannot count as Buddhism" (4n.10. See also 235–238). In Chapter 6 I develop that idea in relation to debates about Buddhist nuns' identities.

22. Terms such as *non-Asian origin* or *Western origin* are far from adequate. However, I use them broadly speaking, as a means to differentiate those of "Asian origin."

CHAPTER 1

1. All references to Cheng in this chapter are to her book, *Buddhist Nuns*.

2. This is evidenced in the introduction to the first edition of *Unspoken Worlds*; it became clear that she and Falk had to turn to the work of anthropologists when they discovered that their "fellow historians of religion could not command materials on women's religious lives in enough different areas of specialization" for their book (xvi).

3. There are many criticisms of her work. Some of the criticisms are based on the observations that Gross has been unable to step outside the limits of a

somewhat narrow definition of religion and the history of what we know in
the academy today as the discipline of religion. Clearly, Gross has inadequately
engaged postcolonial and subaltern studies. Such problems continue to pervade
and circumscribe the study of religion. As I have noted, Gross recognized some
of the limits of the discipline when she asked anthropologists to contribute to
her co-edited volume *Unspoken Worlds*.

4. The reference to Muller's citation also appears in another work by Gross—a
   1991 essay (reprinted in 1999 in *Cross Currents* online).

5. For further deliberation on how such thinking is articulated in Muller's engagement with the study of religion, see Fitzgerald 34–35; Mandair 165–169; Kwok,
   "Gender" 16–19; and King 122.

6. Gross's thinking on the idea of comparative equivalence appears to have
   changed somewhat in her later works, where she suggests that scholars who
   assume the existence of a "transcendental" in all religions tend to forget how
   Eurocentric and Christian-centered interpretations have molded the study of
   religion (*Garland* 74–75, 109).

7. For a discussion of the idea of "extent" or scale as a colonial construct, see Kwok
   "Gender" 26.

8. For example, see my critique of Nancy Falk's essay in Chapter 3.

9. This is a variation on Gayatri C. Spivak's well-known statement "White men are
   saving brown women from brown men" ("Can the Subaltern Speak" [1988] 296–
   297). That statement reminds us of the kind of project identified by Spivak and
   is recognized by scholars working in different contexts (see, for example, Kwok
   "Unbinding Our Feet" and Gandhi, "Postcolonialism"). Kumari Jayawardene
   has also discussed that notion of saving in relation to the development of "feminist" and "civilizational" ideals in colonial South Asia (*White Woman's Other
   Burden*). In current scholarship on Buddhist women, it is often a case of white
   women saving brown women from brown men.

10. See, for example, her essay "Buddhist Women"; M. Falk 245; Mohr "Sakyadhita"
    21; and of course Cheng.

11. This chapter appears to be a revision of a 1991 essay entitled "Buddhism after
    Patriarchy?" that was published in *After Patriarchy*. Here I reference her later
    publication of the chapter.

12. Here, by implying that "Buddhism" is responsible for a "relative lack of atten-
    tion" to its lay members, Gross proposes a need for the transformation of
    Buddhism. That is the kind of curative and colonial project that we must ques-
    tion. Indeed, following her quote, it is difficult to imagine how Buddhist prac-
    titioners would incur a "relative lack of attention" in regard to themselves! That
    may explain her reification of Buddhism as some kind of agent.

13. Her main interest in segregating Western and Asian Buddhisms and develop-
    ing a feminist Buddhism for the West depends on an underlying distinction
    between Western Buddhism and Asian Buddhism. The distinctions she makes,
    involving assumptions about social realties with which she is unfamiliar, are

problematic—for example: "The greatest difference between Asian and Western Buddhism... is the obvious and frequent presence of women in meditation halls, a place where they are rarely seen in many forms of Asian Buddhism" (*Feminism* 215). Here she not only seeks to make an Asian/Western distinction that is unhelpful but does so without a knowledge of the centrality of women meditators in Asian contexts. For more on women meditators, see Bond's *The Buddhist Revival* and M. Falk.

14. In 1983 when I first began interviewing *sil matas* in Sri Lanka, a university professor asked me why I would want to study them, since "they are like beggars." That Buddhist nuns were seen as unworthy of serious study is also noted in Sid Brown's research in Thailand (28). In a similar vein, in her 2000 publication, Kawanami notes the denigration of nuns in Myanamar, who are referred to as beggars (161).

15. Another master narrative deployed by Bartholomeusz is a liberal feminist one that I discuss in the next chapter.

16. Another book that relies heavily on Pali textual models to inform research on contemporary nuns is Sid Brown's study of female renunciation in Thailand.

17. It is interesting to note how in this passage, Bartholomeusz calls the nuns of the nineteenth century "pious laywomen." "Pious laywoman" is a common translation of the word *upasika*, which refers to a devotee who is not a fully ordained monastic. Bartholomeusz's reference to pious laywomen (as nuns) renders them similar to both women living in households as well as to *bhikkhunis*, maintaining a questionable lay/monastic distinction and circumventing the need to find accurate and nuanced renderings of renunciant identities.

18. Interestingly, Bartholomeusz, though omitting mention of any such interest on the part of the Sinhalese-speaking nuns, focuses on a discussion of the Sinhalese elite's preoccupation with the *bhikkhuni* order as well as its attempt to "control" or subordinate the nuns to gender-determined activities, such as the teaching of weaving and hygiene (116–128). Female renunciation is thus considered to be a "problem": "Once the women had renounced, the *problem* of how to cope with female world-renouncers became of paramount importance" (128; emphasis added).

19. How scholars continue to assume that seemingly self-evident notion of Buddhist reform is discussed at some length in Abeysekara's review essay "Buddhism, Power, Modernity."

20. Although Mohanty proceeds in the rest of this statement to focus on the question of agency, what I wish to emphasize is that such a homogenization of women obscures the distinctive conditions in which women live their lives in different contexts. My concern is not that nuns, because of a loss of agency, appear to be pawns but that who nuns are remains hidden. How subjects of research might have their agency robbed is another matter that has led to some debate in the field. For further discussion on that, see Ananda Abeysekara's article "Sri Lanka."

21. I refer here to Martha Nussbaum's idea of capability that Asad critiques (*Formations* 149–151).

22. Cheng, in using this term, assumes a certain homogenization in which the category of Asian Buddhists is distinct. Even though she consistently attempts to acknowledge differences among the nuns she studies, her continual self-description as an Asian Buddhist makes her vulnerable to Aihwa Ong's criticism that questions placing "non-Western women" as an "unproblematic universal category" and that invites pitting "Western modernity" against "Third World traditionalism"(82). Similarly, Mohanty argues that there is no such thing as an "average Third World woman" (22), as does Enloe (*Bananas, Beaches* 175 and 198–199).

23. There are methodological problems with her surveys (e.g., the comparative data are often based on much smaller numbers of Sri Lankan nuns than of Taiwanese nuns). These questions, significant as they are for their impact on Cheng's conclusions, are not my primary concern here.

24. That kind of repetition of perspectives that are critiqued also appears in Sasson's article "Politics of Higher Ordination," which explicitly criticizes Gross and the idea of "feminist rights" yet continues to interpret nuns' lives in terms of a liberal feminist framework invoking the notions of freedom to be gained in renunciation, choices that are made, and problems that need solutions.

25. In my research I have observed that some *bhikkhunis* prefer not to participate in such rituals.

26. This framework is clearly affirmed in the conclusion of her book, where she refers to Ibsen's play *A Doll's House*. Here Cheng explains how empowerment in feminism is related to a "transformation" of relations involving "patriarchal constraints" of marriage and housekeeping. The maids in the play who remain in the household are viewed as comparable to the Asian nuns she studies (199–200).

27. Although Cheng has attempted to use what she terms "Western feminist critiques on Buddhism" (3) and "feminism" to better explain the emergence of the *bhikkhuni* ordinations, she seems to have difficulty explaining how that emergence works and whence it derives. This is evidenced in her claim that "the *bhikkhuni* movement is generated not by the Sri Lankan Buddhist establishment"—by which she must mean the state and the well-established senior monks who are heard by government officials—"but by feminists (e.g., Sakyadhita), Buddhists from abroad (e.g., Foguangshan)," and *bhikkhus* such as the prominent Inamaluwe Sumangala (185). Interestingly, although Cheng connects feminism with the higher ordination of women in Buddhism, here she sees the transnational organization Sakyadhita as "feminist," whereas that title is not ascribed to the monk Sumangala. It would appear that Cheng, much like the Western scholars she discusses, equates feminism with the "freedom" to receive the *upasampada*, but she cannot adequately explain how, according

to her subjects, their lives as *bhikkhunis* involve the fulfillment of that feminist ideal.

28. Kusuma may be considered an exception. She is unlike the other nuns ordained at the time in that she is bilingual. Moreover, the circumstances in which she accepted the *bhikkhuni* ordination were quite different from those of the other nuns.

29. Institutional capture is explained more fully by Dorothy E. Smith, who defines it as taking place "when both informant and researcher are familiar with institutional discourse, know how to speak it, and hence can easily lose touch with the informant's experientially based knowledge" (*Institutional Ethnography: A Sociology* 225).

CHAPTER 2

1. Although I refer to "a" liberal feminine narrative and "a" colonial narrative, I recognize that there are multiple narratives like those. That multiplicity is not something I can take up here, however.

2. Collins also notes that the use of the term *public* in relation to Buddhist renunciation is misleading (*Civilisation* 19). Nevertheless, by replacing the domestic/public dichotomy with the domestic/non-domestic dichotomy, he maintains an opposition that is not so clear-cut in renunciant practice.

3. Unless otherwise stated, the names of interviewees have been changed throughout this book to preserve anonymity.

4. Even scholarship on monks that does not have a feminist focus (e.g., recent studies by Blackburn and McDaniel) uses a similar kind of vocabulary about freedom and agency.

5. An interesting example of this kind of narrative is found in the book by Sid Brown. Brown's work, in addition to deploying a dichotomous public/private structure to frame nuns' lives, cites a passage from a Buddhist text at the beginning of each chapter. She uses such passages, together with events from the life story of the Buddha, to provide a framework for interpreting the lives of various individuals, including the nun Mae chi Wabi. Hence, Brown, rather than centering on renunciant lives themselves, turns to feminist thinking and an analysis of textual themes to produce meaning in relation to accounts of renunciation.

6. For an interpretation of the idea of universal capability see Asad's *Formations*, 149–151.

7. For example, in Sri Lanka female "renunciants" who observe the Eight Precepts and live in hermitages would be observing the same precepts as "householders," who might observe them on a more temporary basis either at home or at a temple. Female renunciants who are robed alike in saffron may follow either the Ten Householder Precepts or the Ten Renunciant Precepts. While some *sil*

matas who observe the ten renunciant precepts today claim that those precepts have been followed since Sudharmachari returned from Myanmar in the late nineteenth century, those ten renunciant precepts are now also associated with novice (*samaneri*) ordinations as well. For more on these two versions of the Ten Precepts, see Chapter 4.

8. By Catholicism here, my reference is specifically to Roman Catholicism.

9. In his now classic study, Heinz Bechert also finds recourse to the term "*lay*" (*Laie*) or "lay adherent" (*Laienanhänger*) (vol.1, 13–14). He refers to female renunciants in Sri Lanka (*Dasasīla-Upāsikās*) as well as those in Myanmar (*Thila-shing*) as laywomen in order to distinguish them from *bhikkhunis* or "ordained nuns" (vol. 2, 53–54).

10. The *Encyclopedia of Monasticism* notes that even in early Christianity, the difference between monks or nuns and clerics was not always as distinct as it now appears to be in Catholicism (Derwich).

11. Bhikkhuni Kusuma for example, wore white and lived a renunciant life while staying in different households (including her own) for well over a decade before she received the *bhikkhuni* ordination. Other Sri Lankan nuns discussed in this book have also lived renunciant lives in the homes of householders while attired in white or the yellow-orange robes most commonly associated with nuns. Also see Sasson, "Politics" 64–65.

12. It is perhaps because of a focus on *Vinaya* texts that scholars assume a well-defined category of *bhikkhu/bhikkhuni*. However, other texts, such as the *Dhammapada* describe the *bhikkhu* differently. A lay/monastic dichotomy, deriving perhaps from textual studies of the *Vinaya* and cited so often by scholars of contemporary Buddhist practice, overlooks more nuanced relationships between renunciants who live in a household and those who do not.

13. Gutschow makes a bid for "reimagining" Buddhist monasticism in terms of "engagement with the world" (256), and yet she maintains subsequently that the sacred/profane distinction is important for monastics. Her work bears witness to the confusion that ensues from adopting certain dichotomies in relation to Buddhist practice.

14. Van Esterik attempts to explain the oppositions in terms of contrasts between ordained and not ordained, asceticism and sensuality, and detachment and attachment rather than as strict male and female differences (58–59).

15. Collins and McDaniel explain how this dichotomy is primarily a *textual* one. Although they indicate that it has had "complex and varying relations to practice" (1376) and they introduce a notion of "Third Statuses" for female renunciants, the dichotomous structure itself remains present in their analysis of contemporary practice.

16. The term *chi/ji*, "is an honorific…, used for any person who occupies a position of respect" (Collins and McDaniel 1384).

17. Havnevik states that *"ani* is also used to denote father's brother's wife" (209, note 29) and cites S. C. Das: *"jomo* can also mean 'the female head of the household, a woman that governs as mistress of her own servants'" (209, note 30).

18. For example, she says that some nuns "might have stayed in nunneries for part of their life, but found it difficult to adjust to monastic life" (45), suggesting that those nuns may have lived in households. Also see her description of how some nuns stay at home to support their families (57). Nevertheless, Havnevik describes "lay" life as though it is something quite distinct from the life of nuns (46).

19. Elsewhere she says that there is indeed a clear distinction between "laymen and laywomen and those who belong to the Buddhist Order, e.g., monks and nuns" (44).

20. I refer here to discussions with nuns, such as Mae chi Kanittha, reported by Sid Brown (34–36) and Monica Falk (230–236), as well as the numerous writings of Karma Lekshe Tsomo and Chatsumarn Kabilsingh, later known as Dhammananda. While such well-known nuns articulate attempts to overcome a perceived subordination, it is interesting to note that nuns who speak differently do not consider their "situation" a problem. The latter nuns often see no need for the *upasampada* (Collins and McDaniel; M. Falk 30; Sasson "Politics").

21. Asad in *Genealogies* states this well: "Discourse involved in practice is not the same as that involved in speaking about practice. It is a modern idea that a practitioner cannot know how to live religiously without being able to articulate that knowledge" (36).

22. Sid Brown indicates that Thai women are ideally wives and mothers but at the same time they may work on farms and in factories (68, 100); Bartholomeusz, writing at a time when new forms of employment became available for women in Sri Lanka, singles out rural women as those who become renunciants because of limited "choices": they become either housewives or nuns (130–133).

23. That nuns remain closely connected with family is evident in the accounts presented by Brown (18, 40, 77–81, 85). Also see Bartholomeusz (247, note 51). Bartholomeusz, like Brown, overlooks that in her analysis of female renunciation.

24. This distinction appears to be the difference between those who worship as devotees in a temple and those who preach in public. Elsewhere in her book there are references to female preachers in robes who "moved from the private sphere, the sphere of temple worship and support, into the public sphere" (26). Similarly, contemporary nuns who participate in activities like those of a village monk are considered to have entered the public sphere: those who are "preachers, teachers and ritual specialists…demonstrate that Buddhism is able to create a space for women in public, religious life" (131).

25. Joanna Cook's study, which also follows this pattern, endeavors to rethink how power works for nuns (*mae chis*) in Thailand. Despite her attempt to find

"alternative ways" (151) of thinking about them, she "does not question that *mae chee* are hierarchically inferior to monks and…lead challenging and economically disadvantaged lives" (151). Her finding that *mae chis* do not see themselves in that light leads her to a critical awareness of previous literature on nuns and renunciation and an attempt to explain nuns' practice in terms of the cultivation of the "monastic self." Nevertheless, her statement about the purported "inferiority" and "disadvantaged lives" of nuns is complicit in suggesting a need for rectification.

26. According to Havnevik, Western nuns have "brought attention to the inferior position of the Tibetan nuns" (204).

27. For example, Brown (26–36); Gutschow (240–250); and Havnevik (195–202).

28. Havnevik hints at the appropriateness of such a comparison when she says that the "gap in status between a pious laywoman and a nun may not be as great as the difference between a pious layman and a monk" (183).

29. For more on Palmo and her activities, see Dutch Foundation.

30. One may also discern private/public distinctions in Falk's summary of Kirsch's studies on Thailand (M. Falk 33). Recall that Pateman notes how the public/private difference may appear in different forms.

31. As evidenced in her research, even the conventional identification of the recipient of alms as "ordained" and the giver as "lay" is undermined, since there "is nothing unusual about monks and *mae chiis* giving *dana* [alms] to other monastics or to lay people" (157). That identification is one that Gregory Schopen had already questioned in his research on early Buddhist inscriptions in India (30–32).

32. The idea that nuns are "subordinate" is often reiterated in studies of the Eight Conditions (M. Falk 26). I focus on understandings of the Eight Conditions in the next chapter.

33. In *Genealogies* Asad explains how liberal theory construes problems in lived lives—problems that appear to need a cure (280).

34. Following usage prescribed by the Modern Language Association, I have generally dropped honorifics and titles when used together with monastic names (e.g., Sil Mata, Bhikkhuni, Venerable, Thera, etc.) unless it is necessary to make specific monastic distinctions. I have also omitted diacritics for names of individuals. No disrespect is intended.

35. Much has already been written about the feminized labor and jobs that were available to women in Sri Lanka during this time. For more on those, see Chapter 5.

36. The word *prashna*, which may also be translated as "problem," literally means "question" or, by extension, "issue." It does not have the meaning of a problem that needs solving in the liberal or curative sense of the English word; rather, it refers to that which has arisen at a particular time and cannot be ignored.

37. *Kalakirima* has been translated as an "act of being disheartened or disgusted" and as "displeasure, dissatisfaction; disgust" ("Kalakirīma"). Dhamma used the word most often as a noun. The more commonly used verb form, *kalakirenavā* also includes a sense of being "wearied or fatigued" or "dejected" (Kalakirenavā). The multiple connotations of this word are difficult to convey in a simple English term.

38. What she described happened at a time of economic hardship in Sri Lanka that began in the 1960s when Prime Minister Sirimavo Banaranaike's socialist-oriented economic policies were implemented. During that time, the distribution of food staples such as rice, flour, and sugar was controlled by a system of ration cards. Only those fortunate enough to have their own estates or cultivated land were allowed to collect produce for their households, although even that came under strict governmental control. Violations of regulations incurred severe penalties.

39. It became clear to me later that her family members discouraged her from renouncing because they had concerns about their "little one" staying at a hermitage that lacked the comforts she had at home.

CHAPTER 3

1. This chapter is a revised version of my article, "Eight Revered Conditions: Ideological Complicity, Contemporary Reflections and Practical Realities," first published in the *Journal of Buddhist Ethics* 15 (2008): 177–213. It is reprinted here, with changes, with permission from the *Journal of Buddhist Ethics*.

2. I am not assuming a strict division between scholars and practitioners, as those two groups may overlap (as scholar-practitioners). Yet, how practitioners articulate their practice of the Conditions is often quite different from what has been assumed by the scholarly focus on them.

3. As I argue in Chapters 6 and 8, what is meant by "Theravada" is not clear-cut. The same may be said of "Sri Lanka." Scholars and Buddhist practitioners dwelling in Sri Lanka both impact and are impacted by scholarship and Buddhist practices outside the geographical area that is Sri Lanka. Theravada Buddhist women (from within and without Sri Lanka) train for the *upasampada* in Sri Lanka, India, Taiwan and elsewhere, and even the very label "Theravada" is contested.

4. Scholars often draw on ideas about rules in order to interpret cultural and institutional organizations. In so doing, they may, as Bourdieu argues, "explain a social practice that in fact obeys quite different principles" (*Outline* 19). The apparent (mis)practices of the Eight Conditions today provide us with new ways of thinking about how the Conditions might have been understood in the lives of early Buddhist monastics.

5. See Kate Blackstone's article for an interesting literary analysis of this simile.

6. This statement, which has provided one rationale for the recent *bhikkhuni upasampadas* in a "single ordination" (given by monks alone), is well known in Sri Lanka, as is the suggestion made here—that the Conditions were given only to Mahapajapati Gotami, not to the other five hundred women. However, according to my research, the preceding assertion—that the Eight Conditions were presented to the *bhikkhunis* in general as a means of containment—is generally ignored.

7. The *uposatha* is the day of the full moon and the new moon when *bhikkhus* and *bhikkhunis* were expected to hold a ritual that involved reciting codes of conduct and acknowledging faults. *Bhikkhunis* were also responsible for approaching monks and making arrangements to receive instruction (*ovāda*) from them every half-month.

8. This ceremony, held at the end of the rainy season, involves satisfactorily addressing specific questions about proper conduct.

9. Insight into the context and possible meanings of this word are provided by Chung (227–234).

10. See Alice Collett's article for a thoughtful critique of Horner's work.

11. Unlike Wijayaratna, Kusuma, in her doctoral thesis on the *Vinaya*, notes that several Conditions presuppose the existence of particular *vinaya* rules that were not in place until *after* the *bhikkhuni sangha* had been established; she argues that that is a reason to take issue with the very authority of the Conditions. Neither Horner nor Wijayaratna problematizes the chronological discrepancy that Kusuma has observed. Kusuma's question, arising from a comparison of the fourth *garudhamma* with a similar *vinaya* rule, is relevant to other *garudhammas* and their *vinaya* parallels: "How could such a *vinaya* rule be applicable as a *garudhamma* even before the arising of the *Bhikkhuni* Order?" (48).

12. Interestingly, Gutschow, possibly influenced by Nancy Falk, uses the same language, suggesting that the Conditions, which she refers to as "rules," "permanently subordinated" nuns to monks (170). Gutschow references those "rules" in asserting a "message of inferiority" pertaining to contemporary Tibetan nuns even though nuns themselves are ignorant of that, for "nuns have reproduced these rules for subsequent generations without knowing their content" (185). Monica Falk, who also refers to the Conditions as "rules," states that they "left the *bhikkhuni* permanently subordinated to monks" (26). Nancy Barnes, though citing Nancy Falk, is sensitive to the possible difference between text and practice, but she also echoes her articulation of the "rules" ensuring nuns' "subordinate position" and impeding their leadership in the sangha (108). Gross also adopts Falk's terminology (*Patriarchy* 37–38).

13. See *Discipline and Punish* for his analysis of power. A thoughtful essay that problematizes conceptualizations of power in contemporary Buddhism may be found in Abeysekara's article "Buddhism, Power, Modernity."

14. It is possible that Horner might consider Mahapajapati as a knowing subject since she states that Mahapajapati had "feministic instincts" and questioned this first Condition (121). However, according to Horner, the views at the time in India were such that "the humiliation of the women [i.e., the first *bhikkhunis*] would have been more bitter" had they thought differently from the views of the time which were "impregnated with the superiority of men" (121). In other words, if the early nuns had *known* the degree of their humiliation caused by the Conditions, they might have responded differently. Wijayaratna also suggests that the early *bhikkhunis* did not *recognize* their oppression when he lists the Conditions and mentions that "the new community [of nuns] was to conform to the norms of the society of the day" (18) and also reminds us that according to the canonical text, "Mahā-Pajāpatī Gōtamī was very happy when she was presented with these conditions" (19).

15. I suggest that scholars in this section indirectly contest the ideologies represented in the previous section. Some scholars in this section may draw heavily on those in the previous section (for example, Gross from Falk and Husken from Horner), but unlike those discussed earlier, they clearly question the account of the Eight Conditions and its implications for early Buddhism.

16. See Koppedrayer's review essay for a useful overview of studies on Buddhism and gender published in mid-1990s.

17. The launching in the 1980s of the publication of the newsletter NIBWA (the Newsletter on International Buddhist Women's Activities which was later called *Yasodhara*) and also the activities of the Sakyadhita International Association of Buddhist Women bear witness to this new concern.

18. Husken follows Horner's example in comparing several of the Eight Conditions with later *vinaya* injunctions (see her discussion of Conditions two, three, four, and seven in particular).

19. As Abeysekara argues, what is in question here is the very translatability of life and religion which is assumed by some scholars, as though life and religion are objects that are merely *available* for interpretation and translation ("Un-translatability").

20. My reference here is to celibate Buddhist women who observe a list of Ten Precepts, wear saffron robes, and often live in ascetic communities. Also see Chapter 4.

21. Acknowledging the relationship between scholarly research and practice is necessary as we might note, for example, in Cheng's frustrated attempt to study attitudes to the Eight Conditions in Taiwan (*Buddhist Nuns* 85–90).

22. It is noteworthy perhaps that publications appearing in Sri Lanka at this time, such as those by Dewaraja, Kariyawasam, and Hecker paid scant, if any, attention to the text of the first ordination account, unlike the publications that appeared about a decade later.

23. See for example: "Move to Reestablish Order"; "Govt. Will Help Set Up Order"; "Govt. Will Help to Revive"; "Buddhist Nuns in China Today."

24. Here I use terms such as *revival* and *reviving* in relation to the *bhikkhuni sasana* since such terms were commonplace in the media at the time. However, one must understand that the lives of the *bhikkhunis* in India and/or Sri Lanka in the past centuries, cannot simply be translated into a contemporary present where questions about the so-called revival of the *bhikkhuni* lineage have their own particularities.

25. *Sil matas* appeared in the TV news on 6 May 1985 which announced a new program to help educate nuns as missionaries. On 7 July 1986 the television news reported that for the first time special classes for *sil matas* to study for the prestigious Buddhist (*pracīna*) examination would begin. On 2 May 1985 the minister for Cultural Affairs appeared on the television news broadcast with a large group of Chinese nuns. One purpose of his visit was to consider the possibility of bringing the *bhikkhuni* order to Sri Lanka from China.

26. For example, see Sirisena, and D. A. Weeraratne, "Bhikkhuni Order."

27. A particularly virulent public debate ensued for a period of six months in 1989 in the popular Buddhist paper *Budusarana*. Interestingly, that debate, focusing on Sri Lankan history and the appropriateness of establishing a Theravada *bhikkhuni* order with the assistance of Mahayana *bhikkhunis*, ensued, not uncoincidentally, in the context of increasing political turmoil and civil disobedience in the predominantly Buddhist south of Sri Lanka.

28. Also see Abhayasundara (43–45) and "Bhikṣunī Upasampadāva Budusasunṭa Apala Da?" for other publications in Sinhalese including accounts about the Conditions.

29. It is difficult to categorize the work of Bhikkhuni Kusuma as either Western or Sri Lankan, because it is arguably both. The essay I refer to here, "Inaccuracies in Buddhist Women's History," was first presented in English in Phnom Penh, Cambodia, and was published in the United States.

30. My subjects include a senior Buddhist monk who has participated in the ordination of *bhikkhunis*: six *bhikkhunis*, one novice nun shortly before her *upasampada*, and one Ten-Precept mother. The *samaneri* and *bhikkhunis* interviewed in this section are all significantly influential head nuns in their own hermitages. Discussions took place in Sri Lanka in 2002 and 2004.

31. Another *bhikkhuni*, also recently ordained, was equally emphatic about the necessity of accepting the Eight Conditions. However, she was able to recall only three of them.

32. Interestingly, at one training session that I attended with Soma, a monk lecturing on the Conditions explained why they should *not* be considered *Buddhavacana*.

33. Soma returned to question this Condition several times. It was clearly the Condition to which she most objected.

34. *Bhikshunvahanse*. This reference was made without sarcasm, contrary to what might be denoted in the English

35. She said this in regard to the seventh (or eighth) Condition, which she seemed to conflate and interpret to mean that a *bhikkhu* might reprimand a *bhikkhuni*, but not vice versa.

36. A well known senior *dasa sil mata* who supervised a training center for junior *sil matas* and a vibrant Buddhist Sunday school at the time of the interview was also familiar with that controversy.

37. *"No dunna upasampadā ne gatte?"*

38. As Bourdieu states, all too often scholarship tends to see "action as merely *execution* of the model" (*Outline* 29; emphasis in original).

39. Here I include both *bhikkhus* and *bhikkhunis*. Some *bhikkhus* who insist on the observance of the Conditions support *bhikkhunis* who they know are explicitly critical of the Conditions.

CHAPTER 4

1. This chapter is a revised version of my article, "Religious Identities of Buddhist Nuns: Training Precepts, Renunciant Attire, and Nomenclature in Theravāda Buddhism," first published in the *Journal of the American Academy of Religion* 72. 4 (2004): 935–953. It is reprinted here, with changes, with permission from the *Journal of the American Academy of Religion*.

2. In Sri Lanka, a *samaneri* is sometimes also referred to as a *samanera*, a term more commonly used for novice monks.

3. All informants interviewed in this chapter came from Sri Lanka. In addition to interviews, sources of public debates on which this chapter is based include publications that appeared between 1980 and 1997 in Sinhalese and English.

4. The *bō* or *bōdhi* tree (*ficus religiosa*) is sacred to Buddhists and is revered in temples and hermitages.

5. She was attired in the white clothes typically associated with devotees who take the Eight Training Precepts on a full-moon (*pōya*) day. Those precepts are discussed later.

6. A list of the Ten Training Precepts is discussed later. The Five Training Precepts observed by most householders include the first five of the Ten Training Precepts, except that the third in the list of Five involves "refraining from sexual misconduct," rather than observing total celibacy.

7. "Pilgrims to Buddha Gaya."

8. In his fine article "Mahāpajāpatī's Going Forth," Analayo argues that the practices of female renunciants who had shaved heads and wore saffron robes but were not ordained *bhikkhunis* were known and accepted in early Buddhist monasticism (287–291).

9. Interestingly, Richard Gombrich, conducting research in Sri Lanka in the mid-1960s, refers to various terms used for nuns but does not mention the terms *dasa sil mata* or *dasa sil upasika*. A masculine rendering of the latter term

was, however, used for "home-dwelling" and "homeless male renunciants" (*Precept* 79).

10. Those *dhammacharinis* should not be confused with other groups of female renunciants of the same name who practice in India and elsewhere.

11. The better-known list of the Eight Precepts (*sila*) is effectively included in the Ten Training Precepts discussed later. That list of eight excludes only the tenth precept in the latter list; its seventh precept combines the seventh and eighth in the latter. A lesser-known list of eight *sila*, referred to as the *ājīvāṭṭhamakasīla*, is practiced by some. That list, also found in canonical texts, emphasizes correct speech—that is, refraining from false speech, complaints, angry words, and frivolous talk. The four ways of speaking correctly consist of four of the eight stipulations in the *ajivatthamakasila*. While celibacy appears in that list, a significant difference is that the night meal is allowed. The eighth stipulation in the list involves abstention from wrong living (*micchā ājīva*).

12. I have used the following abbreviations for Pali Text Society publications of canonical texts: A.– *Anguttara Nikāya* (see Hardy; Richard Morris); D.—*Dīgha Nikāya*; M.– *Majjhima Nikāya* (see Chalmers; Trenckner); Pu.—*Puggalapaññatti* (see Morris 1883); Vin.—*Vinaya Piṭaka* (see Oldenberg).

13. Although the first four ways of behaving in the list known as *dasa dhamma* are similar to the first four of the Five Training Precepts, the last six are additions that are quite different from the Ten Training Precepts known as the contemporary *dasa sīla or dasa sil*. Also see A.II.220 for a version of that list.

14. I searched for an iteration of the *dasa sikkhāpadāni* in the Latin-alphabet transliteration of the Pali Canon on the *Chaṭṭha Saṅgāyana* CD-ROM. Although that effort yielded only one list in the entire canon, I know of two such lists.

15. I also refer to these as the Ten Renunciant (Training) Precepts.

16. I also refer to these as the Ten Householder (Training) Precepts.

17. My search for these references was also conducted on the CD-ROM mentioned in note 14, this chapter.

18. This is my translation of the Pali version of the list of Training Precepts found in a Buddhist handbook (Narada and Kassapa 18–19).

19. All quotations relating to the ordination ritual of the Ten Renunciant Training Precepts come from a text in Sinhalese called *Sāmaṇera Baṇa Daham Pota*. According to one source cited by Gombrich, this formula, which is not found in the canon, could be as late as the ninth-twelfth centuries ("Temporary Ordination" 63n.7). Those dates coincide with dates given to me by a scholar-monk who explained the derivation of the formula of the Three Refuges, which are part of the text preceding the recitation of the Ten Renunciant Training Precepts. According to him, the entire recitation of the ordination ritual likely dates to about the ninth-twelfth centuries.

20. The Three Refuges known to householders are the same ones ordinands recite when undertaking the Ten Householder Training Precepts: "I go to the Buddha

as my refuge; I go to the Dhamma as my refuge; I go to the sangha as my refuge"; for a second time, "I go to the Buddha as my refuge," and so on: (*Buddhaŋ Saraṇaŋ Gacchāmi, Dhammaŋ Saraṇaŋ Gacchāmi, Saŋghaŋ Saraṇaŋ Gacchāmi, Dutiyampi Buddhaŋ Saraṇaŋ Gacchāmi*).

21. The one recited first is referred to as the "going for the refuges with the *aṃ* ending" (*makārānta saraṇāgamanaya*) and the one recited second as the "going for the refuges with an *aŋ* ending" (*niggahītānta saraṇāgamanaya*). The latter has the same wording as the Three Refuges recognized by most householders. The wording of the former, however, shows a Sanskrit influence in the replacement of the Pali *aŋ* ending of *Buddhaŋ*, *Dhammaŋ*, and *Saŋghaŋ* with the Sanskrit *aṃ* ending, as in *Buddhaṃ*, *Dhammaṃ*, and *Saŋghaṃ*. The monk with whom I discussed that suggested that the Sanskrit ending was brought by Sri Lankan monks from Thailand around the eleventh century, when the *upasampada* was reintroduced to Sri Lanka. He stated that the Sanskrit usage was present in the Thai *upasampada* ritual. According to him, the decision to include both forms of the Three Refuges in the *upasampada* was made in Sri Lanka later. For another discussion of the recitation of the Three Refuges, see Bizot 49–59.

22. Malalgoda indicates that the Novice (i.e., Renunciant) Training Precepts are the ones that were supposedly observed by the white- or saffron-clad ascetics or *gaṇinnānses*, who basically served as monks in the seventeenth and eighteenth centuries in Ceylon, at a time when the *upasampada* of monks had been discontinued (59).

23. Interestingly, the commentary to the *Khuddaka Pāṭha* also mentions that non-monastic devotees (*upasakas*) might take the Five Training Precepts as one rule, much as ordinands undertake the Ten Training Precepts as one rule (H. Smith 28).

24. Unlike *sil matas*, novice nuns may receive such training.

25. *Sil matas* who can currently trace their own ordination back to her and are themselves ordained in the Ten Renunciant Training Precepts confirmed this in interviews with me.

26. Their first eight precepts are identical to the Eight Training Precepts, and their tenth precept is the same as the tenth of the Ten Training Precepts listed earlier. However, their ninth precept is a phrase wishing loving-kindness (*mettā*) on all beings.

27. Interview conducted in August 2002 with an elderly *sil mata* from her lineage.

28. According to another account, Sudharmachari and her nuns wore "a dress of apricot over an under-dress of white" (Woolf 85).

29. Today nuns in Myanmar wear pinkish salmon-colored robes, possibly the same color worn by nuns there when Sudharmachari received her ordination.

30. Interview conducted in August 1997.

31. The color of the robes of nuns from Myanmar also changed over time. That caused a fierce debate in Myanmar in the early nineteenth century. Eventually, officials declared that either the white or the red robes were suitable for those nuns (Jordt, "Bhikkhuni"37).

32. See "Sil māṇivaruṇṭa kahavat dārīma?"; "Dasasil māṇivaru" and "Sil māṇivarun kerehit."

33. "Sil māṇivaruṇṭa kahavat dārīma?" The use of the word *pärāde* is interesting. The Pali equivalent is *pārājika*, which refers to the most serious transgressions, which result in expulsion from the sangha.

34. D.A. Weeraratne "Dasa Sil Matas."

35. Some debaters suggest that both *kaha* and *kasa* refer to a yellow color (in Sinhalese the *h* and *s* are often interchangeable). But one writer suggests that there is a difference, explaining that although *kaha* refers to the color yellow, *kasa* refers to a type of yellow or orange dye used for the robes. That writer further suggests that although renunciants should not wear the complete *kaha* attire, they should wear the specially dyed robes. "Kasāvat dārīma?"

36. Interview conducted in July 1997.

37. Interestingly, a 1907 article in the *Dinamiṇa* newspaper used the term *āvāsaya* or "dwelling" to refer to a residence of nuns (qtd. in Bartholomeusz 102).

38. Devasara; Dhammavasa.

39. Dhammavasa.

40. Uncoincidentally, this *sil mata* did not support the *bhikkhuni upasampada*.

41. Interview conducted in August 1997.

42. They argued that the terms *Precept Mother* and *Mother* were commonly used to refer to women who serve at the shrines of the gods. See also Obeyesekere's *Medusa's Hair* (22–30) on this usage of the term *Mother* (*maniyo*). One nun pointed out that the word *Mother* (*mātāva*) could also be used to refer to a midwife (also known as a *vinnambu mātāva*).

43. My reference to the conceptualization of "messy" here is found in McDaniel's *Lovelorn Ghost* (230).

CHAPTER 5

1. My study of Sinhalese-language papers during the 1980–1999 period indicates only one occurrence of the term *movement* (*vyāpāra*) in relation to *sil matas*. Ironically, this term was used by Biyagama Sudharma, who was then well known among *sil matas* for her rejection of the need for a *bhikkhuni upasampada*. See Sudharma. "Dasasil mātāngṭa."

2. Here Jordt makes a distinction between the (lack of) *intended* political goals and the actual *outcome* of the movement. But this again raises the question of the usefulness of the term *movement* in relation to the religious practices she describes.

3. The suggestion that Buddhist monastics do not lead normal lives appears frequently in discussions of Buddhism. It assumes a secular idiom about normality that all too often remains unquestioned. That perspective is also present in the pathologization of female renunciation that is depicted in the 2007 movie *Uppalavanna* (directed by Sunil Ariyaratne), which is about a young woman whose love affair causes family turmoil and results in her seeking refuge as a Buddhist nun.

4. I have noticed that confusion about *sil matas'* status in several newspaper articles that have appeared since the 1970s. Even more recently, the term *bhikkhuni* has sometimes been used mistakenly in reference to *sil matas*. See, for example, L. B. Senaratne's article that describes how "*bhikkhunis*" celebrating the "Sil Matha Conference" processed in the streets. Also see "Thirty-five Foreign Bhikkhunis," which describes how "unordained bhikkhunis" from abroad, also referred to as "bhikkhunis," meet with their "counterparts" in Sri Lanka.

5. *Sil matas'* "organizations" or loose networks that emerged in the 1970s are still well remembered by senior *sil matas* for their pioneering, albeit uneven, efforts to create liaisons between female renunciants. Thamel dates the founding of one such organization, the Samasta Lanka Dasa Sil Matha Saṅgamaya (All Lanka Dasa Sil Mata Association) to 1972 (118). That association was to become more prominent in the 1980s when it served as a center for state communications with *sil matas*. Names of several renunciants involved in such associations in the 1970s appear in copies of the *Meheṇi Udāva*, a monthly newsletter discussed below.

6. For a thoughtful analysis of the violence that took place at the time, see Jagath Senaratne's work.

7. Note that most of the female renunciants I interview in this book decided to become renunciants before the 1980s, so events of the 1980–2000 decades would not have influenced their *initial* decision to renounce. However, what transpired in the country during that period would have impacted their thinking about the *subject* of female renunciation.

8. An entire chapter of her thesis is devoted to texts about the origins of the *bhikkhuni* order in India and its later history in Sri Lanka.

9. According to Thamel, only about 620 *sil matas* registered with the ministry. She states that many *sil maniyos* she visited "were not willing to co-operate with the authorities, attributing many reasons for their indifference" (117). Kusuma Devendra (now Bhikkhuni Kusuma), whose research was conducted a few years after that of Thamel, estimates that the number of *sil matas* at the time ranged from three thousand to four thousand (Kusuma, *Dasa Sil* 121). Bloss provides a more conservative estimate of 2,500 (17).

10. Rohana's name is mentioned in interviews with her here and elsewhere with her permission.

11. For a brief biography of Mavichari, see Kusuma, *Dasa Sil* 114–120.

12. Ratwatte happened to be a classmate of Devendra's husband and welcomed her visits to the ministry.

13. This article considers how so called third-world countries might develop strategies of resistance to the domination of developed countries. Note however, that a focus on resistance can be misleading in the context of female renunciation.

14. This discourse is present in a few earlier newspaper reports. See "Govt. Will Help to Revive."

15. Escobar states that "new types of power and knowledge are being deployed in the Third World which try to insure the conformity of its peoples to a certain type of economic and cultural behavior (broadly speaking, that embodied in 'the American way of life')" (382).

16. See, for example, the article by Abhaya Weerakoon, then the commissioner for Buddhist affairs, which calls for donations to ensure a secure livelihood and education for *sil matas*. On January 28, 1985, the Buddhist affairs department initiated a flag day to collect funds for *sil matas*.

17. The article "Udav illā kolomba," tells how a *sil matas* and a lay supporter visit the newspaper office. The article describes the living conditions of the nun and appeals for help from the general public. The ill-conceived attempts of two German nuns to become *bhikkhunis* drew the attention of prominent Sri Lankan Buddhists associated with the World Federation of Buddhists, and thus heightened interest in *sil matas'* "status" ("WFB to Study Revival").

18. Tharu and Niranjana, focusing on the analysis of specific "events" in India in the early 1990s, state that "suddenly 'women' are everywhere" (232). They point out that the 'new visibility of women' at that time was based on certain humanistic assumptions about the liberal citizen and occluded important particularities of caste, class, and community (233–237). Their analysis helps us think more carefully about how we might begin to read the activities of *sil matas* in the 1980s and 1990s and go beyond the usual explanations of "feminist protest" and "Buddhist revival."

19. See, for example, Veragoda's article, which includes interviews with several *sil matas* who, without proper lodgings, shelter under the sacred trees in the ancient city of Anuradhapura. One of the *sil matas* claims to have lived in that manner for forty years. What is interesting is the humanist appeal of the article, which questions whether it is "right" for *sil matas* to have to live in that manner. Bartholomeusz suggests that, unlike in the 1980s, there was in the early 1990s an "increase" in the number of homeless *sil matas* in that area (191). That is disputable; she has neither accounted for the seasonal variation in pilgrimages to Anuradhapura nor given evidence of comparative data on "homelessness" among *sil matas*.

20. See the article "Dasa sil mātā abhivṛddhiyaṭa," which celebrates *Unduvap Poya* (the full moon day commemorating Sanghamitta's historic arrival in Sri Lanka and the first recorded establishment of a *bhikkhuni* order in the country in the third century B.C.E). It calls attention to the inadequate lodging, food, clothing, and education for *sil matas* and suggests that temples for *sil matas* be established in every village. Also see Welihinda's article, which describes how *sil matas* serve their community well despite their inadequate residential facilities, and "Sil mātāvangē tattvaya," which provides early evidence of a global adoption of the discourse of deprivation in relation to *sil matas*. It questions why *sil matas* live like beggars and tells how the Sakyadhita organization in Sri Lanka is attempting to improve their situation and provide them with an education.

21. See, for example, "Dasa Sil Mathas Face a Dilemma," which cites officials from the Cultural Affairs Ministry who deplore the inadequate accommodation and alms for *sil matas*. It also mentions the officials' discussions on the "possibility of establishing a Buddhist nuns' order in Sri Lanka."

22. See Chapter 4.

23. A group of women from Colombo that worked for the "uplift" of the *sil matas* was known as the Dhammacharinis. According to one member, they wished to ensure that the nuns learn English and not "roam about." In 1997 a senior executive member of that group whom I interviewed spoke of their attempts to assist the *sil matas* (in much the same way as did "the Professor" mentioned below: "We have been looking for nuns.... But they like to be where they are." Although the president of the Dhammacharinis eventually became ordained as a *bhikkhuni*, the organization itself made no official statement on the *bhikkhuni upasampada*.

24. Between the 1970s and 2000, there were changes of government as well as new appointments of state officials working with *sil matas*. Such changes influenced how state attitudes to *sil matas* varied. Those varying attitudes to the *sil matas* may also be understood in relation to the debates about them as well as to the state's attempt to maintain good relations with the *bhikkhus*, who were important political players at that time of unprecedented violence and civil strife.

25. Bartholomeusz says that the interest in reviving the *bhikkhuni* ordination was strong in the '70s but "decreased dramatically in the eighties" (147). However it is evident from the debates that took place at the time, that that interest was particularly prevalent in the 80s, both in the print media and also on national television and radio.

26. "Move to Reestablish."

27. Nemsiri Mutukumara, "Plans to Set Up Bhikkhuni Sasana." This article describes government support of programs to train *sil matas*. The cultural affairs minister is quoted as saying, "Mahanayaka Theras...have expressed their complete accord for the conferring of Upasampada...to...qualified Buddhist nuns." Buddhist prelates present at the opening ceremonies for those programs

"advised that action should be taken to initiate [the nuns] in the proper order as *bhikkhunis*." At that time, Buddhist texts from China were also being translated into Sinhalese "so that the cultural minister himself [would] be able to confirm the possibilities of restoring the Order of *bhikkhunis*" (Salgado, "Female Religiosity" 232).

28. One *sil mata* who favored the *bhikkhuni upasampada* explained the then Madiwela head *sil mata*'s disapproval of the *upasampada* in terms of the latter's everyday renunciant practice. She said that that Madiwela *sil mata* (whom she knew well) lived in a populous area that had a well-informed constituency and had told her that her potential *bhikkhuni* status would be under careful observation; if she were to break even minor rules as a *bhikkhuni*, the consequences could be severe. In other words, it was considered easier by the Madiwela nun to cultivate her everyday disciplinary practices as a *sil mata* than it would have been for her to do so as a *bhikkhuni*.

29. President Chandrika Kumaratunga Bandaranaike, who became president some time after Premadasa, was well known among *sil matas* for what they perceived to be a lack of interest in their concerns as well as those of Buddhists in general. Meanwhile the Department of Buddhist Affairs continued to sponsor the meetings and classes for *sil matas* and accept the advice of senior monks who opposed the *upasampada* of *bhikkhunis*.

30. "Dasasil mātāvangē yahapataṭa" For more on the Buddhist Congress, see Bond, *Buddhist Revival* 117–119.

31. The state inaugurated classes for *sil matas* between 1984 and 1986. In the first centers, at Nugegoda and Ratmalana, *sil matas* attended classes in Pali, English, and health science, whereas in Gampaha they attended classes in Sinhalese, Pali, English, and Buddhism. *Sil matas* also took states-sponsored classes at centers in Colombo and Kalutara. Class attendance varied from ten to forty and classes were taught by *bhikkhus* and other qualified individuals (Salgado, "Female Religiosity" 230–231).

32. These details are based on interviews conducted with state officials at the Department of Buddhist Affairs in the mid-1980s and in 1995. At the time of writing, the Kurunegala district *bhikkhunis* claimed that their district had more *bhikkhunis* than any other in the country. That is not surprising since that district is one of the most populous in the country. Sri Lanka's Department of Census and Statistics *Demographic Survey 1994* showed that excluding the Northern and Eastern provinces, for which numbers were unavailable, the Kurunegala district was the third most populated district in Sri Lanka (8–11). The 2011 survey which included all twenty-five districts in the country, still listed Kurunegala as the third most populated.

33. Although previous organizations of *sil matas* may have claimed to be of "all Lanka," as did the one centered in Madiwela, this was the first one that included *sil matas*' official state representation from *all* districts where *sil matas* were

known to live in significant numbers. (Areas in the war-torn north and east were excluded).

34. I attended two state-sponsored meetings in Colombo. The first one I attended was held in the mid-'80s and was for *sil matas* of the Colombo area alone. It was very unlike the 1995 meeting, which was national in scope. At the latter, I observed an electoral process in which a committee of *sil matas* elected representatives for the national organization. It was clear that during a decade of district and national state-sponsored meetings, the *sil matas* had cultivated the skills needed not only to communicate effectively but also to run elections and administer and plan their own district and national organizations. The state infrastructure was fundamental in encouraging senior *sil matas* to work together and in developing programs to hone their administrative and communicative skills. Some of those *sil matas* later become *bhikkhunis*.

35. At the time this *sil mata* was an elected official of the SMJM executive committee.

36. In an earlier article, I elaborate on how state officials celebrated the *sil matas* in peace marches and promoted an image of the female renunciant that was unpopular with both laypeople and *sil matas* in general (Salgado, "Buddhist Nuns"). State recognition of *sil matas* (directly and indirectly) also involved naming *Unduvap Poya* as "National Women's Day," the celebration in 1993 of the 2,300th anniversary of Sanghamitta's arrival in Sri Lanka, and the state postal service's 1996 issue of a first-day cover and stamps with images of early *bhikkhunis*. Amarasiri Weeraratne, a longtime advocate of the *bhikkhuni* order, lamented that Catherine de Alwis, "the founder of the Dasa Sil Mata Nun movement in Sri Lanka," was not also commemorated. See "Stamps to Honor Buddhist Nuns."

37. The need for a clear definition of the "*sil mata*" was likely associated with an attempt to avoid the abuse of state patronage that covered *sil matas*' travel and educational expenses, as well as the state's attempt to regulate *sil matas*.

38. These were not the first attempts by non-monastics to regulate who could be a female renunciant and what she should do (Bloss 12–15; Bartholomeusz 113).

39. A 1988 document entitled *Dasa Sil Mata Vädapiḷiveḷa* ("*Dasa Sil Mata* Regulations") attested to one attempt by government officials to define the female renunciant (Bartholomeusz 249, n.78). The details include stipulations concerning physical and mental health, character, education, age, religious training, and acceptance of ordination on the part of parents or guardians and a senior *sil mata* (149–150).

40. The regulation of *sil matas* was also of concern to some monks. Note for example how one monk appealed to the state to establish a code of conduct for *sil matas* on the basis that they were being mistaken for *bhikkhunis*. He worried that they were allowed to accept donations and participate in rituals only meant then for *bhikkhus* (Vipulasara).

41. Note that the 1989 and 1995 documents to which I refer are not the same as the 1988 document which Bartholomeusz mentions (149). The drafting of these documents may be seen as different attempts to define and regulate the female renunciant subject.

    The *"dhammacharinis"* referred to in the state deliberations about and with *sil matas* should not be confused with the Colombo-based Buddhist women's group formed in June 1995, whose members call themselves *dhammacharinis*. See "Anagarika Women's Group Formed." My interviews with members of that group indicate that in the mid-'90s, that group numbered thirty women, thirteen of whom were married. At that time they hoped to assist *sil matas* but had not come to a consensus concerning the appropriateness of reviving the *bhikkhuni* order.

    The question of the subject of who a renunciant was and the activities that might be permissible for her continued to be raised throughout the 1990s. See, for example, the 1994 newspaper article, by Sheila Uduwara.

42. Department of Buddhist Affairs, "*Dhammacārinī Saŋsthāva*" (*Dhammacharini* Institute) n.d. (1).

43. See "Silmāṇivaru puhuṇu karana ārāmayak."

44. This concerns a recommendation that *sil matas* be between the ages of sixteen and sixty on entry into the renunciant life.

45. For example, it calls for stipulations concerning the ownership of the land on which renunciants live and states that "things [*dravya*] at the *aramaya* should not be used for [*gihiyo*] householders."

46. In this respect, Ambala Rohana Gnanashila may be considered an exception.

47. For example, that "*sil mata* institutions of education should be registered" and that "benefits that the state gives to the *bhikkhus* should also be given to the *sil matas*" (as read to me by officiating *sil matas* in November 1995 from the *Sil Mata* Codes of Conduct).

48. *Sil matas* on the executive committee of the SMJM explained to me with some resentment that a bus seat was generally reserved for male clergy and, more recently, for pregnant women. *Sil matas* were neither. *Sil matas* also requested that there be separate wards for *sil matas* in government hospitals, akin to what *bhikkhus* enjoy (a privilege that has since been granted in some districts).

49. Also see the letter sent then by the vice president of the SMJM (Rohana Gnanashila). That letter, addressed to the president of Sri Lanka, makes twenty recommendations "for the sake of the establishment of the *bhikkhuni* lineage" (37).

50. Although the media debates on the *bhikkhuni upasampada* were at their height during this period, those debates, unlike what is sometimes assumed, did not include a significant collective of female renunciants themselves. Recall that Rosalind O'Hanlon has warned against reading into groups the presence of a resistant ideology and a collective consensus that is in fact absent (164–166).

51. When I asked her about the difference between being a *sil mata* and a *bhik-khuni*, she responded, "Earlier we could not accept a *saŋghika dāna* (alms-giving for the sangha) and accept an *aṭapirikara* [eight standard requisites used by members of the sangha: three robes, an almsbowl, a belt, a needle, a razor, and a water strainer]. A *dasa sil maniyo* cannot participate in a *sanghika danaya*. Now we can accept the *aṭapirikara* . . . and a *sanghika danaya*, and we can go and deliver a sermon and participate in the *pāṇsakūla* [funerary rite involving the donation of white cloth to the sangha and offering of merit to the departed]. And the *bhikshunvahanses*, [reverend monks] if they go to serve the dispensation, we too can go; both the *bhikshus* [fully ordained monks] and the *bhikshunis* [fully ordained nuns] can do that. . . . Unlike pre-viously, in the time of being *dasa sil matas*, our religious responsibilities are greater."

52. Not infrequently I have heard the term *koṭiyak samvara sīla* (immeasurable dis-cipline of morality) used to indicate that the monastic rules of the *Vinaya* are congruent with an inner discipline that is incomparable and suggestive of dis-ciplinary and moral growth. However, that is not what Nanda Bhikkhuni meant in her later conversations with me.

53. A particularly virulent public altercation entitled *"Bhikṣuṇī śāsana vādaya"* ("Bhikshuni Shasana [Dispensation] Debate") took place between Amarasiri Weeraratne and the monk Baddegama Vimalavangsa in the *Budusaraṇa* papers between December 1988 and May 1989. Weeraratne (in a personal communica-tion) informed me that the debate became so heated that the newspaper editor ended it by refusing to publish his latest response. Although that debate fore-grounded the subject of the *bhikkhuni* at the time, it actually became a contesta-tion between an erudite proponent of *bhikkhunis* (Weeraratne) and a monk. *Sil matas* themselves did not participate in that debate. The *Budusaraṇa* is a paper that is popular among nuns who read the papers.

54. "Lakdiva bhikṣuṇī śāsanaya." For narratives on Sudharma, also see Bloss 15–17; Kusuma, *Dasa Sil* 162; Bartholomeusz 123–125; and Gombrich and Obeyesekere 280–286.

55. According to her, he announced that the *bhikkhuni sasana* could not be reestab-lished until the coming of the next Buddha (Maitreya), and that *sil matas* who wore yellow robes deserved a rebirth in hell.

56. Gnanashila, "Meheni sasana labāganna gaha."

57. See Weeratne. This article, a review of the *Meheni Udāva*, states that the author is the "Meheni Association of the District of Hambantota."

58. The first (1989) issue—of twenty-five pages, published by the "Meheni Association of the District of Hambantota," of which Rohana was president—was in fact funded by Rohana. The second issue was funded by family supporters of Rohana, and in 1993 there was no publication because of a lack of funds. The later issues of the annual newsletter received financial support from well-known proponents

of the *bhikkhuni upasampada*. I have come across a total of five issues of the annual *Meheṇi Udāva*. The 1990 issue was thirty-nine pages long, the 1991 issue sixty-nine pages, the 1992 issue forty-six pages, and the 1994/1995 issue sixty-four pages. In the 1992 issue one article introduces the discourse of "human rights" to Buddhism. In general, the articles in the later issues are informational and educational in their attempts to make a case for the *bhikkhuni upasampada*. The front-cover images of some of the later issues are especially provocative. The 1990 issue depicts two hands, one holding a *bo* sapling and the other a fan, typically associated with monks. Splitting the fan in two as it emerges is a sacred *bo* sapling, reminiscent of Sanghamitta, who first brought it to the country. The cover of the 1991 issue depicts four pillars of a building of which one is broken and held by three women. One of them also uses her hand as a pillar to uphold the roof, visually recalling the text in which the Buddha states his intention to establish the fourfold retinue of *bhikkhus, bhikkhunis, upasakas,* and *upasikas* as pillars of his dispensation before his passing.

59. The first issue was cyclo-styled on acidic paper and included stylistically unrefined handwritten pieces that were formulated in the written or spoken idiom of the Sinhalese language, whereas subsequent issues were printed in typescript on better quality paper and were more consistent in style and content.

60. The first issue mentions the Indian king Asoka and his missionary activities and gives recognition to Weerakoon and the wife of then president Premadasa for their service to contemporary *sil matas*. The deceased *guru maniyo* of Rohana is also acknowledged. Some compositions describe the material needs of hermitages and deplore the absence of *bhikkhunis*, observing that the well-known founding *bhikkhunis* Sanghamitta and Anula obtained freedom (*nidahas*) for Eastern women long before it was known in the West (21). The absence of a *bhikkhuni* order is implicitly connected to the "downfall" of the country at present (12, 20). Although some may interpret the compositions in the first issue as promoting an ideology of Sinhalese Buddhist nationalism, what predominates is the attempt to portray the *sil matas* with reference to historical role models, as renunciants who are deserving of social recognition. I have had several discussions with Rohana on the then ongoing Tamil-Sinhalese tensions and civil strife in the country. Her opinions are not supportive of a militant Sinhalese Buddhist nationalism but rather indicate a commitment to addressing the needs of minority communities without engaging in warfare. It is possible to read into the first issue intimations of a discourse of deprivation and a call for the *upasampada* of nuns. Yet there is no indication of a plan to ordain *bhikkhunis*. Overall, the issue lacks a clear ideology and is more simply a call for reflection on and representation of female renunciants in Sri Lanka, as articulated by three *sil matas*.

61. Piyasena's monthly newsletter was continued for about four years.

62. I mention the late Piyasena's actual name with his prior permission.

63. This information did not trouble her, because, she said, Piyasena "took it over in a way that I could accept."

64. For example, the ordination controversy in the previously mentioned debate that began in the *Budusaraṇa* paper in 1989 now emerged in this newsletter, not in the form of debate but rather in the form of a summation of the concerns and their relationship to the wider world. *Dhammavedi* was another widely disseminated Sinhalese newsletter that supported the *bhikkhuni upasampada* in the late 1990s. Its editor worked closely with Inamaluwe Sumangala for several months.

65. The Professor commented that although his goal was to help train *sil matas* and make the *upasampada* available to them, the *sil matas* he contacted were more interested in how he could help them improve their individual hermitages. Their thinking, according to him, was very narrow, and "it was extremely difficult to get them over this way of thinking." The nuns seemed more focused on cultivating their renunciant everyday, which was of the most immediate concern to them, rather than on addressing the question of the *upasampada*, which interested the Professor. Also note that Rohana did not seek the *upasampada* for herself, even after it became a possibility in the country. In fact, when she was invited to receive it, she initially dismissed the possibility of doing so as she was preoccupied with repairing some damage at her hermitage. She received the *bhikkhuni upasampada* only after attending to the repair.

66. I conducted interviews with these renunciants as they trained in Dambulla, less than a year after the 1996 Sarnath *bhikkhuni upasampada*.

67. The term *sarthaka* could also be interpreted as "successful." I prefer to translate it as "meaningful," because its literal significance is "with meaning" and centers on the relevance of *bhikkhuni* ordination attempts rather than their success or failure in terms of a "movement."

CHAPTER 6

1. See, for example, Gethin; Harvey.

2. In their otherwise thoughtful articles on "Theravada Studies," Crosby and Choompolpaisal, in keeping with most works on the subject, have assumed the category of Theravada without questioning it.

3. This is somewhat similar to the understanding of Theravada found in Gombrich's earlier book, *Theravada Buddhism*, which suggests that the designation *Theravada* is associated with the primacy of monasticism, Pali texts, certain beliefs and practices, and specific countries where it is predominant, and is also differentiated from "Mahayana." However, that book describes Theravada as an "ordination tradition" (168) and also assumes that Theravada Buddhism has a long history of more than 2500 years (21).

4. That is something that they state in addressing the question of the *bhikkhuni upasampada*. We may infer the authors' support for the *bhikkhuni upasampada* in their assertion that Theravada/Mahayana differences are not about "monastic tradition" or ordination lineage—an assertion that Sri Lankan proponents of the ordination also make.

5. Another book that appears to share a similar understanding of Theravada is *Constituting Communities* by Holt et al. The essays in the book discuss beliefs and practices laid out in Pali texts as well as the particular cultures of South and Southeast Asia that are generally identified as Theravada. In that book an explanation of what "Theravada" itself means is absent.

6. Anil Sakya, in his paper "Contextualising Thai Buddhism" (cited with permission), makes interesting comments about the idea of Theravada. He suggests that the modern use of the term "Theravada" was introduced in 1950, at the first conference of the World Fellowship of Buddhists (WFB) in Colombo, Sri Lanka. That conference, attended by representatives from twenty-seven countries, was held as part of an attempt to overcome the pejorative connotations of the term "Hinayana." Sakya also discusses a paper by Peter Skilling that has since been revised and published. Skilling's publication states that though the term "Theravada" is often taken for granted today, it should not be, because it "is rare in Pali literature, . . . and for nearly a millennium it was rarely used in the Pali or vernacular inscriptions, chronicles, or other premodern texts" ("Theravāda" 61). According to Skilling, "as a *type of Buddhism*, the very idea of Theravada is a by-product of globalization" ("Theravāda" 62; emphasis in original). Skilling proposes (like Bechert but unlike Gombrich and Obeyesekere) that the history of "Theravada" does not concern doctrine but rather "ordination lineages" (64). For further reflection on the genealogy of Theravada see the recent work, *How Theravāda is Theravāda?* by Skilling et al.

7. See, for example, "Bhikkhuni Order" and sources mentioned below.

8. For support of this procedure, see "Ordination of Dasa Sil Matas," and the article by Kumar Piyasena.

9. I use the terms "Sarnath (group) *bhikkhunis* or nuns" and "Bodhgaya-Dambulla (group) *bhikkhunis* or nuns" to also refer to those female renunciants who have received training (and often also the *upasampada*) from *bhikkhunis* from one of these groups.

10. One must understand that debates about a (Theravada) *bhikkhuni* ordination of Sri Lankan nuns took place in the context of contestations about the question of what did or did not constitute a "pure" Buddhism in Sri Lanka. Those contestations were prevalent in the country throughout the 1980s and 1990s. As Abeysekara indicates, neither the meaning of Theravada nor the idea of a pure Buddhism should be considered self-explanatory (*Colors* 109–142).

11. The question of monastic precedence was noted quite publicly in a 2010 event organized by the Sri Lankan monk Bodagama Chandima and Taiwanese *bhikkhunis* that was heralded as the "First all Sri Lanka Bhikkhuni Dana (alms giving ceremony)." Sri Lankan monks, Taiwanese monastics, and approximately 2,900 Sri Lankan nuns (*bhikkhunis*, *samaneris*, and *sil matas*) received alms. Although some senior Sri Lankan *bhikkhunis* were excited about participating in such an event, others with whom I have talked mentioned their concern about the inadequate observance of monastic precedence between monks and nuns as well as between nuns themselves. Also see Cheng, "Cross-Tradition" and Theravada Samadhi Education Association.

12. Although the determination of seniority among *sil matas* in discrete hermitages is generally straightforward, at Dambulla, where nuns from different hermitages gathered for training, it was to be rearranged partly according to the precedence of the novice and higher ordinations and also according to the performance of individual nuns at the required *bhikkhuni* qualifying examination. I later learned that the *sil mata* ordination precedence is often taken into account when nuns from one hermitage receive the higher ordination at Dambulla on the same day.

13. The term *golaya* means more than "pupil" or "student." It refers to an individual who owes moral allegiance and loyalty to a teacher or mentor who serves as a guiding authority in life. Teachers are usually older than their *golayas* by a generation and are comparable to parents who share with their progeny their life experiences and social connections.

14. This nun used the term *samanera* or "novice monk" for novice nuns or *samaneris*, and I followed suit by using it in a similar manner in my conversations with her.

15. For subsequent preparations for the higher ordination of a Theravada nun in the United States, also see Nemsiri Mutukumara, "Sri Lankan, Thai Bhikkhus." Deegalle Mahinda, a Buddhist monk from Sri Lanka who was studying in the United States at the time and also considered it important to address the needs of the mission abroad published an article in a national Sri Lankan newspaper, suggesting that the establishment of a Theravada *bhikkhuni* order would "prove that women have equal status in Buddhism even today" and also potentially assist with the "quick acceptance and progress of Theravada Buddhism in Western countries."

16. According to one informant, discussions for the ordination at Sarnath began in a very preliminary fashion when female practitioners working to "uplift" what he referred to as the *tattvaya*, or status, of *sil matas* and enhance their acceptance among Buddhists as worthy recipients of donations decided that those goals could be accomplished with the institution of a *bhikkhuni upasampada*. Those practitioners spoke persistently about the need for the *bhikkhuni upasampada* with Vipulasara, who at that time (the 1980s) was at the Parama Dhammachaitya

Pirivena in Ratmalana, where a Korean *bhikkhuni* was also residing and studying. (The Korean *bhikkhuni*, Sang Wong, chief incumbent of the Bo Myunsa
temple in Seoul, South Korea, is now referred to as the *Mahā Bhikkhuni* ["Great
Bhikkhuni"]; it was she who initiated plans for the *bhikkhuni* ordination that
took place in Sarnath in 1996.) Although Vipulasara had long-term associations
with Korean monastics, the conversations between Vipulasara and the Korean
monastics concerning the *bhikkhuni upasampada* appear to have begun in
Ratmalana. It would be inaccurate to suggest, as has Goonatilake, that the ini-
tiative for the *bhikkhuni upasampada* began as a result of the Sakyadhita conference of 1993 in Colombo, Sri Lanka (44–45). Vipulasara's intentions to prepare
sil matas for the *upasampada* and for missionary work abroad were publicized
later in 1996 in the Sri Lankan media. See "Maha Bodhi Society."

17. "The Ordination of Dasa Sil Matas." This interview was broadcast nationally on
the *Buddhist Review* radio program the same (full-moon) day.

18. I interviewed four Sri Lankan *bhikkhunis* shortly after their ordination at Sarnath.
Although they had been following the renunciant life for several years, none of
them had had long-term aspirations to become fully ordained *bhikkhunis*. Their
acceptance of the *upasampada* points to the "contingent conjunctures" (to use
Abeysekara's terminology) that resulted in the Sarnath ordination. The efforts
leading up to the Sarnath ordination are not unlike those led by individuals
such as Piyasena and the Professor mentioned earlier. One difference is that the
attempts of the latter were led by householders rather than monastics. Those
efforts were stymied by an absence of accepting and suitably prepared *sil matas*.
The Sarnath ordination, led by monastics of transnational stature raised similar
concerns about the preparedness of the *sil matas*.

19. Kusuma, "How I Became a Bhikkhuni" (17). Kusuma conveyed to me that there
were many reasons that Vipulasara made this request of her: he knew her to
be a strong meditator and scholar; he knew of her linguistic abilities in Pali,
English, and Sinhalese and of her educational background in the sciences; and
he trusted that her maturity as an older woman would enable her to handle
being the target of imminent public criticism.

20. This questionable idea of *struggle* in which *bhikkhunis* are pitted against opposing Buddhist monks has appeared frequently in the media. See, for example,
Frances Harrison's article.

21. For an extended account of the Foguangshan monastery and its interest in *bhikkhuni* ordinations, see Chandler.

22. Sarvodaya is a well-known non-governmental organization working at a grassroots level in Sri Lanka that was then training householders as well as *sil matas*
in an attempt to improve living standards in villages. For more on Sarvodaya,
see Bond's *Buddhism at Work* and Macy. Sarvodaya's initial involvement with *sil
matas*, though predating that of Sumangala, was part of a larger effort to "uplift"
villages rather than promote a *bhikkhuni upasampada*.

23. See Seelananda's article. This article calls for unity among *bhikkhunis* throughout Sri Lanka: "My fervent and kind appeal is, please do not make divisions and do not let others...make divisions in the Bhikkhuni Order as in [the] Bhikkhu Order in Sri Lanka." This article mentions the Sarnath ordination, a proposal from Taiwan to confer a higher ordination on nuns, and, indirectly, the efforts in Dambulla.

24. Those procedures included details such as reversion to the white attire of a temporary renunciant or householder before accepting the attire and requisites of a fully ordained monastic—a practice associated with Sri Lankan higher ordinations. Unlike the Sri Lankan *bhikkhunis* ordained in Sarnath in 1996, who wore Korean-style monastic robes associated by some with "Mahayana," the Sri Lankan *bhikkhunis* ordained in 1998 in Bodhgaya wore Sri Lankan-style monastic robes.

25. According to one Sri Lankan *bhikkhuni* who received this ordination, these personal questions were asked by Taiwanese *bhikkhunis*, with the Sri Lankan *bhikkhuni* serving only as a translator.

26. Although we need to be cautious about raising questions that appear relevant to the ordination of nuns both in Tibetan and Theravada Buddhism, it is interesting that the notion of monastic precedence is also important to Tibetan nuns. A Tibetan nun of Asian origin talked to me about the matter in some detail. This nun did not seek to receive the higher ordination, but she knew of the efforts of Tibetan nuns of Western origin to do so. She observed that at a particular ritual session, the participating Western nuns, who were very junior to some of the Asian Tibetan nuns present, assumed monastic seniority by (inappropriately to their junior station) sitting in front of the latter. "Just because they are Western nuns they want to sit ahead.... They know very well they should not be there and they are doing it anyway." She indicated that such nuns, who as novices did not observe proper behavior in respect to monastic seniority, should not even consider trying to become ordained as *bhikkhunis*, who are even more restricted. According to her, the debate about the *bhikkhuni* ordination ultimately concerned who could or could not sit in "the front seat row."

27. "Meheni sasna yali."

28. See Rupasinghe. The assertion that no Theravada *bhikkhuni* order existed before the 1998 Dambulla ordination centers on the idea of *where* the ordination can take root. Sumangala has dismissed the 1996 Sarnath ordination by citing a passage from the *Mahāvaṃsa* that, according to him, asserts that the *bhikkhuni* ordination can only be established when a renunciant is ordained "on Sri Lankan soil." His interpretation has been contested by a scholar-*bhikkhuni* who indicates that the passage refers not to renunciants ordained "*on* Sri Lankan soil" but rather to renunciants "*of* Sri Lankan soil"—renunciants who were born in Sri Lanka but may be ordained anywhere in the world. Unlike the former interpretation, the latter suggests that the "rebirth" of the Sri Lankan

bhikkhuni order "after 800 years" first took place in Sarnath in 1996 rather than in Dambulla in 1998.

29. See, for example, Vidanagama, and Weerasinghe.

30. See the articles by I. B. Wijayasiri, G.A.D. Sirimal, and D. Amarasiri Weeraratne, "Mahanayakas."

31. This forty-one-page booklet describes eight methods of ordination acceptable in a Pali text and makes a case for the contemporary establishment of the higher ordination for women in Sri Lanka. It also cites verbatim (31–39) a conference paper I presented at the fifth Sakyadhita International Conference on Buddhist Women, Phnom Penh, 1997. That paper was later revised and published as "Unity and Diversity."

32. Reasons for the nuns' discontinuing their practices as *bhikkhunis* relate first to an absence of real interest among the nuns themselves in becoming *bhikkhunis* (Bartholomeusz 182), a lack of training and education in what the higher ordination meant, and inadequate preparations for the nuns to continue their practice after returning to Sri Lanka. *Bhikkhunis*, following stricter rules than *sil matas*, are not in a position to observe certain *vinaya* regulations (e.g., concerning restrictions on food preparation and the observance of the *patimokkha*) without the support of householders and monks.

33. That the Korean ordination lineage has also been traced to the Chinese was not a matter I raised with him.

34. These include necessary rituals performed by *bhikkhus* and *bhikkhunis* in community, such as the *patimokkha* recitation and the *kathina* (ritual held at the end of the rainy-season retreat).

35. Although several Bodhgaya-Dambulla *bhikkhunis* have affirmed that Sumangala said this and that they follow his recommendations, I know that some *bhikkhunis* do not comply with this. In one such instance, a *bhikkhuni* ordained at Dambulla appeared at a Sarnath *bhikkhuni* ritual and planned to officiate. She was turned away by senior Sarnath nuns because she lacked the "character qualifications" to participate.

36. For purposes of maintaining their anonymity, I have not included their actual names here.

37. I have identified Sumangala by name, as he requested. He indicated that the ordinations he was conducting were part of a "big event" with which he wanted his name to be identified.

38. Also "on the sly" or "deceptively."

39. Sumangala attempted to invalidate the ordination in Taiwan because of what he viewed as the insincerity and money laundering of its sponsors, not because it was "Mahayana." If he had dismissed it as Mahayana, I would have had the opportunity to present him with a counter-narrative potentially invalidating the Bodhgaya ordination. Because the Foguangshan temple in Taiwan had been central to both the Bodhgaya and the Taiwan ordinations of Sri Lankan nuns,

undercutting the validity of the Taiwan ordination would effectively have done the same to the Bodhgaya and Dambulla ordinations.

40. According to some, the two junior *sil matas* (*golayas*) received their *sil mata* training and ordination from her, and according to others, they did not. But my informants all agree that, according to their *sil mata* ordination, the two nuns who had associated closely with her were junior to Seelavatie. That the dispute involved a notion of seniority that was questioned when the junior *sil matas* became *bhikkhunis* was also confirmed directly by the three nuns involved in the dispute.

41. On her return to Sri Lanka, Seelavatie Bhikkhuni trained nuns for *bhikkhuni* ordinations and has since participated in ordinations associated with the Sarnath group.

42. The confusion about Buddhist practices and their associations with different countries is common among practitioners in Sri Lanka. Another nun associated with Dambulla who also refuted the Mahayana ordinations seemed to think that Taiwan and Thailand were one country. Also see Cheng (*Buddhist Nuns* 180–185). Unlike Cheng, I wish to focus on this matter not to indicate the significance of "ignorance" among subjects, but rather to argue that knowledge of what kind of Buddhism is practiced where is just not a primary concern. What is at stake here is the question of recognition of an *authentic* Sri Lankan (Theravada) *bhikkhuni upasampada* that is opposed to something else.

43. This confusion may have been prompted by her knowledge that Kusuma, whose ordination was conducted by Korean monastics, was also present at the Taiwan ordination.

44. Such questions may well have entered into the first ordination of Thervada *bhikkhunis* in Australia in 2009 in which Ajahn Brahm of the Thai Wat Pa Pong Buddhist community participated. Within weeks of the ordination, Thai monks of that community declared the ordination invalid and expelled Ajahn Brahm. See "History in the Making?"

CHAPTER 7

1. Such ways of thinking about autonomy may help one understand the activities of Buddhist nuns to some extent. Yet, we should keep in mind that those ways of thinking are limited, because they do not assume the same kind of idea of self (or no-self) as that which is found in Buddhist practice. Additionally, it would be mistaken to suppose that Buddhist nuns seek autonomy as an end in itself.

2. Henceforth in this chapter "colonial" and "colonialism" refer specifically to British colonialism.

3. Let us keep in mind that female renunciants may have lived within familial households long before they began to live communally with other nuns in hermitages.

4. Buddhism, when studied, is often viewed as being in a state of revival or reform. As Abeysekara (*Colors* 71–80) and Scott (85) have noted, ideas such as reform and revival are analytically problematic and should not be accepted at face value.

5. By "pursuing" such a life, I do not mean that these renunciants made a decision about *available* choices and that their lives were guided by perceivable options. Rather, in pursuing such a life, renunciants *were* the path of life that they made; they were *living* a choice instead of *choosing* a way to live.

6. Also see Cheng (*Buddhist Nuns* 107); Devendra (*Dasasil* 121); M. Falk (55).

7. Commonly used words for *nun* and *devout female householder* (*upāsikāmmā, mǎṇiyō*) in Sri Lanka are akin to those used for *mother*. That is also true in Thailand, where one word for *nun, mae chii*, means *honorable mother*. In Tibetan, a nun with the novice ordination may be referred to as *ani*, which also means "aunt" (Havnevik 44). Such terms emphasize a closeness between the supposedly distinct "lay" and "monastic" categories.

8. Gombrich and Obeyesekere also point out that marriage and divorce practices changed significantly with the introduction of new colonial laws (*Buddhism Transformed* 256).

9. For a more detailed discussion of how this works, see Salgado ("Teaching Lineages" 175–178).

10. According to him, "competition for religious power owes its specificity . . . to the fact that what is at stake is the *monopoly of the legitimate exercise of the power to modify, in a deep and lasting fashion, the practice and world-view of the lay people,* by imposing on and inculcating in them a particular *religious habitus*" (Bourdieu, "Legitimation" 126; emphasis in original).

11. The phrase "good-faith" may carry too much of a Christian connotation to be exactly applicable to Buddhist nuns. Nonetheless, what Bourdieu generally says about such relations may aid reflection on the ways that relationships between nuns and their supporters work.

12. Bourdieu explains how the (materially) wealthy exert their power in the form of symbolic capital. I suggest that in the case of monastics, the "wealth" may be seen in terms of their providing religious services, the performance of which appears to build up symbolic capital.

13. See Chapter 5 for how Nanda speaks about the *bhikkhuni* ordination. I give another account of Nanda in a previous article ("Teaching Lineages" 180–183).

14. Note that the Sinhalese verb meaning *want* (*ōnä*) is identical to the verb meaning *need.*

15. A *buduge* is a shrine housing a Buddha image. *Poyage* literally means "full-moon house." This is a free-standing building constructed according to *vinaya* regulations for the use of *bhikkhus* or *bhikkhunis* conducting specific rituals. For an earlier account of Mettika see my previous article ("Teaching Lineages" 183-187).

16. This assassination took place in the 1970s, when the JVP first became a serious threat to the government. For a useful account of JVP activities at that time, see the work by Alles.

17. The *maniyos* who related this incident suggested that since the leopard was accustomed to their yellow attire and did no harm to them, the man probably assumed that the yellow robes would protect him too from the leopard.

18. For Sumana's thoughts on the higher ordination, see Chapter 5. Of the seven nuns who were under her tutelage in 2010, when I last visited her, two had received the *upasampada*. One was still a *sil mata*, and the others had no plans for becoming *bhikkhunis*.

CHAPTER 8

1. See, for example, Dhammananda's outline of developments in recent ordinations and Vishvapani's description of the Los Angeles ordination as part of an ongoing "movement."

2. Some have suggested that those nuns were unwilling to continue to live in Sri Lanka as higher ordained nuns because they lacked support from other monastics and householders and were criticized for having received a Mahayana ordination.

3. The terms *global* and *transnational*, which have gained currency in recent years, may be understood in different ways. There is a vast literature discussing what they are and how they work. (See, for example, the works of Peter Beyer, Stuart Hall et al., Ulf Hannerz, Jonathan Inda and Renato Rosaldo, Joseph E. Stiglitz, and Steven Vertovec.) I use the terms more or less interchangeably. My focus in this chapter is not on theorizing about globalization and transnationalism per se but rather on understanding transnational discourses about female renunciation and its supposed empowerment. I use the term *international* somewhat loosely, in connection with its usage in gatherings that call themselves international, rather than to convey a meaning the same as or different from that of *global* or *transnational*.

4. There are of course some nuns of Asian origin who might speak differently. See, for example, Seeger's article concerning Thai nuns' articulations of equality and rights (*Bhikkhuni Ordination* 160–161).

5. One Sri Lankan monk recalls that serious discussions about organizing an ordination of *bhikkhunis* took place among senior monks at Vidyalankara University in Sri Lanka as early as 1963. Another Sri Lankan monk, who frequently participates in transnational forums, traced the inception of the idea of an international ordination of Theravada *bhikkhunis* at Bodhgaya to the mid-1980s, when the members of the Buddha's Light International Association (BLIA), connected with Foguangshan, held a meeting in Toronto. Participants at that meeting suggested uniting the different branches of Buddhism as one Buddha vehicle, or *Buddhayāna*. He stated that at an international meeting held in Taiwan a few years later, participants decided "to bring the *bhikshuni shasana* to those countries that did not have it." He maintained that, at that time, Sakyadhita was

not as organized as it is now and had no influence in the matter. Also see the chapter "The Bhikkhuni Order" in Piyananda's book for an interest in promoting the higher ordination for women among Sri Lankan monastics that was not initiated by SIABW, as well as Yuchen Li, for a similar interest in Taiwan before the founding of SIABW (190).

6. Needless to say, a discourse of development (outlined in Chapter 5) resonates in these transnational forums. The forums have witnessed the initiation of projects to help provide for the nuns materially and to educate them in various countries.

7. Scholars have criticized Said himself for making that kind of distinction (Loomba 48–49). Sujato, an ICBW participant, is sensitive to the difference, as shown by his comment on an ICBW session: "This discussion highlighted the difference in the Tibetan community between Western and Tibetan nuns. Language gets tricky here, as not all of the bhikkhunis are Western, nor are all the Tibetan nuns 'Tibetan.' ... But leaving the labeling difficulty aside, the difference is clearly one of scope: a local versus an international perspective" ("Dark Matter" 6). Because it is necessary to emphasize a difference of *perspective* rather than a difference of geographical *place*, I focus on globalatinized ways of talking that practitioners of non-Western origin may or may not assume.

8. Despite engaging in gendered practices, nuns may not consider themselves gendered but rather may see themselves as renunciants who are beyond gender. Note however that it is the focus on *female* identity that evinces the liberal rhetoric of ordination, equality, and rights.

9. Mohanty's remarks are part of a critique of the notion of global sisterhood described in Robin Morgan's book *Sisterhood Is Global*. For another thoughtful analysis of cultural translation in relation to the idea of global feminism and narratives on gender, see Vron Ware's article.

10. One may often forget that most nuns living in Sri Lanka (and certain other countries) neither take an interest in nor can afford access to computers and the Internet, which are essential for specific kinds of transnational conversations. At the same time, some nuns living in Asia attend transnational gatherings with an aim of raising funds for their home hermitages.

11. Although this citation refers to the sameness of humans and the ontological difference of gender, we might consider how it applies to the conceptualization of a sisterhood of nuns, where sameness may be seen as that of male and female monastics and ontological difference as that of gender *and* where sameness may be seen as that of female renunciants and ontological difference as that of the first-world and third-world distinction mentioned by Mohanty.

12. Keep in mind Mandair's thinking on the notion of language and translatability of such concepts as "law" (100–101). On the question of law and necessity, see Abeysekara ("Sri Lanka").

13. For a useful discussion of the relationship between colonialism, discourse, and domination, see Loomba 20–69.

14. Tsedroen and Tathaloka are both *bhikkhunis* who are strong advocates of the *upasampada*, as are Lekshe Tsomo and Dhammananda (formerly Kabilsingh). The latter two nuns have received the higher ordination twice.

15. There are of course differences between nuns in these apparently disparate lineages or schools of Buddhism. For an account of distinct practices among diverse groups of Tibetan nuns, see Havnevik 37–59.

16. Such comparisons often emerge in SIABW discussions, as they did at the ICBW in Hamburg. Also see Tenzin Palmo, and Tsomo, "Almost Equal."

17. We may think of this as what Asad calls the "European project," in which "the translation of particular moral-legal relations that crystallized…into "universal" principles…gave us the individual as an inviolable subject of rights" ("Comment" 35).

18. Note that even when the four main Tibetan Buddhist schools hold discussions about the question of higher ordination for nuns, the Dalai Lama or his representatives seem to preside over such discussions. See "High-Level Scholarly Committee."

19. For the importance of recognizing and deconstructing such seemingly universal narratives, see Chakrabarty 27–46.

20. In his work, Mandair further explains how the notion of comparative equivalence translates into the affirmation of colonial discourse.

21. I am not suggesting that notions of equality and rights are exclusively Eurocentric, a perspective Spivak asks us to note in "Righting Wrongs" (525). My concern here is that the focus on ideals such as rights and equality in the context of the higher ordination of nuns forces a certain interpretation of nuns' concerns and tends to detract from an understanding of their renunciant everyday. For a thoughtful analysis of interpretations of human rights, also see Asad's chapter, "Redeeming the 'Human' through Human Rights" in his *Formations*.

22. This is not say that those discourses are simply pejorative. They have far-reaching consequences for an unintended politics of violently removing the subjects (nuns) from the conditions of life that make possible what they do.

23. For more on the idea of those distinctions, see Abeysekara, *Politics*, and Fitzgerald, "Who Invented Hinduism?"

24. In support of this statement, she cites Kusuma's article, "Inaccuracies," which makes no mention of the higher ordination as a basic human right. As noted in Chapter 6, Kusuma does not invoke the language of rights in the account of her own ordination.

25. In 2006 the Dalai Lama gave her 50,000 Swiss francs, which she used to help fund the ICBW. More details on these activities and the plans of the Vinaya Research Committee are outlined in Tsedroen's article, "Activities of the Vinaya Research Committee."

26. "Background and Objectives."

27. For more on these alternatives, see the works of Petra Kieffer-Pulz and Heng-ching Shih as well as the archives of Alexander Berzin.

28. One participant presiding at the session, clearly attuned to this problem, found himself intervening several times to ensure that translations of comments into Tibetan from English became available. (English proved to be the lingua franca of the evening).

29. There was some discussion about implementing the practice of *daḷhīkamma* or ("strengthening procedure") mentioned in Pali texts. This procedure permits a monastic ordained in one Buddhist ordination lineage to practice as a fully ordained monastic in another. Interestingly, the *daḷhikamma* procedure is not generally implemented among monastics in Sri Lanka and is not commonly known to many *bhikkhus* and *bhikkhunis* living there. Of course, it received more attention from monastics in Sri Lanka and elsewhere *after* the Hamburg conference.

30. She went so far as to draw a comparison to the issues of abortion and euthanasia, suggesting that she would support the "right" of another person to engage in these activities even though she herself might not agree with them in principle.

31. Her reference was to the word *upasampada*, which she explained in these terms.

32. Not being conversant in Tibetan, I cannot ascertain whether this particular point was a suggestion made by the Tibetan-speaking monastic or an elaboration of the latter's speech by the volunteer translator.

33. Some organizers of the conference had expected Asian Tibetan nuns involved with the Tibetan Nuns Project (TNP) to attend the conference and were surprised when other Tibetan nuns attended instead. According to one informant, the Tibetan nuns associated with the TNP had previously indicated their willingness to receive the *bhikkhuni* ordination, and the decision to send other Tibetan nuns was one that senior Asian Tibetan nuns made somewhat unexpectedly (to some), and probably to maintain parity among nuns in exile communities.

34. This conference participant evidently meant *Asian* Tibetan nuns.

35. That silence was unheard. Such silence highlights what Asad calls the "inequality of languages [that] is a feature of the global patterns of power created by modern imperialism and capitalism" (*Genealogies* 199). It is also reminiscent of Spivak's ideas about subaltern speech and representation.

36. Here, rather than using the term *Western*, he named individual Tibetan nuns of Western origin. The latter have argued that a higher ordination in the Tibetan lineage would allow nuns ordained in that lineage to participate in certain ritual practices and fully engage the Tibetan *Vinaya*, which they would otherwise be barred from doing.

37. After the conference, a monastic participant of Asian origin suggested that the question of monastic seniority may have prompted the Dalai Lama's inconclusive comments. That monastic suggested that because senior Tibetan nuns of Western origin had already received the *bhikkhuni* ordination in the Dharmaguptaka lineage, they might be considered senior to senior Tibetan nuns of Asian origin who would be ordained for the first time according to ordination procedures acceptable in the Mulasarvastivadin *Vinaya*. The monastic argued that nuns of Asian origin would not favor the prospect of positioning the Western Tibetan *bhikkhunis* (or *gelongmas*) as senior to the Asian Tibetan *bhikkhunis* (or *gelongmas*). Another monastic of Asian origin suggested that it was unlikely that the Dalai Lama would have publically pronounced a decision for the higher ordination in Germany (of all places). That monastic suggested such a pronouncement would more likely happen in an Asian country. Indeed, in his opening remarks at the Hamburg congress, the Dalai Lama declared that it would be "even better...if such [an international Buddhist] conference should take [place] either in India in or some of the Buddhist countries" (chuckling). He added, "but anyway it is wonderful [that an] international Buddhist conference take[s] place in Christian countries, that [is] also nice" (laughter from the audience) (Maria Jepsen).

38. The emphasis on "roles" is evident in comments made throughout the film *Women and the Buddha Potential*, made in conjunction with the ICBW, as well as in the title of the congress itself, which emphasized "Buddhist Women's Role in the Sangha." Although the Asian Tibetan nuns were put in a position of engaging the dominant concerns of the congress and addressing issues of identity, they evaded doing so. The question of the higher ordination was simply not important to them. Asad indicates that the conceptualization of *representations* of the self (roles), as distinct from the development of the *moral* self, involves "a meditation not on virtue but on power" (*Genealogies* 65). While some conference participants articulated the debate in terms of power and an idiom of roles and equality, others focused on everyday practice and the development of the moral self.

39. At the ICBW the question of the higher ordination of nuns was grounded in the symbolic meaning of the ritual status of higher ordained nuns rather than in the embodiment of disciplinary practices integral to religious lives. That difference reflects the "fundamental disparity between a 'ritual' that organizes practices aimed at the full development of the monastic self and a 'ritual' that offers a *reading* of a social institution" (*Genealogies* 78; emphasis in original). The latter is intrinsic to how the higher ordination is talked about in the transnational forums I have attended.

40. Although I pressed the topic on the nuns, the higher ordination clearly sparked no interest for them. The nuns were keener on talking to me about their everyday lives.

41. For more on Buddhism in Mongolia in recent decades, see Kollmar-Paulenz, Shakspo, Jerryson and *Bakula Rinpoche: In Commemoration.*

42. One scholar who lived and worked in Mongolia and was critical of the transnational projects to promote Buddhism there was troubled to find that the form of Tibetan Buddhism being endorsed by such projects since the 1990s differed from Mongolian Buddhism. The scholar mentioned that although senior foreign lamas (Tibetan monks) visited and preached increasingly frequently, the Buddhist practice they advocated diverged significantly from that historically practiced in Mongolia.

43. When I asked the nuns what they thought of the efforts of SIABW, they burst into laughter and then fell silent.

44. For another account of these ordinations, see Le Vine and Gellner (187–193). Their account does not address the perspectives Jenti outlined here.

45. I have avoided using the term *local* in contrast to *global* or *transnational*, because it erases the discursive element of power those terms imply. For more on the use of the term *local* see Asad (*Genealogies* 5–12).

46. On the idea of international competitions to establish *bhikkhuni* ordination lineages, also see Yuchen Li (178–179).

47. I queried her about the possibility of *bhikkhunis* in Nepal sharing sleeping quarters with a nun who had not received the full ordination (a limitation involving a *vinaya* rule observed by *bhikkhunis* in Sri Lanka). She assured me that, unlike the case with Sri Lankan *bhikkhunis*, her *bhikkhuni* ordination in Nepal did not forbid her from doing so. That *bhikkhuni* ordination has little meaning for the renunciant everyday of Nepalese nuns is affirmed by Le Vine and Gellner, who state that "few would claim that being fully ordained bhikkhunis makes a significant difference in their daily lives" (195).

48. For a discussion of the *bhikkhuni* ordination in Myanmar, see Kawanami, "*Bhikkhunī* Ordination." It is one of the few scholarly articles that begins to explain the tensions between nuns who embrace liberal ideologies and those who do not.

49. As Asad points out, the concept of "'choice" is not self-evident: "Choices and desires make actions before actions can make 'history.' But predefined social relations and language forms, as well as the body's materiality, shape the person to whom 'normal' desires and choices can be attributed. That is why questions about what it is possible for agents to do must also address the process by which 'normal persons' are constituted" (*Genealogies* 13).

50. The Asian Tibetan nuns I have met have themselves attended transnational conferences or become active in transnational projects. Yet, what the nuns conveyed to me was different from the thinking which seemed to dominate the

transnational venues in which we met. This is not to say that nuns' perspectives cannot or will not appear to change as they (possibly) continue to engage transnational projects and as the conjunctures in which their lives are debated continue to shift. As Michael Lempert's recent work argues, the interface of liberal subjectivity and liberal ideals with Tibetan Buddhism is a complicated one.

51. Paradoxically, I myself have engaged in this comparison to some extent, but here it is with the aim of demonstrating *why* it is questionable.

Works Cited

Abhayasundara, Vimal. *Ādima Yugayehi Bauddha Kantāvō* (Buddhist Women of Ancient Times). Colombo: Godage, 1999. Print.

Abeysekara, Ananda. "Buddhism, Power, Modernity." Rev. of *Gathering Leaves and Lifting Words: Histories of Buddhist Monastic Education in Laos and Thailand*, by Justin Thomas McDaniel. *Culture and Religion* 12.4 (2011): 489–497. Print.

———. *Colors of the Robe: Religion, Identity, and Difference*. Columbia: U of South Carolina P, 2002. Print. Studies in Comparative Religion Ser.

———. *The Politics of Postsecular Religion: Mourning Secular Futures*. New York: Columbia UP, 2008. Print. Insurrections: Critical Studies in Religion, Politics and Culture Ser.

———. "Sri Lanka, Postcolonial 'Locations of Buddhism,' Secular Peace: Sovereignty of Decision and Distinction." *Interventions: International Journal of Postcolonial Studies* 14.2 (2012): 211–237. Print.

———. "The Un-translatability of Religion, the Un-translatability of Life: Thinking Talal Asad's Thought Unthought in the Study of Religion." *Method and Theory in the Study of Religion* 23 (2011): 257–282. Print.

Alles, A. C. *Insurgency, 1971: An Account of the April Insurrection in Sri Lanka*. Colombo: Colombo Apothecaries, 1976. Print.

Almond, Philip C. *The British Discovery of Buddhism*. Cambridge: Cambridge UP, 1988. Print.

Analayo, "Mahāpajāpatī's Going Forth in the *Madhyama-āgama*." *Journal of Buddhist Ethics* 18 (2011): 267–317. Web. 27 May 2012.

———. "Theories on the Foundations of the Nuns' Order: A Critical Evaluation." *Journal of the Center for Buddhist Studies, Sri Lanka* 6 (2008): 105–142. Print.

"Anagarika Women's Group Formed." *Daily News* 13 June 1995: 2. Print.

Anderson, Carol. "Defining Women's Bodies in Indian Buddhist Monastic Literature." *Refiguring the Body: Embodiment in South Asian Religions*. Ed. Barbara A. Holdrege and Karen Pechilis. Albany, N.Y.: SUNY P, forthcoming.

Anuradhapura Shri Sarananda Maha Pirivena. *Sāmaṇera Baṇa Daham Pota* (Book of *Dhamma* Sermons of Novice Monks). Colombo: Anuradhapura Shri Sarananda Maha Pirivena, 1995. Print.

Arai, Paula Kane Robinson. *Women Living Zen: Japanese Sōtō Buddhist Nuns*. Oxford: Oxford UP, 1999. Print.

Ariyaratne, Sunil, dir. *Uppalavanna: A Contemporary Theri-Gatha*. Torana Music Box, 2007. DVD.

Armstrong, Aurelia. "Beyond Resistance: A Response to Zizek's Critique of Foucault's Subject of Freedom." *Parrhesia: A Journal of Critical Philosophy* 5 (2008): 19–31. Web. 10 Sept. 2011.

Asad, Talal. "A Comment on Aijaz Ahmad's *In Theory*." *Public Culture* 6.1 (1993): 31–39. Print.

———. *Formations of the Secular: Christianity, Islam, Modernity*. Palo Alto, Calif.: Stanford UP, 2003. Print. Cultural Memory in the Present Ser.

———. *Genealogies of Religion: Discipline and Reasons of Power in Christianity and Islam*. Baltimore: Johns Hopkins UP, 1993. Print.

———. "Modern Power and the Reconfiguration of Religious Traditions." *Stanford Electronic Humanities Review* 5.1 (1996): n. pag. Web. 21 Apr. 2011.

"Avasthāva." *The Shorter Sinhalese-English Dictionary*. 1949. Print.

"Background and Objectives." Proc. of First International Congress on Buddhist Women's Role in the Sangha: Bhikshuni Vinaya and Ordination Lineages with H.H. the Dalai Lama, 18–20 July 2007, U of Hamburg. Web. 10 Apr. 2010.

Bakula Rinpoche: In Commemoration of the 91st Birth Anniversary of HH Bakula Rinpoche. Ulaanbaatar: Penthub Buddhist Center, 2008. Print.

Bannerji, Himani. *Inventing Subjects: Studies in Hegemony, Patriarchy and Colonialism*. London: Anthem P, 2002. Print. Anthem South Asian Studies Ser.

Barnes, Nancy Schuster. "Buddhism." *Women in World Religions*. Ed. Arvind Sharma. Albany, N.Y.: SUNY P, 1987. 105–134. Print. McGill Studies in the History of Religions Ser.

Bartholomeusz, Tessa J. *Women under the Bō Tree: Buddhist Nuns in Sri Lanka*. New York: Cambridge UP, 1994. Print. Cambridge Studies in Religious Traditions Ser. 5.

Bechert, Heinz. *Buddhismus, Staat und Gesellschaft in den Ländern des Theravāda-Buddhismus*. Vol. 1. *Grundlagen: Ceylon*. Frankfurt am Main: Metzner, 1966. Print. Schriften des Instituts fur Asienkunde in Hamburg Ser. 17.

———. *Buddhismus, Staat und Gesellschaft in den Ländern des Theravāda-Buddhismus*. Vol. 2. *Birma, Kambodscha, Laos, Thailand*. Wiesbaden: Harrossowitz, 1967. Print. Schriften des Instituts fur Asienkunde in Hamburg Ser. 17.

Belsey, Catherine. *Critical Practice*. 2nd ed. London: Routledge, 2002. Print.

Bermann, Sandra, and Michael Wood, eds. *Nation, Language, and the Ethics of Translation*. Princeton, N.J.: Princeton UP, 2005. Print. Translation/Transnation Ser.

Berzin, Alexander. *A Summary Report of the 2007 International Congress on the Women's Role in the Sangha: Bhikshuni Vinaya and Ordination Lineages.* Parts 1–4. *Berzin Archives: The Buddhist Archives of Dr. Alexander Berzin, 2003–2012.* Web. 30 May 2012.

Beyer, Peter. *Religion and Globalization.* London: Sage, 1994. Print. Theory, Culture and Society Ser.

Bhabha, Homi K. *The Location of Culture.* London: Routledge, 1994. Print.

———. "The Other Question: Difference, Discrimination, and the Discourse of Colonialism." *Black British Cultural Studies: A Reader.* Ed. Houston A. Baker Jr. et al. Chicago: U of Chicago P, 1996. 87–106. Print.

Bhadra. *Higher Ordination and Bhikkhuni Order in Sri Lanka.* Dehiwala, Sri Lanka: Sridevi, 2001. Print

Bhadra, Vakada. *Nivan Maga Heli Karana Upasampadāva.* (The Higher Ordination which Leads the Way to Nibbana). Ratmalana: Vishva Lekha, 2001. Print.

"Bhikkhuni Order—Can It Be Re-established?" *The Sun* 12 June 1986: 7. Print.

"Bhikṣunī Upasampadāva Budusasunṭa Apala Da? Sapala Da?" (Is the Higher Ordination of *Bhikkhunis* Unproductive or Productive for the Buddhist Dispensation?) *Dhammavedi* 3.4 (July 1999): 20–23. Print.

Bizot, François. *Les Traditions de la pabbajjā en Asie du Sud-Est: recherches sur le bouddhisme khmer,* 4. Gottingen: Vandenhoeck & Ruprecht, 1988. Print. Abhandlungen der Akademie der Wissenschaften in Gottingen. Philologisch-historische Klasse, F. 3, Nr. 169.

Blackburn, Anne M. *Locations of Buddhism: Colonialism and Modernity in Sri Lanka.* Chicago: U of Chicago P, 2010. Print. Buddhism and Modernity Ser.

Blackstone, Kate. "Damming the Dhamma: Problems with Bhikkhunīs in the Pāli Vinaya." *Journal of Buddhist Ethics* 6 (1999): 292–312. Web. 15 Apr. 2012.

Blake, E. "A Buddhist Nun." *Buddhist Review.* 7 (1915): 47–58. Print.

———. "The Sacred Bo Tree." *The Nineteenth Century and After.* 76 (July-Dec. 1914): 660–673. Print.

Bloch, Esther, Marianne Keppens, and Rajaram Hegde, eds. *Rethinking Religion in India: The Colonial Construction of Hinduism.* London: Routledge, 2010. Print.

Bloss, Lowell W. "The Female Renunciants of Sri Lanka: The Dasasilmattawa." *Journal of the International Association of Buddhist Studies* 10.1 (1987): 7–31. Print.

Bodhgaya International Full Ordination Ceremony. Taipei: Foguang Cultural Enterprise, 1998. Print.

Bond, George D. *The Buddhist Revival in Sri Lanka: Religious Tradition, Reinterpretation and Response.* Columbia: U of South Carolina P, 1988. Print.

———. *Buddhism at Work: Community Development, Social Empowerment and the Sarvodaya Movement.* Bloomfield, Conn.: Kumarian. 2004. Print.

Boserup, Ester. *Woman's Role in Economic Development.* New York: St. Martin's. 1970. Print.

Bourdieu, Pierre. *Language and Symbolic Power*. Ed. and Introd. John B. Thompson. Trans. Gino Raymond and Matthew Adamson. Malden, Mass.: Polity, 1991. Print.

Bourdieu, Pierre. "Legitimation and Structured Interests in Weber's Sociology of Religion." Trans. Chris Turner. *Max Weber, Rationality and Modernity*. Ed. Sam Whimster and Scott Lash. London: Allen and Unwin, 1987. 119–136. Print.

———. *The Logic of Practice*. Cambridge: Polity, 1990. Print.

———. *Outline of a Theory of Practice*. Cambridge: Cambridge UP, 1977. Print. Cambridge Studies in Social Anthropology Ser.

Brown, Sid. *The Journey of One Buddhist Nun: Even against the Wind*. Albany, N.Y.: SUNY P, 2001. Print.

Brown, Wendy. *States of Injury: Power and Freedom in Late Modernity*. Princeton, N.J.: Princeton UP, 1995. Print.

Bstan-'dzin-rgya-mtsho, Dalai Lama XIV. Comments on reviving the full ordination of Tibetan nuns. "Wisdom Compassion Peace: His Holiness the 14th Dalai Lama at Smith College." Buddhist studies faculty seminar moderated by Jamie Hubbard. Smith College, 9 May 2007. Jamie Hubbard's home page. Web. 10 July 2011.

———. "Opening Speech of His Holiness the Dalai Lama." Tsomo, *Sakyadhītā* 39–46.

Buddha Shasana Rajya Amathayanshaye Lekam. (Secretary to the Ministry of Buddha Sasana). "Silmāṇivaru puhuṇu karana ārāmayak ārambha karanavā" (Opening a Training Hermitage for *Sil Manis*). *Dinamiṇa* 19 Dec. 1989: 13. Print.

"Buddhist Nuns in China Today." *Sunday Observer* 15 February 1981:9. Print.

Butler, Judith. *Undoing Gender*. New York: Routledge, 2004. Print.

Calman, Leslie J. *Toward Empowerment: Women and Movement Politics in India*. Boulder, Colo.: Westview, 1992. Print.

Carter, John Ross, and Mahinda Palihawadana. *The Dhammapada: A New English Translation, with the Pali Text and First English Translation of the Commentary's Explanation of the Verses*. New York: Oxford UP, 1987. Print.

CENWOR (Centre for Women's Research). *The Hidden Face of Development: Women, Work and Equality in Sri Lanka*. Proc. of National Convention on Women's Studies, 1–3 Mar. 1989, CENWOR. Colombo: CENWOR, 1989. Print.

———. *The UN Decade for Women: Progress and Achievements of Women in Sri Lanka*. Colombo: CENWOR, 1985. Print.

Chakrabarty, Dipesh. *Provincializing Europe: Postcolonial Thought and Historical Difference*. Princeton, N.J.: Princeton UP, 2000. Print. Princeton Studies in Culture/Power/History Ser.

Chalmers, Robert, ed. *The Majjhima-Nikāya*. Vol. 2. Oxford: Oxford UP, 1993. Print. Pali Text Society Text Ser. 61.

———, ed. *The Majjhima-Nikāya*. Vol. 3. Oxford: Oxford UP, 1994. Print. Pali Text Society Text Ser. 62.

Chandima. "Dasasil Peḷapāliya." (A Procession of Ten-Precept Nuns). *Meheṇi Udāva* (Dawn of the *Meheni*) 3 (1991): 36–38. Print.

Chandler, Stuart. *Establishing a Pure Land on Earth: The Foguang Buddhist Perspective on Modernization and Globalization*. Honolulu: U of Hawai'i P, 2004. Print. Topics in Contemporary Buddhism Ser.

Chaṭṭha Saṅgāyana (The Six *Dhamma* Councils). 3rd version. Vipassana Research Institute, 1999. CD-ROM.

Cheng, Wei-Yi. *Buddhist Nuns in Taiwan and Sri Lanka: A Critique of the Feminist Perspective*. London: Routledge, 2007. Print. Routledge Critical Studies in Buddhism Ser.

———. "A Cross-Tradition Exchange between Taiwan and Sri Lanka." *Journal of Buddhist Ethics* 18 (2011): 249–267. Web. 24 July 2012.

Choompolpaisal, Phibul. "Constrictive Constructs: Unravelling the Influence of Weber's Sociology on Theravada Studies since the 1960s." *Contemporary Buddhism* 9.1 (2008): 7–51. Print.

Chung, Jin Il. "Gurudharma und Aṣṭau Gurudharmāḥ." *Indo-Iranian Journal* 42.3 (1999): 227–234. Print.

Cohn, Bernard S. *Colonialism and Its Forms of Knowledge: The British in India*. Princeton, N.J.: Princeton UP, 1996. Print.

Collett, Alice. "Buddhism and Gender: Reframing and Refocusing the Debate." *Journal of Feminist Studies in Religion* 22.2 (2006): 55–84. Print.

Collins, Steven, and Justin McDaniel. "Buddhist 'Nuns' (Mae Chi) and the Teaching of Pali in Contemporary Thailand." *Modern Asian Studies* 44.6 (2010): 1373–1408. Print.

Collins, Steven. *Civilisation et femmes célibataires dans le bouddhisme en Asie du Sud et du Sud-Est: Une " étude de genre."* Paris: Cerf. 2011. Print. Les Conférences de l' École Practique des Hautes Études Ser.

———. "Monasticism, Utopias and Comparative Social Theory." *Religion* 18.2 (1988): 101–135. Print.

———. *Selfless Persons: Imagery and Thought in Theravāda Buddhism*. Cambridge: Cambridge UP, 1982. Print.

Cook, Joanna. *Meditation in Modern Buddhism: Renunciation and Change in Thai Monastic Life*. Cambridge: Cambridge UP, 2010. Print.

Copleston, Reginald Stephen. *Buddhism, Primitive and Present in Magadha and in Ceylon*. London: Longmans, Green, 1892. Print.

Crosby, Kate. "Changing the Landscape of Theravada Studies." Editorial. *Contemporary Buddhism* 9.1 (2008): 1–6. Print.

"Dasasil mǎṇivaru" (Dasasil Manis). *Budusaraṇa* 28 April 1991: 4. Print.

"Dasa sil mātā abhivruddhiyaṭa viśeṣa vāda piḷiveḷak ōnä" (A Special Program Is Needed for the Development of *Dasa Sil Matas*). *Dinamiṇa* 12 Dec. 1989: 8. Print.

"Dasa Sil Mathas Face a Dilemma." *Weekend* 20 Apr. 1986: 3. Print.

"Dasasil mātāvangē yahapataṭa Bauddha Samuluwa idiripat veyi" (Buddhist Congress Steps Forward for the Well-Being of *Dasasil Matas*). *Budusaraṇa* 26 Feb. 1981: 15. Print.

Davids, T. W. Rhys, and William Stcdc. *The Pali Text Society's Pali-English Dictionary*. London: Pali Text Society, 1921–1925. Print.

de Alwis, Malathi. "The Changing Role of Women in Sri Lankan Society." *Social Research* 69.3 (2002): 675–691. Print.

———. "Gender, Politics and the 'Respectable Lady.'" *Unmaking the Nation: The Politics of Identity and History in Modern Sri Lanka*. Ed. Pradeep Jeganathan and Qadri Ismail. Colombo: Social Science Association, 1995: 137–157. Print.

de Certeau, Michel. *The Practice of Everyday Life*. Berkeley: U of California P, 1984. Print.

Deegalle, Mahinda. "Does Feminism Challenge Buddhism?" *The Island* 29 Apr. 1991: 4. Print.

De Kock, Leon. "Interview with Gayatri Chakravorty Spivak: New Nation Writers Conference in South Africa." *ARIEL: A Review of International English Literature* 23.3 (1992): 29–47. Print.

de Mel, Neloufer. *Militarizing Sri Lanka: Popular Culture, Memory and Narrative in the Armed Conflict*. New Delhi: Sage, 2007. Print.

Derrida, Jacques. *Acts of Religion*. London: Routledge, 2002. Print.

Derwich, Marek. "Monk-Bishops." *Encyclopedia of Monasticism*. 2000. Print.

Devasara, P. "Sil mātāvan 'anagārikā' namin amatamu" (Let Us Call *Sil Matas* "Homeless Ones"). *Budusaraṇa* 27 April 1987: 3. Print.

DeVido, Elise Anne. *Taiwan's Buddhist Nuns*. Albany, N.Y.: SUNY P, 2010. Print.

Dewaraja, L. S. *The Position of Women in Buddhism*. Kandy, Sri Lanka: Buddhist Publication Society, 1981. Print. The Wheel Ser. 280.

Dhammaloka, Talalle. *Mahāprajāpatī Gōtamiya Saha Bhikṣuṇī Sāsanaya*. (Mahaprajapati Gotami and the *Bhikshuni* Dispensation). Sakyadhita Jatiyantara Kantha Saṇvidhānaya, 1998. Print.

Dhammananda. "Keeping Track of the Revival of Bhikkhuni Ordination in Sri Lanka." *Yasodhara: Newsletter on International Buddhist Women's Activities* 1 Oct. 2006. *The Free Library*. Web. 28 Mar. 2010.

Dhammaratana, Induragare. "Kantāva Pilibanda Bauddha Nirvachanaya" (A Buddhist Explanation in Relation to Women). *Nivan Maga* 25 (Vesak 2538/1994): 1–10. Print.

Dhammavasa, Kotugoda." "Sil mātāvan 'anagārikā' namin amatamu" (Let Us Call *Sil Matas* "Homeless Ones"). *Budusaraṇa* 21 Feb. 1987; 9. Print.

Dhammavihari. *Woman in Buddhism: Studies on Her Position and Role*. Kandy, Sri Lanka: Buddhist Publication Society, 2003. Print.

Donaldson, Laura E., and Pui-lan Kwok. Introduction. Donaldson and Kwok 1–38.

———, eds. *Postcolonialism, Feminism, and Religious Discourse*. London: Routledge, 2002. Print.

Dubuisson, Daniel. *The Western Construction of Religion: Myths, Knowledge, and Ideology*. Trans. William Sayers. Baltimore: Johns Hopkins UP, 2003. Print.

Dutch Foundation for Ladakhi Nuns. Cordaid, 2011. Web. 20 September 2011.

Engler, Steven. "Modern Times: Religion, Consecration and the State in Bourdieu." *Cultural Studies* 17.3 (2003): 445–467. Print.

Enloe, Cynthia. *The Curious Feminist: Searching for Women in a New Age of Empire*. Berkeley: U of California P, 2004. Print.

———. *Bananas, Beaches, and Bases: Making Feminist Sense of International Politics*. Berkeley: U of California P, 1989. Print.

"Empower." *The New Shorter Oxford English Dictionary on Historical Principles*. 1993. Print.

Escobar, Arturo. "Discourse and Power in Development: Michel Foucault and the Relevance of His Work to the Third World," *Alternatives* 10 (winter 1984–1985): 377–400. Print.

Falk, Monica Lindberg. *Making Fields of Merit: Buddhist Female Ascetics and Gendered Orders in Thailand*. Seattle: U of Washington P, 2007. Print. Critical Dialogues in Southeast Asian Studies Ser.

Falk, Nancy Auer. "The Case of the Vanishing Nuns: The Fruits of Ambivalence in Ancient Indian Buddhism." Falk and Gross 155–165.

Falk, Nancy Auer, and Rita M. Gross. "Introduction to the First Edition: Patterns in Women's Religious Lives." Falk and Gross xiii–xviii.

———, eds. *Unspoken Worlds: Women's Religious Lives*. Belmont, Calif.: Wadsworth, 1989. Print.

Fenn, Mavis, and Kay Koppedrayer. "Sakyadhita: A Transnational Meeting Place for Buddhist Women." *Journal of Global Buddhism* 9 (2008): 45–79. Web. 6 Aug. 2012.

Findly, Ellison Banks, ed. *Women's Buddhism, Buddhism's Women: Tradition, Revision, Renewal*. Boston: Wisdom, 2000. Print.

"First All Sri Lankan Bhikkhuni Dana." Theravada Samadhi Education Association. Bodagama Chandima. n.d. Web. 24 July 2012.

"The First International Conference on Buddhist Nuns." Tsomo, *Sakyadhītā* 31–37.

Fitzgerald, Timothy. *The Ideology of Religious Studies*. Oxford: Oxford UP, 2000. Print.

———. "Who Invented Hinduism? Rethinking Religion in India." Bloch, Keppens, and Hegde 114–134.

Foucault, Michel. *Discipline and Punish: The Birth of the Prison*. New York: Pantheon, 1977. Print.

———. "The Subject and Power." *Critical Inquiry* 8.4 (1982): 777–795. Print.

Friedman, Marilyn. "Autonomy and Social Relationships: Rethinking the Feminist Critique." *Feminists Rethink the Self*. Ed. Diana Tietjens Meyers. Boulder, Colo.: Westview, 1997. 40–61. Print. Feminist Theory and Politics Ser.

Gamburd, Michele Ruth. *The Kitchen Spoon's Handle: Transnationalism and Sri Lanka's Migrant Housemaids*. Ithaca, N.Y.: Cornell UP, 2000. Print.

Gandhi, Leela. "Postcolonialism and Feminism." *Postcolonial Theory: A Critical Introduction.* New York: Columbia UP (1998): 81–101. Print.

Gethin, Rupert. *The Foundations of Buddhism.* Oxford: Oxford UP, 1998. Print.

Gnanarama, Pathegama. "Bhikshunī Śāsanaya Nävata Äti Kala Häkiya." (It is Possible to Reinstate the Bhikshuni Dispensation). Weeraratne, Tuduvage, and Dinapala 205–212.

Gnanashila, Ambala Rohana. "Letter to the President." *Meheṇi Udāva.* (The Dawn of the Sri Lankan *Meheni Sasna*). 2. (1990): 37–39. Print.

———. "Meheṇi sasna labāganna gaha bäna gannada kiyannē?" (Do You Mean We Should Debate and Fight to Establish the *Meheni Sasana?*) *Tharuṇī.* 7 Aug. 1985: 8–9. Print.

———. *Sirilak Meheṇi Udāva (The Dawn of the Sri Lankan Meheni Sasna).* Ambala Shri Rohana Gnanashila, 2004. Print.

Gombrich, Richard F., and Gananath Obeyesekere. *Buddhism Transformed: Religious Change in Sri Lanka.* Princeton, N.J.: Princeton UP, 1988. Print.

Gombrich, Richard F. *How Buddhism Began: The Conditioned Genesis of the Early Teachings.* London: Athlone, 1996. Print.

———. *Precept and Practice.* Oxford: Clarendon, 1971. Print.

———. "Temporary Ordination in Sri Lanka." *Journal of the International Association of Buddhist Studies* 7.2 (1984): 41–65. Print.

———. *Theravada Buddhism: A Social History from Ancient Benares to Modern Colombo.* London: Routledge & Kegan Paul, 1988. Print. Library of Religious Beliefs and Practices Ser.

Goodwin, Jeff, and James M. Jasper, eds. *The Social Movements Reader: Cases and Concepts.* Malden, Mass.: Blackwell, 2003. Print. Blackwell Readers in Sociology Ser. 12.

Goonatilake, Hema. "Women Regaining a Lost Legacy: The Restoration of the Bhikkhunī Order in Sri Lanka." Tsomo, *Out of the Shadows* 42–47.

Gothoni, Rene. *Modes of Life of Theravada Monks: A Case Study of Buddhist Monasticism in Sri Lanka.* Helsinki: Societas Orientalis Fennica, 1982. Print. Studia Orientalia Ser. 52.

"Govt. Will Help Set Up Order for Buddhist Nuns Says President." *Times of Ceylon* 16 Jan. 1974: 3. Print.

"Govt. Will Help to Revive Bhikkhuni Sasana—President." *Ceylon Daily Mirror* 16 Jan. 1974: 3. Print.

Gross, Rita M. "Buddhism after Patriarchy." *After Patriarchy: Feminist Transformations of the World Religions.* Ed. Paula M. Cooey, William R. Eakin, and Jay B. McDaniel. New York: Orbis. 1991: 65–86. Print.

———. *Buddhism after Patriarchy: A Feminist History, Analysis and Reconstruction of Buddhism.* Albany, N.Y.: SUNY P, 1993. Print.

———. "Buddhist Women as Leaders and Teachers: Gender Bias and Democratization." Tsomo, *Out of the Shadows* 356–362.

———. *Feminism and Religion: An Introduction.* Boston: Beacon, 1996. Print.

———. *A Garland of Feminist Reflections: Forty Years of Religious Exploration*. Berkeley: U of California P, 2009. Print.

———. "Religious Diversity: Some Implications for Monotheism." *Cross Currents* 49.3 (1999): n. pag. Web. 21 May 2011.

———. "Response: A Rose by Any Other Name…: A Response to Katherine K. Young." *Journal of the American Academy of Religion* 67.1 (1999): 185–194. Print.

Grossholtz, Jean. *Forging Capitalist Patriarchy: The Economic and Social Transformation of Feudal Sri Lanka and Its Impact on Women*. Durham, N.C.: Duke UP, 1984. Print. Duke Press Policy Studies Ser.

Gunawardene, R.A.L.H. *Robe and Plough: Monasticism and Economic Interest in Early and Medieval Sri Lanka*, Tucson: U of Arizona P, 1979. Print. Monographs of the Association for Asian Studies Ser. 35.

Gutschow, Kim. *Being a Buddhist Nun: The Struggle for Enlightenment in the Himalayas*. Cambridge, Mass.: Harvard UP, 2004. Print.

Hall, Stuart, David Held, and Tony McGrew, eds. *Modernity and Its Futures*. Cambridge: Polity, 1992. Print. Understanding Modern Societies Ser.

Hannerz, Ulf. *Transnational Connections: Culture, People, Places*. London: Routledge, 1996. Print. Comedia Ser.

Hardy, E., ed. *Anguttara Nikāya*. Parts 3–4. London: Pali Text Society, 1958. Print.

Harrison, Frances. "'Rebel' Nuns Battle Monks' Scorn." *BBC News* 29 Jan. 2004. Web. 23 Dec. 2011.

Harvey, Peter. *An Introduction to Buddhism: Teachings, History and Practices.*Cambridge: Cambridge UP, 1990. Print.

Havnevik, Hanna. *Tibetan Buddhist Nuns: History, Cultural Norms and Social Reality*. New York: Oxford UP, 1990. Print.

Hecker, Hellmuth. *Lives of the Disciples: Buddhist Women at the Time of Buddha*. Kandy, Sri Lanka: Buddhist Publication Society, 1982. Print. The Wheel Ser. 292/293.

Heirman, Ann. "Becoming a Nun in the Dharmaguptaka Tradition." *Buddhist Studies Review* 25.2 (2008): 174–193. Print.

———. "Fifth Century Chinese Nuns: An Exemplary Case." *Buddhist Studies Review* 27.1 (2010): 61–76. Print.

———. "Where Is the Probationer in the Chinese Buddhist Nunneries?" *Zeitschrift der deutschen morgenländischen Gesellschaft* 158.1 (2008): 105–137. Print.

Hekman, Susan J. *Private Selves, Public Identities: Reconsidering Identity Politics*. University Park: Pennsylvania State UP, 2004. Print.

Hewamanne, Sandya. *Stitching Identities in a Free Trade Zone: Gender and Politics in Sri Lanka*. Philadelphia: U of Pennsylvania P, 2007. Print. Contemporary Ethnography Ser.

"High-Level Scholarly Committee Meets to Discuss Gelongma Ordination." *Phayul. com*. Phayul. 6 Aug. 2012 Web. 8 Aug. 2012.

"History in the Making?" *Go Beyond Words*. Wisdom Publications, 3 Nov. 2009. Web. 30 Aug. 2012.

Holt, John Clifford, Jacob N. Kinnard, and Jonathan S. Walters, eds. *Constituting Communities: Theravada Buddhism and the Religious Cultures of South and Southeast Asia.* Albany, N.Y.: SUNY P, 2003. Print. SUNY Series in Buddhist Studies.

Horner, I. B. *Women under Primitive Buddhism: Laywomen and Almswomen.* Delhi: Motilal Banarsidass, 1989. Print.

Husken, Ute. "Die Legende von der Einrichtung des buddhistischen Nonnenordens im Vinaya-Pitaka der Theravādin." *Studien zur Indologie und Buddhismuskunde:* Ed. Reinhold Grunendahl, Jens-Uwe Hartmann, and Petra Kieffer-Pulz. Festgabe des Seminar für Indologie und Buddhismuskunde für Professor Dr. Heinz Bechert zum 60 Geburtstag, 27 June 1992, Bonn: Indica et Tibetica, 1993. 151–170. Print.

Inda, Jonathan Xavier, and Renato Rosaldo, eds. *The Anthropology of Globalization: A Reader.* Malden, Mass.: Blackwell, 2002. Print. Blackwell Readers in Anthropology Ser. 1.

Inden, Ronald B. *Imagining India.* Bloomington: Indiana UP, 1990. Print.

Ismail, Qadri. *Abiding by Sri Lanka: On Peace, Place, and Postcoloniality.* Minneapolis: U of Minnesota P, 2005. Print. Public Worlds Ser. 16.

Jayawardena, Kumari. *The White Woman's Other Burden: Western Women and South Asia during British Rule.* New York: Routledge, 1995. Print.

Jepsen, Maria. "H.H. the Dalai Lama." Proc. of First International Congress on Buddhist Women's Role in the Sangha, 18–20 July 2007, U of Hamburg. Auditorium-Netzwerk, 2007. CD-ROM. Disc 2.

Jerryson, Michael, K. *Mongolian Buddhism: The Rise and Fall of the Sangha.* Chiang Mai, Thailand: Silkworm, 2007. Print.

Jordt, Ingrid. "Bhikkhuni, Thilashin, Mae-Chii: Women Who Renounce the World in Burma." *Crossroads* 4.1 (1988): 31–39. Print.

———. *Burma's Mass Lay Meditation Movement: Buddhism and the Cultural Construction of Power.* Athens: Ohio UP, 2007. Print. Ohio University Research in International Studies: Southeast Asia Ser. 115.

Jutima. "The Amazing Resurgence of Woman Sangahood in Sri Lanka." *Sunday Times* 2 Mar. 2003. Web. 5 July 2011.

Kabilsingh, Chatsumarn. *Thai Women in Buddhism.* Berkeley, Calif.: Parallax, 1991. Print.

"Kalakirīma." *The Shorter Sinhalese-English Dictionary.* 1949. Print.

"Kalakirenavā." *The Shorter Sinhalese-English Dictionary.* 1949. Print.

Kariyawasam, Tilokasundari. *Theravada Buddhism and Feminism.* Colombo: Ministry of Education, 1987. Print.

"Kasāvat därīma sil māṇivaruṇṭa tahanamda?" ("Are *Sil Manis* Forbidden to Wear Yellow Attire?"). *Budusaraṇa* 23 Dec. 1992: 4. Print.

Kawahashi, Noriko. "Buddhism after Patriarchy: A Feminist History, Analysis and Reconstruction of Buddhism." *Japanese Journal of Religious Studies* 21.4 (1994): 445–449. Print.

Kawanami, Hiroko. "The *Bhikkhunī* Ordination Debate: Global Aspirations, Local Concerns, with Special Emphasis on the Views of the Monastic Community in Burma." *Buddhist Studies Review* 24.2 (2007): 226–244. Print.

———. "Patterns of Renunciation: The Changing World of Burmese Nuns." Findly 159–171.

———. "The Religious Standing of Burmese Buddhist Nuns (Thilá-Shin): The Ten Precepts and Religious Respect Words." *Journal of the International Association of Buddhist Studies* 13.1 (1990): 17–39. Print.

Kieffer-Pulz, Petra. "Presuppositions for a Valid Ordination with Respect to the Restoration of the Bhikṣuṇī Ordination in the Mūlasarvāstivāda Tradition." *Dignity and Discipline: Reviving Full Ordination for Buddhist Nuns.* Ed. Thea Mohr and Jampa Tsedroen. Boston: Wisdom, 2010. 217–225. Print.

King, Richard. *Orientalism and Religion: Postcolonial Theory, India and the "Mystic East."* London: Routledge, 1999. Print.

Kiribamune, Sirima, and Vidyamali Samarasinghe, eds. *Women at the Crossroads: A Sri Lankan Perspective.* New Delhi: International Centre for Ethnic Studies, 1990. Print.

Klein, Anne C. *Meeting the Great Bliss Queen: Buddhists, Feminists, and the Art of the Self.* Boston: Beacon, 1995. Print.

Kodikara, Vatsala, M. *Buddha Kantāvagē Samāja Kāryabhārya* (Social Obligations of Buddhist Women). Colombo: Godage, 2000. Print.

Kollmar-Paulenz, Karenina. "Buddhism in Mongolia after 1990." *Journal of Global Buddhism* 4 (2003): 18–34. Web. 27 May 2012.

Koppedrayer, Kay. "Feminist Applications of Buddhist Thought." *Journal of Feminist Studies in Religion* 23.1 (2007): 121–140. Print.

Krey, Gisela. "On Women as Teachers in Early Buddhism: Dhammadinnā and Khemā." *Buddhist Studies Review* 27.1 (2010): 17–40. Print.

Kusuma. "The Bhikkhunī Vinaya: A Study of the Vinaya Rules of Bhikkhunīs and Translation of the Pali Bhikkhunī Pāṭimokkha with Commentarial References." Diss. Buddhist and Pali U of Sri Lanka, 1999. Print.

———. *Bhikṣunī Vinaya.* Ratmalana, Sri Lanka: Vishva Lekha, 2003. Print.

———. *The Dasasil Nun: A Study of Women's Buddhist Religious Movement in Sri Lanka with an Outline of Its Historical Antecedents.* Diss. U of Sri Jayawardenepura, 1987. Dehiwala, Sri Lanka: Kusuma, 2010. Print.

———. "How I Became a Bhikkhuni." *Sakyadhita International Association of Buddhist Women* 16.2 (2008): 16–18. Print.

———. "Inaccuracies in Buddhist Women's History." Tsomo, *Innovative Buddhist Women* 5–12.

Kwok, Pui-lan. "Gender, Colonialism, and the Study of Religion." Donaldson and Kwok 14–28.

———. "Unbinding Our Feet: Saving Brown Women and Feminist Religious Discourse." Donaldson and Kwok 62–99.

"Laity." *The New Shorter Oxford English Dictionary on Historical Principles*. 1993. Print.

"Lay." *The New Shorter Oxford English Dictionary on Historical Principles*. 1993. Print.

Leach, Edmund Ronald. *Pul Eliya, a Village in Ceylon: A Study of Land Tenure and Kinship*. Cambridge: Cambridge UP, 1961. Print.

Lempert, Michael. *Discipline and Debate: The Language of Violence in a Tibetan Buddhist Monastery*. Berkeley: U of California P, 2012, Print.

LeVine, Sarah, and David N. Gellner. *Rebuilding Buddhism: The Theravada Movement in Twentieth-Century Nepal*. Cambridge, Mass.: Harvard UP, 2005. Print.

Li, Yuchen. "Ordination, Legitimacy, and Sisterhood: The International Full Ordination Ceremony in Bodhgaya." Tsomo, *Innovative Buddhist Women* 168–198.

Loomba, Ania. *Colonialism-Postcolonialism*. London: Routledge, 1998. Print. The New Critical Idiom Ser.

Lynch, Caitrin. *Juki Girls, Good Girls: Gender and Cultural Politics in Sri Lanka's Global Garment Industry*. Ithaca, N.Y.: Cornell UP, 2007. Print.

Macy, Joanna. *Dharma and Development: Religion as Resource in the Sarvodaya Self-Help Movement*. West Hartford, Conn.: Kumarian, 1983. Print.

"Maha Bodhi Society Will Boost Dasa Sil Mathas' Image—Thera." *Daily News* 29 Jan. 1996: 12. Print.

Mahmood, Saba. *Politics of Piety: The Islamic Revival and the Feminist Subject*. Princeton, N.J.: Princeton UP, 2005. Print.

Malalgoda, Kitsiri. *Buddhism in Sinhalese Society, 1750–1900: A Study of Religious Revival and Change*. Berkeley: U of California P, 1976. Print.

Mandair, Arvind-Pal Singh. *Religion and the Specter of the West: Sikhism, India, Postcoloniality, and the Politics of Translation*. New York: Columbia UP, 2009. Print. Insurrections: Critical Studies in Religion, Politics, and Culture Ser.

Mas, Ruth. "Refiguring Translation in Religious Studies." *Method and Theory in the Study of Religion* 23.2 (2011): 143–159. Print.

Masuzawa, Tomoko. *The Invention of World Religions; or, How European Universalism Was Preserved in the Language of Pluralism*. Chicago: U of Chicago P, 2005. Print.

McAdam, Doug, John D. McCarthy, and Mayer N. Zald, eds. *Comparative Perspectives on Social Movements: Political Opportunities, Mobilizing Structures, and Cultural Framings*. Cambridge: Cambridge UP, 1996. Print. Cambridge Studies in Comparative Politics Ser.

———. "Introduction." McAdam, McCarthy, and Zald 1–20.

McCarthy, John D. "Constraints and Opportunities in Adopting, Adapting and Inventing." McAdam, McCarthy, and Zald 141–151.

McCoy, Liza. "Keeping the Institution in View: Working with Interview Accounts of Everyday Experience." *Institutional Ethnography as Practice*. Ed. Dorothy E. Smith. 109–125.

McDaniel, Justin. *Gathering Leaves and Lifting Words: Histories of Buddhist Monastic Education in Laos and Thailand*. Seattle: U of Washington P, 2008. Print. Critical Dialogues in Southeast Asian Studies Ser.

McLeod, John. *Beginning Postcolonialism*. Manchester: Manchester UP, 2000. Print. Beginnings Ser.

Meeks, Lori. *Hokkeji and the Reemergence of the Female Monastic Orders in Premodern Japan*. Honolulu: U of Hawai'i P, 2010. Print. Kuroda Institute Studies in East Asian Buddhism Ser. 23.

"Meheṇi sasna yali Sirilak pihiṭa vu vagayi!" (An Account of the Reestablishment of the *Meheni Sasana* in Sri Lanka!). *Dinamiṇa* 12 March 1998: 15. Print.

Mitragnanissari, Panagoda. "Sil mātā saṇvidhānayē aitihāsika pasubima saha ehi vartmāna tattvaya" (Historical Background of the *Sil Mata* Organization and Its Present State). Weeraratne, Tuduvage, and Dinapala 128–144.

Mohanty, Chandra Talpade. *Feminism without Borders: Decolonizing Theory, Practicing Solidarity*. Durham, N.C.: Duke UP, 2003. Print.

Mohr, Thea. "Sakyadhita: Empowering the Daughters of the Buddha." Tsomo, *Bridging Worlds* 20–30.

———. *Weibliche Identität und Leerheit: Eine ideengeschichtliche Rekonstruktion der buddhistischen Frauenbewegung Sakyadhītā International*. Frankfurt am Main: Peter Lang. 2002. Print. Theion: Jahrbuch fur Religionskultur Ser. 13.

Mohr, Thea and Jampa Tsedroen, eds. *Dignity and Discipline: Reviving Full Ordination for Buddhist Nuns*. Boston: Wisdom, 2010. Print.

Morris, Richard, ed. *The Aṅguttara-Nikâya*. Part 1. Ed. A. K. Warder. 2nd ed. London: Luzac, 1961. Print.

———, ed. *The Aṅguttara-Nikâya*. Part 2. London: Luzac, 1955. Print.

———, ed. *The Puggala-Paññatti*. Part 1. London: H. Frowde, 1883. Print. Pali Text Society Publications Ser. 6.

Morris, Rosalind C, ed. *Can the Subaltern Speak? Reflections on the History of an Idea*. New York: Columbia UP, 2010. Print.

"Move to Reestablish Order of Bhikkhunis in the Island." *Ceylon Daily News* 21 Oct. 1972: 9. Print.

Mrozik, Susanne. "A Robed Revolution: The Contemporary Buddhist Nun's (Bhikṣuṇī) Movement." *Religion Compass* 3.3 (2009): 360–378. Print.

Muller, F. Max. *Introduction to the Science of Religion: Four Lectures Delivered at the Royal Institution in February and May 1870*. London: Longmans, Green, 1899. Print. Collected Works of the Right Hon. F. Max Muller Ser. 14.

Murcott, Susan. *The First Buddhist Women: Translations and Commentaries on the Therigatha*. Berkeley, Calif.: Parallax, 1991. Print.

Mutukumara, Nemsiri. "Plans to Set Up Bhikkhuni Sasana." *Daily News* 19 Apr. 1986: 3. Print.

———. "Sri Lankan, Thai Bhikkhus in US Revive Bhikkhuni Order." *Daily News* 26 May 1997: 15. Print.

———. "Udav illā kolomba ā sil mātāva" (The *Sil Mata* Who Came to Colombo Asking for Help). *Budusaraṇa* 28 Mar. 1983:13. Print.

Nandy, Ashis. *At the Edge of Psychology: Essays in Politics and Culture*. Delhi: Oxford UP, 1980. Print.

Narada and Kassapa. *The Mirror of the Dhamma*. Ed. Kassapa. 2nd ed. Colombo: A.B. Gomes Trust, 1975. Print.

Nissan, Elizabeth. "Recovering Practice: Buddhist Nuns in Sri Lanka." *South Asia Research* 4.1. (May 1984): 32–49. Print.

Obeyesekere, Gananath. *Land Tenure in Village Ceylon: A Sociological and Historical Study*. London: Cambridge UP, 1967. Print. Cambridge South Asian Studies Ser.

———. *Medusa's Hair: An Essay on Personal Symbols and Religious Experience*. Chicago: U of Chicago P, 1981. Print.

O' Hanlon, Rosalind. "Recovering the Subject: *Subaltern Studies* and Histories of Resistance in Colonial South Asia." *Reading Subaltern Studies: Critical History, Contested Meaning and the Globalization of South Asia*. Ed. David Ludden. London: Wimbledon, 2002. 135–186. Print. Anthem South Asian Studies Ser.

Oldenberg, Hermann. *The Vinaya Piṭakaṃ: One of the Principal Buddhist Holy Scriptures in the Pâli Language*. Vol. 1. London: Williams and Norgate, 1879. Print.

Ong, Aihwa. "Colonialism and Modernity: Feminist Re-Presentations of Women in Non-Western Societies." *Inscriptions* 3–4.(1988): 79–93. Print.

"Ordination of Dasa Sil Matas." *Daily News* 23 Jan. 1997: 16–17. Print.

Palmo, Tenzin. "Thus Have I Heard: The Emerging Female Voice in Buddhism." Tsomo, *Bridging Worlds* 17–19.

Pateman, Carole. *The Disorder of Women: Democracy, Feminism, and Political Theory*. Palo Alto, Calif.: Stanford UP, 1989. Print.

Paul, Diana Y., and Frances Wilson. *Women in Buddhism: Images of the Feminine in the Mahayana Tradition*. 2nd ed. Berkeley: U of California P, 1985. Print.

Pennington, Brian K. *Was Hinduism Invented: Britons, Indians, and the Colonial Construction of Religion*. Oxford: Oxford UP, 2005. Print.

Perera, Pearl. "Aṣṭa Garu Dharma Pilibanda Vimasumak" (An Analysis of the Eight Revered Conditions). *Nivan Maga* 25 (Vesak 2538/1994): 45–50. Print.

Piyananda, Walpola. *The Bodhi Tree Grows in L.A.: Tales of a Buddhist Monk in America*. Boston: Shambhala, 2008. Print.

"Pilgrims to Buddha Gaya." *The Buddhist*. Dec. 28.1894: 400. Print.

Piyasena, Kumar. "Theravādaya" (Theravada/The debate on 'Thera'). *Sirilankā Meheṇī Udāva* Jan. 1994: 11. Print.

Quli, Natalie E. "Western Self, Asian Other: Modernity, Authenticity, and Nostalgia for 'Tradition' in Buddhist Studies." *Journal of Buddhist Ethics* 16 (2009): 1–38. Web. 27 May 2012.

Rhys Davids, T. W., and W. Stede. *The Pali Text Society's Pali-English Dictionary*. London: Pali Text Society, 1986. Print.

Risseeuw, Carla. *Gender Transformation, Power, and Resistance among Women in Sri Lanka: The Fish Don't Talk about the Water*. Delhi: Manohar, 1991. Print.

Rupasinghe, Upali. "Rebirth of the Bhikkhuni Order in Sri Lanka." *Daily News* 24 Feb. 1998: 9. Print.

Ruwanpura, Kanchana N. *Matrilineal Communities, Patriarchal Realities: A Feminist Nirvana Uncovered.* Ann Arbor: U of Michigan P. 2006. Print.

Said, Edward W. *Orientalism.* New York: Vintage, 1979. Print.

Sakya, Anil. "Contextualising Thai Buddhism." Korea-Thai Buddhist Cultural Forum 2010, Gyeongju. 1–2 April 2010. Web. 10 May 2012.

Salgado, Nirmala S. "Buddhist Nuns, Nationalistic Ideals and Revivalist Discourse." *Nēthrā* 2.2 (1998): 32–64. Print.

———. "Eight Revered Conditions: Ideological Complicity, Contemporary Reflections and Practical Realities." *Journal of Buddhist Ethics* 15 (2008): 177–213. Web. 28 Apr. 2012.

———. "Female Religiosity: Case Studies of Buddhist Nuns in Sri Lanka." 1986. Colombo: International Centre for Ethnic Studies. Print.

———. "Religious Identities of Buddhist Nuns: Training Precepts, Renunciation Attire, and Nomenclature in Theravāda Buddhism." *Journal of the American Academy of Religion* 72.4 (2004): 935–953. Print.

———. "Teaching Lineages and Land: Renunciation and Domestication among Buddhist Nuns in Sri Lanka." Findly 175–200.

———. "Unity and Diversity among Buddhist Nuns in Sri Lanka." Tsomo, *Innovative Buddhist Women* 30–41.

Saparamadu, Rupa. *Siŋhala Gāhāniya* (The Sinhalese Woman). Kohuwela, Sri Lanka: Tisara Prakasakayo, 2003.

Sasson, Vanessa R. "Peeling Back the Layers: Female Higher Ordination in Sri Lanka." *Buddhist Studies Review* 27.1 (2010): 77–84. Print.

———. "Politics of Higher Ordination for Women in Sri Lanka: Discussions with Silmātās." *Journal for the Study of Religion* 20.1 (2007): 57–71. Print.

Schopen, Gregory. *Bones, Stones, and Buddhist Monks: Collected Papers on Archaeology, Epigraphy, and Texts of Monastic Buddhism in India.* Honolulu: University of Hawai'i P, 1997. Print. Studies in the Buddhist Traditions Ser.

Scott, David. *Refashioning Futures: Criticism after Postcoloniality.* Princeton, N.J.: Princeton UP, 1999. Print. Princeton Studies in Culture/Power/History Ser.

Seeger, Martin. "The Bhikkhunī-Ordination Controversy in Thailand." *Journal of the International Association of Buddhist Studies* 29.1 (2008): 155–183. Print.

Seelananda. "Let There Be No Divisions in the Bhikkhuni Order." *The Island* 15 July 1997: 6. Print.

Semmens, Justine. "Does The Buddha Wear Yellow?: Custodial Orientalism, Conventual *Dasa Sil Matas,* and the Buddhist Revival in Ceylon at the Turn of the Twentieth Century. *Sri Lanka Journal of the Humanities.* XXXIII. 1 and 2. (2007): 71–96. Print.

Senaratne, Jagath P. *Political Violence in Sri Lanka, 1977–1990: Riots, Insurrections, Counterinsurgencies, Foreign Intervention.* Amsterdam: VU UP, 1997. Print. Sri Lanka Studies Ser. 4.

Senaratne, L. B. "Bhikkhunis Meet in Kandy." *Daily Mirror* 24 Dec. 2001: 3. Print.

Shakspo, Sonam Wangchuk. *Bakula Rinpoche: A Visionary Lama and Statesman*. New Delhi: Sonam Wangchuk Shakspo, 2008. Print.

Sharma, Arvind. *Women in World Religions*. Albany, N.Y.: SUNY P, 1987. Print. McGill Studies in the History of Religions Ser.

Shaw, Miranda. *Passionate Enlightenment: Women in Tantric Buddhism*. Princeton, N.J.: Princeton UP, 1994. Print.

Shih, Heng-ching. "Three Options: Reestablishing the Bhikshuni Lineage in the Tibetan Tradition." Proc. of First International Congress on Buddhist Women's Role in the Sangha: Bhikshuni Vinaya and Ordination Lineages with H.H. the Dalai Lama, 18–20 July 2007, U of Hamburg. N. pag. Print.

"Sil māṇivarun kerehit dharmānukūla visandumak onä" (A Religious [dharmic] Solution concerning *Dasasil Manis* Is Necessary). *Budusaraṇa* 22 July 1992: 4. Print.

"Sil māṇivaruṇṭa kahavat dārīma sudusuda?" (Is It Appropriate for *Sil Manis* to Wear Yellow?). *Budusaraṇa* 31 Mar. 1980: 4. Print.

"Sil mātāvan anagārikā namin amatamu" (Let Us Call *Sil Matas* "Homeless Ones"). *Budusaraṇa* 21 Feb. 1987: 9. Print.

"Sil mātāvangē tattvaya nangalīma aramuṇu karagat" (Making It a Goal to Uplift the Status of *Sil Matas*). *Tharuṇiya* 10 Nov. 1993: 3. Print.

Sirimal, G.A.D. "Mahanayakas and [the] Bhikkhuni Order." *The Island* 28 July 1998: 6. Print.

Sirisena, U.D.I. "The Cry for a Bhikkhuni Order." *Daily News* 24 April 1986: 13. Print.

Skilling, Peter. "Theravāda in History." *Pacific World: Journal of the Institute of Buddhist Studies* 3.11 (Fall 2009): 61–93. Print.

Skilling, Peter, Jason A. Carbine, Claudio Cicuzza and Santi Pakdeekham, eds. *How Theravāda is Theravāda? Exploring Buddhist Identities*. Chiang Mai, Thailand: Silkworm Books. 2012. Print.

Smith, Dorothy E. *The Conceptual Practices of Power: A Feminist Sociology of Knowledge*. Boston: Northeastern UP, 1990. Print. Northeastern Ser. in Feminist Theory.

———. *The Everyday World as Problematic: A Feminist Sociology*. Boston: Northeastern UP. 1987. Print.

———. "Incorporating Texts into Ethnographic Practice." D. Smith *Institutional Ethnography as Practice* 65–88.

———. *Institutional Ethnography: A Sociology for People*. Walnut Creek, Calif.: AltaMira, 2005. Print. Gender Lens Ser.

———, ed. *Institutional Ethnography as Practice*. Lanham: Rowman & Littlefield, 2006. Print.

Smith, Helmer, ed. *The Khuddaka-Pāṭha, together with Its Commentary Paramatthajotikā I*. Comp. Mabel Hunt. London: Milford, 1915. Print. Pali Text Society Ser.

Spivak, Gayatri Chakravorty. "Can the Subaltern Speak?" Ed. Rosalind C. Morris. 21–78.

————. "Can the Subaltern Speak?" *Marxism and the Interpretation of Culture*. Ed. and Introd. Cary Nelson and Lawrence Grossberg. Urbana, Ill.: U of Illinois P, 1988. 271–313. Print.

————. "Can the Subaltern Speak?" *The Post-Colonial Studies Reader*. Ed. Bill Ashcroft, Gareth Griffiths, and Helen Tiffin. London: Routledge, 1995. 24–28. Print.

————. *A Critique of Postcolonial Reason: Towards a History of the Vanishing Present*. Cambridge, Mass.: Harvard UP, 1999. Print.

————. "Righting Wrongs." *South Atlantic Quarterly* 103.2–3 (2004): 523–581. Print.

————. "Subaltern Talk: Interview with the Editors (1993–1994)." *The Spivak Reader: Selected Works of Gayatri Chakravorty Spivak*. Ed. Donna Landry and Gerald MacLean. New York: Routledge, 1996. 287–308. Print.

Sponberg, Alan. "Attitudes toward Women and the Feminine in Early Buddhism." *Buddhism, Sexuality, and Gender*. Ed. Jose Ignacio Cabezon. Albany, N.Y.: SUNY P, 1992. 3–36. Print.

Sri Lanka. Dept.of Census and Satistics. "Census of Population and Housing 2011: Enumeration Stage Feb.-Mar. 2012. Preliminary Report (Provisional)—1." 20 Apr. 2012. Web. 24 Aug. 2012.

————. *Demographic Survey 1994 Sri Lanka: Report on Demographic Characteristics of the Population*. Release 3. Colombo. Depart. of Census and Statistics, 1997. Print.

"Stamps to Honor Buddhist Nuns." *Daily News* 25 May 1996: 11. Print.

Stiglitz, Joseph E. *Globalization and Its Discontents*. New York: Norton, 2002. Print.

Sudharma. "Dasasil mātāngṭa tänak nädda?" (Don't *Dasasil Matas* Have a Place?). *Budusaraṇa* 23 Oct. 1980: 10. Print.

————. "Lakdiva bhikṣuṇī śāsanaya" (The *Bhikkhuni* Dispensation of the Island of Lanka). *Dinamiṇa* (*Unduvap Atireka*) 22 Dec. 1958: IV. Print.

Sugirtharajah, Sharada. "Colonialism and Religion." Bloch, Keppens, and Hegde 69–78.

Sujato. "Dark Matter." *Monastic Life*. Thubten Chodron's home page. 4 Aug. 2007. Web. 5 July 2011.

Sunder Rajan, Rajeswari. "Death and the Subaltern." Ed. R. Morris 117–138.

————. *Real and Imagined Women: Gender, Culture and Postcolonialism*. London: Routledge, 1993. Print

Tarrow, Sidney G. *Power in Movement: Social Movements, Collective Action, and Politics*. Cambridge: Cambridge UP, 1994. Print. Cambridge Studies in Comparative Politics Ser.

Thamel, K.M. Lily Beatrice. "A Study of the Das-Sil Māniyo (Consecrated Women) in the Buddhist Society of Sri Lanka." Diss. U of the Philippines, 1983. Print.

Tharu, Susie, and Tejaswini Niranjana. "Problems for a Contemporary Theory of Gender." *Subaltern Studies IX: Writings on South Asian History and Society*. Ed. Shahid Amin and Dipesh Chakrabarty. New Delhi: Oxford UP, 1996. 232–260. Print.

Theravada Samadhi Education Association. "First All Sri Lankan Bhikkhuni Dana." *Theravada Samadhi Education Association*. TSEA, n. pag. n.d. Web. 24 July 2012.

"Thirty-five Foreign Bhikkhunis on Mercy Mission." *Observer* 25 Feb. 1999: 1. Print.

Trainor, Kevin. "In the Eye of the Beholder: Nonattachment and the Body in Subhā's Verse (Therīgāthā 71)." *Journal of the American Academy of Religion* 61.1 (1993): 57–79. Print.

Trenckner, V., ed. *The Majjhima-Nikāya.* Vol. 1. Oxford: Pali Text Society. 1993. Print. Pali Text Society Text Ser. 60.

Tsedroen, Jampa. "Activities of the Vinaya Research Committee: A Report on the Last Three Years (1987–90)." *Sakyadhita Newsletter* 2.2 (1991): n. pag. Web. 10 Apr. 2010.

Tsing, Anna. "Conclusion." *The Anthropology of Globalization: A Reader.* Ed. Jonathan Xavier Inda and Renato Rosaldo. Malden, Mass.: Blackwell, 2002. 453–485. Print. Blackwell Readers in Anthropology Ser. 1.

Tsomo, Karma Lekshe. "Almost Equal: Obstacles on the Way to an International Bhikṣuṇī Sangha." *Bridging Worlds* 177–183. Ed. Tsomo.

———, ed. *Bridging Worlds: Buddhist Women's Voices across Generations.* Taipei: Yuan Chuan P, 2004. Print.

———, ed. *Buddhist Women across Cultures: Realizations.* Albany, N.Y.: SUNY P, 1999. Print. SUNY Series, Feminist Philosophy.

———, ed. *Buddhist Women and Social Justice: Ideals, Challenges, and Achievements.* Albany, N.Y.: SUNY P. 2004. Print. SUNY Series, Feminist Philosophy.

———, ed. *Innovative Buddhist Women: Swimming against the Stream.* Richmond, Surrey: Curzon 2000. Print. Curzon Critical Studies in Buddhism Ser.

———. "Introduction." Tsomo, *Innovative Buddhist Women* xvii–xxviii.

———, ed. *Out of the Shadows: Socially Engaged Buddhist Women.* Delhi: Sri Satguru, 2006. Print. Bibliotheca Indo-Buddhica Ser. 240.

———, ed. *Sakyadhītā: Daughters of the Buddha.* Ithaca, N.Y.: Snow Lion, 1988. Print.

———. *Sisters in Solitude: Two Traditions of Buddhist Monastic Ethics for Women: A Comparative Analysis of the Chinese Dharmagupta and the Tibetan Mūlasarvāstivāda Bhikṣuṇī Prātimokṣa Sūtras.* Albany, N.Y.: SUNY P, 1996. Print. SUNY Series, Feminist Philosophy.

Uduwara, Sheila. "Dasasil matāvanṭa ācāra dharma paddhatiyak" (A Dharmic Code of Ethics for *Dasasil Matas*). *Dinamiṇa.* 17 Dec. 1994: 11. Print.

Vajira, Panadure. *Bhikṣuṇī Vaŋśaya* (The *Bhikshuni* Lineage). Anuradhapura, Sri Lanka: Gunasekara, 1992. Print.

Vajira, Panadure. *The Enlightened Nuns of the Buddha Era.* Colombo: National Book Development Council of Sri Lanka, 1994. Print.

Vajiragnana, M. "International Ordination at Bodhgaya." *Bodhgaya International Full Ordination Ceremony.* Taipei: Foguang Cultural Enterprise, (1998): 44–46. Print.

Van Esterik, Penny. "Lay Women in Theravada Buddhism." *Women of Southeast Asia.* Ed. Penny Van Esterik. Rev. ed. DeKalb: Northern Illinois University Center for Southeast Asian Studies, 1996. 42–61. Print. Monographs Series on Southeast Asia, Occasional Paper 17.

Vangisa, Urugamuve. *Bhikṣuṇī Śāsanaya* (The *Bhikshuni* Dispensation). Dehiwala, Sri Lanka: Makandure Sirisumaṇa, 1986. Print.

VanLoo, Babeth, dir. *Women and the Buddha Potential.* Buddhist Broadcasting Foundation, 2008. DVD.

Veragoda Arachchi, Padma. "Kusaṭa āhārak, hisaṭa vahalak näti anurāpura sil māṇivaru" (The Anuradhapura *Sil Manis* with Neither Food in Their Bellies nor a Roof over Their Heads). *Divayina* 31 Mar. 1985: 9. Print.

Vertovec, Steven. *Transnationalism.* London: Routledge, 2009. Print. Key Ideas Ser.

Vidanagama, Sena. Picture. *Daily News* (AFP) 14 March 1998: 1. Print.

Vipulasara. "Dasa sil matavan sandahā cariyā paddhatiyak onä" (A Code of Conduct Is Needed for *Dasa Sil Matas*). Letter. *Dinamiṇa* 8 May 1989: 9. Print.

Vishvapani. "Bold Step for Nuns." *Dharmalife* 19 (2002): n. pag. Web. 28 Mar. 2010.

Ware, Vron. "Info-War and the Politics of Feminist Curiosity." *Cultural Studies* 20.6 (2006): 526–551. Print.

Weerakoon, Abhaya. "Dasasil mātā abhivruddhiyaṭa pahasukam aväsiyi" (Necessity of Facilities for the Development of *Sil Matas*). *Dinamiṇa* 28 Jan. 1985: 4. Print.

Weeraratne, D. Amarasiri. *Bhikṣuṇī Śāsanaya nävata pihiṭuviya nohäkida?* (Is It Not Possible to Re-establish the Dispensation of *Bhikshunis?*). Mahanuvara, Sri Lanka: Samastha Lanka Janōpakāra Bauddha Saṉgamaya, 1992. Print.

———. *Buddhist Nuns in Sri Lanka.* Kandy, Sri Lanka: Janōpakāra Buddhist Society, 1994. Print.

———. "Bhikkhuni Order." *Sunday Observer* 8 July 1984: 20. Print.

———. "Dasa Sil Matas and Their Robes." *The Island* 18. Sept. 1990: 6. Print.

———. "Mahanayakas and the Bhikkhuni Order." *The Island* 7 July 1998: 7. Print.

Weeraratne, D.G., Sirisena Tuduvage, and Padma Dinapala, eds. *2300 Saṉghamittā Jayanti Saṉgrahaya* (2,300th Sanghamitta Commemorative Volume). Colombo: Buddhist Affairs Department, 1993. Print.

Weerasinghe, Chandrasiri. Picture. *The Island* 14 March 1998: 1. Print.

Weeratne, Theja. "Journal from Dasa Sil Mathas." *Daily News* 9 July 1991: 19. Print.

Welihinda, Rukshani. "Stoic Observance." *Midweek Mirror* 29 Oct. 1997: 8. Print.

"WFB to Study Revival of Bhikkhuni Order." *Weekend* 13 Apr. 1986: 1. Print.

Wickramasinghe, Nira. *Sri Lanka in the Modern Age: A History of Contested Identities.* Honolulu: U of Hawai'i P, 2006. Print.

Wijayaratna, Mohan. *Buddhist Nuns: The Birth and Development of a Women's Monastic Order.* Colombo: Wisdom, 2001. Print.

Wijayasiri, L. B. "Mahanayake Theras Disapprove [of] Bhikkhuni Order." *Daily News* 12 Apr. 1998: 6. Print.

Wijebandara, C. "Anagārika jīvitayak gevana vatman silmātāvan magin ätikala häki āgamika prabōdaya" (A Spiritual Awakening That Can Be Realized through the

Present-Day *Sil Matas* Who Lead a Homeless Life). Weeraratne, Tuduvage, and Dinapala 117–126.

Wilson, Liz. *Charming Cadavers: Horrific Figurations of the Feminine in Indian Buddhist Hagiographic Literature*. Chicago: U of Chicago P, 1996. Print. Women in Culture and Society Ser.

Woolf, Bella Sidney. *How to See Ceylon*. 4th ed. Colombo: Times of Ceylon, 1929. Print.

Young, Iris Marion. *Intersecting Voices: Dilemmas of Gender, Political Philosophy, and Policy*. Princeton, N.J.: Princeton UP, 1997. Print.

Young, Katherine K. "Having Your Cake and Eating It Too: Feminism and Religion." *Journal of the American Academy of Religion* 67.1 (1999): 167–184. Print.

Young, Robert. *Postcolonialism: An Historical Introduction*. Oxford: Blackwell, 2001. Print.

Index

Abeysekara, Ananda, 167, 215, 235n4,
    239n19, 239n20, 246n13,
    268n4, 270n12, 271n23
    Colors of the Robe, 14, 151–152, 237n21,
    262n10
    See also conjunctures
activists, 13, 62, 64, 124, 133, 137, 143–144
agency, 1, 3, 5–6, 8, 80, 123, 239n20,
    241n4
    Eight Conditions and, 10–11
    gender or feminism and, 3, 5, 10–11,
    21–23
    Mahmood on, 53, 185, 197
    of nuns or renunciants, 6, 75, 84–85,
    140, 239n20
    of women, 52
    See also Asad, Talal; lived lives
All Ceylon Buddhist Congress, 89,
    135. *See also* Sri Lanka Buddhist
    Congress
alms (*dāna*), 2, 66, 82–83, 108, 153–155,
    191, 204, 208, 222, 244n31,
    255n21, 259n51, 263n11
Ambala Rohana Gnanashila. *See*
    Gnanashila, Ambala Rohana
anagārika, 112, 117
Analayo, 32, 249n8
androcentrism, 27–28, 82, 86
anis, 58, 211, 226–227, 243n17, 268n7

Anula, Queen, 32–33
Arjun, xii, 297
Asad, Talal, 5, 47, 215, 233, 235n4,
    236n12, 240n21, 271n17, 272n35,
    273n38, 274n45
    on consciousness, 22
    on curative treatment or project, 65,
    244n33
    on everyday practice or life, 2
    Formations, 241n6
    Genealogies, 243n21, 274n49
    on human rights, 271n21
    interview by Mahmood, 21–22
    on narrative, 2, 21
Asgiriya (Nikaya), 134, 166–167, 170, 179
associations. *See* organizations
aṭṭhagarudhammā, 77, 81, 94–95. *See*
    also *garudhamma*; *dhammā*
    (conditions, rule); Eight
    Conditions
attire, renunciant, 53, 56, 103, 105, 107,
    110, 113, 121, 211, 231, 235n2
    brown (*guru*), 7, 57, 107, 114–115, 231
    Korean-style, 167, 265n24
    in Myanmar, 251n29, 252n31
    red or maroon, 231, 252n31
    of Sudharmachari, 114, 251n28
    textual or *vinaya* sources on, 113–114,
    116

white, 104–107, 113–115, 138, 242n11,
    249n5, 251n22, 252n31, 265n24
yellow or saffron, 33, 107, 113–115, 133,
    207, 231, 241n7, 242n11, 247n20,
    249n8, 251n22, 252n35, 259n55,
    269n17
Australia, 36, 267n44
authenticity, 4, 13, 32, 40, 45–47, 146,
    236n10
    Theravada, 14, 154, 158–159, 161, 165,
        167–170, 175–176, 180, 267n42
authority, 121, 141, 192–193, 226, 231,
    263n13
    of Dalai Lama, 216, 221
    of Eight Conditions, 82, 84, 86, 93,
        100, 246n11
    of monks or monastic, 166–167, 180,
        199, 202, 216
    power and, 45
    symbolic, 199
    of texts, 216
    of women, 188–189
authors, 10, 75, 77–79, 82, 88, 99
autonomy, 5, 51, 209, 215
    of nuns or renunciants, 53, 63, 74, 77,
        86, 185, 187, 191, 197, 209, 267n1
    relational, 187
Bartholomeusz, Tessa, 9, 21–23, 31–40,
    44–45, 47–48, 55, 59–60, 90,
    110, 239n15, 239n17, 239n18,
    243n22, 243n23, 254n19, 255n25
    on Mahāvamsa view of history, 32–33
    Women under the Bō Tree, 32–39
Belsey, Catherine, 79, 87
Bengal, 133, 187–188
Bhabha, Homi, 50, 64
Bhadra, Vakada, 91, 170, 175–176
bhikkhunī (bhikṣuṇī)
    ahistorical claims about, 35–38, 44
    alms (dāna) or support for, 154–155,
        259n51, 263n11

ancient, early, or past, 2, 32–33, 35–38,
    40, 44, 77, 81, 84–85, 88, 92–93,
    128, 150, 164, 216–217, 247n14,
    248n24, 249n8, 257n36
attire of, 55, 107, 114–115, 160, 167, 231,
    265n24
Bodhgaya-Dambulla (group of), 161,
    166–167, 171, 174–179, 266n35
Burmese, 230
Chinese, 134, 150, 164, 223
Dambulla (see bhikkhunīs: Bodhgaya-
    Dambulla [group of])
debates on higher ordination of (see
    bhikkhunī upasampadā: debates
    on)
defined, notion of, or terms for, 12, 17,
    48, 117–120, 140–141, 233, 235n2,
    242n12
East Asian, 150
Eight Conditions and, 78, 80–81, 84,
    91–95, 97–99, 246n6, 246n12,
    247n14, 248n31, 249n35,
    249n39
empowerment of (see under
    empowerment)
"failed" or lapsed, 38
fully ordained, 15, 38, 107, 119, 214,
    264n18, 274n47
gender of, 7
hermitages or aramayas of, 160–161,
    204, 233
idea of the, 141–142, 147
ideal(ized), 12, 15, 128, 144, 164,
    213–214, 233
identity of, 98–99
(in)equality and, 64
Kaoutaramaya, 179
Korean, 164, 178–179, 263–264n16
lineages of (see lineages)
in Mahāvamsa, 32
Mahayana, 14, 171, 248n27

monastic precedence or seniority and, 14, 154–160, 176, 179, 267n40

narratives about, 88, 128, 161

in Nepal or Nepalese, 227–228, 232, 274n47

novice (see *sāmaṇerīs*)

order of (see *bhikkhunī* order)

organizations of, 136

rituals or ritual services performed by, 55, 142, 154, 158, 240n25, 246n7, 266n34, 266n35, 268n15

Sarnath group of, 150, 154, 158, 167, 169, 177–179, 266n35, 267n41

senior, 6–8, 95–96, 98, 176, 178, 180, 263n11

sil mātās and, 38, 97, 120, 128, 137, 140–142, 144–145, 154–159, 174, 176, 180, 253n4, 256n28, 257n40, 259n51, 266n32, 267n40

Sinhalese-speaking, 44

Sri Lankan state and, 42

Sri Lankan, 6, 45, 92, 105, 130, 150, 164–165, 168–171, 177, 180–181, 231–232, 263n11, 264n18, 265n23, 265n24, 265n25, 265n28, 274n47, 256n32

Sri Lankan–East Asian ordination of, 150

Sri Lankan–Korean ordination of, 150, 163–164, 167, 171, 178–179, 228

Sri Lankan–Taiwanese ordination of, 150, 166, 168, 170–171, 173–174, 176, 179, 266n39

status of, 37–38, 42, 48, 55, 95, 112, 126, 130, 142, 155, 213, 256n28

"struggle" of or to become, 165, 264n20

as subject or subjectivity of, 11–12, 90–91, 93, 95, 98, 142–143, 145, 214, 259n53

Taiwanese, 150, 170–171, 263n11, 265n25

textual sources on, 32, 128, 140, 213

Thai, 64

Theravada (identity of), 13, 45, 88, 91, 133, 150, 152, 158–159, 164–168, 171, 180, 211, 227, 229, 231–233, 267n44

Tibetan, 272n36, 273n37

training, 153, 159, 163, 165–166, 168–170, 173, 176

Vinaya on, 83, 128, 160, 242n12, 266n32

Western, 231, 270n7

bhikkhunī order, 98, 115, 127–128, 162, 220, 235n5, 239n18, 246n11, 248n25, 253n8, 257n36, 265n23

absence, end, or decline of, 33, 128, 235n5, 260n60

debates on, 127

establishment or revival of, 34–35, 39, 83, 89–90, 128, 134, 142, 170–171, 220, 248n24, 255n20, 255n25, 2556n27, 258n41, 263n15, 266–67n28

Theravada, 90, 171, 248n27, 263n15, 265n28

bhikkhunī sāsana, 2, 95, 117–118, 134–135, 137, 144, 248n24, 259n55, 269n5

defined, 236n6

bhikkhunī upasampadā, 110, 114, 117–119, 246n6, 255n23, 264n18, 264n22

(dis)interest in, 6, 8, 13, 15–16, 35–38, 42, 48, 50, 64, 124, 126, 128, 130, 137, 140, 144–147, 212, 215, 218, 221–227, 230, 233, 243n20, 266n32

Cheng on, 42, 240n27

bhikkhunī upasampadā (*Cont.*)
  Dambulla-organized (*see* Dambulla)
  debates on, 1–2, 5, 11–13, 16, 48, 98,
      104, 107–108, 116, 121, 127, 139–
      140, 142, 144, 147–148, 150, 166,
      181, 211–213, 223, 255n25, 258n50,
      261n64, 262n10, 265n26
  Eight Conditions and, 78, 89, 91, 93,
      95–98
  feminism and, 40, 42, 240n27
  Mahayana, 13, 211
  monks' role in, 13, 34, 162, 166, 168,
      174–175, 179, 223
  as movement, 5–6, 12–13, 45, 124, 126,
      137, 165, 261n67
  need or "struggle" for, 33, 45, 50,
      123, 126, 140, 142, 147, 162, 165,
      214–215, 222
  as opportunity, 6, 42
  opposition to, 12–13, 98, 107, 119, 121,
      134, 142, 158, 166–167, 180, 186,
      256n28, 256n29
  quorum for, 2, 179
  ritual, 150, 251n21
  sil mātās and, 6, 13, 46, 105, 112, 114,
      119–121, 124, 126, 128, 132, 137,
      139–147, 153–154, 163, 176, 180,
      252n40, 252n1, 256n28, 261n65,
      263–264n16
  Sri Lankan, 6, 13, 36, 99, 104–105, 121,
      141, 144, 150, 232, 245, 251n21
  state or government and, 42, 134,
      137, 139, 146, 163, 170, 186, 230,
      240n27
  status and (*see* status: of *bhikkhunīs*)
  support for, 89, 91, 93, 95, 98, 107,
      121, 132, 137, 142–144, 150, 166,
      256n28, 260n58, 261n64,
      262n4, 271n14
  Theravada, 13–14, 46, 119, 166–168,
      171, 175–178, 180, 230, 267n42
      (*see also* ordination: Theravada
      identity and)

  Tibetan, 216, 220–222, 226, 230
  training or preparations for, 6, 95,
      97, 108, 112, 119, 121, 150, 153–154,
      163, 166, 176, 245n3, 262n9,
      264n16
Bloss, Lowell, 90, 110, 123, 128–130, 142,
      253n9
bō tree, 105, 194, 203, 206–207, 249n4,
      260n58
Board of Sri Lanka *Bhikshuni* Order, 45.
      See also Dambulla
Bodhgaya, ordination at, 146, 150, 166,
      168–171, 174–176, 227–228,
      265n24, 266n39, 269n5
Bodhgaya-Dambulla group, 150, 156,
      158, 161, 166, 170–171, 174, 176,
      178–179
  defined, 262n9
Bond, George, 89, 239n13, 256n30,
      264n22
Bourdieu, Pierre, 14, 98, 191–193, 196,
      200, 245n4, 249n38, 268n10,
      268n11, 268n12
Brahm, Ajahn, 267n44
brahmacārī, 113, 117, 138
Brown, Sid, 59–61, 239n14, 239n16,
      241n5, 243n20, 243n22, 243n23
Brown, Wendy, 10, 53, 214
Buddha, the, 2, 81, 83, 87, 91–92, 95–96,
      108–109, 120, 167, 172, 178, 217,
      219, 241n5, 250–51n20, 260n58
Buddha, word of. See *Buddhavacana*
Buddhavacana, 78, 82–86, 88–91, 93–
      94, 98–99, 248n32
  defined, 11
Buddhism
  Asian, 28–31, 39, 86, 238–239n13
  authentic, 32, 40, 45–47, 175, 179 (*see
      also* authenticity: Theravada)
  early, 11, 77, 82, 86, 99–100, 149,
      247n15
  feminist, 21, 23, 28–29, 238n13 (*see
      also* feminism: Buddhist)

Mahayana (*see* Mahayana Buddhism)
"post-patriarchal," 31, 42
Protestant, 33, 149
reform or revival of, 6, 33, 35–36, 188,
    239n19, 254n18, 268n4
Sinhalese, 149, 260n60
Sri Lankan, 35–36, 88, 150, 164–165,
    209, 240n27, 254n17
textual, 11, 29
Theravada (*see* Theravada Buddhism)
Tibetan in Mongolia, 226–227,
    274n42
Tibetan, 10, 58, 216–217, 225, 227,
    274n42, 275n50
Western, 23, 27–31, 86, 219–220, 223,
    238–239n13
Buddhist Congress. *See* All Ceylon
    Buddhist Congress; International
    Congress on Buddhist Women's
    Role in the Sangha; Sri Lanka
    Buddhist Congress
budugē, 204, 268n15
Canavarro, Miranda de Souza, 34–36
canon, Buddhist, 2, 108–109, 113,
    250n12, 250n14, 250n19
capital
    economic, 192, 200
    symbolic, 192, 196, 200, 203
capitalism, 24–25, 127, 188, 190–191, 193,
    199, 209, 272n35
Cariyāpaddhati. See Codes of Conduct
categories, 47, 51, 109, 112
    analytical, 16–17, 38, 45, 70, 219
    of *bhikkhunīs*, nuns, or renunciants,
        38, 57–58, 70, 107–108, 134, 138,
        215, 242n12, 268n7
    Buddhist, 240n22
    dichotomously opposed, 53, 55 (*see
        also* dichotomies)
    Mahayana, 45, 151
    "movement" as a, 125–126
    for religion, 4, 24–26, 236n8
    resistance, 185

Theravada, 14, 17, 44–45, 149, 151–152,
    181, 261n2
universal, 47, 196, 240n22
usefulness of, 10
Western feminist, 4
"women," 38, 240n22
Catholicism, 34, 55–56, 60, 242n8,
    242n10
celibacy, 7, 55, 103–104, 108–109, 113,
    117, 138, 151, 247n20, 249n6,
    250n11
Ceylon Buddhist Congress. *See* All
    Ceylon Buddhist Congress
chaityas, 105, 199, 204
Chakrabarty, Dipesh, 133, 271n19
Cheng, Wei-Yi, 9, 21–23, 39–48, 180,
    238n10, 240n22, 240n23,
    240n26, 240n27, 247n21,
    267n42
    on empowerment, 39–43
    feminist discourse and, 39–40,
        42–43, 47
    on nuns' welfare, 39–43, 47
    on ordination, 40, 42, 240n27
    on unfolding history, 44–45
China, 134, 150, 171–172, 221, 223, 227–
    228, 248n25, 256n27
choices, 34, 60, 74, 215, 224, 231–232,
    240n24, 243n22, 268n5,
    274n49
Christianity, 3, 21, 29, 56, 219, 236n8,
    236n12, 238n6, 242n10, 268n11,
    273n37
Christianization, 3
chronicles, Sri Lankan, 32–33
Codes of Conduct
    Cariyā Dhamma Paddhatiya, 138
    Sil Mātā Cariyāpaddhati, 139, 257n40,
        258n47
    Vinaya. See Vinaya
colonial event, 4, 10, 31, 50
colonialism, 14, 26, 188–190, 209,
    236n7, 267n2, 271n13

comparisons, cross-cultural, 3, 16–17,
    23–24, 40, 211
conferences
    Hamburg (*see* International Congress
        on Buddhist Women's Role in
        the Sangha)
    SIABW (*see* Sakyadhita International
        Conferences)
    transnational, 15, 212–213, 230,
        274n50
conjunctures, 12, 88, 90, 93, 141, 151–152,
    264n18, 275n50
    defined, 151, 237n21
consciousness, 22–23, 47, 218
cooking, 2, 73
curative project. *See* projects: curative
curative treatment. *See under* Asad, Talal
Dalai Lama, 216–217, 220–221, 223–
    226, 230, 271n18, 271n25, 273n37
Dambulla, 45, 145, 177
    bhikkhunī training at, 121, 146–148,
        153, 159, 173, 263n12
    ordinations at, 136, 146, 161, 165–166,
        170, 174, 178, 180, 263n12, 266n35
    temple, 136, 165–167, 179
    See also Bodhgaya-Dambulla *bhikkhunīs*;
        Bodhgaya-Dambulla group
dasa sil māṇiyō. See *sil mātās: dasa
dasa sil mātās*. See *sil mātās: dasa
dasa sil*. *See* Ten Precepts
Dawn of the *Meheṇi* (*Meheṇi Udāva*),
    131, 142–143, 253n5, 259n57,
    259–260n58
de Certeau, Michel, 14, 193
Department of Buddhist Affairs, 129,
    131, 137, 139, 256n29, 256n32
deprivation. *See* discourses: of
    deprivation
Derrida, Jacques, 1, 3, 24
development, 6, 13, 44, 47, 61, 126,
    130–131
    discourse of (*see* discourses:
        development[al])

rhetoric of, 12–13, 132
Devendra, Kusuma, 123, 128–130, 135–
    136, 142, 164–165, 253n9, 254n12.
    See also Kusuma, Bhikkhuni
dge slong ma (*gelongma*), 217, 273n37. *See
    also* nuns: fully ordained
dhammā (conditions, rules), 80–81,
    96, 250n13. *See also* Eight
    Conditions
dhamma (teachings of the Buddha), 56,
    63, 107–108, 115, 138, 149, 163,
    251n20
Dhamma Paddhatiya. *See* Codes of
    Conduct: *Cariyā Dhamma
    Paddhatiya*
dhammacārinī, 63, 138, 250n10, 255n23,
    258n41
    defined, 107
Dhammaloka, Talalle, 91, 170
Dhammananda, 243n20, 269n1, 271n14
dharma. *See dhamma*
Dharmaguptaka, 150, 164, 221, 223,
    273n37
Dharmapala, Anagarika, 34, 38, 162–
    163, 188
dichotomies
    female/male, 49, 51, 62, 65
    householder/renunciant, 5, 9–10,
        29–30, 49, 51–53, 55, 57–58,
        60, 62–65, 103, 106, 110, 235n3,
        239n17, 242n12
    liberal feminism and, 49–50
    in narratives about nuns or
        renunciants, 10, 49, 63–65,
        74–75, 241n5
    public/private or domestic, 9, 29–30,
        49–54, 57–59, 62, 65, 70, 75,
        241n2, 241n5
    religious/domestic, 30, 51, 57, 59, 62,
        64–65
    religious/secular, 49, 52
    sacred/profane, 30, 57, 242n13
    samsara/nibbana, 49, 52–53, 65

this-worldly/otherworldly, 9, 30, 49,
    51, 53
world affirmation/world
    renunciation, 5, 57
See also Pateman, Carole
Dīpavaṃsa, 32–33
discourses
    colonial, 3–4, 9, 21, 26–27, 32, 39, 50,
        215, 236n7, 271n20
    curative, 39
    of deprivation, 59–60, 130–131, 133,
        147, 255n20, 260n60
    development(al), 6, 13, 40, 42–43, 123,
        130, 132, 214, 270n6
    global, 212
    imperialistic or Orientalist, 9, 29,
        236n7
    institutional, 10, 34, 42, 53–55, 57,
        241n29
    institutional defined, 54
    liberal or secular-liberal, 4, 9, 16, 74,
        84, 131, 192, 210, 232
    liberal feminist, 47
    on nuns or female renunciants, 187,
        218, 269n3
    postcolonial, 3–4, 6, 10
    of power, 104, 121
    relation to lived lives, 54
    of rights or equality, 208, 212,
        260n58
    scholarly, 1, 47, 98
    Western feminist, 39–40, 43,
        254n13
    of "women and development," 6, 13,
        47
    of "world religions," 24
discussions, transnational or global, 15,
    216–217, 220, 232, 269n3
disempowerment, 88, 94
domestic. *See* dichotomies: religious/
    domestic
dukkha, 10, 52–54, 63, 65, 69–73, 75
    samsara and, 10, 53, 69–70, 189

economics, 131. *See also* capitalism;
    capital: economic; economy;
    nuns: economic condition or
    background of
economy, 51, 126–127, 188, 190,
    196, 200, 245n38. *See also*
    capitalism
education
    Cheng's research on nuns', 40–43
    English, 15
    of *mae chi*, 60
    of nuns, 15, 39–40, 42–43, 54, 61–62,
        75, 134, 158, 208, 218, 228,
        248n25, 270n6
    ordination and, 15, 266n32
    of renunciants, 37, 64, 131, 257n39
    of *sil mātās*, 89, 135–136, 144–145,
        158, 254n16, 255n20, 257n37,
        258n47
    women and, 7, 52, 218
egalitarianism, 26, 217–219
Egypt, 28, 185
Eight Conditions
    accounts or narratives of, 11, 77–78,
        80–82, 86–88, 90–92, 98–99,
        217, 246n11
    aṭṭhagarudhammā or
        aṣṭaugurudharmāḥ, 40
    as *Buddhavacana*, 11, 78, 82–83, 85–86,
        88–91, 93, 98–99
    as conditions, 80, 83
    debates on, 10–11, 78, 80–81, 85,
        89–92, 98–99
    discourse about identity and, 11
    feminist view of, 10, 84, 86
    as interrogative text, 79, 99
    list of, 81–82
    Mahapajapati Gotami and, 80–81, 83,
        90–92, 94, 97, 99, 246n6
    monks on, 93, 95, 98
    observance of or in practice, 78–80,
        84, 91, 93–100, 245n4

Eight Conditions (*Cont.*)
  ordination or *upasampadā* and, 78,
    80, 84–86, 93–94, 98–99
  practitioners on, 10–11, 78, 80, 86, 88,
    90–93, 99–100, 245n2
  as rules, 80, 82–83, 87, 246n12
  scholars on, 10–11, 77, 79–80, 82–87,
    93, 99–100, 245n2, 246n12,
    247n15
  translation of (*aṭṭha*)*garudhammā*,
    77, 80
Eight-Precept renunciant, 241n7
Eight Precepts, 34, 63, 108, 241n7,
  250n11, 251n26
Eight Training Precepts, 107–109, 112–
  113, 249n5, 251n26
empirical studies, 21, 23, 31, 40, 50, 53,
  75, 77–78
empowerment
  agency or autonomy and, 5, 8, 77
  bhikkhunīs, nuns, or renunciants and,
    5, 8, 14–16, 42–43, 185–186, 191,
    196–197, 199, 208–209, 212–214,
    218, 232–233, 236n11
  defined, 186, 210, 236n11
  discourse about, 218, 269n3
  Eight Conditions and, 77
  feminist views of, 15, 185–186,
    240n26
  liberal discourse or idea of, 77, 84,
    185, 196
  ordination and, 8, 40, 42, 121, 186,
    212, 232–233
  renunciant everyday and, 14, 185
  ritual, 62
  secular notions of, 5, 209, 236n11
  universal, 233, 236n11
  women's, 41–42, 209–210, 212, 214
England, 36, 170
Enloe, Cynthia, 127, 240n22
equality, 42, 47, 50, 222, 273n38
  discourse on, 84, 208, 212

Eight Conditions and, 10–11, 84, 96,
  99
feminism and, 21, 39, 42, 215
gender, 4, 11, 26, 63–65, 96, 214, 225
liberal notion of, 21, 48, 54, 64, 77,
  99, 186, 199, 211, 270n8
ordination and, 6, 42, 211, 213–215,
  226
rights and, 4, 36, 51, 64, 208, 213–214,
  218, 269n4, 271n21
as universal value or essential human
  quality, 16, 215
equivalence, 25, 44, 216, 218, 238n6,
  271n20
Escobar, Arturo, 12, 130, 254n15
ethnographies, 1–2, 9, 17, 53, 151
event, colonial. *See* colonial event
everyday lives, 2, 9, 17, 23, 29, 40, 42,
  69, 154, 159, 176, 274n40
everyday practice, 7, 38, 187, 233,
  273n38
Falk, Monica Lindberg, 62–65, 243n30,
  246n12
Falk, Nancy Auer, 23, 27, 84, 86, 238n8,
  246n12
family
  extended, 66, 71, 187–188, 190, 200,
    209
  patriarchal, 68, 187
  renunciation and (*see* renunciation:
    family relations and)
feminism(s), 10, 15, 22–24, 39, 41, 51, 85,
  132, 219, 240n26, 240n27
  as academic method vs. social vision,
    27
  Buddhist, 21–24, 27–32, 40, 42, 61
    (*see also* Buddhism: feminist)
  discourse of (*see* discourses: feminist)
  global, 85, 214, 270n9
  liberal, 2, 9–10, 14–16, 21, 30, 40, 42,
    47, 49–50, 63, 65, 75, 185–186,
    214, 216, 239n15, 240n24

second- or third-wave, 47, 124

secular or secular-liberal, 5, 11, 21, 30, 47, 219

strīvādī ("woman-ism"), 6

Western, 4, 23, 37, 39, 41, 219

field research, 1, 41, 52, 63

Fitzgerald, Timothy, 9, 24–26, 31

Five (Training) Precepts, 104–105, 107–108, 113, 249n6, 250n13, 251n13

Foguangshan, 166, 172–173, 240n27, 264n21, 266n39, 269n5

forums, transnational, 15–16, 29, 213–214, 217–218, 224, 230–233, 269n5, 270n6, 273n39

Foucault, Michel, 5, 12, 84, 130, 197, 214

frameworks, 16, 26, 31, 38, 57, 137, 209. *See also* narrative disjunction

  Bartholomeusz's use of, 9, 22–23

  binary oppositions or dichotomies in, 50–51, 55, 65, 241n5

  Cheng's use of, 9, 22, 40–41, 43, 45

  Gross's use of, 22, 26, 31

  interpretive or theoretical, 2, 9, 241n5

  (liberal) feminist, 2, 8, 240n24

  narrative, 9, 22, 74

  textual, 23, 128

freedom

  agency and, 8, 197, 241n4

  equality and, 16, 186, 199, 211, 226

  feminism and, 22, 47, 51

  feminist and/or liberal(ist), 14–16, 21, 30, 50, 52, 77, 185–186, 191, 199, 209, 211, 226, 232, 236n11

  Mahmood on, 185, 197

  power and, 197

  religious (*vimukti*) or religious view of, 52, 91

  secular notion or discourse of, 8, 74

garudhamma, 82, 90, 92, 94–98, 246n11

  defined, 80–81

  See also Eight Conditions

gelongma (*dge slong ma*), 217, 273n37

gender, 1

  agency and, 3, 11, 21

  Eight Conditions and, 83, 92

  equality (*see under* equality)

  liberal concerns or presuppositions about, 11, 53

  nuns', 7–8, 237n17, 270n8, 270n11

  relations in Sri Lanka, 126–127, 189

  renunciation and, 4, 21, 40, 187

  study of Buddhism and, 1, 5–9, 16, 21–28, 40, 43, 47, 247n16

Germany, 36, 92, 212, 220, 273n37

gihiyō/gihī. See householders

globalatinization, 3. *See also* idioms: globalatinized; vocabulary: globalatinized; voices: globalatinized

globalization, 6, 124, 180, 230, 260n6, 269n3

Gnanashila, Ambala Rohana, 36, 91, 129, 142–143, 253n10, 258n49, 259n58, 260n60, 261n65

goduragama, 202

gōlayā, 129, 156–158, 160, 176–177, 179–180, 198–199, 204, 207–208, 267n40

  defined, 263n13

Gross, Rita, 9, 21–31, 39, 237–238n3, 238n6, 238n12, 240n24

  Buddhism after Patriarchy, 29–30, 86

  Cheng and, 40–41

  on Eight Conditions, 86

  Feminism and Religion, 23, 26–27, 29

  on "real Egyptians," 28

  on *sangha*, 30

  Unspoken Worlds, 23, 27, 237n2, 237n2, 238n3

Gutschow, Kim, 59–62, 106, 242n13, 246n12

Hamburg, 15, 212, 220–221, 224, 226, 271n16, 272n29, 273n37

Havnevik, Hanna, 58–59, 61, 243n18, 244n26, 244n28

healing, 105, 206, 208

hermitages, 2, 13, 34, 73–74, 117, 140, 153–155, 157–161, 194, 227, 230, 233, 241n7, 245n39, 249n4, 260n60, 267n3, 270n10
  of *bhikkhunīs* (see under *bhikkhunī* [*bhikṣuṇī*])
  Bodhgaya-Dambulla, 159, 161
  establishment or development of, 2, 107, 190, 195, 204, 207
  food grown at, 191, 198, 208
  Lady Blake, 112,
  litigation about, 205–208
  ownership of, 195, 198–200, 203–206, 258n45
  samnak chi, 63
  of *sil mātās*, 38, 118, 129, 132, 143, 147, 163, 201–202, 261n65, 263n12

homes, 69, 104, 132, 154, 241n7, 242n11, 243n18, 245n39

homogenization, 37–38
  of Buddhists, 240n22
  of nuns or female renunciants, 37, 213–214
  of women, 38–39, 213, 239n20

Horner, I. B., 82–85, 87, 89, 246n10, 246n11, 247n14, 247n18

householders
  full-moon day observances of, 108
  identity or status of, 12, 57, 113, 121
  moral code of, 56 (*see also* Ten Precepts: Householder [Training])
  renunciants conflated with, 12, 56, 107, 112–113, 119–121, 160, 241n7

renunciants contrasted with, 58, 103–104, 113, 115, 120–121, 138, 160, 235n3
  support for renunciants or monastics from, 162, 191, 194–196, 198, 200–202, 266n32, 269n2
  view of monastics or renunciants of, 42, 97, 103, 117–118, 120, 151

human rights. *See under* rights

Husken, Ute, 87, 247n18

ICBW. *See* International Congress on Buddhist Women's Role in the Sangha

identity
  Abyesekara on, 151–152
  ambiguous, 103
  collective, 124–126, 218
  gendered, 7–8, 59
  Mahayana, 40
  oppression and, 215
  politics of, 4
  renunciant or monastic, 8, 13, 37, 104–105, 107, 120, 137–138, 140, 226, 229, 239n17 (*see also* nuns: identity of)
  Theravada, 13–14, 45, 150–152, 159, 161, 165–167, 178 (*see also* authenticity; see also under *bhikkhunī upasampadā*)
  Tibetan, 226

ideology, 3, 24–26, 49, 79, 80, 82, 87, 99, 151, 220, 233, 258n50, 260n60, 274n48

idioms
  English, 225
  globalatinized, 4, 8, 14, 16, 107, 225, 232, 235n1
  Latin or latinized, 3, 15
  of liberal feminism, 186
  of rights and/or equality, 218, 273n38
  secular, 253n3

imperialism, 25, 220, 236n7, 272n35

Inamaluwe Sumangala. *See* Sumangala, Inamaluwe

institutional capture, 34, 47, 241n29

International Congress on Buddhist Women's Role in the Sangha (ICBW), 15, 212, 220–221, 226, 273n38, 273n39

Internet, 212, 270n10

Janōpakāra Saṅgamaya [Samasta Lankā Janōpakāra Bauddha Saṅgamaya], 143–144, 146

Jayawardene, J. R., 127, 135

jomo, 58, 243n17

Jordt, Ingrid, 125, 252n2

JVP, 206, 208, 268n16

kalakirīma, 70–72, 75, 245n37

Kandy, 146, 166

Kanittha, 60, 243n20

Kaoutaramaya, 172–173, 176–177, 179

karma, 40–41, 47, 206, 209

Kawanami, Hiroko, 112, 239n14, 274n48

Khuddaka Pāṭha, 108, 111, 251n23

Koppedrayer, Kay, 24, 247n16

Kusuma, Bhikkhuni, 90–93, 96, 110, 163, 165, 241n28, 242n11, 246n11, 248n29, 253n9, 264n19, 267n43, 271n24. *See also* Devendra, Kusuma

Kwok, Pui-Lan, 24–26

labor, 7, 59, 127, 190, 196, 244n35

laity, 34, 36, 55, 110, 125, 192, 242n9
   defined, 56

land ownership. *See* ownership

Latin, 1, 3, 15, 235n1

liberalism, 9, 24, 193, 214, 218
   assumptions or traditions of, 4, 24
   secular, 4, 9–11, 16, 30, 47, 74, 78

liberal ecumenical theology, 9, 25
   See also Fitzgerald, Timothy

lineages
   bhikkhunī, 2, 14, 117, 150, 158, 169, 173, 221, 224, 228, 248n24, 258n49, 274n46
   of *dasa sil mātās*, 108, 120
   Dharmaguptaka, 150, 164, 221, 223, 273n37
   East Asian, Chinese, or Korean, 150, 164, 223, 227, 266n33
   lost or broken, 13, 158
   Mahayana, 14
   monastic, 120, 191, 216, 233
   Mūlasarvāstivādin, 223
   in Nepal, 228
   ordination, 2, 14, 149–150, 164, 167, 216, 221, 262n4, 262n6, 272n29, 274n46
   paramparāva, 173, 191
   Sri Lankan, 2, 14, 112, 150, 167
   Theravada, 90, 117, 158, 167, 169, 211, 216–217
   Tibetan, 211, 216–218, 223–225, 233, 272n36

lived lives, 4–5, 10–11, 22, 30, 47, 49, 54, 65, 80, 98, 122, 217, 244n33

Madiwela, 134, 256n28, 256n33

mae chi, 57–60, 62–64, 214, 243–244n25, 244n31
   defined, 57–58, 268n7

Mahapajapati Gotami, 45, 80–81, 83, 90–92, 94, 97, 99, 216–217, 246n16, 247n14

Mahāvaṃsa, 32–34, 265n28

Mahayana Buddhism, 4, 40, 44–47, 149–150

Mahmood, Saba, 5, 10, 53, 185
   Asad interview by, 21–22

Malalasekera, G. P., 89, 188

Malwatte, 166–167

Mandair, Arvind-Pal, 5, 9–10, 31–32, 50, 270n12, 271n20
   on globalatinization, 3–4

Mandair, Arvind-Pal (*Cont.*)
  on *religio*, 24
  Religion and the Specter of the West, 3–4
māṇiyō, 12, 72–73, 105–106, 119, 141,
    144–146, 197, 200, 202, 205,
    253n9, 259n51, 268n7
  defined, 12, 116, 252n42
  guru, 141, 159, 176, 197, 200–201, 204,
    205, 208
  poḍi, 153, 198, 203–204, 206–208
marriage, 14, 59, 68, 106, 186, 188–190,
    240n26, 268n8. *See also* wives
mass media
  English-language, 11, 143
  Sinhalese-language, 11, 169, 252n1
  Sri Lankan, 11–12, 88–89, 117, 131–132,
    134, 142–145, 170, 248n25,
    259n53, 260n64
Masuzawa, Tomoko, 9, 24, 31
meditation, 2, 7, 10, 37, 64, 100, 125,
    206, 208, 239n13
meheṇis, 12, 116–120, 144
Meheṇi Udāva (Dawn of the *Meheni*),
    131, 142–143 253n5, 259n57,
    259–60n58
missionaries
  Buddhist, 13
  Christian, 26, 236n8
  nuns as, 163, 248n25, 264n16
  Sri Lankan Buddhist, 165
  Theravada Buddhist, 162–163 (*see also*
    Theravada identity)
  Tibetan Buddhist, 227
modernity, 3, 24, 43, 49, 133, 231,
    240n22
Mohanty, Chandra T., 5, 27, 37, 213,
    239n20, 240n22, 270n9, 270n11
Mohr, Thea, 218–220
monastic precedence or seniority, 14,
    152–160, 166, 170, 176, 180,
    202, 205, 228, 263n11, 265n26,
    273n37

monasticism, 10, 55, 62, 151, 192, 221,
    236n12, 242n13, 249n8, 261n3
monastics, 91, 108, 142, 158, 178, 197,
    221, 230, 242n13, 244n31,
    264n18, 268n12, 269n2, 270n11
  Asgiriya, 170
  Asian, 16, 213, 222, 225, 228, 273n37
  attire of, 113, 116, 265n24
  (Bodhgaya-)Dambulla, 169–170, 175
  Buddhist, 93, 113, 180, 202, 213, 225,
    253n3
  community of (sangha), 11, 103
  competition of, 228
  defined, 235n2
  early Buddhist, 245n4
  East Asian, 150
  Eight Conditions and, 11, 78–80, 90,
    93–94, 98, 245n4
  fully ordained, 141, 229, 239n17
  Korean, 163–164, 175, 179, 227–228,
    264n16, 267n43
  Mahayana, 13, 46, 150, 162, 175
  mainland Chinese, 227
  male, 78, 137, 139, 195, 208, 236n5
  non-English-speaking, 222
  non-monastics and, 30, 55
  Precepts and, 108, 116
  prominent, 8
  Sarnath-group, 154
  seniority or precedence of, 153
  Sri Lankan, 14, 165, 174, 270n5,
    272n29
  Taiwanese, 168, 175, 227–228, 263n11
  textual sources on, 55
  Theravada, 150, 162, 169, 216, 232
  Tibetan, 216, 222–226
  Western, 213, 221, 225, 228
  Zen, 230–231
Mongolia, 226–227, 274n41, 274n42
monks
  Asgiriya, 134, 166–167, 170, 179
  criticism of, 96, 151

family relations and, 52
fully ordained, 96, 121, 142, 259n51
head, 95, 165–166, 170, 179, 191, 201
land ownership by, 191, 202
Mahanayaka, 163, 255n27
novice, 62, 108, 110–112, 114, 118–119, 121
senior, 95, 98, 158, 163, 170–171, 240n27, 256n28, 269n5
Sri Lankan, 13, 228, 263n11, 269n5
Thai, 62
Tibetan, 223
moral discipline (*sīlaya*), 96, 111
mothers (*māṇiyō*). See *māṇiyō*
mothers, 30, 34, 37, 59–60, 62, 68, 70, 74, 103, 243n22, 268n7
movements
defined, 6, 123, 126
feminist, 1
global or transnational, 6, 220
ordination or renunciation and, 5–6, 12, 47, 123–124
resistance, 13, 142
social, 5–6, 124–126, 137, 165
Muller, F. Max, 25, 238n4, 238n5. *See also* religions: world
Myanmar, 15, 112, 125, 149–150, 214, 230, 233, 242n7, 242n9, 251n29, 252n31, 274n48
Nandy, Ashis, 14, 187
narrative disjunction, 9–10, 23, 41, 49, 75
narratives
colonial, 8, 47, 49, 51, 241n1
competing or contesting, 14, 165, 167, 175, 179–180, 237n21
on culture, 2
of erasure, 47
globalatinized, 4
(liberal) feminist, 2, 10, 21, 49, 241n1
liberal or secular-liberal, 10, 152

liberalism's, 65
master or grand, 9, 21, 32–33, 38, 40, 47–48, 176, 239n15
normative moralist, 49
of nuns (*see under* nuns)
Orientalist, 4, 8
scholarly, 4–5, 7–8, 21, 35, 50, 54, 79
"native," 3–4, 16, 26
need(s), 132
for categories of analysis, 16
for curative treatment, 65
for education, 15, 39
for equality, 4, 64, 214
for empowerment, 212
for (feminist) transformation, 42, 64, 238n12
for problems' solution or cure, 10, 46, 75, 240n24, 244n33, 244n36
for resistance, 58
of *sil mātās*, 132, 135, 142
Sinhalese verb for, 268n14
for *upasampadā*, ordination, or *bhikkhunī order*, 8, 33, 35, 50, 61, 64, 215, 222, 224, 229–230, 263n16
for Western intervention or assistance, 75
Nepal, 15, 226–229, 232, 274n47
networks
family or kinship, 7, 15, 29, 186, 191
global or transnational, 5, 16, 212, 216
of power (relations), 45, 151, 187, 209
social-movement theorists on, 136
newspapers. *See* mass media
nibbana, 5, 40, 49, 51–54, 60, 63, 75, 94, 110, 142, 178, 198
Nikayas, 134, 170, 173, 177
nirvana. *See* nibbana
novices. *See* *sāmaṇeras*; *sāmaṇerīs*

nuns
  ahistorical claims about, 35–37, 40,
    44, 217
  alms (*dāna*) or support for, 2, 43,
    62, 153–155, 191, 194–200, 202,
    205–209, 222, 263n11, 269n2
  American, 15, 38, 230–231
  ancient (see *bhikkhunī*: ancient, early,
    or past)
  as agents or agency of, 6, 10–12, 75,
    85, 123, 140, 147, 239n20
  Asian, 9, 15, 54, 61, 214, 217, 225–226,
    230, 232–233, 240n26, 269n4
  assumptions or generalizations
    about, 1, 4, 16, 40, 43–44, 79
  attire of, 7, 33, 53, 103–106, 114–115,
    167, 211, 231, 235n2, 242n11,
    252n31
  authentic or traditional, 4, 122
  autonomy of, 185, 187, 191, 197,
    267n1
  Bodhgaya-Dambulla, 156, 178, 181,
    262n9
  Burmese, 15, 129, 214, 230, 233
  Catholic, 55
  Chinese, 248n25
  contrasted to monks, 7–8, 52,
    191–192
  Dambulla (see nuns: Bodhgaya-
    Dambulla)
  debates on higher ordination of (see
    bhikkhunī upasampadā: debates
    on)
  defined, 55–56, 235n2
  "disempowered," 88, 94
  duties of, 2, 206
  economic condition or background
    of, 43, 61, 244n25
  education of (see *under* education)
  empowerment of (see *under*
    empowerment)
  English word, 55, 58

  English-speaking or English-
    educated, 4, 15, 33, 59, 61, 65,
    237n13, 255n23
  everyday lives of, 42, 154, 209,
    274n40
  "failed" or lapsed, 36–38
  family relations and, 15, 52, 59, 72,
    104, 185–187, 191–192, 195, 197,
    206, 209, 217, 243n18, 243n23,
    253n3
  Five-Precept, 105–106
  foreign or Western, 33, 36–38, 61,
    223, 244n26, 265n26
  frameworks for study of (see *under*
    frameworks)
  freedom of (see renunciation:
    freedom of)
  fully ordained, 2, 103, 160, 214, 217–
    218, 229, 259n51
  gender, bodies, or sexuality of, 7–8,
    46, 237n17, 270n8
  higher ordination of (see *bhikkhunī
    upasampadā*)
  idealized or idea of, 120, 211
  identity of, 1, 7, 10, 12, 46, 59, 103,
    121–122, 126, 210, 215, 237n21,
    273n38
  "ignorant," or "uneducated," 103
  "indigent" or "impoverished," 75,
    214, 217
  (in)equality and, 10, 39, 42, 54,
    84, 186, 199, 211, 214 (*see also*
    monastic precedence; nuns:
    monastic precedence or
    seniority and)
  invisibility of, 106
  junior, 153, 155–156, 158–161, 176, 179,
    228, 265n26, 267n40
  Ladakhi, 61
  lay or householder, 12, 32–33, 35–38,
    55, 60, 117, 137
  lineages of (see lineages)

as "liminal," 103

Mahayana, 14, 40

monastic precedence or seniority and, 14, 153–161, 180, 228, 265n26

names for, 12, 53, 55, 107, 116–122, 249n9, 268n7 (see also *ani; bhikkhunī; dge slong ma; jomo; mae chi; māṇiyō; meheṇi;* nuns: English word; *sāmaṇerī; sil mātā; thiláshin*)

narrative disjunction and, 9–10, 49, 75

narratives about, 1, 4–5, 8–10, 35–36, 40–41, 49–50, 54–55, 59, 61, 65, 75, 152, 167, 233

in Nepal or Nepalese, 15, 226–229, 232, 274n47

novice, 114–115, 248n30, 251n24 (see also *sāmaṇerīs*)

order of (see *bhikkhunī* order)

ordination rituals of, 13–14, 151, 168, 228, 233

"problems" of, 4–5, 8, 10, 37, 54, 60–61, 75, 156–157, 228, 233, 239n20, 240n24, 243n20

residences of, 53, 117, 185, 191–192, 194–195, 197, 200, 203, 252n37 (see also hermitages)

rituals performed by, 2, 7, 55, 62, 154, 160

rules or precepts of (see Codes of Conduct; Ten Precepts; *Vinaya*)

senior or head, 118–119, 154–158, 166, 205, 248n30

Sinhalese-speaking, 6, 33, 36, 60, 65, 175, 177, 180, 273n13

Sri Lankan in India (see Sarnath; Bodhgaya)

Sri Lankan in USA, 161–162

Sri Lankan state and, 131, 134–135, 137, 163

Sri Lankan–Korean ordination of, 163–164, 167, 171, 228

state or government and, 54, 64, 216 (see also nuns: Sri Lankan state and)

as subjects (see renunciant subjects)

subordinate, 10, 39–40, 54, 59–60, 84, 99, 217, 222, 239n18, 243n20, 244n32, 246n12

Taiwanese, 9, 39–40, 43

Ten (Training) Precept Mothers (see *sil mātās: dasa*)

textual sources on, 1–2, 11, 16, 34, 217, 236n5, 239n16

Thai, 15, 65, 217, 269n4 (see also *mae chi*)

Theravada identity of Sri Lankan, 13, 150, 152, 161, 165, 176–180, 262n10

Theravada, 14, 16, 32, 40, 90, 150–151, 216–217, 226–228, 230–231, 233, 263n15

Tibetan, 1, 10, 16, 58–62, 74, 106, 211, 216–217, 220–227, 230–231, 233, 244n26, 246n12, 265n26, 270n7, 271n15 (see also *anis*)

Tibetan of Asian origin, 211, 216, 221–227, 229–230, 265n26, 272n33, 272n34, 273n37, 273n38, 274n50

Tibetan of Western origin, 218, 220, 222–226, 265n26, 270n7, 272n36, 273n37

welfare of (see *under* Cheng, Wei-Yi)

Western (see nuns: foreign or Western)

See also monastics; renunciants, female

Obeyesekere, Gananath, 116, 149, 236n5, 252n42, 268n8

"opportunities," 61–62, 65–67, 74, 222 *avasthāva* defined, 65–66

oppression, 22, 59, 74, 84–85, 88, 187, 213–215, 247n14

ordained woman, defined, 117–120

ordination
  bhikkhunī, 6, 14, 36, 38–40 (see also
    bhikkhunī upasampadā)
  Bodhgaya-Dambulla, 146–147, 159,
    166
  Bodhgaya-Nepalese, 227–228
  caste and, 166–167
  Dambulla (*see* Dambulla: ordinations
    at; ordinations: Bodhgaya-
    Dambulla)
  dual, 221, 223–224
  higher (see *bhikkhunī upasampadā*)
  householder, 110, 112
  international, 13, 38, 164, 168–169,
    227–228, 269n5
  Kaoutaramaya, 172, 176
  Kushtanagara, 177
  lineage and, 13–14, 149–150, 158,
    164, 167, 169, 212, 215–217, 221,
    223–225, 227, 231, 233, 262n4,
    262n6, 266n33, 272n29,
    272n36, 273n37, 274n46
  Los Angeles, 161–162, 170, 211, 269n11
  mahaṇavīma, 110, 118
  Mahayana, 13–14, 45, 158–159, 171, 175,
    177, 179, 269n2
  mainland China, 227–228
  novice, 55, 58, 112, 118, 242n7, 268n7
  opposition to or rejection of, 13, 36,
    42, 46, 50, 134–135, 142, 158, 166,
    170, 176, 180
  renunciant, 110–112, 118
  rituals or ceremony of, 110–111, 114,
    150–151, 161, 166, 168–170, 179,
    221, 223, 228, 233, 250n19
  Sarnath (*see* Sarnath)
  Sri Lankan, 2, 6, 11–13, 38, 45
  Theravada identity and, 159, 161,
    165–167, 178
  Theravada, 13–14, 150, 158, 160–161,
    167, 169, 179–180, 232

upasampadā (see *bhikkhunī*
    upasampadā)
organizations
  of nuns or *bhikkhunīs*, 136, 147, 166
  of *sil mātā*, 13, 88–89, 114–115, 118,
    134–136, 139–140, 146–147, 163,
    199–200, 253n5, 256n33, 257n34
  women's, 85, 127, 247n17 (*see also*
    Sakyadhita International
    Association of Buddhist Women)
orientalism, 3, 16, 213, 236n7. *See also*
  discourses: imperialistic or
  Orientalist
other, the, 4, 8, 50, 187
ownership, 14–15, 185, 194–195, 198–203,
    205–206, 208–209, 258n45
  capitalism and, 190–191, 193, 199
  of temples, 166, 191, 201
  by women, 188, 190
pabbajjā, 103, 108, 110, 159. See also
    pävidi
Pali, 12, 32, 56, 104, 216, 237n12, 251n21,
    252n33
  accounts of Eight Conditions, 81, 86
  canon, 250n14
  classes or sermons in, 135, 256n31
  depictions of *bhikkhunīs* or nuns, 34,
    140, 239n16
  ordination and, 86, 169, 266n31,
    272n29
  precepts, 111, 250n18
  Theravada and, 149, 152, 261n3,
    262n5, 262n6
  Vinaya or *pāṭimokkha*, 32, 150, 161,
    168
paramparāva, 173, 191
Pateman, Carole, 10, 51, 57, 244n30
patriarchy, 11, 14–15, 31, 52, 54, 61, 86,
    96, 127, 209, 219
pävidi, 11, 103–105, 108–112, 114–115,
    117–121, 160

People's Liberation Front. *See* JVP

Piyananda, Walpola, 162, 170, 270n5

Piyasena, Kumar, 143–144, 146, 260n61, 261n62, 261n63, 264n18

pluralism, 24, 212

poverty, 60, 74, 131–133

power
  authority and, 45
  Bhabha on, 50
  discourse of, 104, 121
  Foucault on, 84, 130, 197, 214, 246n13
  freedom and, 197
  gender and, 192
  knowledge or recognition and, 85, 87–88, 130, 254n15
  liberal(ist) notions of, 85, 185, 236n11
  monastic seniority and, 157, 180
  of narrative construction, 77
  negative sense of, 84–85
  (networks of) relations of, 45, 127, 151, 187, 209
  nuns' or *sil mātās'* "lack" or "loss" of, 5, 15, 35, 37
  religious practice or subjectivity and, 197, 209
  scholarly practices and, 27
  separation of discourse from, 152
  state or bureaucracy and, 140, 186, 216
  subjectivity and, 214
  symbolic, 191–192, 196, 199, 202, 205
  of women, 188–190, 214, 220

pōya (full moon day), 108–109
  Unduvap, 255n20, 257n36

pōyagē, 204, 268n15

practices
  (Buddhist) women's, 23, 29–30, 47, 53
  everyday renunciant, 145, 212, 230, 236n11, 256n28
  everyday, 7, 187, 233, 273n38

gendered or gender and, 7–8, 47, 270n8
  knowledge and, 79, 85–86, 88
  (moral or) disciplinary, 5, 8, 23, 44, 103, 119, 126, 216, 236n12, 256n28, 273n39
  religious, 13, 15, 23, 53, 149, 188, 190, 193, 209, 227, 230, 235n2, 253n2
  renunciant, 15, 36, 115, 120, 193, 197
  ritual (*see under* ritual)

praśna/prashna. *See* questions

Precepts. *See* Five (Training) Precepts; Eight Precepts; Ten Precepts

private sphere, 51–52, 54, 71, 243n24

projects
  curative, 5, 10, 238n12
  European, 271n17
  transnational, 226, 229, 233, 274n42, 274–275n50
  Western, 211, 233

property, 15, 186, 189–193, 196, 198, 200, 205–206, 208

protests, 126, 137, 146

public sphere, 42, 50–51, 54, 59, 61, 63–65, 133, 243n24

questions (*praśna/prashna*), 66–69, 75, 154, 156, 160
  defined, 244n36

Rāja Mahā Vihāraya. *See* temples: historic royal

Ratwatte, Eardley, 130, 135, 254n12

regime of truth, 50, 131

religio, 24. *See also* Derrida, Jacques; Mandair, Arvind-Pal

religions
  Asian, 9, 24, 26, 29
  colonial (Orientalist) discourse and, 9–10, 16, 24–26, 236n8
  concept, classification, or category of, 24–25, 236n8

religions (*Cont.*)
  "native" or "indigenous" vs. world, 26
  "objective" study of, 9, 24, 26–27
  phenomenological studies of, 25–26
  scholarship on or theorizations
      about, 3, 9, 23–25, 53, 236n8,
      238n3, 238n6
  study of, 9, 25–27, 39, 124, 236n8
      (*see also* Fitzgerald, Timothy;
      Gross, Rita; Masuzawa, Tomoko;
      Muller, F. Max)
  translation of, 3–4, 24
  world, 23–26, 31 (*see also* Masuzawa,
      Tomoko)
renunciant everyday, 2, 5–7, 14, 185,
      200, 211, 213, 232, 261n65, 271n21
  defined, 7, 126, 235n3
  ordination and, 6, 16, 126, 146,
      274n47
renunciant subject, 9, 40, 48, 79–80,
      123, 134, 138–139, 258n41
  creation or construction of, 3, 11–13,
      37, 77, 84, 88, 93, 99–100, 124,
      126–127, 138–139, 257n36
  "(dis)empowered," 88
  epistemic, 11, 99–100
  female, 11, 87, 124, 126, 137, 209,
      258n41
  respectable, 134, 137, 139, 144
renunciants, female
  autonomy or freedom of, 53, 63, 74,
      77, 187, 209
  attire of, 33, 133, 249n8, 252n35
  canonical literature on, 108–109
  defined, 103, 235n2
  discourse on, 187
  "(dis)empowerment" of, 15, 82,
      212–213
  economic condition or background
      of, 8, 68–71, 132, 189
  Eight-Precept, 104, 241n7
  English-speaking or English-
      educated, 4, 60, 107

epistemic, 11
  everyday lives of, 176
  family relations and (*see* renunciation:
      family relations and)
  hermitages or land of, 107, 191
  householder or laity vs., 55–56
  idealized, 35, 161, 213
  identity of, 8, 12–13, 37, 57, 59, 104–
      105, 107, 120, 212–213, 218
  "ignorant" or "uneducated," 214
  "indigent" or "impoverished," 8, 132
  (in)equality and, 11, 16, 50, 64, 84
  invisibility of, 99, 106
  live in household, 242n12, 267n3
  "movement" of, 48, 123, 126
  names used for, 12, 55–58, 107, 116–
      122, 242n9
  narratives about, 3, 49–51, 58, 61,
      64–65, 77–78, 80, 82, 88, 197,
      239n11
  pävidi, 103–105, 109, 115, 117–121
  practices of, 5, 10, 16, 123
  "problems" of, 61, 63, 239n18
  reasons for renunciation of, 189
  Sinhalese-speaking, 39
  Sri Lankan, 32, 65, 72, 106, 189
  state and, 134–138, 186
  status of, 48, 56, 186
  studies of, 31, 49, 51, 55, 58
  "struggles" of, 64
  as suffering subjects, 133
  ten-precept (*dasa sil mātā*) (see *sil
      mātās: dasa*)
  ten-precept (*sikkhamats*), 63
  textual sources on or representations
      of, 213
  Thai, 57, 60, 63
  Tibetan, 51, 58
  upasampadā and, 13, 215, 218, 229
renunciants, male. *See* monks
renunciation
  "abnormality" or "deviance" of, 50,
      62–65, 253n3

category or conceptualization of, 54–55

compared to funeral, 73–74

defined or "meaning" of, 11, 103, 107

empowering, 5

family relations and, 2, 5, 14–15, 29–30, 50–53, 59, 63, 66, 68–74, 186–187, 189, 193–195, 197–200, 231, 235n2

as feminist act, 51

freedom of, 14–16, 35, 37, 50–53, 64, 68, 74, 186, 189, 191, 195–199, 209, 211, 226, 231, 240n24, 240n27

of home, 104

laity and female, 55

ordination debates and, 48

reasons for, 2, 5, 15, 51–54, 63–65, 70–72, 187, 189

resistance, 3, 13–14, 50–52, 54, 58–59, 68, 70, 123, 140, 185, 209, 215, 219, 254n13

resistant subject, 145

rights, 205–209, 272n30

  feminist, 240n24

  human, 127, 131–132, 147, 214, 218, 220, 223, 260n58, 271n21, 271n24 (*see also* Asad, Talal; Spivak, Gayatri C.)

Risseeuw, Carla, 14, 188–190

ritual, 7, 42, 126, 142, 147, 154, 158, 160, 177, 188, 246n7, 236n12, 240n25, 257n40, 265n26, 266n34, 266n35, 268n15, 273n39

  empowerment, 62

  of ordination, 104, 110–111, 114, 119, 150–151, 161, 168–169, 176, 223, 228, 233, 250n19, 251n21

  practices, 206, 216, 272n36

  services, 55, 154

  specialists, 243n24

  subordination, 89

Rohana. *See* Gnanashila, Ambala Rohana

Said, Edward, 3, 217, 270n7

Sakyadhita International Association of Buddhist Women (SIABW), 86, 212, 216, 218, 240n27, 247n17, 255n20, 269–270n5, 271n16, 274n43

Sakyadhita International Conferences, 15, 92, 212, 219–220, 230, 264n16

Sakyadhita, 171–173, 176

sāmaṇeras, 114, 159–161, 235n2, 249n2, 263n14

sāmaṇerīs, 168, 263n11, 263n14

  attire of, 114

  defined, 104, 235n2, 249n2

  Eight Conditions and, 78, 94

  monastic precedence or seniority and, 154–156, 159–160

  ordination, 56, 156, 168, 242n7

  word *sāmaṇera* used for, 159–161, 249n2, 263n14

  status of, 115

Samasta Lankā Janōpakāra Bauddha Saṇgamaya, 143–144, 146

samsara, 5, 51–53, 65, 75, 198

  detachment from, 55–56

  dukkha or suffering of, 10, 53, 69–70, 189, 198

  fear of, 104, 120

  nibbana vs., 49, 52–53

sangha, 30, 33, 35, 55, 87, 125, 172, 246n12, 251n20, 252n33

  attire of members of, 113

  bhikkhu or *mahā*, 81, 91, 95

  bhikkhunī, 37–38, 44, 92, 117, 246n11

  dual, 82

  householders vs., 11, 103, 110

  Mahayana, 150

  pūjā or *dāna* for, 201, 259n51

  Taiwanese, 40, 46, 179

  upasampadā and, 110, 112, 119–121

  World Buddhist Sangha Council, 162

Sanghamitta, 32–33, 45, 91, 255n20, 257n36, 260n58, 260n60

Sanskrit, 25, 251n21

Sarnath, 89, 121, 130, 140, 146–147, 150, 161–171, 173–177, 181, 228, 261, 263–264n16, 264n18, 265n23, 265n24, 265n28, 266n35

   group, 150, 154, 158, 167, 169, 177–179, 267n41

   group defined, 262n9

Sarvodaya, 166, 264n22

sāsana, 162, 199. See also *bhikkhunī sāsana*

sati, 187–188

Scott, David, 14, 268n4

secularism, 3–4, 24. *See also* liberalism: secular; feminism: secular-liberal

Seelavatie, 176–177, 267n40

sexuality, 7, 30

Shearer, Catherine, 34–35

sikkhamats, 63

Sil Mātā Cariyāpaddhati (*Sil Mātā Code of Conduct*), 139, 257n40, 258n47

sil mātās

   alms or donations and, 154–155, 255n21, 259n51, 263n11, 263n16

   attire of, 7, 110, 113–116, 160, 167, 259n55

   Bartholomeusz on, 59, 90

   bhikkhunīs and (see *bhikkhunī: sil mātās* and; *bhikkhunī upasampadā: sil mātās* and)

   dasa, 6, 48, 88–90, 97, 105–106, 108, 110–121, 128–130, 133–134, 136–138, 140–142, 159, 163, 173, 249n9, 259n51

   discourses on, 131–132

   duties or work of, 147

   education of, 89, 135, 144, 248n25, 254n16, 258n47

   everyday lives of, 159

   families of, 66–68, 70–74, 104, 129, 197–200, 206, 208

   homeless, 112, 117, 254n19

   "indigent," 132

   junior, 153–154, 159, 176, 249n36, 267n40

   land of, 15, 201 (*see also* hermitages: of *sil mātās*)

   lineages of, 108, 120

   living with or near family or householders, 66, 104, 111

   names or titles used for, 116–120, 138

   novice monks and, 111–112, 119, 121

   precedence and, 153–154, 158–160, 176, 263n12, 267n40

   precepts observed by, 105, 108–112, 114–116, 118, 120, 241–242n7

   regulation of, 137–138, 257n39, 257n40

   as renunciants or renunciant status of, 104–105, 109–113, 115–116, 118–121, 137, 139, 253n4, 254n17

   rituals of, 259n51

   state or government and, 42, 89, 128–131, 133–140, 147, 199, 208, 253n9, 255n24, 255n27, 256n29, 256n31, 257n34, 257n36, 257n37, 257n39, 257n40, 258n48, 258n49, 260n60

   studies of, 90, 128, 130, 136, 239n14

   upasampadā and (see *bhikkhunī upasampadā: sil mātās* and)

sīla, 5, 8, 15, 56, 103, 141, 185, 189, 196–197

   defined, 236n12

Sinhalese speaking, 6, 33, 36, 39, 44, 60, 65, 168, 175, 177, 180

   defined, 237n13

sisterhood

   global, 16–17, 211–212, 214, 220, 230, 233, 270n9

   international Buddhist, 212

of nuns or renunciants, 16, 213–214,
220, 230, 270n11
transnational, 6, 211
universal, 214
Smith, Dorothy E., 5, 10, 34, 54, 75, 77,
241n29
SMJM [*Sil Mātā Jātika Maṇḍalaya*], 136,
139, 139, 142, 146, 258n48
Spivak, Gayatri C., 238n9
on rights, 270n21
on subaltern, 6, 236n9, 237n14,
237n15, 272n35
Sponberg, Alan, 86–87
Sri Lanka Buddhist Congress, 162.
See also All Ceylon Buddhist
Congress
Sri Lanka, 32, 34, 60, 149–150, 245n38,
245n3
colonial-era, 188–189, 209
gender relations in, 126–127, 189
status
of *bhikkhunīs*, 36–38, 42, 48, 55,
95, 98, 112, 126, 130, 141–142,
155, 209, 213, 233, 256n28,
273n39
of *bhikkhus* or monks, 58, 104, 117,
244n28
of female renunciants, 48, 56, 103,
122, 186
higher ordination and (*see* status: of
bhikkhunīs)
householder, 12, 104, 113
of land, 202–203
of nuns, 5, 7, 12, 36, 42, 58, 103, 112,
117, 121, 209, 244n28, 273n39
ordained, 118
renunciant, 12, 103–104, 110–113,
116–118, 120
ritual, 273n39
of *sil mātās*, 104, 109, 111–112, 115–121,
139, 253n4, 254n17, 263n16
of women, 62, 172, 263n15

subalterns, 6, 236n9, 237n14, 237n15,
272n35
subjectivity
of *bhikkhunīs*, 98, 214
Chakrabarty on, 133
female (renunciant), 133, 209
liberal notions of, 48, 275n50
power and, 209, 214–215
subjects, renunciant. *See* renunciant
subjects
subordination
institutional vs. spiritual, 86
of nuns (*see under* nuns)
of women (*see under* women)
Sudharma of Biyagama, 130, 142, 252n11
Sudharmachari, 33, 112, 114, 117, 242n7,
251n28
Sugirtharajah, Sharada, 25
Sumangala, Inamaluwe, 145, 147,
165, 167–171, 174–176, 178, 180,
240n27, 261n64, 264n22,
265n28, 266n35, 266n37,
266n39
Sunita (non-monastic), 172–173
Sunita (nun), 72–74
tactics, 193, 196, 209
Taiwan, 39–40, 43, 46, 170–172, 174,
176, 178–179, 229
television. *See* mass media
temples, 162, 171, 194, 197, 207, 228,
231, 243n24, 249n4, 255n20,
264n16
Asgiriya, 167, 170, 179
Dambulla, 136, 165–167, 179
duties or work at, 106, 136, 147–148,
157
Foguangshan (*see* Foguangshan)
historic royal, 201–202
Hsi Lai, 211, 229
monks', 97, 191, 201, 204
precepts observed at, 108–109, 113,
241n7

Ten (Training) Precept Mother. See *sil mātā: dasa*

Ten Precepts, 33–34, 97, 108, 111, 118, 193, 197, 242n7, 247n20
  anagārika, 112
  Householder (Training), 108–113, 115–116, 118, 241n7, 250n16, 250n20
  pävidi, 112
  Renunciant (Training), 104, 109–112, 119, 159, 241–242n7, 250n15, 250n19, 251n22, 251n25
  Training, 103, 105, 107–114, 116–118, 120, 249n6, 250n11, 250n13, 251n23, 251n26

textual studies, 1–2, 9, 11–12, 16, 23, 29, 31–32, 64, 78, 95, 104, 113, 239n16, 242n15
  of Eight Conditions, 77, 80–81, 83–84, 86–87, 90–92, 98–99
  of precepts, 108–109, 111, 120
  of *Vinaya*, 242n12

Thailand, 15, 57–60, 62–64, 149–150, 215, 217, 239n14, 239n16, 243n25, 244n30, 251n21, 267n42, 268n7

Thamel, K.M. Lily Beatrice, 90, 106, 128–129, 253n5, 253n9

theology, liberal ecumenical, 9, 23–25. *See also* Fitzgerald, Timothy

theories
  of *différance*, 50
  liberal, 5, 16, 51–52, 244n33
  social-movement, 5, 12, 123–126, 136

Theravada Buddhism, 1, 4, 13, 149, 152, 162–163, 170, 180, 216 263n15, 265n26
  authentic or purist, 14, 40, 44–45, 47, 151
  category of (*see under* categories)
  defined, 149–150, 161, 180, 261n3, 262n6. *See also* Dambulla

thiláshin (*thila-shing*), 112, 214, 242n9

"third world," 6, 13, 43–44, 47, 61, 130, 185–186, 214, 254n13, 270n11

Three Refuges, 111, 250n19, 250–51n20, 251n21

Tibet, 106, 223

Tissa (monk), 198

Tissa (nun), 230–231

translation, 3–4, 12, 16, 58, 107, 133, 217, 222–223, 225–226, 233, 247n19, 270n12, 271n17

transnational conferences. *See* conferences, transnational

transnational discussions. *See* discussions, transnational or global

transnational forums. *See* forums, transnational

transnational projects. *See* projects: transnational

Tsedroen, Jampa [Carola Roloff], 220, 271n14

Tsomo, Karma Lekshe, 218, 243n20

United States, 15, 24, 36, 38, 65–66, 144, 170, 226, 230

universal capability, 53, 241n6

upāsakas, 56, 108–109, 113, 251n23, 260n58

upasampadā
  bhikkhunī (see *bhikkhunī upasampadā*)
  of monks, 108, 110–111, 119, 121, 251n22

upāsikāmmās, 106, 268n7

upāsikās, 48, 104, 108, 194, 260n58
  attire of, 57, 113, 138
  bhikkhunīs or nuns as, 117
  brahmacārī, 117
  canonical texts on, 113
  contrasted with *bhikkhunīs*, nuns, or *sil mātās*, 115, 119–120, 229, 239n7, 242n9
  dasa sil, 249n9
  defined, 56–58, 239n17

sil mātās as, 119
    Sri Lankan state and, 138
uposatha, 81, 246n7
vāḍa, 2, 147
Vakada Bhadra. *See* Bhadra, Vakada
Van Esterik, Penny, 57–58, 242n14
Vangisa, Urugamuve, 89–90, 92
Vinaya, 7, 38, 55, 80, 83, 87, 108, 114–
    116, 120, 128, 149, 158, 160, 171,
    223, 246n11, 247n18, 259n52
    Bhikkhunī, 92
    karmaya, 141, 171–172
    Mūlasarvāstivādin, 217, 221
    Pali or Theravada, 32, 150, 161, 168
    Tibetan, 272n36
Vipulasara, Mapalagama, 162, 164–166,
    169–170, 263–264n16, 264n19
vocabulary
    globalatinized, 122, 180, 229
    of religion, 3
    secular, 52
voices
    biblical prophetic, 28
    globalatinized, 211, 221, 232
    (un)silenced, 27–28, 41, 222, 226
warfare, 127, 260n60
Weber, Max, 49, 57, 186, 192
Weerakoon, Abhaya, 135–137, 254n16,
    260n60

widows, 133, 187–188, 190
Wijayaratna, Mohan, 83–85, 246n11,
    247n14
wives, 30, 34, 37, 52, 58, 60, 62,
    70–71, 74, 103, 127, 187, 243n22,
    243n17
women
    Asian or non-Western, 9, 187, 209,
        218–220, 240n22
    construction of subject or category
        of, 28, 38
    cross-cultural studies of, 23
    discourse on, 6, 13, 28–29, 47
    in development or and development,
        6, 13, 126
    economic condition or activities of,
        52, 62, 188–190, 218
    independence of, 5, 40
    nuns contrasted to, 7
    Sri Lankan, 60, 71, 126–127, 133, 188–
        189, 209, 243n22, 244n35
    as "subordinate," "disempowered," or
        "oppressed," 40, 63–64, 84, 187,
        209, 213
    Thai, 62–65, 243n22
    "third world," 37–38, 214, 240n22
    Western, 34, 61, 187, 219–220
women's studies, 9, 27
Young, Katherine, 27, 210